Swing Trading For Dummies®

Cheat Sheet

Assessing Industry Strength

If you determine what stage the economy is in (see Chapter 1) and then use that info as you review the following chart, you'll have a good idea which economic sectors are likely to lead the market in the near future.

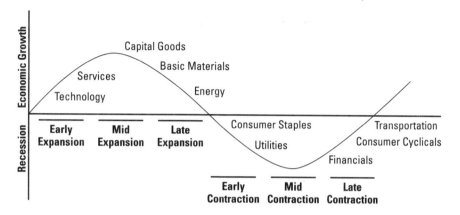

Seven Signs You've Found a Good Swing Trading Candidate

✔ **The market is on your side.** You've determined that the market is trending in the same direction you want to swing trade. (If it isn't, you may need to find a different trending market entirely.)

✔ **The industry group is on your side.** If the security's industry group is trending strongly in the same direction you want to swing trade, chances are your trade will be profitable.

✔ **If you're trend trading, the candidate is moving out of a base.** The candidate should be in an existing uptrend or downtrend that has pulled back in the short term. Use the ADX indicator to determine whether a trend exists.

✔ **If you're trading ranges, the candidate has just bounced off of support/resistance with a technical indicator confirmation.** Watch for the technical indicator (an oscillator) to generate a buy or sell signal. Divergences between your oscillator and the price action signal higher-confidence trades.

✔ **The fundamentals back the technicals.** Verify the important items, such as financial health, return on equity, P/E ratio, and expected earnings growth rates.

✔ **The stop loss level is near your desired execution price.** The closer your desired entry price is to your stop loss level, the less you stand to lose if matters turn ugly.

✔ **You allocate the right amount to the trade.** Set your position size in accordance with your trading plan, which should put an absolute ceiling on your position size and set a maximum percentage of capital you're willing to lose.

BESTSELLING
BOOK SERIES

Swing Trading For Dummies®

Cheat Sheet

Reviewing Fundamentals: The Six-Step Dance

Use the six-step process outlined here to size up a company in a short period of time:

1. **Know the company's overall industry.**

   Industry classification helps determine price multiples.

2. **Check the firm's financial stability.**

   A firm should be able to meet short-term obligations (check current ratio) and long-term obligations (check long-term debt to equity).

3. **Review the company's historical earnings and sales growth.**

   Stability (that is, predictability) in earnings and sales growth tends to be rewarded with higher price multiples, as are high growth rates.

4. **Learn how well the firm meets earnings and sales expectations.**

   The higher the expectations, the higher the multiple the security deserves.

5. **Find out who the company's competitors are and how they're valued.**

   Use the Ratios section of Reuters's finance site (www.reuters.com/finance/stocks).

6. **Calculate a rough estimate of the firm's value.**

   Estimate using a reasonable P/E ratio or price-to-cash-flow ratio.

Managing Your Risk: A Checklist

The most important determinant of whether you'll be a successful swing trader is how well you manage risk. Ask yourself these questions before placing a trade to ensure you don't cut corners:

❏ **Is the security liquid?**

❏ **Is the security a penny stock (hopefully not)?**

❏ **Are you prepared to limit losses at the individual stock level?** Check the box next to whichever precautionary measure you've taken:

  ❏ I set the position size based on the percentage I'm willing to lose (0.25 percent to 2 percent of total assets).

  ❏ I set the risk level as a straight percentage of assets and that percentage doesn't exceed 10 percent of my total portfolio.

❏ **Is your portfolio diversified?** Make sure your positions are spread among different market capitalizations (for example, large cap, mid cap, and small cap), sectors, and asset classes (not to mention domestic and international securities).

❏ **Have you limited your total portfolio losses to 7 percent?** Cover all your bases by confirming that

  ❏ Each security in the portfolio has a risk amount equal to the difference between the current price and stop loss level.

  ❏ The difference on an individual security level is tight — around 0.50 percent.

  ❏ The sum of those differences doesn't exceed 7 percent of the total portfolio value.

  ❏ The stop loss levels are at a level representing a profit (barring a gap in prices, of course).

Remember: Cut losses when your stop loss is hit — no questions asked.

For Dummies: Bestselling Book Series for Beginners

Wiley, the Wiley Publishing logo, For Dummies, the Dummies Man logo, the For Dummies Bestselling Book Series logo and all related trade dress are trademarks or registered trademarks of John Wiley & Sons, Inc. and/or its affiliates. All other trademarks are property of their respective owners. Copyright © 2008 Wiley Publishing, Inc. All rights reserved. Item 9368-3. For more information about Wiley Publishing, call 1-800-762-2974.

Swing Trading

FOR

DUMMIES®

Swing Trading

FOR

DUMMIES®

by Omar Bassal, CFA

Wiley Publishing, Inc.

Swing Trading For Dummies®

Published by
Wiley Publishing, Inc.
111 River St.
Hoboken, NJ 07030-5774
www.wiley.com

Copyright © 2008 by Wiley Publishing, Inc., Indianapolis, Indiana

Published simultaneously in Canada

No part of this publication may be reproduced, stored in a retrieval system, or transmitted in any form or by any means, electronic, mechanical, photocopying, recording, scanning, or otherwise, except as permitted under Sections 107 or 108 of the 1976 United States Copyright Act, without either the prior written permission of the Publisher, or authorization through payment of the appropriate per-copy fee to the Copyright Clearance Center, 222 Rosewood Drive, Danvers, MA 01923, 978-750-8400, fax 978-646-8600. Requests to the Publisher for permission should be addressed to the Legal Department, Wiley Publishing, Inc., 10475 Crosspoint Blvd., Indianapolis, IN 46256, 317-572-3447, fax 317-572-4355, or online at http://www.wiley.com/go/permissions.

Trademarks: Wiley, the Wiley Publishing logo, For Dummies, the Dummies Man logo, A Reference for the Rest of Us!, The Dummies Way, Dummies Daily, The Fun and Easy Way, Dummies.com and related trade dress are trademarks or registered trademarks of John Wiley & Sons, Inc. and/or its affiliates in the United States and other countries, and may not be used without written permission. All other trademarks are the property of their respective owners. Wiley Publishing, Inc., is not associated with any product or vendor mentioned in this book.

LIMIT OF LIABILITY/DISCLAIMER OF WARRANTY: THE PUBLISHER AND THE AUTHOR MAKE NO REPRESENTATIONS OR WARRANTIES WITH RESPECT TO THE ACCURACY OR COMPLETENESS OF THE CONTENTS OF THIS WORK AND SPECIFICALLY DISCLAIM ALL WARRANTIES, INCLUDING WITHOUT LIMITATION WARRANTIES OF FITNESS FOR A PARTICULAR PURPOSE. NO WARRANTY MAY BE CREATED OR EXTENDED BY SALES OR PROMOTIONAL MATERIALS. THE ADVICE AND STRATEGIES CONTAINED HEREIN MAY NOT BE SUITABLE FOR EVERY SITUATION. THIS WORK IS SOLD WITH THE UNDERSTANDING THAT THE PUBLISHER IS NOT ENGAGED IN RENDERING LEGAL, ACCOUNTING, OR OTHER PROFESSIONAL SERVICES. IF PROFESSIONAL ASSISTANCE IS REQUIRED, THE SERVICES OF A COMPETENT PROFESSIONAL PERSON SHOULD BE SOUGHT. NEITHER THE PUBLISHER NOR THE AUTHOR SHALL BE LIABLE FOR DAMAGES ARISING HEREFROM. THE FACT THAT AN ORGANIZATION OR WEBSITE IS REFERRED TO IN THIS WORK AS A CITATION AND/OR A POTENTIAL SOURCE OF FURTHER INFORMATION DOES NOT MEAN THAT THE AUTHOR OR THE PUBLISHER ENDORSES THE INFORMATION THE ORGANIZATION OR WEBSITE MAY PROVIDE OR RECOMMENDATIONS IT MAY MAKE. FURTHER, READERS SHOULD BE AWARE THAT INTERNET WEBSITES LISTED IN THIS WORK MAY HAVE CHANGED OR DISAPPEARED BETWEEN WHEN THIS WORK WAS WRITTEN AND WHEN IT IS READ.

For general information on our other products and services, please contact our Customer Care Department within the U.S. at 800-762-2974, outside the U.S. at 317-572-3993, or fax 317-572-4002.

For technical support, please visit www.wiley.com/techsupport.

Wiley also publishes its books in a variety of electronic formats. Some content that appears in print may not be available in electronic books.

Library of Congress Control Number: 2008933744

ISBN: 978-0-470-29368-3

Manufactured in the United States of America

10 9 8 7 6 5 4 3 2 1

WILEY

About the Author

Omar Bassal, CFA is the head of Asset Management at NBK Capital, the investment arm of the largest and highest rated bank in the Middle East. There, he oversees all asset management activities for institutional and high net worth individuals investing in the equity markets of the Middle East and North Africa (MENA). Prior to joining NBK Capital, Mr. Bassal was a portfolio manager at Azzad Asset Management, where he managed mutual funds and separately managed accounts. Mr. Bassal also worked as an analyst at Profit Investment Management and launched a socially responsible hedge fund in 2002. He holds an MBA with honors in finance, management, and statistics from the Wharton School of Business at the University of Pennsylvania. Additionally, he graduated summa cum laude with a Bachelor's of Science degree in Economics, also from the Wharton School. He has appeared on CNBC and has contributed articles to *Barron's* and *Technical Analysis of Stocks & Commodities*.

Dedication

To my mother, my mother, and my mother — Maha Al-Hiraki Bassal. To my father, Dr. Aly Bassal. And my sisters, Suzie and Sarah. To my loving wife, Salma, and my brother-in-law, Hisham. And to my beloved nephew, Mostafa. They have always supported me in easy and difficult times.

Author's Acknowledgments

I don't believe any experience could possibly have prepared me for the rigorous schedule required to write a book. I can't tell you how many weekends, evenings, and holidays were required to write *Swing Trading For Dummies.* The effort was, of course, worth it. But I did miss several episodes of *Lost, The Office,* and other shows. Alas, the cost of writing books isn't measured in time alone.

Before I turn this section into an autobiography (which I should pitch to Wiley as my second book, come to think of it: Omar Bassal For Dummies!), let me thank those who deserve thanks (give credit where credit is due, I'm told, is the way the kids are putting it these days). I first learned of this opportunity through Susan Weiner, CFA — a skilled and professional investment writer. Susan told me about a search Wiley was conducting to find an author for this book. Marilyn Allen, my agent, pitched me to Wiley. I'm honored Wiley offered me the opportunity to write this book. Thank you, Stacy Kennedy, for your confidence in me and your buy-in.

Writing the book, as you may have gleaned from my previous comments, was a grueling, tough process, and Kristin DeMint was an invaluable resource. She was my project editor and made sure the book progressed. She often joked that she knew nothing about swing trading. But her "weakness" was in reality a strength. Not being an expert in the subject meant Kristin could offer helpful comments on what might confuse a novice when I made assumptions or didn't properly explain ideas. Kristin also kept a watchful eye when deadlines approached. Oh how I didn't want to draw her ire. (I'm half joking. She's actually a very sweet person . . . as long as I didn't miss my deadline!)

As my trading mentor, Ian Woodward, once said: Many hands make light work. In addition to Kristin, many Wiley staff members worked behind the scenes. Russell Rhoads, the technical editor, ensured I wasn't making things up, and other editors — Todd Lothery, Jennifer Tucci, and Elizabeth Rea — made sure my grammar made cents. (They must've missed this part!)

Though not involved directly in my project, per se, my family supported me throughout. That meant a lot. It's not something I can put into words — even as a writer.

Publisher's Acknowledgments

We're proud of this book; please send us your comments through our Dummies online registration form located at www.dummies.com/register/.

Some of the people who helped bring this book to market include the following:

Acquisitions, Editorial, and Media Development

Project Editor: Kristin DeMint

Acquisitions Editor: Stacy Kennedy

Senior Copy Editor: Elizabeth Rea

Copy Editors: Todd Lothery, Jennifer Tucci

Assistant Editor: Erin Calligan Mooney

Technical Editor: Russell Rhoads

Editorial Manager: Michelle Hacker

Editorial Assistants: Joe Niesen, Jennette ElNaggar

Cover Photo: © ACE STOCK LIMITED/ Alamy

Cartoons: Rich Tennant (www.the5thwave.com)

Composition Services

Project Coordinator: Erin Smith

Layout and Graphics: Stacie Brooks, Reuben W. Davis, Nikki Gately, Melissa K. Jester, Christine Williams

Proofreaders: Laura Albert, Context Editorial Services

Indexer: Potomac Indexing, LLC

Publishing and Editorial for Consumer Dummies

    Diane Graves Steele, Vice President and Publisher, Consumer Dummies

    Joyce Pepple, Acquisitions Director, Consumer Dummies

    Kristin Fergusan-Wagstaffe, Product Development Director, Consumer Dummies

    Ensley Eikenburg, Associate Publisher, Travel

    Kelly Regan, Editorial Director, Travel

Publishing for Technology Dummies

    Andy Cummings, Vice President and Publisher, Dummies Technology/General User

Composition Services

    Gerry Fahey, Vice President of Production Services

    Debbie Stailey, Director of Composition Services

Contents at a Glance

Introduction 1

Part 1: Getting into the Swing of Things 7

Chapter 1: Swing Trading from A to Z 9
Chapter 2: Understanding the Swing Trader's Two Main Strategies 25
Chapter 3: Getting Started with Administrative Tasks 41

Part II: Determining Your Entry and
Exit Points: Technical Analysis 57

Chapter 4: Charting the Market 59
Chapter 5: Asking Technical Indicators for Directions 89
Chapter 6: Analyzing Charts to Trade Trends, Ranges, or Both 117

Part III: Digging Deeper into the
Market: Fundamental Analysis 141

Chapter 7: Understanding a Company, Inside and Out 143
Chapter 8: Finding Companies Based on Their Fundamentals 163
Chapter 9: Six Tried-and-True Steps for Analyzing a Company's Stock 181

Part IV: Developing and Implementing
Your Trading Plan 201

Chapter 10: Strengthening Your Defense: Managing Risk 203
Chapter 11: Fine-Tuning Your Entries and Exits 231
Chapter 12: Walking through a Trade, Swing-Style 247
Chapter 13: Evaluating Your Performance 263

Part V: The Part of Tens 277

Chapter 14: Ten Simple Rules for Swing Trading..279
Chapter 15: Ten Deadly Sins of Swing Trading 289

Appendix: Resources 299

Index 309

Table of Contents

Introduction *1*

About This Book 2
Conventions Used in This Book 3
Foolish Assumptions 3
How This Book Is Organized 4
   Part I: Getting into the Swing of Things 4
   Part II: Determining Your Entry and Exit Points:
      Technical Analysis 4
   Part III: Digging Deeper into the Market: Fundamental Analysis 4
   Part IV: Developing and Implementing Your Trading Plan 5
   Part V: The Part of Tens 5
Icons Used in This Book 5
Where to Go from Here 6

Part 1: Getting into the Swing of Things *7*

Chapter 1: Swing Trading from A to Z 9

What Is Swing Trading? 10
   The differences between swing trading and
      buy-and-hold investing 11
   The differences between swing trading and day trading 12
What Swing Trading Is to You: Determining Your Time Commitment ... 13
   Swing trading as your primary source of income 13
   Swing trading to supplement income or improve investment
      returns 14
   Swing trading just for fun 15
Sneaking a Peek at the Swing Trader's Strategic Plan 15
   The "what": Determining which securities you'll trade 16
   The "where": Deciding where you'll trade 18
   The "when" and the "how": Choosing your trading
      style and strategy 19
Building Your Swing Trading Prowess 24

**Chapter 2: Understanding the Swing Trader's
Two Main Strategies** 25

Strategy and Style: The Swing Trader's Bio 25
   Two forms of analysis, head to head 26
   Scope approach: Top down or bottom up? 27
   Styles of trading: Discretionary versus mechanical 28

Wrapping Your Mind around Technical Theory 29
    Understanding how and why technical analysis works................29
    Sizing up the technical advantages and disadvantages................31
    The two main aspects of technical analysis....................................33
Appreciating the Value of the Big Picture: Fundamental Theory...........34
    Understanding how and why fundamental analysis works...........35
    Surveying the fundamental advantages and disadvantages 36
    Looking at catalysts and the great growth/value divide 38

Chapter 3: Getting Started with Administrative Tasks 41

Hooking Up with a Broker 42
    Choosing a broker...42
    Opening an account...45
Selecting Service Providers 46
    Providers to do business with 46
    Providers to avoid 50
Starting a Trading Journal 52
Creating a Winning Mindset 56

**Part II: Determining Your Entry and
Exit Points: Technical Analysis 57**

Chapter 4: Charting the Market 59

Nailing Down the Concepts: The Roles of Price and
    Volume in Charting..60
Having Fun with Pictures: The Four Main Chart Types.......................61
Charts in Action: A Pictorial View of the Security Cycle of Life 64
    The waiting game: Accumulation..64
    The big bang: Expansion..66
    The aftermath: Distribution..67
    The downfall: Contraction...69
Assessing Trading-Crowd Psychology: Popular
    Patterns for All Chart Types...70
    The Darvas box: Accumulation in action.......................................71
    Head and shoulders: The top-off 73
    The cup and handle: Your signal to stick around for coffee..........74
    Triangles: A fiscal tug of war 76
    Gaps: Your swing trading crystal ball 77
Letting Special Candlestick Patterns Reveal Trend Changes 80
    Hammer time! 80
    The hanging man (Morbid, I know) 82
    Double vision: Bullish and bearish engulfing patterns 82
    The triple threat: Morning and evening stars 83

Measuring the Strength of Trends with Trendlines 85
    Uptrend lines: Support for the stubborn bulls............................... 86
    Downtrend lines: Falling resistance 87
    Horizontal lines: Working to both support and resist 88

Chapter 5: Asking Technical Indicators for Directions.............89

All You Need to Know about Analyzing Indicators Before You Start 90
    You must apply the right type of indicator 90
    Not all price swings are meaningful 90
    Prices don't reflect volume, so you need to account for it 92
    An indicator's accuracy isn't a measure of its value...................... 92
    Two to three indicators are enough.. 93
    Inputs should always fit your time horizon.................................. 94
    Divergences are the strongest signals in technical analysis.......... 95
Determining Whether a Security Is Trending 95
Recognizing Major Trending Indicators 97
    The compass of indicators: Directional Movement Index (DMI)...98
    A mean, lean revelation machine: Moving averages 100
    A meeting of the means: MACD.. 105
Spotting Major Non-Trending Indicators.. 107
    Stochastics: A study of change over time.................................... 108
    Relative Strength Index (RSI): A comparison
       of apples and oranges... 111
Combining Technical Indicators with Chart Patterns 114
Using Technical Indicators to Determine Net Long or Net
    Short Positioning... 115

Chapter 6: Analyzing Charts to Trade Trends, Ranges, or Both.....117

Trading Trends versus Trading Ranges: A Quick Rundown 118
Trading on Trends.. 120
    Finding a strong trend 120
    Knowing when to enter a trend... 122
    Managing your risk by setting your exit level 124
Trading Ranges: Perhaps Stasis Is Bliss?.. 125
    Finding a security in a strong trading range 125
    Entering on a range and setting your exit level 127
Comparing Markets to One Another: Intermarket Analysis.................. 128
    Passing the buck: The U.S. dollar 128
    Tracking commodities.. 130
    Watching how bond price and stock price
       movements correlate.. 133
Putting Securities in a Market Head-to-Head:
    Relative Strength Analysis 134
    Treating the world as your oyster: The global scope................. 135
    Holding industry groups to the market standard....................... 137

Part III: Digging Deeper into the Market: Fundamental Analysis 141

Chapter 7: Understanding a Company, Inside and Out 143

Getting Your Hands on a Company's Financial Statements 144
    What to look for 144
    When to look 145
    Where to look 146
Assessing a Company's Financial Statements 146
    Balance sheet 147
    Income statement 151
    Cash flow statement 153
Not Just Numbers: Qualitative Data....................................... 156
Valuing a Company Based on Data You've Gathered 158
    Understanding the two main methods of valuation.................... 158
    Implementing the swing trader's preferred model...................... 159

Chapter 8: Finding Companies Based on Their Fundamentals 163

Seeing the Forest for the Trees: The Top-Down Approach.................. 163
    Sizing up the market... 164
    Assessing industry potential 170
Starting from the Grassroots Level: The Bottom-Up Approach 172
    Using screens to filter information..................................... 173
    Assessing your screening results 179
Deciding Which Approach to Use 179

Chapter 9: Six Tried-and-True Steps for Analyzing a Company's Stock 181

The Six Step Dance: Analyzing a Company 181
Taking a Company's Industry into Account.................................. 183
    Scoping out markets you're familiar with........................ 184
    Identifying what type of sector a company is in............... 184
Determining a Company's Financial Stability 187
    Current ratio.. 188
    Debt to shareholders' equity ratio 188
    Interest coverage ratio 189
Looking Back at Historical Earnings and Sales Growth 190
Understanding Earnings and Sales Expectations 192
Checking Out the Competition 194
Valuing a Company's Shares... 197
    Gauging shares' relative cheapness or expensiveness.............. 197
    Figuring out whether the comparative share-price difference is justified 198

Part IV: Developing and Implementing Your Trading Plan 201

Chapter 10: Strengthening Your Defense: Managing Risk 203

Risk Measurement and Management in a Nutshell 205
First Things First: Measuring the Riskiness of Stocks
    before You Buy 205
    Assessing the beta: One security compared to the market 206
    Looking at liquidity: Trade frequency 207
    Sizing up the company: The smaller, the riskier 208
    Avoiding low-priced shares: As simple as it sounds 209
Limiting Losses at the Individual Stock Level 209
    Figuring out how much you're willing to lose 210
    Setting your position size 211
Building a Portfolio with Minimal Risk 215
    Limit all position losses to 7 percent 215
    Diversify your allocations 217
    Combine long and short positions 220
Planning Your Exit Strategies 221
    Exiting for profitable trades 221
    Exiting based on the passage of time 225
    Exiting based on a stop loss level.. 225

Chapter 11: Fine-Tuning Your Entries and Exits 231

Understanding Market Mechanics 231
Surveying the Major Order Types 233
    Living life in the fast lane: Market orders 233
    Knowing your boundaries: Limit orders 234
    Calling a halt: Stop orders 234
    Mixing the best of both worlds: Stop limit orders 234
Placing Orders as a Part-Time Swing Trader 236
    Entering the fray 236
    Exiting to cut your losses (or make a profit) 237
Placing Orders if Swing Trading's Your Full-Time Gig 237
    Considering the best order types for you 238
    Taking advantage of intraday charting to time
        your entries and exits 238
    Investigating who's behind the bidding: Nasdaq
        Level II quotes 241

Chapter 12: Walking through a Trade, Swing-Style 247

Step 1: Sizing Up the Market.. 247
    Looking for short-term trends on the daily chart........................ 248
    Analyzing the weekly chart for longer-term trends...................... 249

Step 2: Identifying the Top Industry Groups............................250
Step 3: Selecting Promising Candidates.................................251
    Screening securities 252
    Ranking the filtered securities and assessing chart patterns 252
Step 4: Determining Position Size...255
    Setting your stop loss level 256
    Limiting your losses to a certain percentage..............257
Step 5: Executing Your Order..258
Step 6: Recording Your Trade..259
Step 7: Monitoring Your Shares' Motion and Exiting
   When the Time is Right 259
Step 8: Improving Your Swing Trading Skills 261

Chapter 13: Evaluating Your Performance....................263

No Additions, No Withdrawals? No Problem!.............................263
Comparing Returns over Different Time Periods:
   Annualizing Returns 264
Accounting for Deposits and Withdrawals:
   The Time-Weighted Return Method 266
    Breaking the time period into chunks.......................268
    Calculating the return for each time period..............270
    Chain-linking time period returns to calculate a total return 271
Comparing Your Returns to an Appropriate Benchmark............272
Evaluating Your Trading Plan 276

Part V: The Part of Tens.............................. 277

Chapter 14: Ten Simple Rules for Swing Trading...............279

Trade Your Plan..279
Follow the Lead of Industry Groups as Well as the Overall Market......281
Don't Let Emotions Control Your Trading! 282
Diversify!..283
Set Your Risk Level..283
Set a Profit Target or Technical Exit 284
Use Limit Orders...284
Use Stop Loss Orders...285
Keep a Trading Journal 286
Have Fun! 287

Chapter 15: Ten Deadly Sins of Swing Trading 289

Starting with Too Little Capital...289
Gambling on Earnings Dates 291
Speculating on Penny Stocks 291

Changing Your Trading Destination Midflight 292
Doubling Down 293
Swing Trading Option Securities 294
Thinking You're Hot Stuff 295
Concentrating on a Single Sector 296
Overtrading 296
Violating Your Trading Plan 297

Appendix: Resources 299

Sourcing and Charting Your Trading Ideas 299
    Trading ideas: MagicFormulaInvesting.com 299
    Trading software: *High Growth Stock Investor* 300
    Financial newspaper with stock ideas:
        Investor's Business Daily 301
    Charting software: *TradeStation* 302
Doing Your Market Research 303
    PIMCO's Bill Gross commentary 303
    Barron's weekly financial newspaper 304
Keeping Tabs on Your Portfolio and the Latest Market News 305
    Yahoo! Finance portfolio tool 305
    Yahoo! Economic Calendar 305
Fine-Tuning Your Trading Techniques 306
    Technical Analysis of Stocks & Commodities magazine 307
    The Black Swan: The Impact of the Highly Improbable 307

Index 309

Introduction

1 wish I could tell you that swing trading is fast and easy and leads to overnight profits that will make you an instant millionaire. Just buy my five CDs today to discover how you can swing trade to massive riches! Or attend one of my training conferences coming soon to a hotel near you: "How I Swing Trade in My Bathing Suit!" (Film cuts to a testimonial from an "actual" client wearing a Hawaiian T-shirt: "I've tried the Omar Bassal Swing Trading Technique [this is patented, of course] and I made more than $5,000 on one trade alone!")

Okay, back to reality. Swing trading isn't going to lead to overnight wealth. Period. Anyone who tells you different is either lying or has made an incredibly risky trade that turned out positive by the grace of God. You can go to Las Vegas and bet $10,000 on the color black at the roulette table and possibly double your money (your odds are slightly less than 50 percent). But is that a sound plan?

Of course not. And it's no different when it comes to swing trading.

At best, as a novice swing trader, you'll produce market returns in line or slightly above the overall market. If you're really besting the markets, it may be because you're taking an inordinate amount of risk that may eventually wipe away your account assets. And even as a stellar swing trader, expect to produce returns of 20 percent or possibly 30 percent annually. (If you want quick profits, first make sure you're an impeccable market timer, and then look into day trading.)

Unlike day traders, swing traders hold positions over several days and sometimes for a few weeks. But similar to day traders, swing traders rely heavily on signals from chart patterns and technical indicators to time their entries and exits from securities. The goal of *swing trading* is to profit from short but powerful moves on the long side (buying) and short side (selling) of the stock market.

Swing trading also differs from the buy-and-hold approach to investing. Long-term investors may hold a security through periods of weakness that may last several weeks or months, figuring that the tide will eventually turn and their investment thesis will be proven correct. Swing traders don't care for such poor performance in the near term. If a security's price is performing poorly, swing traders exit first and ask questions later. They're nimble and judicious in choosing potential opportunities.

About This Book

In *Swing Trading For Dummies,* I introduce you to the strategies and techniques of the swing trader. Moreover, I cover topics given short shrift in some trading textbooks — topics that largely determine your swing trading success. For example, whereas many textbooks focus on chart patterns and technical indicators used in buying or shorting stocks, this book goes one step further to cover the importance of money management, journal keeping, and strategy planning. Although these subjects are less glamorous than looking at charts, they're actually more important — because even exceedingly skilled chart readers will fail if they devise a flawed system, take unnecessary risks, and don't learn from their mistakes.

Here are some of the subjects this book covers:

- **Calculating investment returns:** This is one of those unglamorous topics, but if you don't properly calculate your returns, you'll never know whether you're doing any better than the overall market. The process is simple if you're not adding or taking away funds from your account, but the procedure can get more complex if you frequently withdraw or add funds.

- **Keeping a journal:** The word *journal* seems to be a lot less offensive to people's sensibilities than *diary.* A journal is like a trading coach, telling you what you did wrong or right in past trades and helping you to avoid repeating mistakes you made previously. Just knowing the symbol, price, and date of your trades isn't going to cut it. This book shows you the key features of a valuable trading journal.

- **Managing your risk:** The most important chapter in *Swing Trading For Dummies* is Chapter 10, where I explain how to manage your portfolio's risk. As remarkable as this may sound, even if you get everything wrong except your risk management, you can still make a profit. Van K. Tharp, a trading coach, once said that even a totally random entry system can be profitable if your risk management system is sound.

- **Focusing on fundamentals:** This book differs from other swing trading books in its emphasis on the fundamentals of securities. All too often, swing traders pay attention only to the chart and disregard the company behind the chart. You don't need to spend 20 hours a day analyzing a company's financial statements — swing traders don't have that kind of time on their hands. But it's essential to find out the basics and apply the most important measures in your trading.

- **Paying attention to the popular (and easy) chart patterns to trade:** Dozens of chart patterns appear from time to time in securities' price patterns, but not all of them are sound or based on investor psychology. That's why I focus on the tried-and-true chart patterns to give you the critical ones to look for.

✔ **Outlining your swing trading plan:** A trading plan must outline when you're in the market and when you're not. It must detail your criteria for entering and exiting securities. Your plan should also cover what to do when a trade doesn't work out, as well as how much you risk and how you handle your profits.

Conventions Used in This Book

I use the following conventions to assist you in reading this text:

✔ **Bold** terms are for emphasis or to highlight text appearing in bullet point format.

✔ *Italics* are used to identify new terms that you may not be familiar with. I also use italics to highlight a difference between two approaches (for example, *higher* than the first case).

✔ Monofont is used as text for Web sites.

Charts and figures used in this book have text next to them explaining the essential point the figure conveys. These captions make it easy to skip to different charts and take away the critical point made in each one.

Foolish Assumptions

I made several assumptions about you when I was writing this book. I'm assuming that you

✔ Know how to trade securities online

✔ Plan on trading stocks or exchange traded funds

✔ Have little or no experience swing trading but are well versed in the basics of trading in general

✔ Are able to access and use Internet Web sites that cover research, charting, news, and your portfolio account

✔ Have the will to change your current trading approach

✔ Don't have an MBA, CFA charter, or CMT designation and need some terms and techniques explained clearly

✔ Aren't a genius and don't think of yourself as the character Matt Damon plays in *Good Will Hunting*

✔ Appreciate humor and popular movie references

If you want to trade other types of securities — like currencies or commodities — you may want to pick up *Currency Trading For Dummies* by Mark Galant and Brian Dolan, or *Commodities For Dummies* by Amine Bouchentouf (both published by Wiley).

How This Book Is Organized

This book has five main parts. You may not need to start at Part I and proceed from there. You may be better served beginning at Part II or Part III if you already know the basics of swing trading.

For that reason, I explain the five parts as follows so you can determine which part or parts you need to focus on.

Part 1: Getting into the Swing of Things

Swing trading can be a rewarding endeavor for those who have the time and interest in trading securities over the short term. But you need to pack your backpack before you set out on the journey. Part I helps you do just that. This part introduces you to swing trading and provides an overview of the investment landscape. You also discover the brokers that cater to swing trading and the two main trading strategies (fundamental analysis and technical analysis).

Part II: Determining Your Entry and Exit Points: Technical Analysis

Swing traders rely heavily on *technical analysis:* the art and science of trading securities based on chart patterns and technical indicators. But it's easy to get lost in the world of technical analysis given how many different chart patterns and indicators exist. When should you use this indicator over that one? Part II explains the ins and outs of technical analysis for everyone from the neophyte to the market expert.

Part III: Digging Deeper into the Market: Fundamental Analysis

Fundamental analysis is given short shrift in most swing trading books, but I introduce you to the important fundamental measures you may be overlooking.

Fundamental analysis doesn't have to be a scary science that only institutions use to their advantage. You, too, can profit from simple fundamental ratios and measures. In this part, I cover the basics of financial statements and the criteria you can use to screen for under- or overvalued stocks.

Part IV: Developing and Implementing Your Trading Plan

Your trading plan is your map in the swing trading world — or your GPS, if you prefer to have directions read to you. Your trading plan outlines what you trade, how often you trade, how many positions you own, and so on. In creating your plan, you must decide how much to risk on each position and when to exit (for a profit or a loss). You also need to know how to calculate your performance so you can tell whether you're ahead or behind the overall market.

Part V: The Part of Tens

The Part of Tens includes "Ten Simple Rules for Swing Trading." Stick to these rules and you're unlikely to make any major mistakes that take you out of the game. But you need to know more than what to do; you must also know what to avoid at all costs. "Ten Deadly Sins of Swing Trading" covers ten "sins" that are sure to lead to subpar performance. Maybe not today or tomorrow, but eventually, these sins will catch up with you.

And what would a book be without an appendix? In this book's appendix, I recommend several valuable resources you should use to help you with your swing trading.

Icons Used in This Book

I use icons throughout the book to highlight certain points. Here's what each one means:

This may be somewhat self-explanatory, but the Remember icon references subject matter you should remember when swing trading. Often, the Remember icon highlights a nuance that may not be apparent at first glance.

I don't use the Warning icon often, but when you see it, take heed. As a swing trader, you must always take action to ensure you're able to swing trade another day. I use this icon to point out subject matter that, if ignored, can be hazardous to your financial health.

The Trader's Secret icon signals that the material presented is quite technical in nature. Most often, the technical tidbits are my own personal insights based on experience.

A Tip icon marks advice on making your life easier as a swing trader. If *Swing Trading For Dummies* were a second grade classroom, this icon would signal my jumping to the end of the fairy tale *Goldilocks and the Three Bears* and telling you how it ends. The Tip icon cuts through the fluff and tells you exactly what you need to know.

Where to Go from Here

Like all *For Dummies* books, this book is modular in format. That means you can skip around to different chapters and focus on what's most relevant to you. Here's my recommendation on how best to use this book depending on your skill level:

- ✔ **For a newcomer to swing trading:** I strongly encourage you to begin with Part I and proceed to Parts II and IV. You can skip Part III if you plan on exclusively using technical analysis in your swing trading.

- ✔ **For the swing trader looking to refine his or her skills:** Parts III and IV will likely be of most value to you because you probably already have a good bit of technical analysis under your belt. Help in designing your trading plan, which I cover in Part IV, may be the best way to improve your results. Remember, Chapter 10 is the most important chapter in this book.

- ✔ **For the swing trading expert:** You may benefit most by using this book to target specific areas for improvement. The index or table of contents can help you identify which parts of the book to target.

Part I
Getting into the Swing of Things

"I like the faster pace of swing trading. It shortens the agony/ecstasy cycle."

In this part . . .

If you're just embarking on your swing trading journey, then this is the part for you. In the next few chapters, I help you figure out how much time you're willing to devote to swing trading and clue you in to the lingo you need to know. I also introduce you to the rules of the swing trading game, the steps you can take to get ready to play, and some recommended strategies for growing your portfolio into a swing trading success story.

Chapter 1

Swing Trading from A to Z

In This Chapter

▶ Contrasting swing trading with other types of trading

▶ Deciding how much time you want to devote to swing trading

▶ Getting strategic by preparing your trading plan

▶ Avoiding the mistakes that many swing traders make

*Y*ou can earn a living in this world in many different ways. The most common way is by mastering some skill — such as medicine in the case of physicians, or computers in the case of information technology experts — and exchanging your time for money. The more skilled you are, the higher your compensation. The upside of mastering a skill is clear: You're relatively safe with regard to income. Of course, there are no guarantees. Your skill may become outdated (I don't believe that many horse carriage manufacturers are operating today), or your job may be shipped overseas. You also have a maximum earning potential given the maximum hours you can work without exhausting yourself.

But there's another way to make a living. Swing trading offers you the prospect of earning income based not on the hours you put in but on the quality of your trades. The better you are at trading, the higher your potential profits. Swing trading takes advantage of short-term price movements and seeks to earn a healthy return on money over a short time period.

Swing trading is a good fit for a minority of the population. It involves tremendous amounts of responsibility. You must rely on yourself and can't be reckless or prone to gambling. If you're not disciplined, you may end up with no income (or worse).

This book is a guide for those of you interested in swing trading. To understand swing trading, you should understand what it is and what it isn't.

What Is Swing Trading?

Swing trading is the art and science of profiting from securities' short-term price movements spanning a few days to a few weeks — one or two months, max. Swing traders can be individuals or institutions such as hedge funds. They're rarely 100 percent invested in the market at any time. Rather, they wait for low-risk opportunities and attempt to take the lion's share of a significant move up or down. When the overall market is riding high, they go long (or buy) more often than they go short. When the overall market is weak, they short more often than they buy. And if the market isn't doing all that much, they sit patiently on the sidelines.

Uncle Sam differentiates between trading time frames

What would a discussion of swing trading be without mentioning our good old friend Uncle Sam? He has a say in your profits and losses because you presumably pay taxes. And he treats profits and losses differently depending on whether you're a day/swing trader or the buy-and-hold variety.

The factor that determines how you're taxed is based on your holding period. If you hold a position for 366 days (one year and one day) and then sell it, any profits from that position are taxed at a lower rate than your ordinary income tax rate (which can be as high as 35 percent). Presently, this rate is 15 percent for most people (5 percent for lower-income individuals, as defined by the federal government). However, this rate can change due to tax law changes. The 15 percent tax rate is set to expire at the end of 2010.

Swing traders, of course, are unlikely to qualify for this lower tax rate on positions. Holding periods for swing traders are measured in days, not years. Short-term profits are likely to be taxed at an individual's ordinary income tax rate.

But there's an exception. The government provides special tax treatment to people it considers pattern day traders. *Pattern day traders* must trade four or more round-trip day trades in five consecutive business days. Pattern day traders must also maintain a brokerage account with at least $25,000 worth of equity (cash and stock). The government allows pattern day traders to treat profits and losses as costs of doing business. This means you can categorize home-office expenses as business expenses (and lower your overall tax rate). More important, you can convert capital gains and losses into ordinary gains and losses under the IRS accounting rules.

A swing trader who trades part time may have difficulty convincing the IRS that he or she is a pattern day trader. But if you're a full-time swing trader, you should be able to take advantage of the special treatment of pattern day traders. Otherwise, expect to pay taxes on profits at your ordinary income tax rate.

However, swing trading in tax-deferred accounts — like in an Individual Retirement Account (IRA) or a 401(k) Plan — takes care of the tax issue. Gains and profits in such accounts aren't paid until the account holder withdraws the assets (usually at retirement). Because taxes change often and depend on an individual's situation, I strongly recommend consulting an accountant or tax professional to understand how swing trading will affect your taxes.

Swing trading is different from day trading or buy-and-hold investing. Those types of investors approach the markets differently, trade at different frequencies, and pay attention to different data sources. You must understand these differences so you don't focus on aspects that are only relevant to long-term investors.

The differences between swing trading and buy-and-hold investing

If you're a buy-and-hold investor in the mold of Warren Buffett, you care little for price swings. You don't short because the overall market trend has generally been up. You study, study, and study some more to identify promising candidates that will appreciate over the coming years. Short-term price movements are merely opportunities to pick up securities (or exit them) at prices not reflective of their true value. In fact, buy-and-hold investors tend to have a portfolio *turnover rate* (the rate at which their entire portfolio is bought and sold in a year) below 30 percent.

Buy-and-hold investing is an admirable practice, and many investors should follow this approach, because it's not as time-intensive as swing trading and not as difficult (in my opinion). But if you have the work ethic, discipline, and interest in swing trading, you can take advantage of its opportunities to

- ✔ **Generate an income stream:** Buy-and-hold investors are generally concerned with wealth preservation or growth. They don't invest for current income because they sometimes have to wait a long time for an idea to prove correct. Swing trading, on the other hand, can lead to current income.

- ✔ **Time your buys and sells and hold a basket of positions to diversify your risk:** The majority of people aren't interested in closely following their finances and are best served by investing in a basket of domestic and international mutual funds covering stocks, commodities, and other asset classes. Swing traders can hold a few securities across asset classes or sectors and generate higher profits than those who invest passively.

- ✔ **Profit from price declines and excessive euphoria through shorting, which buy-and-hold investors simply can't replicate:** The essence of *shorting* is that it allows traders to profit from price declines as opposed to price increases. But shorting involves risks not inherent in buying. When you buy a stock, your loss is limited to the amount you trade. Your potential profit is unlimited, but you can only lose what you put into the security. Shorting carries the exact opposite payoff. A stock can go up over 100 percent, but the theoretical maximum amount of profit a short position can make is 100 percent if the security's price falls to $0.

Although shorting allows you to profit from the decline of a security, the potential losses from shorting are theoretically unlimited, and the potential gains are limited to the amount you short. So if a security jumps up in price by 30 or 40 percent or more, you may end up owing your broker a tremendous amount of dough.

The differences between swing trading and day trading

Opposite the buy-and-hold investor on the trading continuum is the day trader. Day traders don't hold any positions overnight. Doing so would expose them to the risk of a gap up or down in a security's price that could wipe out a large part of their account. Instead, they monitor price movements on a minute-by-minute basis and time entries and exits that span hours.

Day traders have the advantage of riding security price movements that can be quite volatile. This requires time-intensive devotion on their part. Near-term price movements can be driven by a major seller or buyer in the market and not by a company's fundamentals. Hence, day traders concern themselves with investor psychology more than they do with fundamental data. They're tracking the noise of the market — they want to know whether the noise is getting louder or quieter.

But it's not all cake and tea for day traders. They trade so often they rack up major commission charges, which makes it that much more difficult to beat the overall market. A $5,000 profit generated from hundreds of trades may net a day trader a significantly reduced amount after commissions and taxes are taken out. This doesn't include additional costs the day trader must sustain to support his or her activities.

Swing traders also face stiff commissions (versus the buy-and-hold investor), but nothing as severe as the day trader. Because price movements span several days to several weeks, a company's fundamentals can come into play to a larger degree than they do for the day trader (day-to-day movements are due less to fundamentals and more to short-term supply and demand of shares). Also, the swing trader can generate higher potential profits on single trades because the holding period is longer than the day trader's holding period.

What Swing Trading Is to You: Determining Your Time Commitment

Getting started in swing trading requires some reflection. Before you rush out to buy that slick PC or set up that brokerage account, you need to think about what kind of swing trader you want to be. (Yes, swing traders come in different shapes and sizes.)

Your first step is to determine just how much time you can commit to swing trading. You may be a full-time trader for a firm, in which case you should consider yourself as trading for a living. Or you may be doing this part time for income with the intention (and hope) of becoming a full-time trader.

Many swing traders have full-time jobs and have little time to devote to trading, so they trade primarily to improve the returns of their investment accounts. Or perhaps they're already in retirement and swing trade to grow their assets over time. These swing traders watch the market during the day but rely on orders placed outside market hours to enter or exit their positions. And if they trade in tax-deferred accounts, like an Individual Retirement Account, they can ignore the tax issue.

The point is, you can swing trade whether you have a full-time job or not, but you need to make adjustments depending on whether you're able to watch the market all day. And by the way, watching the market all day long doesn't necessarily improve your returns. In fact, doing so can lower them if it causes you to overtrade or react to market gyrations.

Swing trading as your primary source of income

If you intend to swing trade as your primary means of generating income, be prepared to spend several months — if not years — gaining experience before you're able to give up your job and trade from home full time. Swing traders who trade full time devote several hours a day to trading. They research possible trades before, during, and after market hours. And they handle pressure well.

Many traders find that they can't handle the stress of trading full time. After all, if swing trading is your main source of income, you face a lot of pressure to generate consistent profits. And you may be more tempted to gamble if you encounter a string of losses. What many traders fail to realize is that the correct response to a series of losses isn't *more* trading but *less* trading. Take a step back and evaluate the situation.

Swing trading for a living isn't difficult in the sense that to excel at it requires some kind of amazing IQ level or insane work ethic. Rather, it requires an incredible amount of self-restraint, discipline, and calm. A swing trader who trades for income must always be unemotional. When things don't work out, he or she doesn't try to get even but moves on to another opportunity.

So don't quit your day job just because you generate impressive profits for a few months. The name of this game is to always have enough capital to come back and play again. If you plan on living off of $5,000 per month, for example, you can't expect to generate that kind of profit on $30,000 of capital. That would require a monthly gain of 16.67 percent! Some of the best all-time traders in the world topped out at returns of 20 to 25 percent *annually* over 20 or 30 years.

Swing trading to supplement income or improve investment returns

This category likely applies to the lion's share of swing traders. Swing trading with an eye on earning additional income or improving the returns on your portfolio is less stressful than swing trading for a living. You still have something to fall back on if you make a mistake, and you can swing trade while holding down a full-time job.

Part-time swing traders often do their analysis when they get home from work and then implement trades the following day. Even though they may not be able to watch the market all the time, they can enter stop loss orders to protect their capital.

If you want to eventually swing trade full time, you should go through this phase first. Over time, you'll be able to determine how well you've done. And if you follow the other recommendations in this book (like keeping a trading journal, which I cover in Chapter 3), you'll learn from your mistakes and improve your techniques.

Swing trading part time is suitable for those individuals who

- ✔ Have a full-time job
- ✔ Can devote a few hours a week to analyzing markets and securities
- ✔ Have a passion for financial markets and short-term trading
- ✔ Have the discipline to consistently place stop loss orders
- ✔ Are achieving subpar returns in their current investment portfolios from a financial advisor or third party
- ✔ Don't gamble with their own money and are unlikely to fall prey to doubling down or taking major risks

If you fit these criteria, then part-time swing trading may be for you. When you first start out, I recommend swing trading with just a small portion of your portfolio so any early mistakes don't prove too costly. Although paper trading can be beneficial, it can't compare to the emotions you'll be battling as a swing trader when you put your own money on the line.

Swing trading just for fun

Some swing traders get a rush from buying and selling securities, sometimes profiting and sometimes losing. Their motivation isn't to provide or supplement current income. Rather, these swing traders do it for the excitement that comes from watching positions they buy and sell move up and down. Of course, this can lead to significant losses if they abandon the rules designed to protect their capital — rules that I outline throughout this book (specifically in Chapter 10).

If you want to swing trade solely for fun, my advice is: don't. I recommend you get your kicks at a bowling alley or basketball court. The danger of trading for fun is that you're using real money with real consequences. You may begin to risk more of your capital to satisfy your need for excitement. If you lose, you may take extreme action to prove yourself right in the end, like putting all your money into one or two securities. By then you're really in the realm of gambling.

If you insist on trading for fun, at least restrict yourself to a small amount of your assets and never touch your retirement nest egg. Remember that you're competing with traders who are motivated by profit, not just excitement. That gives them an advantage over someone who just enjoys the game.

Sneaking a Peek at the Swing Trader's Strategic Plan

Plan your trade and trade your plan.

Fail to plan and you plan to fail.

Countless clichés address the importance of a trading plan. A trading plan is the business plan of your trading business. Without the plan, you're likely to fall into the trap of making things up as you go. Your trading will be erratic. You won't improve because you won't have the records on your past trading. You may think your trading plan is in your head, but if you haven't written it down, for all intents and purposes it doesn't exist.

Throughout this book I cover all the important parts of swing trading strategy in detail. In the following sections, I preview the critical parts of the strategy, trimming them all down into one neat little package. (For more on your trading plan, see Chapter 10.)

The "what": Determining which securities you'll trade

Your trading plan should identify the securities you trade. As a swing trader, you can choose from a variety of securities:

✔ **Public equity (stock):** This category is perhaps what you're most familiar with. Common stocks, American Depository Receipts, and exchange traded funds fall under this rubric. Swing traders often trade stocks exclusively because of the variety, ease, and familiarity of trading corporate stocks. Most stocks listed in the United States trade every day, but stocks in foreign markets may trade infrequently (perhaps once a week). To make your entries and exits as painless as possible, you must focus only on those stocks that meet a specified level of volume. Trying to sell 1,000 shares of a stock that trades 5,000 shares in a day can be extremely costly. I recommend you use stocks due to the abundant information on firms domestically and even internationally.

One of the beauties of stocks is how efficient they are to trade, partly because they offer exposure to other asset classes. For example, you can gain exposure to the commodity gold by trading an exchanged traded fund with underlying assets in gold bullion. I stick to stocks myself because that's my area of expertise, and I recommend them because of this exposure to other asset classes and because of the variety of positions you can choose from. But you may wish to trade other asset classes as well — that's your call.

• **American Depository Receipts (ADRs):** ADRs have become increasingly important in today's globalized world. Simply put, an ADR allows U.S. investors to buy shares of foreign companies. ADRs are quoted in U.S. dollars and pay dividends in U.S. dollars. Trading ADRs is much more cost efficient than setting up accounts in several foreign countries, converting your dollars into foreign currencies, and so on. And because the economic growth of emerging nations is outstripping the growth of developed countries, ADRs can offer strong profit opportunities. ADRs of companies based in emerging markets (like Brazil or China) are sometimes highly leveraged to a particular commodity, making ADRs one way to profit from commodity price strength.

- **Exchange traded funds (ETFs):** ETFs are pooled investments. The most common ETFs mirror the movement of an index (such as SPY, a popular ETF that tracks the S&P 500 Index) or a subsector of an index. If you want to ride a coming tech bounce, you may be better served trading a technology ETF than choosing a particular tech company that may or may not follow the overall tech sector. That's because if you're right on the move, you'll profit from a diversified technology ETF. However, a single technology security may buck the trend. ETFs also offer you the ability to profit from international indexes and commodities.

✔ **Closed end funds:** These funds are basically mutual funds that trade on a secondary exchange. Traditional, open end mutual funds are priced according to their *net asset value* — or the value left after subtracting the fund's liabilities from its assets. Closed end funds are different. They're priced according to the supply and demand for shares of that particular fund. Sometimes, a closed end fund will trade for more than its net asset value; other times, it will trade for less. Closed end funds may be an efficient way to profit from international markets.

✔ **Fixed-income markets:** These markets include securities issued by governments on the federal, state, and local level, as well as those issued by corporations. The value of fixed-income securities depends on interest rates, inflation, the issuer's credit worthiness, and other factors. Because the fixed-income market tends to have less volatility than stocks and other asset classes, many swing traders usually avoid trading it.

✔ **Futures contracts:** Standardized contracts to buy or sell an underlying asset on a certain date in the future at a certain price are known as *futures contracts.* Futures are traded on commodities and financial instruments, such as equity indexes. Technically, the buyer and seller don't exchange money until the contract's expiration. However, futures exchanges require traders to post a margin of 5 percent to 15 percent of the contract's value. This means that traders can employ extreme leverage, if they choose, by putting down only a small amount of the contract's value.

I strongly recommend avoiding the use of such extreme leverage because of the potential to lose most, if not all, of your assets due to an unexpected move in a security. Newcomers in particular should avoid using leverage. Even experienced swing traders can become careless or arrogant before the market educates them.

✔ **Commodities:** This security type is perhaps the biggest asset class receiving attention today other than stocks. With the boom in the prices of everything from gold to crude oil, commodities are attracting more money from swing traders. Commodities — including energy commodities, agricultural commodities, and precious metals — are traded in the futures markets.

You can profit from commodity price movements through stocks or exchange traded funds. For example, swing traders wanting to profit from movements in gold prices can trade streetTRACKS Gold shares, which tracks the movement of gold bullion prices. But trading commodities involves risks and issues that differ from trading equities. (See *Commodities For Dummies* by Amine Bouchentouf, published by Wiley, for more information on trading commodities.)

✔ **The currency market:** Often called the foreign exchange market or forex market, the *currency market* is the largest financial market in the world. According to the Bank of International Settlements, the average daily turnover in the foreign exchange markets is $3.21 trillion. Like the futures market, trading in the currency market allows for extreme leverage.

Not all brokers offer trading in foreign exchange, so make sure you check whether your broker has the capability. Unlike stocks, trading in the currency market is concentrated in a few currencies: the U.S. dollar, the euro, the Japanese yen, the British pound sterling, and the Swiss franc. If you plan on using fundamental analysis to complement your technical analysis as a swing trader (see the definitions of both terms in the section "Establishing your analysis techniques" later in this chapter), be prepared to learn about the various factors that affect the value of foreign currencies: inflation, political stability, government deficits, and economic growth — to name a few. (See *Currency Trading For Dummies* by Mark Galant and Brian Dolan, published by Wiley, for more information on trading currencies.)

✔ **Options:** Investment contracts that give the purchaser the option, but not the obligation, to buy an underlying asset at a specified price up until the expiration date are known as *options*. Options are highly risky and not efficient swing trading vehicles because of their illiquidity.

The "where": Deciding where you'll trade

Where you trade depends a great deal on what you trade. Stocks, commodities, currencies, and bonds trade on different markets.

The New York Stock Exchange (NYSE), American Stock Exchange (AMEX), and NASDAQ list stocks based in the United States and abroad (they also list other investment vehicles, like exchange traded funds, that enable you to profit from movements in prices of commodities and other asset classes). The NASDAQ differs from the NYSE and AMEX in that it's completely electronic and allows for efficient transaction and order routing.

Not all stocks trade on these markets. Recently, electronic communication networks (ECNs) have emerged as an efficient way to match buy and sell orders. ECNs connect individual traders with major brokerage firms. You sometimes can get a better price by submitting orders to an ECN instead of a broker. The easiest way to access ECNs is by subscribing to a broker who provides direct access trading.

But swing traders can buy and sell other securities on other markets. For example, if you want to trade an actual commodity, the Chicago Board of Trade (CBOT) lists several commodities: ethanol, gold, silver, corn, oats, rice, soybeans, and wheat. The New York Mercantile Exchange (NYMEX) also lists popular commodities like crude oil, coal, natural gas, and gold. But you must consider the additional risk factors if you venture outside trading stocks. For example, commodities require different margin requirements than stocks. Not properly employing a risk management system can lead to losing your entire capital on a single trade. Commodities also trade on different fundamentals than companies or fixed-income securities.

If you want to trade commodities, currencies, or other investment vehicles, you need to trade via firms authorized to transact in those markets.

The "when" and the "how": Choosing your trading style and strategy

Whether you enter orders during or after market hours affects your entry and exit strategies.

- ✔ Part-time swing traders enter orders when markets are closed and rely on limit and stop losses to execute this strategy.

- ✔ Full-time traders, on the other hand, can execute their entries and exits during the day and incorporate intraday price action into their timing of trades. They also find more trading opportunities because they have more time to devote to swing trading.

How you trade refers to your various trading strategies, which I outline in this section.

Establishing your analysis techniques

Swing traders rely on two major analysis techniques: technical analysis and fundamental analysis. *Technical analysis,* broadly speaking, encompasses chart pattern analysis and the application of mathematical formulas to security prices and volume. *Fundamental analysis* covers earnings, sales, and other fundamentals of a company or a security.

In my experience, most swing traders rely solely or in large measure on technical analysis. However, I explain both analysis techniques in this book because I strongly believe that understanding and using both improves the odds of success.

Both analysis techniques have their advantages:

- ✔ **Technical analysis can be quickly and easily applied to any market or security.** For example, a trained swing trader can use technical analysis to quickly decide whether to buy or sell a security using chart patterns of technical indicators. In contrast, a swing trader relying on fundamental analysis needs more time to read about a company, its business, and its earnings before coming to a conclusion. Whether you're trading commodities, currencies, stocks, or bonds, you can apply technical analysis uniformly to these markets. In other words, if you know how to interpret a chart, then the kind of security being plotted is largely irrelevant. In my opinion, the ease of application is the biggest advantage technical analysis has over fundamental analysis.

- ✔ **Fundamental analysis can answer questions that are beyond the scope of technical analysis, such as, "Why is this security price moving?"** Swing trading on the long and short side based, in part, on fundamentals is like having a head start in the 100-meter dash. Rallies and declines that are driven by fundamentals are more profitable to trade than rallies and declines that are simply the result of noise in the markets (such as a large mutual fund liquidating or buying a position). Over the long term, security movements are driven by the securities' underlying fundamentals. Crude oil prices rise when demand exceeds supply or when supply becomes scarce — not, as technical analysis may superficially indicate, because the chart developed a bullish formation. (Of course, crude oil — or any security — can rise or fall due to non-fundamental reasons. But such rallies and declines are often fleeting and not as strong as fundamentally driven price moves.)

Some swing traders shy away from learning about a company's fundamentals. Generally, fundamental analysis is seen as long, laborious, and not always right. But you can improve your swing trading by getting to the essence of a company's fundamentals, even though it does require extensive reading, researching, and modeling.

Just how much should you care about a company's fundamentals? The general rule of thumb is that the longer your investment horizon, the more important fundamental analysis becomes. The shorter your horizon, the less important fundamental analysis is in trading securities. This is because short-term movements are driven by momentum, noise, and other factors. Over the long term, however, fundamentals always win out.

But just because you understand how to apply fundamentals doesn't mean you'll make money. Markets don't rise simply because they're undervalued, or fall simply because they're overvalued. Markets can remain under- or overvalued for long periods of time. That's why I don't recommend swing trading on fundamentals alone. Fundamental analysis tells you which way the wind is blowing so you're prepared, but technical analysis provides the important timing components.

Choosing candidates to buy

You can find promising securities in two main ways — the top-down approach and the bottom-up approach. Both are covered in detail in Chapter 8, but here's a brief rundown:

- ✔ **Top-down:** Swing traders who prefer the top-down approach identify opportunities beginning at the market level, drill down to the industry level, and finally look at individual companies. If you fit this category, your entry strategy should begin with an examination of the overall markets, then trickle down to the major sectors in the market, and then to the industries within the strongest or weakest sectors. At this point, you rank the securities in the industry on some technical or fundamental measure (more on that in Chapter 8). Then you select the securities that meet your entry strategy.

- ✔ **Bottom-up:** Swing traders who use the bottom-up approach are grassroots-oriented individuals who look for strong securities and then filter promising ones by their industry groups or sectors. If you fit this category, your approach begins with a screen of some sort (a *screen* is a quantitative filter), sometimes depending on whether growth or value stocks are in favor at that particular point in time. If that's the case, you then compare the relative strength of the growth and value indexes (and possibly also the market capitalizations of the market). After identifying which securities rank highest in the screen, you determine which securities meet your entry rules, and then you trade only those securities that reside in leading or lagging industry groups, depending on whether you favor buying or shorting.

Planning your exit

Most swing traders focus almost entirely on their entry strategy, but it's the exit strategy that determines when you take profits, when you take losses, and when you exit a meandering position so you can put the capital to better use. So although planning your entry is important, you need to spend equal (if not more) time on your exit.

Your exit strategy is most likely going to be technically driven, and it's threefold:

- ✔ **Determine when you exit for a profit.** Don't take profits based on a gut feeling — rely on a trigger or catalyst instead. For example, some exit strategies for profits stipulate that the time for departure arrives when prices reach the implied target based on a chart pattern, or when shares close below a moving average.

- ✔ **Determine when you exit for a loss.** Your exit strategy for losses should be based on the breach of a support level, a resistance level (in the case of shorting), or some type of moving average (for example, the nine-day moving average). (*Support levels* are simply price zones where securities stop falling, and *resistance levels* are price zones where prices stop rising.) This keeps your losses limited to some known quantity (barring, of course, a gap up or down in the security price, which must be addressed by proper position sizing and other risk management techniques).

✔ **Determine when you exit if a trade generates neither profits nor losses.** That is, it meanders sideways and results in dead weight. Some swing traders exit a position quickly if it doesn't perform. I prefer to give a position a few days to prove itself one way or the other. So I recommend exiting a position after ten days if it hasn't hit your stop loss level or triggered a profit-taking signal.

You should outline your exit strategy by making sure your trading plan addresses when you exit for profit, loss, and capital redeployment.

Settling on when you'll net long or short

Swing traders sometimes short securities to profit from price declines. If you choose to incorporate shorting into your trading strategy, you must determine when you'll be net long or net short.

Net long means that the majority of assets you've invested in are on the long side of the market. *Net short* means that the majority of assets you've invested in are on the short side of the market. And if your long and short assets are equal, then you're *market neutral.*

Generally, the decision to be net long or net short is driven by the state of the major market index. When the S&P 500, for example, is in a bull market, then most swing traders are net long. When the S&P 500 is falling, most swing traders are net short. And when the market is in a trading range, swing traders may be market neutral.

Preparing your risk management plan

The most important part of your trading plan is how you manage risk. Risk management, which I cover in detail in Chapter 10, addresses how you manage risk on an individual security level and on the portfolio level as a whole. A trading plan with a weak entry strategy and a weak exit strategy can still be profitable if the risk management strategy limits losses and lets profits run.

In order to effectively manage your risk, you need to account for the following aspects of your trading plan:

✔ **How much you risk on an individual position:** Your trading plan must spell out how much you plan on allocating to a single position.

✔ **How much you risk of your overall portfolio:** You determine how much of your total portfolio is at risk on a single position. Generally, this figure should be 0.5 to 2 percent (see Chapter 10).

✔ **How to achieve proper diversification:** Diversification means more than adding several securities. You need to have exposure to different asset classes, sectors, and market capitalizations.

✔ **How you combine long and short positions:** Combining long and short positions enables your portfolio to benefit in up and down markets.

✔ **How you implement the 7 percent rule:** How much you risk on a single position is different from how much you risk of your total portfolio. The 7 percent rule caps your total risk at 7 percent.

✔ **How you determine your exit points:** Your exits should be driven by support and resistance ranges, technical indicators, and profit targets.

✔ **What triggers an exit:** An exit may occur due to a loss, a profit, or a lack of meaningful market action.

✔ **How you manage your emotions:** No matter how effective a risk management system is, it ultimately must be enacted by a human being. Thus, this last point is paramount, because humans are affected by emotions, experiences, and hopes. This fact can cause a swing trader to abandon the stringent rules he or she has fashioned and may have been following for years.

I've found that managing emotions is the most difficult aspect of swing trading. The better you get at trading, the more likely your emotions will convince you to cut corners and abandon the rules that got you to where you are. But emotions can be managed. You can limit their impact by, for example, implementing stop loss orders that get you out of a security without your interference.

The preceding bullets all boil down to two categories of action: position sizing and limiting losses at the portfolio level. So what's the difference between the two? Alexander Elder, a trading expert, once differentiated between losses suffered at the individual stock level and the portfolio level through an analogy of sharks and fish. Specifically, he said that position sizing is done to reduce the risk that your portfolio will suffer a "shark bite" loss from a single position. That is, a single major loss that wipes out your account value.

On the other hand, portfolio risk management is done to prevent *several* small losses from killing you — or as he described it, death by piranha bites. A single small piranha may not be able to kill a larger mammal, but dozens of piranha working together can be deadly.

Similarly, a small loss is not life threatening for a portfolio. The risk is that several small losses may gang up and cause major loss. That's why you must limit losses on an individual stock level (and avoid those shark bites) while also limiting losses on the portfolio level (to prevent death by piranha bites).

Building Your Swing Trading Prowess

Staying on top of your game means you can never stop learning or improving yourself. Sadly, you can't simply become a swing trading extraordinaire and implement your trades with nary a single problem. Heck, a master martial artist doesn't stop after earning his or her black belt — why would a swing trader?

The following action items will help you stay strong throughout your swing trading career:

- ✔ **Admit to losses when they occur.** Markets have a way of humbling even the most skilled traders if they let their egos get in the way of their trading. Some traders hold onto losing positions in the hopes that they can eventually break even — a policy that devastates an account in the long run. A losing position not only may lose more money but it also ties up capital that could be invested in more promising trading opportunities.

- ✔ **Be a student of the markets.** Successful swing traders never stop absorbing information. The markets are always changing, with new investment vehicles appearing and new laws being introduced. As a swing trader, you must maintain intellectual curiosity. Reading books is one way to continually stay informed. Take an interest in understanding your positions and reading the pro and con arguments on them.

- ✔ **Try to insulate yourself as much as possible from others' opinions, whether the person is an Average Joe or a Wall Street analyst.** Remember, Wall Street is a community, and analysts send out their opinion reports to hundreds, if not thousands, of traders and portfolio managers. Reading those reports can lead you to think like the analyst does — and like hundreds of others do. Good performance doesn't come by copying what everyone else is doing.

- ✔ **Don't frequent message boards.** Message boards often foster a group mentality that a position should behave a certain way. You don't want to gather knowledge from just anyone on the Internet. Rather, stick to trusted sources and form your own opinion on matters.

Chapter 2

Understanding the Swing Trader's Two Main Strategies

In This Chapter

▶ Considering different trading strategies and styles

▶ Understanding technical analysis: charts, trends, and indicators

▶ Figuring out fundamental analysis: catalysts, growth stocks, and value stocks

As a soon-to-be swing trader, how do you uncover promising opportunities? And after you uncover those opportunities, how do you time your entries and exits? Very good questions, and I'm glad you asked.

Like all traders, swing traders rely primarily on two main strategies: technical analysis and fundamental analysis. The difference between swing traders and all the rest of 'em, though, is that most swing traders rely on one form of analysis at the exclusion of the other; the majority of swing traders use technical analysis either solely or in conjunction with fundamental analysis.

I encourage you to use both strategies. After all, understanding why stocks move and which ones are likely to move can be just as important as knowing which stocks are moving. After spending years trading and managing money, I believe a swing trader should be well rounded in his or her approach.

Strategy and Style: The Swing Trader's Bio

Technical analysis deals with charting and technical indicators. *Fundamental analysis* is principally concerned with earnings, corporate events (takeovers, acquisitions, and so on), and valuation. Some swing traders are *discretionary* — they use technical and/or fundamental analysis to evaluate each potential trade and make decisions based on the rules they've outlined for themselves. Other swing traders are *mechanical* — they use either or both forms of analysis and make trades using an automated system (they rely on a computer to execute their strategies).

This chapter introduces you to both strategies (technical and fundamental analysis) and both styles of trading (discretionary and mechanical). Only you can determine what kind of trader you want to be based on your interests and expertise.

Two forms of analysis, head to head

Devoid of calculations, reading, or other time-intensive research, technical analysis allows a swing trader to examine *any* security — be it stock, commodity, currency, or something else — and make a decision on its likely short-term direction. The swing trader relying on technical analysis doesn't care about what a company does, how it makes its money, or whether the CEO is embezzling funds — he or she cares for nothing but the ticker tape. After all, swing traders earn profits based on a security's price, not how many widgets a company sells or the academic pedigree of its board of directors.

Technical analysis is particularly important for swing traders with a very short time horizon (that is, a couple of days). The shorter your time horizon, the more prominently technical analysis should figure in your trading plan.

The swing trader who relies on fundamental analysis is a different breed. This trader wants to know what line of business a company is in, whether that industry is on the rocks or gaining momentum, when a company reports its earnings, and what those earnings expectations are. The swing trader using fundamental analysis isn't interested in *every* detail of a company's balance sheet. After all, if you're looking at trading stocks of ten companies in the coming week, you don't have the time to read those companies' annual reports cover to cover. Instead, a high-level overview is enough. Intricate modeling in Excel, though useful, isn't practical for a swing trader who buys and sells stocks over a period of days.

Newcomers to swing trading are typically attracted to technical analysis, for a couple reasons:

- ✔ **Technical analysis doesn't require nearly as much work as fundamental analysis.** A fundamental analyst has more variables to deal with and more calculations to compute. To analyze a firm, a fundamental analyst must understand the dynamics of the firm's industry, its competitors, its cost structure, its management team, and other factors.

- ✔ **Trading decisions based on fundamental analysis takes more time to play out than those based on technical analysis.** A company may be deeply undervalued relative to the market and its industry, but being undervalued doesn't necessarily mean shares will rise tomorrow or the day after. Some companies' shares stay undervalued for weeks, months, or even years. That's why long-term investors rely so heavily on fundamental analysis — they can afford to be patient.

✔ **Technical analysis, because it relies more on charts and indicators, involves less subjectivity than fundamental analysis.** A fundamental analyst can have all relevant information and still come to the wrong conclusion.

Despite the major advantages of technical analysis, my goal is to convince you to use both strategies in your swing trading plan — you tend to get the best investment results when a security's fundamentals line up perfectly with the technicals. Neither fundamental analysis nor technical analysis is perfect, and neither is superior to the other. In fact, many top swing traders use fundamental analysis to trade short term. Why? Because as a swing trader, you need to understand what drives price movements in the securities you trade. Fundamental analysis helps you understand how news impacts the market and the shares you're trading. After all, what drives oil stocks higher is quite different from what drives technology stocks higher. Moves out of such securities can be powerful and longer lasting than securities that pop or fall due solely to technical considerations.

You can integrate technical analysis and fundamental analysis without much difficulty, but don't integrate them for the sake of integration. If you feel more comfortable with one type of analysis (likely technical analysis), then use that method. If you're attracted to using fundamental analysis to the exclusion of technical analysis, then excel at it. You can be a successful swing trader by using one type of analysis alone — as long as you use a strict risk management system (see Chapter 10).

Scope approach: Top down or bottom up?

Regardless of which approach you take, you should also think about whether you want to be a top-down swing trader or a bottom-up swing trader (I don't recommend using both approaches in this case). A *top-down* trader finds securities by beginning at a macro level and drilling down to an industry and then to a particular company. A *bottom-up* trader finds securities by beginning at the bottom (that is, with individual companies) and then selecting the company that has the best industry group and macro-level fundamentals.

Recognizing that you can use technical analysis or fundamental analysis with the top-down or bottom-up approach is important. For example, you can select undervalued securities using fundamental screens (a bottom-up approach, as explained in Chapter 8) and then vet those securities for strong or weak chart patterns. Alternatively, you can identify strong or weak stocks using industry chart patterns (a top-down approach, covered in Chapter 8) and then investigate those securities to find the candidates that are most compelling to buy or short.

Styles of trading: Discretionary versus mechanical

Discretionary swing traders evaluate potential trades based on their trading plan. They use either fundamental or technical analysis to determine whether each trade meets their requirements. Although the discretionary trader's rules are written down, he or she may pass on or take trades based on experience or gut. The discretionary swing trader doesn't follow a program such as, "If A, then B." Instead, he or she synthesizes all available info, weighs items, and then makes a call.

Mechanical swing traders are much different. They map out trading strategies that a computer can execute. The mechanical system can be based on technical inputs (like price, indicators, and so on) or fundamental ones (such as earnings surprises, sales growth rates, and other corporate events). The strategies are programmed into a computer software program that tests them on historical market data. The mechanical swing trader analyzes those results to determine whether the strategy is worth pursuing — if it produces higher profits than the overall market, for example.

As you may've guessed, the two approaches both have advantages and disadvantages:

- ✔ Discretionary trading allows for a fresh look at each situation and the ability to pass on trades when external data that may not be easily captured in a computer program indicates decreased chances of success. However, because the discretionary trader must make a decision on each buy or sell, he or she is more prone to falling in love with trades, becoming emotionally attached, or failing to follow the trading plan.

- ✔ Mechanical trading largely takes the human out of the equation. A computer program, barring some kind of catastrophe, executes the trades as programmed. The only input on the swing trader's part is the amount of capital devoted to each position, the entry signals, and the exit rules. After those factors are determined, the mechanical trader can step back and watch the computer work its magic. But mechanical trading systems also have their drawbacks. Can a system be designed to capture all contingencies or possibilities that may arise? Of course not. And when losses occur, the mechanical swing trader must determine whether the setback is a temporary part of the system or whether it represents a fundamental failure of the strategy.

This text is geared toward discretionary traders. Although hard data on the proportion of swing traders who are discretionary or mechanical is hard to come by, my experience and anecdotal evidence point to discretionary trading as the more common approach. After all, some things, such as recognizing chart patterns, can't be easily programmed into a computer. And most swing traders feel more in control when they evaluate each trade instead of relying on a computer to execute transactions.

Wrapping Your Mind around Technical Theory

Technical analysis is the art of reading a security price chart with volume and determining the security's likely direction based on the strength of buyers and sellers. Technical analysis can range from the simple (interpreting a chart pattern) to the complex (performing intermarket analysis and interpreting indicators based on differential equations). Basic chart interpretation is an important skill, but swing traders typically rely on indicators and intermarket analysis.

The technical analyst is principally concerned with the following questions:

- ✔ Is this security in a bull or bear market in the short and long term?

- ✔ Is the security trending or in a trading range?

- ✔ Who's in control of the market — buyers or sellers?

- ✔ Is the strength of the buyers/sellers increasing or waning?

- ✔ What price point indicates a reversal or failure?

- ✔ What signals the time to enter?

- ✔ What signals the time to exit?

Understanding how and why technical analysis works

So why does technical analysis work? How can examining past price history possibly provide insight into future price movements?

- ✔ **Market participants, acting alone, react similarly to major news.** Technical analysis is partly based on the psychology of crowds. Even though all investors may not be congregated in a single room, they're all human. Hence, they're susceptible to the same emotions all humans share: greed, fear, hope, and the like. Security prices would be very difficult to analyze if everyone trading were Spock-like — perfectly logical with no emotions getting in the way.

- ✔ **Market participants have memory.** Traders, investors, and other market participants have reference points when they buy or sell securities. The price they pay when they buy a security affects when they're likely to sell that security (even though it should have no bearing on that decision). They remember their purchase price and, naturally, want to either make a profit or break even. If the security price swoons after they purchase shares, they're likely to feel pain. And if the price recovers to their original purchase price, many will be happy to sell to break even. What these traders and investors often don't realize is that hundreds, if not thousands, of others are experiencing these same emotions. This fact is why certain price levels are more significant than others. Securities tend to find *support* (a level at which security prices stop falling and begin to rise) and *resistance* (a level at which security prices stop rising and begin to fall) at round numbers.

I'm amazed at how often traders place buy limit or sell limit orders at round price figures. Don't they realize that many other traders may be doing the exact same thing, and that their actions may prevent the price from ever reaching that level? Quite simply, a sell limit of $100 isn't too bright, because other traders or investors likely placed orders at that same round number. And their orders may prevent yours from ever getting executed (the overwhelming supply of shares at that level will force the stock to retreat before reaching $100). On the other hand, a sell limit of $98.71 is smart, because it's unlikely that other traders placed an order at that specific price, and you have a much better chance of your order getting executed.

✔ **Smart investors' actions show up on the chart.** *Smart money* often refers to investment money made by institutional investors who buy or sell securities based on sound, reasoned analysis. These investors have the resources to call the suppliers and customers of firms they invest in and can determine with a high degree of confidence whether a company's earnings are on- or off-track. Smart money also constitutes insiders at a firm who have an information advantage over other market participants and may trade on that information.

Dumb money, on the other hand, refers to investment money made by amateurs who buy or sell securities for the thrill of investment. Dumb money can include retirement plans or corporate plans that divest securities that no longer meet the plans' criteria. This selling pressure pushes prices down for no good reason. Dumb money can also include institutional investors who buy or sell stocks because they fall in love with their investments. Believe it or not, institutional investors are subject to the same whims and emotional swings experienced by all traders.

✔ **Folks with knowledge of a company's prospects can only take advantage of that knowledge by trading on the open market.** Their trading shows up on the ticker tape (it's the law). So if you know that Microsoft is going to have a blowout quarter (by legal means, of course, and not through insider knowledge), you can't profit from that knowledge except by buying shares. And your buying is going to show up as volume on a price chart. Others who may not know about the blowout quarter can, nonetheless, infer that something is up when they see Microsoft's shares rising on heavy volume.

Sizing up the technical advantages and disadvantages

Because the price chart shows all available public and private information, technical analysis can really shine bright when prices diverge from their fundamentals. Opportunity is greatest when you're in the minority, but right. If everyone, including you, expects shares of Coca-Cola to do well, you won't make much money because everybody else has already come to the same conclusion as you. However, if you think something is terribly wrong at a company and everyone else is on the other side, you stand to make a large profit if you're right and the crowd has to correct its collective opinion by selling stock.

For example, shares of Enron were tumbling in late 2000 despite what appeared to be stellar fundamentals. Price drops were met by upgrades and buy recommendations by Wall Street analysts who, using all available public data, determined that shares represented a major value.

But prices kept falling. A swing trader using technical analysis would conclude that something wasn't right. If everything was peachy, why were shares falling? Something must be up. And sure enough, something was up — something mischievous indeed. Investors using fundamental analysis, on the other hand, are often alerted of underlying cracks in a company's financial position after it's too late.

Despite the advantage technical analysis has of signaling information that you may not know, this strategy isn't a cure-all for your trading woes. Reading a chart involves a degree of interpretation, and sometimes whipsaws or indications can give you one signal, only to reverse a short while later. Moreover, a major event can occur that no one knows about. For these reasons, you'll never know with certainty that a particular chart pattern or indicator will yield a profitable signal. Swing traders (indeed, all traders) have to learn to live with this uncertainty, which also exists in fundamental analysis (or any analysis technique, for that matter). Some swing traders are actually wrong the majority of the time, but still extremely successful. Why? Because the many losers are small, whereas the few winners are huge.

Some of the major advantages of technical analysis are that it

- Applies consistently across time and markets
- Can be used on a single security in a short period of time
- Incorporates the psychology of the crowd, whether rational or irrational
- Allows for support and resistance levels for exits and entries
- Involves low levels of subjectivity in the analysis of charts

Is technical analysis valid?

Despite being viewed by portfolio managers as useful in some respect, charting has largely been rejected in the world of academia. Professors generally believe that chart reading is a lot of smoke and mirrors and hocus pocus. Academics and some portfolio managers hold the belief that Peter Lynch, the legendary Fidelity mutual fund manager, succinctly expressed: "You can't see the future through a rearview mirror." I couldn't agree more. I wouldn't drive my car looking in the rearview mirror — unless, of course, I had the car in reverse.

Burton Malkiel, professor of economics at Princeton University, is a proponent of the notion that investors can't outperform the market using technical analysis (in fairness, he also feels that fundamental analysis won't help you outperform the market either). So are Lynch and Malkiel correct in their conclusions against technical analysis? Is technical analysis a fool's game? I think not. Of course, my voice doesn't carry the same weight as Lynch's or Malkiel's, so I'll consult my own expert, who comes to a very different conclusion.

Professor Jeremy Siegel of the Wharton School of Business finds that chart reading and technical analysis can assist in the timing of buying and selling securities. Others have come to similar conclusions: Technical indicators can be shown to add value to trading.

Many successful mutual fund and hedge fund managers use charts to profit on a short-term and long-term basis. And as a portfolio manager overseeing assets of exceeding $1 billion, I can tell you firsthand that chart reading can and does work. (This in no way means that other techniques — such as fundamental analysis, which I cover in Part III of this book — don't work.)

So just why does technical analysis work? Because it

✔ **Helps you identify areas of support and resistance:** When breached, these areas often signal important changes in security prices. The areas can be horizontal (to identify stationary levels of support or resistance), rising, or falling.

✔ **Highlights the commitment of traders through volume:** The higher the volume, the more committed bulls or bears are to the position in question. Light volume indicates indifference or agreement on a security's value. Heavy volume can signal the beginning or end of a trend.

But technical analysis also has some glaring weaknesses. For example, it

✔ Ignores a security's fundamentals

✔ Allows traders to be on the side of irrationality

✔ Assumes the market is always right

✔ Fails to incorporate major corporate events (earnings, acquisitions, and so on)

The two main aspects of technical analysis

This book covers the two major aspects of technical analysis: charting and using technical indicators. Reading charts and using indicators are of equal importance to the swing trader who uses technical analysis, so you should be adept at both. (Keep in mind that technical indicators are largely unhelpful if you don't understand basic chart pattern interpretation.)

Reading charts

Charting, which I cover in Chapter 4, is the analysis of securities based on patterns, which security prices trace, as well as volume. The appeal of stock charts for many is their ease of use. Even fundamentals-based investors who don't believe in or use technical analysis bring up a stock chart before buying a new position just to see where the security has been recently. Managers with no background in charting whatsoever still use it to some extent. As a swing trader, you can use dozens of chart types, including line charts, bar charts, and candlestick charts.

In this book, I break the discussion of patterns in two, though I cover both topics in the same chapter:

- ✔ **Popular chart patterns:** The patterns you'll find most useful in your swing trading, like head-and-shoulders and cup-and-handle formations, may show up whether you're using a line, bar, or candlestick chart.

- ✔ **Candlestick-specific chart patterns:** These chart patterns, like morning and evening stars and bearish engulfing patterns, are easily detected when using candlestick charts

Using technical indicators

A technical indicator is like a compass: It helps steer you in the right direction. The act of using technical indicators, which I cover in Chapter 5, is a two-step process:

1. **Apply technical indicators to security prices.**

    Technical indicators are mathematical formulas that, when applied to security prices, clearly flash either buy or sell signals. They largely remove subjectivity from the analysis of chart patterns. Technical indicators primarily fall into two categories: trending and non-trending.

    - *Trending indicators* are designed to look for significant changes in direction and allow you to ride through *noise* (unimportant changes in security prices) that may happen over the course of a few days. They measure the strength of these trends and signal reversals, so you should apply trending indicators to securities that are consistently rising or falling.

- *Non-trending indicators* measure the strength of buyers and sellers where changes in direction occur frequently. They often standardize recent price history — say, by establishing the high and low prices during the period — and measure the security's relative position within that standardized range. Non-trending indicators also generate overbought and oversold signals. *Overbought* simply means the security has risen too high and is due for a course correction, and *oversold* means the security has fallen too low and is due for a reversal. You should apply non-trending indicators to securities that oscillate between two price levels, when the market participants largely agree on the security's value and the swings between the two price extremes.

Not all indicators tell you whether a security is in trending mode or non-trending mode, but relying on the ones that do is useful. Not all indicators are appropriate at a single point in time. Technical indicators are subject to user inputs. These questions partly explain why no indicator is always going to give the correct signal. Many swing traders seek out the Holy Grail indicator or system that yields the correct signals every time, but no such indicator exists. You must rely on your understanding of the security in question and apply indicators judiciously.

2. **Analyze the strength of the security relative to the overall market.**

   Relative strength analysis involves comparing the performance of a security to an overall market or industry by looking for divergences between the price of the security and the overall market, which you can see after applying technical indicators. A *divergence* occurs when a security's price moves to new highs or new lows, and the technical indicator doesn't confirm that strength or weakness. The indicator is signaling that the security price isn't telling the whole story. Divergences are powerful signals because they communicate information contrary to the perceived trend.

Appreciating the Value of the Big Picture: Fundamental Theory

If you start to sweat when you hear the phrase *fundamental analysis* and get anxious when you consider all the tough work that goes into analyzing a company, don't worry. I follow the K.I.S.S. (Keep It Simple, Stupid) approach when it comes to fundamental analysis.

The material on fundamental analysis that I present in this book won't prepare you for your MBA. Rather, it will guide you through the key parts of a firm's fundamentals that have the biggest impact on share prices.

The fundamental analyst is constantly asking the following questions:

- ✔ What is this company's value relative to its peers?
- ✔ What is this company's growth rate?
- ✔ What are this company's returns on capital and debt levels?

When you find the answers to these questions, you begin to get an idea of what price the company's shares should reasonably trade at. You're not going to arrive at the intrinsic values that Wall Street analysts slave over calculating (*intrinsic value* refers to the true value of a company and is distinguished from *market value,* which is the value the market is currently assigning to the firm). But you don't need to know the value of the shares you trade down to the cent. If shares are valued at $15, and you know shares should be between $25 and $32, do you really need to spend dozens of hours calculating the exact figure? Nope.

Understanding how and why fundamental analysis works

Understanding how fundamental analysis works is a bit easier than understanding how technical analysis works. Here's why this strategy is effective:

- ✔ **The higher the earnings of a company, the more others will pay for a piece of that company.** If you own a condo that produces $1,000 in income each month, how much would you value that cash flow? Different people would value the condo differently, depending on their risk tolerance levels and the certainty of that cash flow continuing. But obviously, if the condo were producing income of $2,000 per month, it would be worth double what it was worth when it was producing $1,000 per month.

  Fundamental analysis isn't that different, except that instead of producing rental income of $1,000 per month, companies produce earnings and report them quarterly. Of course, shareholders don't usually receive a firm's entire income because much of it is reinvested in the business. But the point is, fundamental analysis works because it measures a company's value based on its expected future earnings.

✔ **Arbitrageurs keep prices in check.** Another important reason fundamental analysis works is that arbitrageurs are looking for riskless profits. For example, suppose a security is trading at $25 per share, and the company is valued at $1 billion. If the firm had $2 billion in cash on its books and no debt, an arbitrageur would step in to take advantage of the mispricing. The arbitrageur could buy the company for $1 billion and then pay for the purchase using the cash the company has on its books. So fundamental analysis works because firms, governments, and individuals are constantly looking for riskless profits.

Okay, you're convinced that fundamental analysis has merit, but can you benefit from it in your swing trading? The answer is yes. But you should be aware of its limitations and how you can address them:

✔ **Unlike technical analysis, you can't uniformly apply fundamental analysis to securities.** A swing trader who understands how to interpret chart patterns and technical indicators goes through the same process whether he or she is trading corn, cotton, gold, oil, stocks, exchange traded funds, or mutual funds. The chart analysis is the same, and resistance and support both apply because market participants behave in similar ways regardless of what they're trading.

Master the fundamental analysis of cotton, however, and you aren't much better off when you come to trading oil. Master the fundamental analysis of telecom shares, and you'll face a new ballgame when it comes to banks. Differences persist between market fundamentals and how you analyze them. For this reason, swing traders who rely on fundamental analysis often must specialize in one or two markets.

✔ **Fundamentals change less often than chart prices.** A company reports its earnings and sales figures once every three months. Swing trading based on a report that's two months old can be hazardous because whatever value the report contained was likely incorporated in the company's price during the first few days after the report was released. This fact doesn't mean you should ignore news of a company that isn't recent. But it does mean that you don't want to buy a security based on a news report issued two months ago that sales are raging. The reason for the purchase has to be a recent catalyst or the convergence of good technicals (a chart) and good fundamentals.

Surveying the fundamental advantages and disadvantages

Fundamental analysis has its pluses and minuses. Some aspects, such as its emphasis on industry dynamics and competition, make it well suited for the swing trader; other aspects, such as its focus on value realization over the long term, make it a poor swing trading tool.

The role of psychology in fundamental analysis

You can see how psychology comes into play with fundamental analysis when analysts under- or overestimate a firm's potential through earnings surprise data. *Earnings surprise figures* show how positively or negatively a company's earnings come in versus Wall Street's consensus expectations. Wall Street analysts consistently underestimate great growth firms' potential, and that underestimation is revealed when those firms post positive earnings surprises. Similarly, Wall Street analysts often overestimate the difficulties at troubled firms, and that overestimation is revealed when those firms post negative earnings surprises.

So how does psychology play a role in these surprises? It turns out that many Wall Street analysts project future events based on information known today that may or may not have

any bearing on those future events. Called *anchoring,* it's a trait we all suffer from. If you bought shares of a security at $15, for example, and watched them fall to $10, you may decide to sell when your shares trade at $15 again. But this may not be the right course of action. You've anchored your expectations of exiting to a past price ($15) that may no longer represent the security's true value. In other words, you may be waiting a long time to break even — just ask shareholders in Nortel Networks, who saw prices fall from more than $800 to $11 in a few years.

I often talk about Wall Street's biases. Just remember that those biases are inherent in you and me, too. So try to guard against falling in love with positions or waiting to break even.

The advantages of fundamentals are centered on the focus on *value* — what a firm is actually worth. Fundamental analysis

- ✔ Estimates a firm's intrinsic value regardless of where the market trades
- ✔ Incorporates industry and market effects, which can drive security prices in tandem
- ✔ Wins out over the long term — fundamentals drive the prices of securities
- ✔ Assumes the market is wrong at times

Of course, fundamental analysis also has its shortcomings because it

- ✔ Can be incorrect in the short term when you most need it
- ✔ Is more subjective than technical analysis
- ✔ Relies heavily on your skill to interpret relevant market information
- ✔ Doesn't provide reference points on exits should your assumptions be incorrect

A fundamentals-based swing trading success story

If you frequently get your business and financial news from the television station CNBC, you've no doubt seen the colorful character known as Jim Cramer, host of the show *Mad Money*. He greets callers on his show with a big "Boo-Yah!" and takes questions on most any company in the market.

Cramer's rise to stardom was predicated on his success at a hedge fund he founded in 1987. Cramer reportedly generated returns of 24 percent per year for a decade after the launch of his firm (he was holding cash during the October crash in 1987) before cashing in during 2001. Though Cramer extols the virtues of buy-and-hold investing on his show, he traded so frequently during his hedge fund years that he likely would've been classified as a swing trader or day trader (his firm often generated the most in commissions among major Wall Street hedge funds). Cramer's books aren't filled with charts and technical indicators. Rather, he talks fundamentals. He was a short-term trader — *very* short term.

Cramer was a contrarian who took long positions (bought) in stocks that had fallen a significant amount, or took short positions in stocks that had risen a significant amount. He traded securities whose price was affected by corporate news, such as an upgrade or downgrade by a Wall Street firm. Sometimes he traded securities before they reported earnings if he felt he knew which way the reports would go. His trading was fundamentals-based — if Home Depot announced poor earnings, it may signal that Lowes's earnings would also disappoint. However, he diverged from the traditional day or swing trader in his use of the media to get his opinions out on securities he owned or was short.

I highlight Cramer as an example of a fundamentals-based short-term trader. He didn't rely on charts or technical indicators. He has even disparaged technical analysis on his TV broadcasts. But his style is instructive in the ways a trader can swing trade on news events that the market gets wrong or that the market reacts too strongly to.

I don't recommend exiting based on a company's fundamentals. All too often, a security's shares make their move before the reasons for that move are fully known. As a swing trader, you're better off basing exits on the strength or weakness in the price chart (depending on whether you're short or long the security). Stock prices fall faster than they rise, and commodities tend to rise faster than they fall. If you're long stocks, you want to exit quickly because of this characteristic. Fundamentals change too slowly to react in a timely manner on an exit. Use stop loss orders in any case to protect your downside.

Looking at catalysts and the great growth/value divide

Fundamental analysis is principally concerned with a company's value (or perhaps more accurately, what a company's value appears to be). But even a company that is undervalued may stay undervalued unless some catalyst occurs to cause other investors to revalue shares higher.

Watching for catalysts

To help make up for the main weakness of fundamental analysis — the issue of timing — swing traders rely on catalysts. *Catalysts* are fundamental events like mergers, acquisitions, new products, and earnings release dates that affect short-term price movement and spur the market to correctly value a company's shares. They can be internal or external, and you should pay attention to both.

- ✔ **Internal catalysts:** Events that a company has direct control over are *internal catalysts.* They come in the form of new services or products (consider the splash that Apple's iPhone made when it debuted) or new management (a change in the CEO position at Hewlett-Packard helped propel shares higher).

- ✔ **External catalysts:** *External catalysts* include such events as consolidation in an industry (when a company is bought out, its competitors are often assigned higher valuations because they're seen as potential targets) or changes in commodity prices (for example, oil or natural gas prices).

As a swing trader, you should look for opportunities to trade when a firm's fundamentals change because of one of these events — or when the perception of a firm's fundamentals changes (such as when a company surprises Wall Street with its earnings report). Consider a real-life example: Homebuilders' shares were overvalued for much of 2005. If you shorted shares of some of the top homebuilders then, you would've had your head handed to you. But if you used fundamental analysis, you may've waited for a catalyst — an event that would cause repricing of homebuilder shares. That event came in August 2005 when, for the first time in many months, the growth rate of contracts for new homes slowed. (Security prices of fast-growing firms often peak when growth rates begin to decline, *not* when growth turns negative.)

Classifying a company according to growth or value

Fundamental analysts usually classify companies as either growth firms or value firms (though many ardent investors argue that growth and value investing are two sides of the same coin). Even though growth investing and value investing are associated with long-term investing, swing traders need to be aware of the differences, because growth stocks and value stocks outperform each other at different times.

- ✔ **Growth stocks:** Companies that typically trade at premiums to the overall market (as defined by price to book ratios or price to earnings ratios) are *growth stocks.* They tend to be in industries that experience high growth rates, like technology and healthcare.

- ✔ **Value stocks:** Companies that typically trade at discounts to the overall market (as defined by price to book ratios or price to earnings ratios) are *value stocks.* They tend to be in the financial sector and the consumer staples sector (for example, companies in the beverage or food industries are considered to be part of the consumer staples industry).

During some years, value is in the lead; during other years, growth is out front. Trading growth stocks when value is in favor, or vice versa, can be like fighting a schoolyard bully with one hand tied behind your back. If you're a great fighter, you can pull it off. But it's not easy.

The reason that value and growth stocks exchange leadership roles lies in investor perception. At times, investors favor companies that pay dividends (such as when the Bush administration cut taxes on dividend payments) or companies that have steady cash flow streams. Value stocks shine during these periods. Other times, investors favor strong earnings growth without as much regard to price. Growth stocks shine at these times.

Is it enough to simply know which horse is in the lead? After all, if you could predict with reasonable accuracy whether growth or value would lead, you could rely on your forecasting abilities rather than historical performance — which, as I'm sure you're well aware, isn't a guarantee of future returns. Forecasting, however, has a problem.

Even if you're right about which style of investing *should* be in the lead based on all known evidence, that doesn't mean that style will actually lead. In other words, the market isn't rational.

I remember meeting with investment consultants in 2005 who quizzed me on whether value stocks would outperform growth stocks in the coming year. In truth, I had no idea. I knew that it was growth's turn to lead because value had been in the driver's seat for several years, and the valuations were compelling on the growth side of the divide. But the market doesn't always agree with my analysis. The only reliable way I know to trade the growth/value divide is by using technical analysis.

Long-term investors care little about who's in the lead because they can afford to wait for the time when their style is in favor and their stocks reflect that value. Fortunately, as a swing trader, you don't have to analyze the economic situation and determine what lies ahead for growth and value stocks. Rather, you can simply analyze recent history and bet with the trend. If matters change, move your chips to the other side of the table.

Chapter 3

Getting Started with Administrative Tasks

In This Chapter

▶ Finding a broker and opening an account

▶ Getting the scoop on those with the scoop — service providers

▶ Tracking your trades with a trading journal

▶ Staying positive to achieve positive results

Swing traders use brokers like any other market participant. But a swing trader needs a different kind of broker than an investor or day trader. What type of broker you choose depends on a number of factors. I break down those factors in this chapter, and I also give you details on how to open a brokerage account.

After you have your account up and running, you need to think about subscribing to certain services to help carry out your analysis. Some services are helpful for conducting screens of the market. Other services chart securities. Still other services help you locate the cream of the crop by focusing on industry group rotation. I recommend some key services in the pages that follow.

I also cover trading journals in this chapter. To be a keen swing trader, I recommend that you keep a journal (not to be confused with a personal diary) of your trades because a journal helps you refine your tactics and improve your trading by allowing you to review what works and what doesn't.

This chapter assumes you have a working knowledge of the financial markets. You should also know how to use the Internet so you can try out some of the brokerage options and service providers that I mention.

Hooking Up with a Broker

Why is the firm that executes all your trades called a *broker?* Not exactly an enticing name, is it?

Despite the name, brokers are necessary for swing trading — or any kind of trading, for that matter. But not all brokers are created equal. Some specialize in offering custom advice and wealth-management services for the high net worth individuals out there. They charge outrageous fees to execute trades because, well, they can. Of course, they'd argue that those outrageous fees simply reflect the cost of their advice.

Swing traders don't use such plush services. Their brokers have more of a no-frills approach. But the nice thing about competition is that even the no-frills brokers are increasingly offering premium services like check-writing privileges and ATM card access to brokerage accounts.

So how do you pick a broker who suits your needs? Read on.

Choosing a broker

When choosing a broker, traders all too often focus on a single factor — commissions — to the exclusion of everything else. Commissions get the limelight because they used to be the main impediment to frequent trading.

Not too long ago, swing trading wasn't possible for the masses due to high commissions. By law, brokers charged fixed trade commissions. But on May 1, 1975 (it's okay if you forget this date after three seconds), securities laws in the United States changed, allowing brokers to charge negotiated trade commissions. Commissions didn't immediately fall to the levels they're at today, but they did fall over time. Today, you may pay a flat $5 to $12 per trade, which *may* be equal to about a penny or less per share, depending on how many shares you trade.

But not all brokers offer such competitive rates, nor do they all provide the same services, so you must carefully consider the factors that are most important to you when settling on a broker. Some of those factors include the broker's charting system, customer service, the ease of placing orders, and the ease of depositing and withdrawing money.

Understanding the different types of brokers

What broker you choose depends on which services you want and how much you're willing to spend on commissions. Here are two classes of brokers to consider:

✔ **Discount brokers:** Discount brokers offer fewer services to their clients than full service brokers do. Instead, they focus on trade execution. You tell them what to buy and sell, and they do it. Of course, trades are usually made electronically today instead of over the phone. You can always speak to a living human being on the phone, but that will cost you more for your trade. Discount brokers may provide some services for free, such as research services or banking services.

✔ **Direct access firms:** Direct access firms allow you to bypass a broker and trade with an exchange or market maker directly. The advantage to this approach is that you have more control because you can see who's offering or bidding for shares of a security and choose with whom you want to trade. Direct access brokers often require you to download software to your computer that provides faster streaming data than you'd receive through a Web site. Some discount brokers are beginning to offer direct access trading.

You may also encounter *full service brokers,* such as Merrill Lynch, who hold their clients' hands, offer a suite of services, and charge enormous commissions. Obviously, full service brokers aren't the choice of swing traders. A swing trader who needs someone else's advice on what to trade shouldn't be in the business of swing trading. Swing trading is about independence, not dependence.

Searching for broker prospects

As a swing trader, you must use either a discount broker or a direct access firm (see the preceding section for details on both). I'm not going to recommend a particular broker for the simple reason that broker rankings change over time, and a broker that provides great service today may not necessarily provide such service in the future.

The major discount brokers you may want to consider include:

✔ *TD Ameritrade* (www.tdameritrade.com)

✔ E*Trade Financial (www.etrade.com)

✔ Scottrade (www.scottrade.com)

✔ Fidelity Active Trader (www.fidelity.com)

The major direct access trading firms you may want to consider include:

✔ *TradeStation* (www.tradestation.com)

✔ Interactive Brokers (www.interactivebrokers.com)

✔ thinkorswim (www.thinkorswim.com)

✔ Open E Cry (www.openecry.com)

Evaluating a potential broker

You need to consider a number of factors before choosing a broker:

- ✔ **Commission rate:** Don't pay more than a $10 flat fee, or more than one to two cents per share for your trades. Trading with commission rates higher than this amount isn't necessary given what you can get from existing brokers. And, more important, the higher the commission rate, the higher your returns have to be to cover the cost of those commissions.

  Although I recommend specific rates in the preceding paragraph, traders tend to put too much emphasis on the commission rate and sometimes neglect other details when choosing a broker. Don't fall into that trap. The commission rate is important, but it's not the sole factor you should consider.

- ✔ **Trading other asset classes:** A broker's ability to offer you other markets is becoming increasingly important. Ask your broker whether he or she can arrange for you to trade international securities, futures contracts, currencies, and so on. Expect to pay a premium for these additional trading options.

- ✔ **Banking services:** Some discount brokers offer banking services like check-writing from your brokerage account or an ATM card that accesses your portfolio. Most brokers allow electronic transfer of assets so you can send and receive money from another bank account. These types of services may or may not be important to you.

- ✔ **Usability:** *Usability* refers to how user-friendly a broker's trading interface is. Some brokers allow swing traders to execute orders through their Web sites; others require traders to download software onto their computers. This factor can really only be addressed by taking a test drive of a broker's trading platform (be it a Web site or trading software). Is it easy to enter orders? Is it easy to watch the market (if you rely on your broker for market data)? I can tell you from experience that *TradeStation* and *TD Ameritrade* have easy-to-use interfaces, but I recommend you try out the brokerage options as you're weighing this point (some brokers allow you to use demo versions of their trading software before opening an account).

- ✔ **Amenities:** Amenities include research services and charting programs. For example, a discount broker may offer you Level II quotes — which enable you to see the order book for Nasdaq stocks; see Chapter 11 for the scoop on using Level II quotes — or stock reports from Wall Street firms for free or for a discounted fee. But I strongly discourage you from relying on research reports. Besides the fact that almost everyone on Wall Street sees them before you do, research reports aren't very useful because they're rarely focused on short-term trading opportunities.

- ✔ **Customer service:** You want to know that you can get someone on the phone — and fast — when you have a trade or problem. How responsive a company is to your complaints is next to impossible to determine without opening an account — unless you use media rankings. I recommend relying in part on such rankings because they can be instructive — the writers share their experiences with a broker's customer service and other issues. *Barron's* and *Technical Analysis of Stocks & Commodities* are two publications that print broker rankings.

✔ **Portfolio analysis and reports:** How much has your portfolio returned year-to-date versus some major index? You can calculate this total on your own (see Chapter 13), but it's nice to have a broker who can run the report for you. And when tax time comes, a broker with extensive tax services can be a lifesaver.

Opening an account

After you've settled on a broker, you need to decide what kind of account you want to open. You have several options, depending on whether you plan to

✔ Borrow money to trade from your broker

✔ Trade futures or options

✔ Place the account in your name alone or in the name of your spouse as well

✔ Designate the account as a retirement account or traditional brokerage account

The next two sections help you answer these questions (save the spouse question . . . that's a discussion you need to have with your significant other — sorry, I'm not that great at relationship advice).

Cash account versus margin account

After selecting your broker, you need to choose between opening a cash account and opening a margin account. *Cash accounts* restrict your investable assets to the cash available in your account. *Margin accounts* allow you to borrow money from your broker to execute trades; they're also necessary if you want to trade options. A swing trader with $50,000 in cash sitting in a margin account can usually borrow $50,000 to trade.

Borrowing is a double-edged sword: It magnifies potential returns but also magnifies potential losses. If you borrow 100 percent of your assets and invest the entire amount (for example, you deposit $50,000 into your brokerage account and trade $100,000 in securities), a 10 percent loss is magnified to a 20 percent loss. Not pretty.

Margin accounts can cause you to be more reckless in your trades. Money that's not yours (but that you have trading discretion over) is easier to gamble with than money that is yours. Margin accounts may lead you to get in over your head. If you're new to swing trading, stick to a cash account — trading only with your own assets is less potentially damaging to your overall portfolio.

Traditional brokerage accounts versus retirement accounts

Another question to ask yourself is whether you want to open a traditional brokerage account or a retirement account. Traditional brokerage accounts offer you easy access to your money. However, you must report your profits on these accounts to the IRS as taxable income, unless the IRS classifies you as a full-time trader, in which case you can convert capital gains and losses into ordinary gains and losses. Why is that important? Because you can deduct ordinary gains and losses against other income. If you're not classified as a full-time trader, the maximum amount of losses that you can deduct annually from pre-tax income is $3,000 (as of the date of this writing).

A retirement account, of course, solves the problem of taxes because it's a tax-deferred account. Unfortunately, the government limits how much you can contribute to an Individual Retirement Account (IRA) in a single year ($5,000 in 2008 if you're age 49 or younger). The government also limits when you can withdraw the money without penalties (usually in the year you turn 59½). So swing trading in a tax-deferred account is preferable if you want to avoid the taxes that result from high turnover, but it isn't preferable if you plan to live off your profits.

Selecting Service Providers

No man (or woman) is an island, and no swing trader can trade without service providers. But not all service providers are created equal. (Okay, okay . . . enough with the clichés!)

Service providers differ in terms of the quality, timeliness, and breadth of the data they supply, among other items. What you want in a provider is some type of service — charting or access to a database of fundamental data, for instance — that you can use for your benefit. In the following pages, I tell you what to look for and what to avoid.

Providers to do business with

Data providers simply provide you with the tools for finding and charting securities and increasing your market intelligence. These tools should be flexible enough to allow you to change inputs, such as what indicators to use for a chart or what criteria to screen for in a database. I classify service providers broadly into those that supply technical data and those that supply fundamental data.

Technical software providers

Every swing trader must have a strong charting system. That charting system must incorporate real-time charting and quotes (charts and quotes that reflect live market data and aren't delayed) if you plan on trading intraday. If you enter orders after the markets close, you don't need a real-time charting service.

The marketplace has many charting providers. Most discount brokers catering to the active trader club offer charting systems, and order entry is often integrated with the charting functions (that is, you can program automatic buys or sells when a certain action occurs in the chart).

Some of the popular charting programs in the marketplace include:

- ✔ *TradeStation* (www.tradestation.com; the charts used in this book are primarily taken from *TradeStation*)
- ✔ *MetaStock* (www.equis.com)
- ✔ *Active Trader Pro* (www.fidelity.com)
- ✔ *eSignal* (www.esignal.com)
- ✔ *E*Trade Pro* (www.etrade.com)
- ✔ *High Growth Stock Investor* (www.highgrowthstock.com)

Several of these charting systems are integrated with brokers to allow for easy order entry.

Which charting system is right for you depends on your needs. For example, if you like to develop new indicators, you need a charting system with that option. You must also consider the system's ease of use and whether the charts are appealing. A charting system should also have a wide array of indicators that you can plot (the most popular indicators are covered in Chapter 5). You should read independent reviews of charting systems to assist you in your selection if you don't already use a charting program regularly. I recommend reviewing the rankings published by *Technical Analysis of Stocks & Commodities* in its annual Reader's Choice Awards.

I use two charting systems: the one provided by my broker and another one in which I conduct much of my own research.

Fundamental analysis software providers

Swing traders who opt to use fundamental analysis in their investment process need to subscribe to data providers that can assist them in their research. Fortunately, much of the fundamental data on a company —historical earnings, returns on capital, expected growth, and the like — is available for free on the Internet. I'm amazed at how much data is free for the taking online (am I dating myself?).

Yahoo! Finance, Google Finance, and Reuters can address many of your fundamental data needs. And all three services provide fundamental data for free. Following are a few more details on all three services:

- ✔ **Yahoo! Finance** (`finance.yahoo.com`): I often begin my fundamental data search at Yahoo! Finance. The Web site offers basic charting; headlines on a selected security; a company profile; competitor information; analysts' estimates (and historical earnings surprises); and financial data from a company's balance sheet, income statement, and cash flow statement. But beware: Yahoo! Finance also has message boards that you should avoid.

- ✔ **Google Finance** (`finance.google.com`): Google is a newcomer to the financial data distribution business. Google doesn't provide as many financial data fields as Yahoo! Finance, but it offers more data on international firms. I visit Google often when Yahoo! Finance doesn't have the data I'm looking for. Google calls its message boards "Discussions," which sounds harmless enough — but not everything is what it seems.

- ✔ **Reuters** (`www.reuters.com/finance/stocks`): Yahoo! Finance and Google simply present data taken from other providers, but Reuters supplies its own data. The main data categories are Stock Overview, Financial Highlights, Ratios, Estimates, Officers & Directors, Financial Statements, Recommendations, and Analyst Research. My favorite category is Ratios, shown in Figure 3-1. At a glance, Reuters provides data on a company versus its peers and the overall market, so you can quickly discern whether a company is priced at a premium or discount, and whether that price is justified based on other ratios, like return on equity or expected earnings growth rates.

In addition to these free research services, a few paid subscriptions are worth your money:

- ✔ ***Investor's Business Daily:*** This daily newspaper provides fundamental data on thousands of stocks. Each security is assigned an earnings rank number and other fundamental data rankings.

- ✔ ***High Growth Stock Investor:*** This software program, also known as *HGS Investor,* provides top-down and bottom-up data services, combining fundamental and technical data. The software is ideal for fundamentals-based traders who screen sectors or the overall market for trading candidates.

- ✔ ***Zacks Investor Software:*** Yahoo! Finance, MSN, and Morningstar — among others — offer stock screening services, but I consider *Zacks* the leader in the business. Many of *Zacks's* screening tools are available online for free at `www.zacks.com/screening/custom`. Certain data fields are available only to subscribers, but you can build effective screens without a subscription. However, if you want to backtest a screen to see how it would've performed historically, you must subscribe to *Zacks Research Wizard* service.

Ratios

Cleveland-Cliffs Inc CLF (NYSE)

Sector: Basic Materials Industry: Metal Mining ▸ View **CLF** on other exchanges

As of 3:01 PM EST	Price Change	Percent Change
$147.91 USD	▲6.10	▲4.30%

Independent Research   Broker Research

Valuation Ratios | Dividends | Growth Rates | Financial Strength
Profitability Ratios | Management Effectiveness | Efficiency

VALUATION RATIOS

	Company	Industry	Sector	S&P 500
P/E Ratio (TTM)	27.51	14.97	21.37	18.70
P/E High - Last 5 Yrs.	NM	41.24	36.35	32.78
P/E Low - Last 5 Yrs.	NM	5.76	11.67	13.68
Beta	2.33	1.74	1.32	1.00
Price to Sales (TTM)	2.82	3.01	2.63	2.57
Price to Book (MRQ)	5.31	4.48	4.26	3.81
Price to Tangible Book (MRQ)	4.94	5.64	7.21	8.21
Price to Cash Flow (TTM)	16.10	10.94	14.28	13.33
Price to Free Cash Flow (TTM)	101.85	45.29	35.98	27.97
% Owned Institutions	95.00	51.07	35.98	72.03

DIVIDENDS

	Company	Industry	Sector	S&P 500
Dividend Yield	0.49	2.52	2.19	2.50
Dividend Yield - 5 Year Avg.	--	3.38	2.12	1.80
Dividend 5 Year Growth Rate	NM	53.72	21.58	14.41
Payout Ratio (TTM)	7.91	37.83	27.95	28.77

GROWTH RATES

	Company	Industry	Sector	S&P 500
Sales (MRQ) vs Qtr. 1 Yr. Ago	42.53	47.73	25.95	17.20
Sales (TTM) vs TTM 1 Yr. Ago	18.40	69.33	23.10	16.00
Sales - 5 Yr. Growth Rate	31.15	39.35	18.79	15.39
EPS (MRQ) vs Qtr. 1 Yr. Ago	32.59	-41.89	-1.10	15.29
EPS (TTM) vs TTM 1 Yr. Ago	-1.26	9.01	1.91	12.84
EPS - 5 Yr. Growth Rate	NM	57.62	31.55	23.15
Capital Spending - 5 Yr. Growth Rate	87.96	41.53	18.91	13.13

PROFITABILITY RATIOS

	Company	Industry	Sector	S&P 500
Gross Margin (TTM)	20.31	42.60	31.25	44.10
Gross Margin - 5 Yr. Avg.	17.64	40.40	29.01	44.08
EBITD Margin (TTM)	21.56	39.49	20.99	23.61
EBITD - 5 Yr. Avg.	17.28	36.23	18.29	22.61
Operating Margin (TTM)	16.85	33.54	16.32	18.87
Operating Margin - 5 Yr. Avg.	14.73	30.46	12.98	19.23
Pre-Tax Margin (TTM)	16.73	23.87	13.24	17.50
Pre-Tax Margin - 5 Yr. Avg.	17.41	28.80	11.49	18.40
Net Profit Margin (TTM)	13.04	21.01	10.36	12.80
Net Profit Margin - 5 Yr. Avg.	14.59	18.02	7.82	12.82
Effective Tax Rate (TTM)	22.09	35.62	28.80	29.55
Effective Tax Rate - 5 Yr. Avg.	16.19	36.27	30.64	30.59

MANAGEMENT EFFECTIVENESS

	Company	Industry	Sector	S&P 500
Return On Assets (TTM)	11.83	15.28	9.42	8.73
Return On Assets - 5 Yr. Avg.	15.09	15.23	7.08	8.06
Return On Investment (TTM)	14.69	17.60	11.54	12.52
Return On Investment - 5 Yr. Avg.	19.84	18.49	8.79	11.70
Return On Equity (TTM)	27.71	28.43	21.06	20.95
Return On Equity - 5 Yr. Avg.	40.67	49.32	20.01	19.60

Figure 3-1:
The Ratios page on the Reuters Web site provides a wealth of data.

Source: Reuters Finance

Providers to avoid

If a service provider is charging exorbitant fees for its services, beware. You can usually purchase top-quality charting programs for a small monthly fee, and sometimes you can get them for free from your broker (assuming you trade often enough with that broker). You can select stocks with software that costs $600 per month, so be wary of high-priced services.

In general, avoid any type of service that tries to do the work for you. For example, a service provider may tell you that ABC is overvalued or XYZ is undervalued. Or it may tell you when to buy and when to sell. But think about it: If that service really was exceptional at predicting when to buy and sell, wouldn't the providers of that service use it for their own profit? Why sell the service? If I developed some model that accurately forecasted when to buy and sell securities, I sure wouldn't sell it to others!

Two types of specific services you should never consult are message boards and newsletters or software programs that issue specific buy or sell recommendations. Both of these services effectively delegate some thinking on the part of the swing trader to someone else. But these services are popular enough that I spend the rest of this section going into more detail.

Message boards: The kiss of death

If you find yourself browsing a message board, you may as well wear a sign on your back that reads, "I'm lost." My advice: Avoid message boards because they won't give you good intelligence and are likely to mislead you. Here's why:

- ✔ **The information on message boards isn't objective.** Generally, the sentiment on message boards is bullish. The majority of people posting are excited about a company's prospects and rave about how the widget the company makes will revolutionize the world. Some people list their target prices and how they recently picked up "another" $10,000 worth of said stock. I'm sure they wouldn't deceive us. (For an example of this sometimes irrationally bullish outlook, see Figure 3-2.)

- ✔ **You can't distinguish between competent and incompetent participants.** No credentials are required to post on the board except a pulse. Although message boards do have intelligent posters mixed in with masses of people who have too much time on their hands, you simply can't read them in the hopes of getting the opinions of the one or two people who actually know what they're talking about.

- ✔ **They're annoying.** You'll get profanity (dressed up in numbers, of course, to get by the Web site's technical censors) and messages that show that some posters are apparently unaware that a keyboard's caps lock can be turned OFF.

Message boards are flooded with rumors and inaccuracies. Don't waste your time (or money) on them.

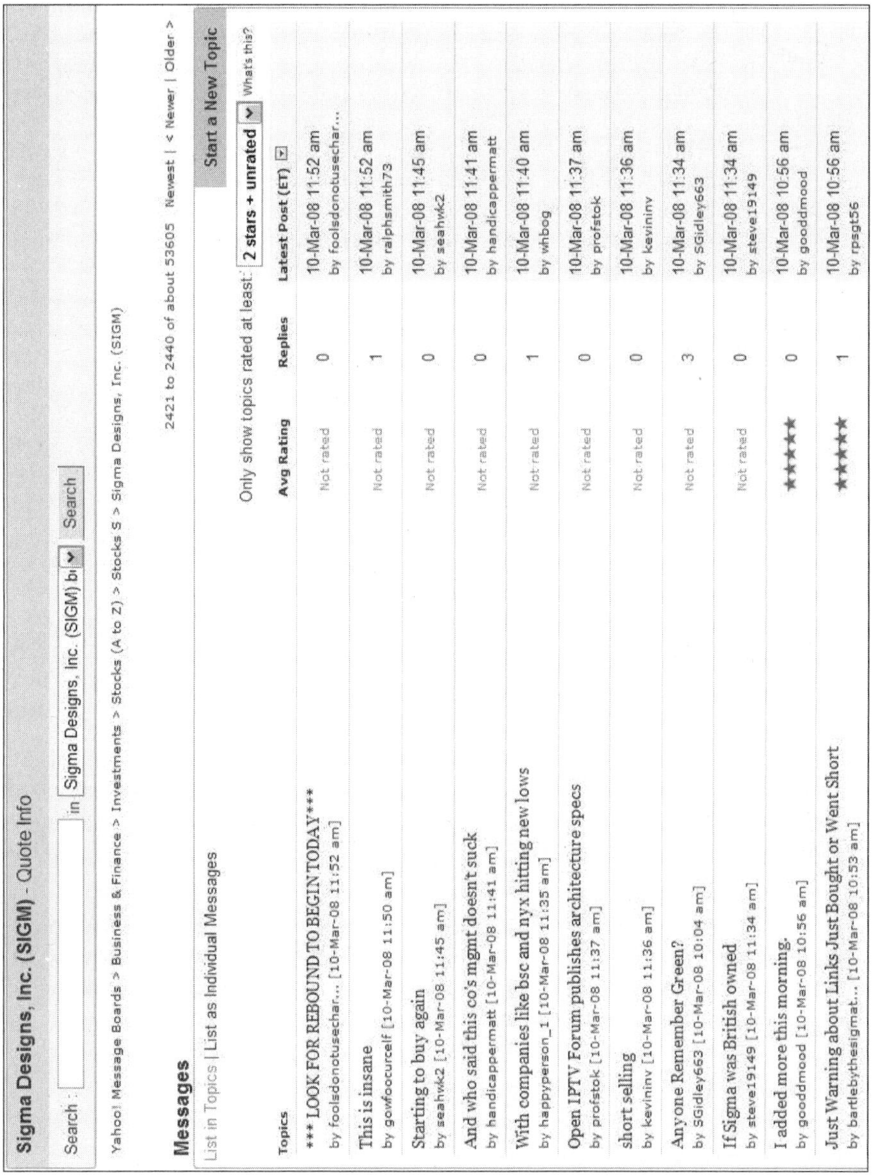

Figure 3-2: Sigma Designs shares declined 60 percent over a few weeks in early 2008, yet message board posters remained bullish as ever.

Newsletters and software programs that issue buy/sell recommendations: The not-so-harmless pack leaders

Many intelligent market experts out there write financial newsletters. Newsletters tend to be of a higher caliber than message boards. Whereas message boards are free to post to, newsletter writers depend on subscribers to continue their service. Hence, it's tougher to make up things when you may lose business as a result.

What I have a problem with are newsletters that recommend you buy or sell this or that stock. As a swing trader, you must be independent. You aren't supposed to rely on anyone else's expertise. Newsletters that stick to the macro picture or industry group analysis are fine. You learn by reading those newsletters.

But don't think for a second that you have an edge in the market if you're simply replicating the buys and sells that a newsletter recommends. Even when the newsletter has a good track record, you shouldn't follow the recommendations blindly. You'd be better off giving your money to a professional manager.

One software tool I suggest you shy away from is *VectorVest.* The service allows you to type in most any publicly traded company and be told what the fundamental and technical picture looks like. It even tells you whether to buy or sell that security. How wonderful. You don't even need to think. *VectorVest* is a quantitative model. It combines quantitative and qualitative factors to determine whether a security is a buy or sell. But what's important is that it's not *your* model — it's someone else's. And anyone who subscribes to that service is going to get the same recommendations as you would if you were to subscribe. So how can you stay ahead of the pack when you're running with it?

Starting a Trading Journal

Any system needs some type of feedback loop to improve itself. For example, employees of most companies must complete annual performance reviews, when their boss sits them down and tells them what they've done well (something? anything?) and what they can improve on.

Your progress as a swing trader is no different. A feedback loop is crucial so you can make adjustments and improvements. Insanity was once defined as doing the same thing over and over and expecting a different outcome each time. If you trade securities without a feedback loop, I view that as a type of insanity.

Your feedback loop should take the form of a trading journal in which you record *all* your trades. The journal entries should be short and combine text that outlines the basics of the trade (like how you found it and what triggered the entry) and charts that show what you saw before entering the trade (which help you spot the readings of technical indicators, where resistance and support levels were, and so on).

After a position closes (meaning you exit for a profit or loss), you can return to the journal entry to discover what you did right or wrong. You may be surprised at what you uncover. You may find that you should let profits ride longer, for example, or take losses faster. Or you may realize that the nine-day moving average isn't such a great tool for signaling the beginning of an uptrend.

Look for commonalities between your winners and losers after you've kept your journal for a few months. If you're like me, you may learn more from your losses than you do from your gains. When you suffer a large loss, it can be helpful to know whether the problem was due to the system itself or your failure to follow the system. Then, if warranted, you can alter your trading plan to improve the odds of success.

Your trading journal should include the following elements:

- ✔ An explanation of how you found each trading opportunity

- ✔ The positions you trade and whether they're long or short

- ✔ A chart of each security with any relevant indicators to assist in analyzing the conditions of the market at the time you executed the trade

- ✔ A miscellaneous section to record any additional information that may be relevant at time of entry, such as concerns you had about executing the position

- ✔ A description of what triggered the entry

- ✔ A post-mortem chart of the security with an explanation of what triggered the exit

- ✔ A rate of return after your exit

A trading journal can, of course, include a lot more information than what I've presented here. For example, I don't include certain items in a journal entry, such as position size, that you can easily obtain from your broker. You can also plot the industry group of the security, if applicable, or a chart of the overall market. But the problem I've found with including too much information is that you may fail to update the journal in a timely manner.

You must strike a balance between including too little information — to the point where the journal isn't useful — and including too much information — to the point where the journal becomes a daunting task you fail to maintain. I believe that if you use the criteria I list, you can achieve that balance. I provide examples of trading journal entries in Figures 3-3 and 3-4.

Figure 3-3:
A sample
excerpt
from a
trading
journal.

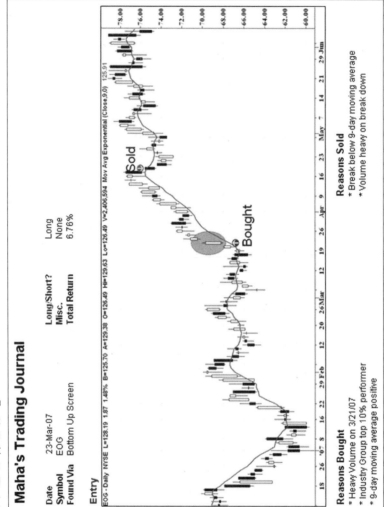

Maha's Trading Journal

Date	23-Mar-07	Long/Short?	Long
Symbol	EOG	Misc.	None
Found Via	Bottom Up Screen	Total Return	6.76%

Entry

EOG - Daily NYSE L=128.19 1.87 1.48% B=125.70 A=129.38 O=126.49 Hi=129.63 Lo=126.49 V=2,406,594 Mov Avg Exponential (Close,9,0) 125.91

Bought

Sold

Reasons Bought
* Heavy Volume on 3/21/07
* Industry Group top 10% performer
* 9-day moving average positive

Reasons Sold
* Break below 9-day moving average
* Volume heavy on break down

Maha's Journal Entry

Date:	March 24, 2008
Security Traded:	FSLR
Long/Short:	Long
Execution Price:	$209.50
Stop Loss Level:	$174.32
How was security found?	Industry group ranked in top 10% of market.
Entry mechanism:	+DMI crossover above -DMI
Miscellaneous:	Overall market looked weak on buy.

Post Mortem: Trade was exited after price target of $300 reached; 43% gain achieved

Figure 3-4:
A sample
excerpt
from a
trading
journal.

Creating a Winning Mindset

The final element you need to get started is a winning mindset. When I first heard this rule of thumb, I thought it was too touchy-feely. But experience and research studies have shown that there's something to it. Fitness experts often focus on a person's mindset because they know that beliefs are translated into action. When your mind believes something, it works to make that belief a reality.

Bill Phillips, in his book *Body for Life,* recounts an intriguing story about beliefs and goal-setting. He refers to a Harvard University study that showed that only 3 percent of the students graduating in 1953 actually wrote down their specific career goals. Twenty years later, the study's researchers interviewed the class of 1953 and discovered that those 3 percent who had written down their goals were worth more than the other 97 percent combined.

Successful swing traders believe they'll succeed. They don't dwell on their past failures but on their past successes. They write down their goals and their trades. They view losses as a normal part of the business of swing trading. They don't become arrogant and overconfident when their trades generate large profits.

It helps to set specific goals, like "I will return 15 percent this year." Write down your goal and read it often. Yes, I know it sounds corny, but I've seen this advice time and time again in investment books, physical fitness books, and other places. And I've seen it work.

So begin swing trading with a winning mindset. Know that you're going to achieve your goals. Be optimistic. Take losses in stride and stay as unemotional as you can. You'll find that a winning mindset helps you become a successful swing trader.

Part II

Determining Your Entry and Exit Points: Technical Analysis

The 5th Wave   By Rich Tennant

"A lot of times he just licks salt off the screen, but once in a while he spots a trending stock."

In this part . . .

Technical analysis is the time-honored tradition of analyzing markets based on price and volume. Here, you discover the ins and outs of reading price charts and applying technical indicators. But with technical analysis, you should note that more isn't necessarily better. All indicators are based on price and volume, so the more indicators you apply, the more noise you hear.

Chapter 4

Charting the Market

. . . .

In This Chapter

▶ Understanding the roles of price, volume, and the security cycle of life in the charting world

▶ Getting up close and personal with four standard charting methods

▶ Making sense of well-known chart patterns

▶ Simplifying security analysis with candlesticks

▶ Using trendlines to guide your swing trading path

. . . .

A picture's worth a thousand words, or so I've heard. The stock chart is, perhaps, the best proof of this old cliché. For centuries, charts have assisted traders in profiting from buying and selling an underlying contract. Candlestick charting, for example, was developed by the Japanese in the 1700s to profit from changes in the price of rice.

Over time, investors became more sophisticated in understanding charts and the information contained within them. In fact, they became so much more sophisticated that they started identifying certain chart patterns and giving them funny names. Would you believe that *head and shoulders* is more than just a shampoo brand, or that *cup and handle* applies to finances and not just your favorite coffee container? Sure, these patterns may be the result of investors and traders staring too long at charts. After all, I sometimes see funny formations in clouds if I stare long enough. But they are useful tools for your swing trading ventures.

In this chapter, I share how you can predict the likely direction of a security — be it sideways, upward, or downward — by understanding the basic cycle of securities and the specific roles price and volume play in what you see on a chart. I also introduce you to several charting patterns every swing trader needs for success. The patterns are presented in order of complexity, so go ahead and skip straight to what you need based on your familiarity with charting. All set? Then chart away, my friend!

Nailing Down the Concepts: The Roles of Price and Volume in Charting

All charts come down to basically two inputs: price and volume. The majority of this chapter focuses on price, because patterns within price are more meaningful than patterns within volume. You're rewarded or punished for being right on price, not volume. But I don't want to gloss over volume. It's a major tool in your swing trading kit and is worth close examination.

Volume communicates conviction on the part of buyers or sellers:

- ✔ A price rise on light volume may signal an absence of sellers, not the presence of buyers.
- ✔ Heavy volume, on the other hand, signals that bulls or bears are committed to the calling.

Look to buy securities on heavy volume (exiting's a different matter). If you're swing trading trends — regardless of the chart pattern you observe — insist on seeing heavy volume. But what is *heavy volume?* My general rule of thumb is that volume 1.5 times the average daily volume over the past 50 days is considered heavy. (Yahoo! Finance and most charting programs report average daily volume statistics.) Volume can also help you determine when to exit. A decline on heavy volume, for example, may signal that the security has farther to fall. If you're swing trading ranges, you want to see light volume, which indicates a lack of interest by bulls and bears.

An old saying on Wall Street notes that amateurs trade at the open and professionals trade at the close. If a security closes higher than it opened, it represents a victory of sorts for the bulls. They were able to overwhelm sellers during the day. On the other hand, if a security closes lower than it opened, that represents a win for the bears, who were able to overwhelm buyers during the day. If a security closes at the same price it opened at, bulls and bears are at a stalemate.

Major institutions that control billions of dollars are in the markets day in and day out. They account for the majority of volume on exchanges. Security prices move when institutions allocate parts of their portfolios to one security or another. So you want to read how they're investing their dollars and ride the inevitable wave that follows as more institutions get into the bathtub. One investment wizard I learned from — Ian Woodward — explained volume in these terms: An institution getting into a security is like an elephant getting into a tub of water. You know the water's going to overflow. Similarly, volume overflows when institutions buy into or sell out of a security.

Having Fun with Pictures: The Four Main Chart Types

Reading a chart isn't difficult, but there are different ways of viewing the same price information, be it a line chart, candlestick chart, or bar chart. Most swing traders choose one chart type and stick to it. The most popular chart type for swing traders is the candlestick chart, because it reveals the most information.

To get the most value out of charting for your swing trading ventures, you first need to be able to recognize the four main types of charts in the finance world and how each can help you — or harm you if you're not careful. Following are the four main chart types and a brief description of each (from the most common and basic to the least common):

- **Line chart:** This chart type simply connects closes from one period to another, and the resulting chart resembles a line. Television news programs often show line charts because of their simplicity. However, critical data is missing. A line chart doesn't show you where a security opened for the day — only where it closed. Nor does it plot the highs and lows that occurred for each period. Line charts do, however, allow you to focus on the most critical piece of information: the day's closing price.

- **Bar chart:** You're likely familiar with traditional bar charts, which show the open, high, low, and close of a specific security. The bar chart addresses many of the shortcomings found in the line chart. Often called an *OHLC bar chart* (which stands for, you guessed it, open-high-low-close), this chart can provide hourly, daily, weekly, or even monthly information. Figure 4-1 shows a representation of a standard bar. A horizontal line protruding from the left of the bar signals the security's opening price, and a horizontal line protruding from the right side of the bar signals the security's closing price. The period's highs and lows are the top and bottom of the bar.

- **Candlestick chart:** This chart type clearly depicts a security price's open, high, low, and close. Traditional bar charts do the same, but candlestick charts do it more effectively. *Candlestick charts* are made up of two components: the range between the open and close (called the *real body*) and price movement above and below the body (called *shadows*). If the security closes higher than its open during that period (a bullish sign), the body is usually white. If the security closes lower than its open during the period (a bearish sign), the body is usually black (**Note:** Different charting programs use different colors to shade in the body.) When prices open and close at the same level, the candlestick body is reduced to a horizontal line, and the remaining parts are the upper and lower shadows. Figure 4-1 shows what typical candlesticks look like.

Candlesticks are a great way to examine charts, and you can use these patterns to assist you when entering and exiting securities. However, I don't know any swing traders who rely on candlestick patterns exclusively. So avoid putting all your eggs in the candlestick basket. Like every technical tool, the candlestick is an imperfect instrument. Look for candlestick patterns as *confirmation* of a trend or reversal, but avoid looking to trade a security primarily because of a candlestick chart pattern.

✔ **Point and figure (P&F) charts:** P&F charts plot security prices using a column of Xs (to represent rising price movements) and Os (to represent falling price movements). The major advantage of P&F charts is that they filter out noise or unimportant price movement by plotting only new Xs and Os when the price of a security moves by a predefined amount. One downside is that they don't reflect the passage of time well. Because new plots are made only when the price exceeds the predetermined threshold, a plot may not be made for days or even weeks if the security in question doesn't move significantly.

The three charts in Figure 4-2 contrast a line chart, bar chart, and candlestick chart. All three charts cover price action for Google (symbol: GOOG) between December 10, 2007 and February 6, 2008. The bottom chart demonstrates a rising trendline, which highlights a support area that, when broken, signals the end of the uptrend. Figure 4-3 shows the other main chart type: P&F.

This book focuses on bar charts and candlestick charts, primarily the latter. Both chart types reveal intraday or intraweek (depending on the time period set) strength of bulls and bears, making them favored tools of swing traders far and wide. Support or resistance areas are also occasionally easier to see with bar charts or candlestick charts.

Figure 4-1:
a) A bar chart. b) A candlestick chart.

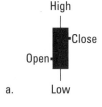

a.

b.

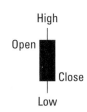

Line Chart

GOOG - Daily NASDAQ L=572.60 -10.41 -1.79% B=0.00 A=0.00 O=579.00 HI=585.00 Lo=571.30 V=4.485.228

Bar Chart

GOOG - Daily NASDAQ

Candlestick Chart

GOOG - Daily NASDAQ

Figure 4-2:
Sample line
chart, bar
chart, and
candlestick
chart
featuring
shares of
Google.

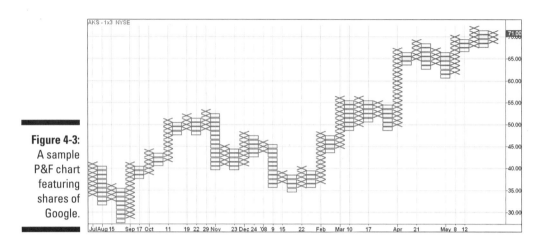

Figure 4-3:
A sample
P&F chart
featuring
shares of
Google.

Charts in Action: A Pictorial View of the Security Cycle of Life

Securities go through a naturally occurring cycle, but not all securities follow this cycle religiously. If you can't characterize which stage a security is in, you're better off skipping it and finding one that's following the normal cycle of accumulation, expansion, distribution, and contraction. Understanding this cycle is helpful, because different phases require different strategies. Swing trading trends, for example, is best achieved during the expansion and contraction phases. Trading ranges, on the other hand, is best achieved in accumulation and distribution phases.

The waiting game: Accumulation

The *accumulation phase* is typically the longest phase a security goes through. During this period, its price neither rises nor declines meaningfully. Instead, its price moves sideways through time. Supply and demand are roughly in balance, and institutional managers or smart money often accumulate shares of an undervalued security. (*Smart money* is typically institutional dollars that are informed by extensive research.)

Volume is usually light, reflecting a general consensus that the security's price is correct. Buyers are unable to push prices higher than a ceiling (a *resistance level*), whereas sellers are unable to push prices below a floor (a *support level*). You can't know in advance with any precision where these ceilings or floors will be found. You can easily identify them, however, by viewing a price chart and looking for price levels that a security is unable to climb above or fall below. These support and resistance areas are usually driven by fundamental reasons. For example, Microsoft's stock may not be able to rise above $35 per share because that movement represents a valuation of $300 billion, and market participants may not feel the company is worth more than $300 billion. Thus, support and resistance levels vary by security and can't be determined until you examine a price chart.

Think of an accumulation phase as a period where most market participants agree on a security's value. Because price isn't moving dramatically, profiting off of securities in the accumulation phase can be difficult. Some swing traders may buy at or near the support level and attempt to sell at the resistance level. This approach only works, of course, when the distance between the support and resistance level is sufficiently wide enough to make the profit worthwhile. It also only works as long as the security continues to trade in the range. If you swing trade trends, you want to look for securities moving out of the accumulation phase and into the expansion phase. However, if you swing trade ranges, you may be content to find accumulation phases and trade them *until* the security ends its accumulation phase.

You can spot accumulation phases on charts of varying time periods. Although accumulation phases are traditionally thought of as occurring over several months, a security can technically be accumulated over a few days. The key factor is time frame. A day trader, for example, looks at intraday charts where each plot represents a five- or ten-minute interval. For day traders, accumulation phases may occur over a two-day period.

As a swing trader, you shouldn't be so close to the bushes. Although you can use intraday charts occasionally to perfect your timing of buys and sells, your default chart period should be measured in days. In these types of charts, an accumulation phase must last several weeks — if not months — to be considered a true accumulation phase. Otherwise, you may be dealing with some other phase of the cycle of the security.

Figure 4-4 highlights a typical accumulation phase when shares of Apache Corporation (symbol: APA) oscillated between two price levels — $75 and $60 — between October 2005 and April 2006. This wide trading range allowed swing traders to buy at support level and sell at resistance level for profits. However, the accumulation phase wasn't perfect. In October 2005, shares rose above the resistance level by a hair for a few days. And then in June 2006, shares fell below the support level of $60 by a hair.

APA - Daily NYSE L=98.47 3.11 3.26% B=97.66 A=99.70 O=96.49 HI=98.74 Lo=95.57 V=3,956,361

Stage 1: Accumulation

Resistance

Support

Figure 4-4:
The accu-
mulation
phase of
APA.

You can't be strict on exact price levels of support and resistance and assume a security's price will immediately stop falling near a support level or imme-diately stop rising near a resistance level. For example, if a security's support level is $35 and its resistance level is $40, you can't assume the security's price will immediately stop falling when it hits $35. It may stop falling at $35.20, $34.90, $34.75, $35.50 — well, you get the idea. Sometimes share prices don't reach either extreme and make turns within the two bands. Swing traders sell long positions or enter short positions near resistance levels.

The big bang: Expansion

The *expansion phase,* also known as the *markup phase,* follows the accumula-tion phase (see the preceding section) and is a period of increasing prices. If the movement out of the accumulation phase is truly an expansion period, the security's price doesn't reenter accumulation. So if you swing trade trends, this is the phase where you want to go long — as soon as possible.

This phase marks the beginning of a change in perception among sharehold-ers and outside investors. A stock expansion may occur as the earnings outlook for a company improves. In the case of companies with a highly suc-cessful product (think Apple and the iPod), shares may begin to rise steadily out of an accumulation pattern after that product's launch.

The expansion phase is ripe with profit opportunities. Swing traders who buy right as the expansion phase gets underway often can ride a strong trend for several days or weeks. The beauty of buying as an expansion gets underway is that the proverbial line in the sand is clearly marked. That is, you know rather quickly whether you bought at the right time based on whether the security's price reenters the accumulation phase. If you buy late, then you risk a large loss if shares of the security rapidly fall to the breakout price level — or worse — fall back into the previous accumulation range. Use the money management strategies outlined in Chapter 10 if you're in this boat.

Look for strong volume at the beginning of the expansion phase as confirmation that it's genuine. If a security emerges from an accumulation phase on weak volume, that may indicate a lack of conviction on the part of buyers. Hence, the rally may be short-lived. For a refresher on the role of price and volume, flip back to the earlier section, "Nailing Down the Concepts: The Roles of Price and Volume in Charting."

For a real-life example of what the expansion phase looks like, check out Figure 4-5, which reflects the expansion of Apache Corporation (symbol: APA). Notice how the breakout from the accumulation phase is on heavy volume, as highlighted in the volume subgraph, and that shares returned to the resistance level established in the accumulation phase. If prices had broken below that level, that'd indicate the expansion breakout had failed. Instead, shares returned to the breakout level and found support. This move is seen as a low-risk entry level. Yet not all breakouts give you such a beautiful gift. Strong breakouts often don't return to the accumulation phase and allow reentry.

Figure 4-5: The expansion phase of APA.

The aftermath: Distribution

All good things must come to an end, including high-flying securities. During the *distribution phase,* the good news that propelled shares during the expansion phase is no longer so surprising to Wall Street. Share prices start to even out and move sideways instead of rising or falling. Think of the distribution phase as the end of the party. The music is bland, the food is stale, and the conversations are getting old. That's the distribution phase in a nutshell.

The folks who built up shares of a security in the accumulation phase unload those shares during the distribution phase. Amateur investors are often buying the security in the distribution phase, having found out about the company or the investment from a front cover on *Forbes.* When everyone knows the story, it usually means the story doesn't have much farther to run.

The distribution phase can resemble the accumulation phase, a misinterpretation that can seriously mess with your swing trading. Confusing the two may prove costly when you're expecting a higher breakout rather than a lower one.

Shares move sideways during the distribution phase, seemingly indicating a consensus on a security's price, and volume tends to taper off. You can tell accumulation from distribution by

- Observing that a markup phase precedes distribution, whereas a markdown phase usually precedes accumulation

- Looking at the security's fundamentals — typically they aren't as strong during accumulation

Companies can sometimes give you a hint that their shares are priced too high. If you see one offering new stock to the public via a secondary offering, you can be sure that management thinks shares are trading at a premium to their true value. Also, you may see a stock split during the distribution phase.

As a swing trader, identifying distribution phases is helpful for knowing when to exit long positions (sell securities you own) and enter short positions (short securities you anticipate declining in value). If you spot a distribution phase, exit immediately if you own the position. You're likely to be stopped out by one of your sell rules during a distribution phase: a moving average crossover or the breaking of a predefined support level, for example. You may also exit based on the passage of time, a strategy I present in Chapter 10.

I don't recommend shorting during a distribution phase. Because distribution resembles accumulation, you may short a security that's only pausing in its ascent. So don't short until you see a security's price exiting the distribution phase and entering the contraction phase (covered in the following section).

Figure 4-6 highlights shares of Sandisk (symbol: SNDK) during a distribution period. Notice that volume tapers off as shares move sideways. This distribution phase followed an expansion phase that occurred in June and July of 2007.

SNDK - Daily NASDAQ L=27.90 2.45 9.63% B=0.00 A=0.00 O=25.63 Hi=27.86 Lo=25.37 V=12,341,268

Stage 3: Distribution

Volume Avg (50,50,Blue,Red) 12341268.00 8739284.10

Volume tapers off...

Figure 4-6:
Shares
of SNDK
during a
distribution
phase.

The downfall: Contraction

The fourth and final stage of a security's price cycle is the *contraction,* or *markdown, phase* that's best summarized as a period of lower highs and lower lows, a time when short sellers rule. (For more on the earlier stages, see the previous three sections.)

Contraction is a dangerous period. Security prices don't fall in straight lines. Instead, they fall, and then rally to attract new buyers who believe a bottom has been hit. Those rallies fail, and the security moves to fresh, new lows. Avoid timing a bottom in a security. Often termed *bottom fishing,* buying a declining security may feel psychologically pleasing because you're buying something that was more expensive only a few days or weeks ago. But it's dangerous because shares can fall off a cliff after being in a contraction phase.

Volume isn't a helpful indicator in periods of contraction. Although heavy volume indicates sellers' conviction, light volume doesn't indicate the opposite. As the old Wall Street maxim says, "A stock can fall on its own weight, but it takes volume to rise." Hence, a contraction period can be met with light volume throughout.

Securities tend to fall faster than they rise. In just a few days, a security can give up gains that it made over the last several months because greed influences price rises and fear influences price declines. Fear's a more potent emotion than greed. If traders fear lower prices, they sell — fast. But when prices are rising, they're not as committed to buying as quickly as possible.

Rallies in a contraction phase are normal and mark entry points for short sellers. Each rally ends at a point that's lower than the previous one. And every decline takes the security's price to a new low. The prudent approach is to wait for clear signs that the contraction phase is complete and that the security's either holding in an accumulation phase or entering an expansion phase. Short sellers should short on the rallies and cover on the declines, a profitable strategy (until it becomes so obvious that it ends). You want to have the wind at your back when you buy a security, and buying in a contraction phase means that wind's going to hit you full in the face.

Figure 4-7 highlights the contraction phase in shares of Sandisk (symbol: SNDK). This contraction followed the distribution phase highlighted in Figure 4-6. Shares of Sandisk rallied in late October and late November as the stock broke to fresh, new lows.

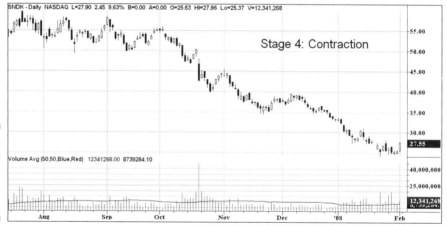

Figure 4-7:
Shares of SNDK enter a contraction phase.

Assessing Trading-Crowd Psychology: Popular Patterns for All Chart Types

Highbrow academics in their ivory towers shun chart patterns because spotting a head and shoulders or cup and handle can be subjective. Just like seeing a pattern in a cloud or the stars, chart patterns are difficult to quantify. To be proven sound, an academic needs to establish rules on spotting these chart patterns, but programming a computer to look for patterns is difficult. Yet reading chart patterns is an essential ability of the successful swing trader.

The solution to the quandary? Trade only patterns that are clear as day. Stick to the tried-and-true chart patterns and you'll avoid the pain of trying to see patterns where none exist.

The following sections describe five major chart patterns: Darvas box, head and shoulders, cup and handles, triangles, and gaps. Rest assured that other chart patterns exist, but these five are, in my opinion, the most common and the most useful. They occur regularly and reflect the psychology of the crowd: day traders, swing traders, position traders, long-term investors, and the like.

The Darvas box: Accumulation in action

The *Darvas box,* a rectangle-shaped pattern, illustrates that security prices tend to trade between two levels before breaching a level and rallying or falling. You may recognize this pattern as the accumulation phase described in the earlier section, "The waiting game: Accumulation."

In a nutshell, the pattern's creator, Nicholas Darvas, looked for securities that traded between two clear price levels: a support level and a resistance level. The support level marked the price point at which buyers stepped in and bought shares, preventing prices from going down. The resistance level marked the price point at which sellers stepped in and sold shares, preventing prices from going up. Darvas didn't waste time with securities that didn't fit nicely into this mold.

After identifying a security as trading between the two price levels, Darvas waited patiently until the security broke out of the upper band on heavy volume. Then he'd buy, placing a stop loss below the support level of the rectangle. If the security rose and formed a new rectangle, he'd raise his stop loss level to the area below the new support level.

The Darvas box works in reverse, too. A falling security may form Darvas boxes on its way down, so short sellers do the opposite of buyers. That is, they identify a security trading between two price levels and then short only after the security breaks below the support level. They place their stop loss level right above the old support level. If a new Darvas box forms, they move the stop loss down to the area above the new resistance level.

Figure 4-8 depicts a typical Darvas box using shares of Philippine Long Distance (symbol: PHI) traded between two clear price levels: $30.50 and $27.30. The excitement came on November 2, 2005, when shares broke out convincingly above $30.50 on heavy volume. This date signaled the beginning of an uptrend (see the later section, "Uptrend lines: Support for the stubborn bulls," for more info on uptrends) and marked the first time shares had exited the Darvas box, indicating an opportune time to buy. Subsequent Darvas boxes would offer the trader a chance to raise the stop loss level.

Figure 4-8:
Shares of
PHI traded
in a Darvas
box in 2005.

In a similar scenario, you could've placed a stop loss level below the support
level of $27.30. However, I'd recommend placing a stop loss level just under
the resistance range, near $30.50. ***Remember:*** If the breakout's genuine, the
security doesn't reenter the Darvas box.

If you're asking yourself why I advise adjusting Darvas's methods, you should
know that Darvas wasn't a swing trader. His time horizon was longer than
that of the swing trader's, and he could afford to wait out a security. As a
swing trader, you don't have the luxury of waiting out a security's consolidation period. Hence, the tighter stop loss level I recommend will keep you in
if the breakout is genuine and get you out if the security decides to take its
sweet time.

Dancing into the investing world: Nicholas Darvas

The Darvas box was popularized by Nicholas
Darvas, a man who turned $25,000 into $2.25
million in 18 months. What made his success
all the more remarkable was that Darvas was
neither a stockbroker nor an investment banker.
In fact, Darvas was in a profession that may be
as far away from investing as you can get: He
was a professional ballroom dancer who trav-
eled the world performing. But in his spare
time, he read books on investing and trading.
He stumbled onto his system after trading for
a few years and reviewing which methods
worked best.

Head and shoulders: The top-off

Not to be confused with the shampoo, the *head-and-shoulders pattern* is a distribution pattern that marks the end of an uptrend, forms for psychologically based reasons, and is among the most reliable of all chart patterns. The Federal Reserve Bank of New York even published a paper called "Head and Shoulders: Not Just a Flaky Pattern." The organization said that the pattern appeared to have some predictive value and produced profits in certain markets.

The head-and-shoulders pattern is composed of three hills, with the middle hill being the tallest and the left and right hills roughly the same height. In this way, the hills resemble a head and shoulders, as you can see in Figure 4-9, which highlights shares of homebuilder Lennar (symbol: LEN).

In January 2007, shares rallied and met resistance at $54 per share. This occurrence formed the left shoulder of the head-and-shoulders pattern. Buyers attempted to raise prices a second time and succeeded, driving Lennar's stock north of $56 per share. Sellers stepped in and brought shares back to the same level as the left shoulder ($52) to complete the head. Finally, buyers attempted once again to raise prices but were only able to push Lennar's stock up to the level established in the left shoulder, a move that completed the right shoulder.

Drawing a trendline through the lows of the left shoulder and the right shoulder establishes the *neckline*. (Flip ahead to the last section for tips on drawing trendlines.) A head-and-shoulders pattern isn't complete until a stock breaks below this point, a movement that's usually followed by lower prices. The head-and-shoulders pattern is typically marked by decreasing volume, which shows a lack of conviction among buyers.

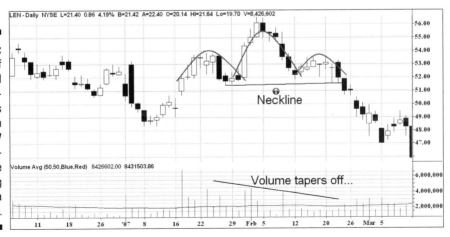

Figure 4-9: Shares of LEN formed a head-and-shoulders pattern in early 2007 that signaled the beginning of a downtrend.

Head-and-shoulders patterns give yardsticks as to how much a security's price will fall after breaking the neckline. Simply measure the distance between the head and the neckline and project that downward to estimate how far the stock will fall at a minimum. In the case of Lennar, the neckline was around $52 and the head was around $56. So you could've expected the stock to fall by at least $4 ($56 – $52) from the neckline ($52) and reach $48. Lennar actually exceeded that estimate.

You should short stocks as they break below the neckline of a head-and-shoulders pattern. Swing traders who hold shares of a company experiencing this pattern should only exit on the break of the neckline or the fulfillment of another selling rule.

An inverse head-and-shoulders pattern, which marks the end of a downtrend, literally looks identical to the head-and-shoulders pattern except that it's turned on its head (pardon the pun). Figure 4-10 highlights an inverted head-and-shoulders pattern in shares of Lan Airlines (symbol: LFL). The measuring technique used in the traditional head-and-shoulders pattern applies to an inverted pattern as well.

The cup and handle: Your signal to stick around for coffee

The *cup-and-handle pattern* is a bullish one that signals shares are being accumulated and the security is preparing for an upward move. Cup-and-handle formations must be preceded by an uptrend, because they're a *continuation formation,* a pattern that indicates the continuation of a trend. (For tips on distinguishing among trendlines, flip to the later section, "Measuring the Strength of Trends with Trendlines.")

Figure 4-10: Shares of LFL formed an inverted head-and-shoulders pattern in July 2006.

The cup and handle first forms after shares rally to some peak. Then for some reason — perhaps fundamental or technical in nature — sellers bring shares down 10 to 20 percent from that peak. Amateur investors who buy near the peak kick themselves for their mistake and agonize over the 10 to 20 percent loss on their investments. They think, "After I break even on this dud, I'll sell."

As it happens, shares of the security give amateur investors that opportunity when they rally back to their previous peak. Then those disgruntled shareholders unload the security en masse, creating a resistance level and leaving shares unable to surpass that peak. However, shares don't fall back to their prior low. Instead, they remain elevated as smart money accumulates shares at a slight discount. Shares may fall 5 percent or so from the peak at this point. On the second attempt to surpass the peak, shares break through and complete the cup-and-handle formation. Volume is key and should rise heavily on the breakout from the handle.

Figure 4-11 illustrates a cup-and-handle pattern in shares of Compania de Minas Buenaventura (symbol: BVN). Shares of BVN rallied to $45 per share in July 2007. Then a general decline in the overall market helped send the shares down to $35, representing a 22 percent loss for shareholders who bought near the peak. Anxious to recoup their losses, these investors unloaded their lot when shares of BVN rose near $45 in September and kept BVN from piercing that level. But the underlying fundamentals of BVN were strong, and investors on the sidelines didn't let BVN decline much — only $5 from the $45 peak. On the second attempt to break through $45, shares sprinted higher and passed that peak on heavy volume.

My selection of numerous foreign securities in this chapter is to illustrate that these patterns occur in both domestic *and* international securities. Moreover, the greatest opportunities, in my opinion, are in foreign securities.

Figure 4-11: Shares of BVN formed a cup and handle in 2007 during an uptrend.

The cup-and-handle pattern isn't as accurate as the head-and-shoulders pattern, which I describe in the preceding section. I've seen it form time and time again only to fail on the breakout. The key question to ask yourself to avoid being a victim of a false breakout is, "What is the security's general market and industry group doing?" The stronger the security's overall market and industry group, the more likely the formation won't fall flat on its face. However, if one or the other is weak, the pattern may be prone to failure.

Triangles: A fiscal tug of war

Triangle chart patterns (shown in Figure 4-12) provide traders with *measurement moves,* an estimate of how far the ensuing trend will travel after breaking out from the triangle. Think of triangles as a reflection of the tug of war that occurs between buyers and sellers. Sometimes buyers have the upper hand; other times sellers have it; and occasionally both sides are evenly matched.

To make use of triangle patterns in your swing trading, you need to get familiar with the three types of triangles and how to calculate price movement with each:

- ✔ **Ascending:** *Ascending triangles* form when buyers maintain a level of strength while sellers continually weaken, so buyers have the upper hand here. Graphically, buyers maintaining their strength is reflected in prices maintaining a certain price level. Each time sellers push prices down, bulls step in and push shares back. Every decline stops at a higher level than the previous decline — a sign that bears are unable to push prices lower. Eventually, buyer strength overwhelms the sellers, and the security breaks upward. To estimate how far, at a minimum, prices will move after a breakout occurs, add the height of the triangle to the breakout price level. The *height of the triangle* is the vertical distance between its support and resistance levels.

- ✔ **Descending:** *Descending triangles* represent the opposite of ascending triangles. Sellers maintain their strength during the formation of the descending triangle, and buyers continually weaken, thus giving sellers the upper hand. Graphically, this weakening is depicted as prices falling to a certain level and subsequent rallies ending at lower peaks. Sellers maintain their strength during the descending triangle, while buyers are unable to push prices to or beyond their previous peaks. Eventually, the buying pressure dries up, and prices break downward. (Think of descending triangles as an amateur boxer fighting a heavyweight. Try as he may, the amateur eventually goes down.) Subtract the height of the triangle from the breakout price level to estimate price movement after a breakout.

✔ **Symmetrical:** *Symmetrical triangles* represent a stalemate; buyers and sellers are evenly matched. Each rally ends at a lower peak than the previous rally, whereas each decline ends at a higher trough than the previous decline. You can't easily tell who's going to win, but you can generally expect prices to continue in the same direction as the trend prior to the formation of the symmetrical triangle. To estimate price movement in this case, add or subtract the triangle's height from the breakout level, depending on which way prices break.

With any triangle chart pattern, be sure to watch for volume on the actual breakout to distinguish between false breakouts and true ones.

Ascending and descending triangles are the easiest triangles to trade because you don't encounter ambiguity on the likely direction of the breakout. Stick to these patterns and skip symmetrical triangles.

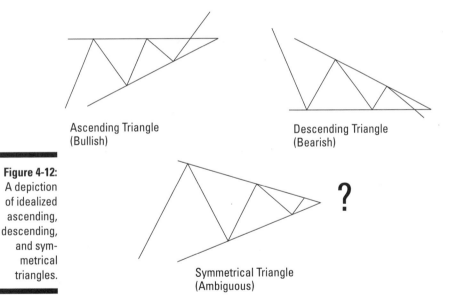

Ascending Triangle
(Bullish)

Descending Triangle
(Bearish)

Figure 4-12:
A depiction
of idealized
ascending,
descending,
and sym-
metrical
triangles.

Symmetrical Triangle
(Ambiguous)

Gaps: Your swing trading crystal ball

Gaps occur frequently in prices; they represent a break in price continuity. For example, a security may be trading in the $19 to $20 range and then gap up to $25. Gaps may represent a seismic shift in the fundamentals of a security, or they may mean nothing. In this section I cover the four types of gaps.

Common gaps

I hate to tell you this, but a *common gap* is meaningless. Prices gap up or down one day but quickly "fill the gap" in a matter of days. This phrase is a simpler way of saying the security's price returns to the area where the gap exists. If a security trades at $50 for several days and gaps higher to $52 the next day, its price fills the gap by trading back down to $50. Figure 4-13 shows two common gaps occurring in late 2006 in a chart of Diana Shipping (symbol: DSX).

Don't trade common gaps. They typically have light volume and don't represent conviction on the part of buyers or sellers.

Breakaway gaps

A *breakaway gap* occurs on heavy volume and indicates seismic shifts are occurring in the security. Often the percentage move up or down is significant (more than 5 percent in a single day), and the volume is at least double the average daily volume. Breakaway gaps are preceded by congestion periods. A security's price trades for several weeks or months in a certain price area and then violently gaps higher or lower one day. The strength of the move indicates a major change is occurring in the way investors value the security. Figure 4-14 highlights a breakaway gap using shares of Contango Oil & Gas Company (symbol: MCF).

Breakaway gaps don't necessarily require swing traders to immediately buy or sell, because several things can happen after the gap, and the gap has to be confirmed. So if you think you see a breakaway gap, take note, but wait for confirmation.

Figure 4-13: Common gaps appeared in shares of DSX in late 2006.

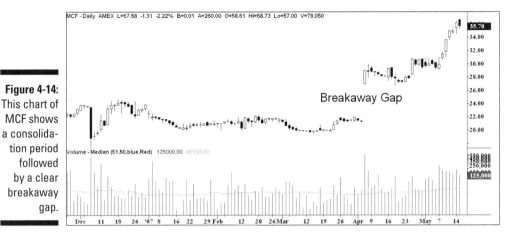

Figure 4-14:
This chart of MCF shows a consolidation period followed by a clear breakaway gap.

Continuation gaps

A *continuation gap* crops up in the midst of an uptrend or downtrend and signals — you guessed it — the continuation of the previous trend. Figure 4-15 highlights a continuation gap that followed a breakaway gap in shares of Flowserve Corp. (symbol: FLS). *Note:* Not all continuation gaps are preceded by a breakaway gap.

Some swing traders actually estimate how far a security will rise or fall based on the price appreciation or depreciation from the beginning of a trend until the continuation gap, and then project that forward. This approach can be somewhat subjective. Instead, look to add or enter a position on a continuation gap in the direction of the gap (for example, buy if the gap is up and short if the gap is down). Place a protective stop loss within the gap. If the gap is truly a continuation gap, shares don't return to fill it.

Figure 4-15:
FLS shares form a continuation gap.

Exhaustion gaps

An *exhaustion gap,* which occurs in the direction of a trend, resembles a continuation gap and marks the end of that trend. If a security has been falling for several weeks and then gaps down, you may think that gap is a continuation gap. However, if the gap fills quickly, it's likely an exhaustion gap. Figure 4-16 offers an example of an exhaustion gap occurring at the end of an uptrend in shares of Sigma Designs (symbol: SIGM).

The exhaustion gap doesn't offer any call to action for you as a swing trader.

Figure 4-16:
An exhaustion gap appears in a chart of SIGM.

Letting Special Candlestick Patterns Reveal Trend Changes

You can find dozens of candlestick chart patterns out there, but I cover only the ones I feel are most accurate. The next four sections feature candlestick chart patterns that are easy to identify and that may signal a change in momentum or a continuation of a trend. (For help discerning one trend from another, flip ahead to "Measuring the Strength of Trends with Trendlines," later in this chapter.)

Hammer time!

A *hammer* represents the bottom of a trend. It looks identical to a hanging man (see the following section) and occurs at the end of a downtrend.

Hammers have small real bodies in the upper portion of the candlestick bar. They have long lower shadows and small upper shadows (if any). Hammers signal that after the price of the security opened on the market, sellers drove it down. By the end of the day, buyers had recouped much of the losses to end the day near or at the high.

I like to see hammers that extend below recent price action. If a hammer occurs within the price action of previous days, I don't consider it a reliable indicator of a bottom.

Figure 4-17 sheds some light on the difference between a hammer that forms below recent price history and one that forms within price history using shares of Western Digital (symbol: WDC), which bottomed on April 10, 2007. Notice how the high and low on that bottoming day were well below recent price history. Contrast this hammer formation to the apparent hammer that formed on March 14, 2007. This second hammer's body was within previous price action, but ultimately, it didn't mark the bottom of the downtrend.

No hammer is complete without confirmation. If the price action directly after the hammer is down, then no hammer has occurred. A true hammer can't have its low violated by subsequent price action. So watch to see how subsequent days unfold before trading a hammer so as to avoid whipsaws.

Volume, again, should be kept in mind. Hammers that form on heavy volume are usually genuine, whereas those that form on light volume probably aren't the real McCoy.

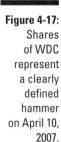

Figure 4-17: Shares of WDC represent a clearly defined hammer on April 10, 2007.

The hanging man (Morbid, I know)

A *hanging man* looks identical to the hammer (see the preceding section). However, it occurs at the end of an uptrend rather than a downtrend. It crops up on heavy volume and is followed by price action confirming the top. If the high of the hanging man is surpassed, then its signal is invalid.

Double vision: Bullish and bearish engulfing patterns

My favorite candlestick charting patterns are the bullish and bearish engulfing patterns, which involve two candlestick bars, not one.

Bullish engulfing patterns occur when a candlestick bar opens lower than the previous candlestick's close and closes higher than the previous candlestick's open. In candlestick terminology, the pattern begins with a candlestick bar that has a small real body and is followed by a candlestick bar whose body engulfs the previous day's body.

Why is this pattern so bullish? It represents a major defeat, so to speak, for bears. When the second candlestick bar opens, sellers are already pushing prices below the prior day's close. However, buyers step in and begin purchasing en masse. Not only are they able to reverse the direction from the open but they also manage to push prices higher than where sellers began the previous day. Think of a bullish engulfing pattern as a surprise victory in a battle where an infantry division loses not only the gains it made in the previous day but also much more.

I've found bullish engulfing patterns to be accurate (otherwise I wouldn't be covering them). Look for subsequent price action to confirm the reversal. If prices trade below the pattern, you can bet your bottom dollar that the pattern failed.

Figure 4-18 highlights a bullish engulfing pattern in shares of NewMarket (symbol: NEU) that fell in mid-2006 from $62 to less than $40. Notice how the open on June 14, 2006, completely engulfed the entire body of the prior day. Subsequent price action confirmed the bottom.

Bearish engulfing patterns occur at the end of uptrends and mark important reversals. They're characterized by two bar formations. The first candlestick consists of a small real body. The second candlestick opens higher than the previous bar's close and closes lower than the previous bar's open, thus engulfing the first candlestick. Figure 4-19 highlights a bearish engulfing pattern that formed in shares of Diamond Offshore (symbol: DO) in late 2007 and signaled the end of the prior uptrend.

Figure 4-18:
Shares of
NEU form
a bullish
engulfing
pattern.

Wait for confirmation before shorting a bearish engulfing chart pattern since not all bearish engulfing patterns lead to lower prices. If the engulfing pattern is genuine, prices should decline after the formation and shouldn't exceed the high of the bearish engulfing bar.

Figure 4-19:
Shares of
DO formed
a bearish
engulfing
pattern in
late 2007 to
mark the
end of an
uptrend.

The triple threat: Morning and evening stars

Morning and evening stars are reversal chart patterns that consist of three candlesticks. *Morning stars* mark the end of a downtrend and the beginning of an uptrend. *Evening stars* mark the end of an uptrend and the beginning of a downtrend.

A morning star occurs at the end of downtrends, which means that sellers (the bears) are in force prior to the reversal, and consists of

- ✔ A long, black-bodied candlestick that pushes the downtrend lower

- ✔ A second candlestick that gaps lower at the open (but doesn't necessarily have to be completely below the first candlestick) and forms a small body

- ✔ A long, white-bodied candlestick that gaps higher from the second candlestick and closes near the upper portion of the first candlestick

Conversely, an evening star occurs at the end of uptrends, reflecting the last gasp of buyers (the bulls), and is made up of

- ✔ A long, white-bodied candlestick that pushes the uptrend higher

- ✔ A second candlestick that gaps higher at the open (but doesn't necessarily have to be completely above the first candlestick) and forms a small body

- ✔ A long, black-bodied candlestick that gaps lower from the second candlestick and closes near the lower portion of the first candlestick

Figure 4-20 is an example of an idealized morning and evening star. Both patterns reflect the inability of the ruling party, bulls or bears, to consolidate previous gains. The star (the middle bar) is an exhaustion attempt by buyers (in the case of an evening star) or sellers (in the case of a morning star) to push prices definitively higher or lower, respectively. That's why the second bar in the morning or evening star formation is small: The day begins with a gap in the direction of the trend, but the initial enthusiasm dies down. The third bar shows a swing in momentum as bulls or bears take over.

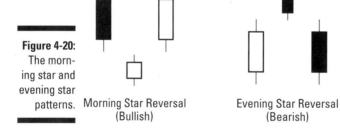

Figure 4-20: The morning star and evening star patterns.

Morning Star Reversal (Bullish)   Evening Star Reversal (Bearish)

To see one of these star patterns in the context of a chart, take a look at Figure 4-21, which shows the evening star reversal in action in shares of China Mobile Limited (symbol: CHL) in February 2007. Notice how the star (the middle candlestick in the formation) gapped higher than the previous bar. The third bar represented a resounding defeat for bulls, as bears were able to push prices to the level of the first candlestick.

Figure 4-21:
Shares
of China
Mobile
Limited
(symbol:
CHL) formed
an evening
star in
February of
2007.

Measuring the Strength of Trends with Trendlines

Quite literally, *trendlines* connect price points together and form either a horizontal, rising, or falling line. They're helpful in establishing support and resistance levels. When a trendline breaks, shares may or may not reverse course. The most you can take away is that the trend in question has ended. A *consolidation period* (sideways movement) may follow, a continuation of the trend may arise, or the trend may reverse. All three scenarios are possible.

The stock market isn't some perfect universe where stocks stop and rally on a dime. There are gray areas, and trendlines should be drawn through them. Of course, trendlines aren't perfect either and may at times intersect with prices. But if trendlines are valid, these intersections shouldn't be significant (in how deeply they intersect) or often (the number of times they intersect with prices.)

Much ink has been spilt on the construction of trendlines, but there's really no science to them. So don't expect one trendline drawn at an angle of 65 degrees to be right and one drawn at 63 degrees to be wrong. The basics of drawing trendlines can be summarized in three simple rules:

✔ **A trendline must touch three different price points to be valid.**
   Otherwise, you can draw a line pretty much anywhere.

✔ **The more times a trendline's touched, the stronger the support or resistance of that line.** A break of a trendline that had been tested several times indicates a serious change in the trend.

✔ **The longer the trendline (measured by time), the more meaningful it is.** The staying power of the trend is measured, in part, by how long the trendline has been in effect.

If you find yourself drawing and redrawing trendlines (on your charting program, not by hand), then you're misusing them.

Don't waste too much time drawing trendlines. Instead, identify support and resistance levels, which are often horizontal lines. Then look for an uptrend or downtrend line that you can draw through the lows or highs to establish a rate of ascent.

In the following sections, I share how to distinguish and use different trendlines.

Uptrend lines: Support for the stubborn bulls

Uptrend lines connect several lows and form a support area for the bulls — the bulls' line in the sand, if you will. They indicate the rate of ascent that buyers have maintained over a certain period of time. If your charts are arithmetically scaled, then the rate of ascent is measured in dollars per time period. If your charts are semi-log or plotted on a log scale, then the rate of ascent represents a percentage change per time period.

You want to draw your uptrend line through the lows, but don't take it to an extreme. If the line intersects prices slightly, that's okay. Consider Figure 4-22, which shows an uptrend line of shares of Sandisk (symbol: SNDK). The uptrend line is drawn through the lows and touches several price points. On an extreme day in the beginning of August, prices fell below the line but basically remained above the trendline. Hence, the trendline stayed intact.

Uptrend lines can be good long entry points for your swing trading. Not only do they offer an entry price but they also offer a clear risk-cutting price. Place a stop loss right below the trendline so that you exit shares if the trendline breaks.

Uptrend lines have another important characteristic: These support lines become resistance lines after being breached. Look again at Figure 4-22. In mid-August, shares of Sandisk broke below the uptrend line that began in June. When shares rallied in September, that support line became a resistance area. After shares rallied to that trendline, they immediately turned around and began declining.

Figure 4-22:
This chart of SNDK shows an uptrend line and a downtrend line.

Downtrend lines: Falling resistance

Downtrend lines connect a series of peaks and represent an area of resistance. Think of them as the line in the sand for the bears. And like uptrend lines, covered in the preceding section, they're more meaningful the more times they're touched by security prices and the longer they've been in effect. Figure 4-23 depicts a downtrend line that occurred shortly after a breakaway gap down in shares of Broadcom (symbol: BRCM).

Because a break of a trendline doesn't necessarily mean the beginning of a new trend, you shouldn't buy or short a security because of a trade trendline break. If you own shares in a stock that's rising and then suffers a break, selling may be warranted. However, don't look to suddenly short because of the break.

Figure 4-23:
In this chart, the downtrend line is touched several times, signaling its importance.

Horizontal lines: Working to both support and resist

Horizontal trendlines depict a stationary support or resistance level. After either of these levels is broken, a trend usually develops. Alternatively, the security may enter a new trading range with horizontal support and resistance levels.

Some common horizontal trendlines you'll encounter as you swing trade are ascending triangles (a horizontal level of resistance) and the Darvas box (a horizontal trendline of support and a horizontal trendline of resistance). These patterns are both described in earlier sections of this chapter.

Chapter 5

Asking Technical Indicators for Directions

In This Chapter

▶ Knowing how to make the most of technical indicators in your swing trading

▶ Identifying popular indicators and using them with chart patterns

▶ Understanding how to use indicators to determine your desired ratio of short and long positions

*S*wing trading used to be far more difficult before the advent of charting programs — many of them now free and online — that calculate technical indicators so that you never need to pick up a pencil and figure them out by hand. In keeping with the technological times, this chapter doesn't linger on how to calculate indicators beyond the basic knowledge necessary to analyze them effectively and understand how price, volume, or both impact their direction. Instead, it introduces you to the popular indicators you can apply to your charts — whether you trade trends, ranges, or both.

No indicator can consistently yield profitable results on all securities under all time frames. That's why this chapter begins with an explanation of what technical indicators are based on and when you should use them. This chapter also helps you grasp the power of combining technical indicators and chart patterns so that you can swing trade successfully.

Even when you know which technical indicators you want to use, you have to know which inputs to use with which indicator. Throughout this chapter, I explicitly state what input variables you should use with the indicators I cover. In most cases, the inputs are the standards most charting programs use. Some of them, however, are different, because they're based on what's most appropriate for a swing trader.

All You Need to Know about Analyzing Indicators Before You Start

Before you dive into the sea of technical indicators, you must remember a few important things, which I run through in this preliminary section.

You must apply the right type of indicator

Often, traders apply trending indicators haphazardly to all security price charts. The problem with this approach is that trending indicators always assume a market is in a trend, and they give false signals when applied to non-trending markets, which are characterized by oscillation between two price levels: a support level and a resistance level. The trending indicator generates false signals because it incorrectly assumes that a price moving to a support or resistance level indicates the beginning of a new trend (when, in fact, these movements are simply normal price fluctuations within an established range value). Therefore, you shouldn't apply trending indicators to markets that oscillate.

Just as trending indicators wreak havoc when applied to non-trending markets, the reverse also holds true. If you apply a non-trending indicator to a trending market, the indicator continually flashes red lights due to an extreme overbought or oversold level. Non-trending indicators, unlike their trending counterparts, assume price stability. The lack of price stability means that non-trending indicators always assume *mean reversion* (the theory that prices will return to the mean, or average). Mean reversion doesn't occur in trending markets.

Figure 5-1 highlights the problems that can arise when you misapply indicators. The figure compares the correct application of a trending indicator (a moving average) in a trending security and the incorrect application of a non-trending indicator (stochastic, located at the bottom of the chart) to the same security. Notice how the moving average keeps the swing trader in for most of the trade, while the non-trending indicator gives premature sell signals. During trending markets, non-trending indicators give false signals.

Not all price swings are meaningful

Technical indicators can go haywire, turning that significant price swing into nothing. Sometimes a price swing on a chart can reflect a data error (which happens more often than you may think), or your charting software provider may fail to account for a stock split. Now and then the price swing is due to an unsubstantiated rumor. That's why you must intelligently judge all price swings.

Figure 5-1:
Applying a non-trend-ing indicator to a trending security leads to premature sell or buy signals.

Figure 5-2 provides an example of how a data error can throw a technical indica-tor off the mark. Shares of SPX Corporation (symbol: SPW) showed a wild price swing on January 22, 2008, when they supposedly opened at $89.50, traded down to $73.31, and then closed at $95.23. However, the intraday chart shows a *bad tick* (an incorrect price) at $73.31. A technical indicator that looks solely at the closing price wouldn't be affected by this price error. However, an indica-tor that incorporates the highs and lows of the day would be affected.

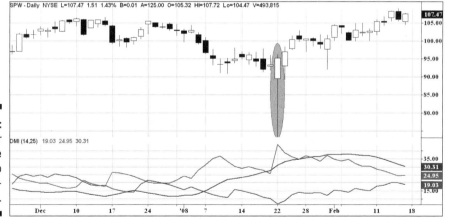

Figure 5-2:
A data error can cause indicators to yield incor-rect signals.

In this case, the Directional Movement Index, or DMI (see "The compass of indi-cators: Directional Movement Index (DMI)," later in this chapter, for details on this indicator) assumes that sellers are in control of shares of SPX Corporation due to the negative price swing. As the company's share price rises, the DMI fails to track this strength due to the data error.

You have a few options to protect yourself from getting messed up by a data error:

- ✔ Rely on an indicator that doesn't incorporate the data error.
- ✔ Ignore that security for trading purposes.
- ✔ Turn to other technical tools, such as chart patterns and candlesticks.
- ✔ Report the data error to the trading system administrator, who can usually correct the error in a day or two.

Prices don't reflect volume, so you need to account for it

Together, price and volume form an important picture for you as a swing trader. Any new information that any single person may possess about a security — be it good or bad — can only be acted upon by buying or selling shares of a security. That buying and selling is reflected on the ticker tape — the price and the volume.

Basing an indicator on price alone does make intuitive sense. After all, a security's price is believed to contain all known information. However, volume explains traders' commitment, which price can't do. Light volume can signal indifference, whereas heavy volume is usually associated with meaningful moves. Also, a security rising on increasing volume has more staying power than a security rising on decreasing volume, and an indicator that looks only at price (that is, the vast majority of indicators) can't distinguish between the two movements. That's why you should have at least one indicator in your arsenal that incorporates volume.

But even if an indicator does look at price and volume, there's always the possibility of an event occurring outside all market participants' knowledge. For example, a company's headquarters may be destroyed due to a hurricane or fire, an incident no one can predict.

An indicator's accuracy isn't a measure of its value

Indicators, like all trading techniques, aren't always accurate. Keep an eye out for *whipsaws,* when prices move violently and throw indicators off, and be sure to plan for and incorporate the possibility that an indicator's signal is a false positive. The simplest way to protect yourself from inevitable whipsaws is to have a risk management system that helps you exit early when a particular trade doesn't go your way.

That said, indicators don't have to be foolproof to be profitable, so accuracy's not a good way to judge whether a particular indicator is valuable. An indicator can generate so-called correct results 30 percent of the time and still be profitable — if the profitable trades far outweigh the losing trades. Consider the trading system of fictitious Trader Josh. He relies on two technical indicators in his trading system. However, his system's usually wrong; the trades he places lose money 70 percent of the time. Is this system worth following?

That question can't be answered without additional information. Swing traders who rely on riding strong trends may be wrong more often than they're right but still generate sizeable profits. Trader Josh's trading log (shown in Figure 5-3) displays his profits, losses, and net gains or losses over the course of ten trading days in January. During this time, Trader Josh lost money on seven days. What a lousy trader, right?

Josh's Trading Log

Beginning Account Value: $100,000

	Profit	Loss	Net Gain/Loss
January 5, 2009	$0	–$400	–$400
January 6, 2009	$300	–$500	–$200
January 7, 2009	$3,000	–$200	$2,800
January 9, 2009	$150	–$500	–$350
January 12, 2009	$290	–$350	–$60
January 13, 2009	$3,500	–$250	$3,250
January 15, 2009	$100	–$150	–$50
January 20, 2009	$320	–$450	–$130
January 21, 2009	$350	–$500	–$150
January 22, 2009	$3,200	–$250	$2,950
Total			$7,660

Figure 5-3: This trading log shows profits and losses over the course of ten days.

Not so fast. Trader Josh made money on three trading days out of the ten. And those three days made up for all the losses and much more. Trader Josh actually generated net profits of $7,660 in those ten trading days — a strong return on a beginning account value of $100,000.

Two to three indicators are enough

Adding an indicator is as simple as clicking your mouse and being dazzled by the charts of many colors that appear quite easily. This simplicity leads some swing traders to incorporate five, six, or even more indicators to a single security. But doing so isn't wise.

The more indicators you add to a system, the more likely your system will fail to generate consistent signals. Rarely do all indicators point in the same direction, because all indicators are based on price, volume, or both. This principle doesn't change, regardless of how many indicators you add to your system. When you apply five or six technical indicators to a security's price chart simultaneously, you amplify the amount of *noise* (unimportant information). Or you wind up not trading anything because the indicators never all point in the same direction.

Stick to three indicators or fewer. Having more than three doesn't add any significant value.

If you're still not convinced, consider the world of regression analysis, which reinforces this point. A *regression* is simply a model that depicts how well one factor or many factors explain something else. For example, housing prices may be a function of location, the number of rooms in the house, and interest rates. Think of housing prices as a security's price, and think of the factors used to predict prices as technical indicators. As a swing trader, you're trying to forecast the direction of prices based on the information contained in the indicators. A model that explains housing prices well is useful for forecasting. One way to improve a regression's ability to explain the variable you're trying to predict is to add additional factors. In this example, you may add the color of the house or the number of garages to the model. If the additional factor doesn't add value, the model's ability to forecast remains unchanged. But if the additional factor adds *some* value — regardless of how minute — the model's effectiveness improves. But that doesn't mean you should forecast using 25 variables when 3 key ones explain most of the variability in housing prices. The same holds true with technical indicators.

Inputs should always fit your time horizon

Practically every technical indicator has settings that can be adjusted. Moving averages, for example, can be set to short-term lengths (4 days and 9 days) or long-term lengths (50 days and 200 days). The smaller the number, the quicker an indicator responds to changes in price. The downside to such quick reflexes is an increased number of *whipsaws,* when prices move violently and throw indicators off. The larger the input figure used in an indicator, the fewer the number of whipsaws.

However, you can't use an unresponsive indicator. Trading based on the 200-day moving average may generate two or three signals a year, and that doesn't help when you're looking to trade in and out of shares over the next week. The input you use should always fit your time horizon.

Some swing traders experiment with each indicator on each security, testing the historical effectiveness of an indicator on a particular security. They may even adjust the technical indicator's inputs for each security they trade. I don't recommend this approach. Besides being complex and time consuming, it doesn't provide a clear payoff in the long run. Customizing indicators for each security also may lead to curve fitting. *Curve fitting* occurs when you try additional input numbers until one of them produces the so-called best fit. But those factors may be the result of chance and have little relevance for future trading.

Divergences are the strongest signals in technical analysis

Divergences represent low-risk entry points — or exits if you're holding a position contradictory to the technical indicator — because the market crowd is convinced that either buyers or sellers are stronger than the other, when in fact the opposite is true. Divergences don't always lead to profitable results, but they're more accurate than most signals coming from indicators.

When a technical indicator, like stochastics, diverges from the price chart, an alert should go off in your mind (ideally relating to the chart you're examining), because divergences represent a contradiction of sorts between the exterior and interior of a security (sounds deep, doesn't it?). The contradiction comes about when prices move in one direction and the indicator moves in another. Well-respected technical analysts, such as Alexander Elder or John Murphy, have said that divergences are the strongest signals in technical analysis.

Unfortunately, divergences are difficult to screen for. You can ask your technical analysis software program to search for securities where this indicator crossed over that one. But divergences usually require an interpretive eye, so score one for humankind versus the machines!

Determining Whether a Security Is Trending

To swing trade successfully, you need to know whether a security is trending so you can apply the right indicator. Because of the importance of correctly applying trending indicators to trending markets and non-trending indicators to non-trending markets, the next logical question you should ask yourself is: How do I know whether the market I'm looking at is trending?

You can answer this question in two ways. Both approaches should yield the same answer if done correctly, so the approach you choose to use doesn't make a huge difference.

One way of determining whether a trend exists is to eyeball a security's chart. If you see a series of higher highs and higher lows or a series of lower highs and lower lows, you know a trend exists. Black and white signals don't exist when it comes to eyeballing a security's price chart and calling a trend or non-trend (that is, trading range). The onus is on you to recognize trending markets and non-trending ones.

When eyeballing a chart, the first question you should ask is: Do I see a series of higher lows and higher highs *or* a series of lower lows and lower highs? If the answer is yes to either question, then you're working with a security that's trending. If the answer's no, then your next question is: Do I see a clear support area that prices consistently rise from and a clear resistance area that prices consistently fall from? If the answer's yes, you're working with a security that's non-trending or in a trading range. *Note:* If the answers to the first and second questions are no, then the security you're looking at can't be classified and should be avoided.

Timeframe affects what you see. You may observe a security's price chart that's set to hourly bars and see a clear trend but switch to a daily bar chart and see an obvious trading range. As a swing trader, you should rely on hourly and daily bar charts. Anything longer is appropriate only for position traders or buy-and-hold investors.

If eyeballing isn't your cup of tea, have no fear — a technical indicator can come to your rescue. The most popular indicator that shows whether a security is trending is the *Average Directional Index* (ADX), which actually measures the strength of a trend rather than its direction. Part of the Directional Movement Index (DMI; see the later section on DMI for details on this indicator), ADX

- ✔ Can be plotted by itself
- ✔ Oscillates between the values of 0 and 100
- ✔ Is the average difference between the two other components of the DMI (covered in more detail later in this chapter)

All ADX examples in this chapter calculate the indicator over a period of 14 days, the standard setting for this popular indicator.

If a security's ADX reading is 20 or below, that security is in a trading range. If the ADX reading is 30 or higher, consider that security to be in a trend. Readings between 20 and 30 are ambiguous. When I see a reading between 20 and 30, I incorporate the direction of the ADX into my analysis to help me determine whether the security's trending. For example, if ADX is rising and above 20, then I consider that as a sign that the security's trending. On the other hand, if the ADX value is below 30 and falling, I consider that as a sign the security may be in or may be entering a trading range.

Figure 5-4 shows ADX applied to a price chart for shares of MEMC Electronic Materials (symbol: WFR). This security experienced a strong uptrend in late 2006 through mid-2007. The ADX indicator was solidly above 20 during this period. However, MEMC Electronic Materials entered into a trading range in May 2007. On May 9, 2007, the ADX indicator fell below 20, a move that signaled a period when non-trending indicators should've been applied.

Figure 5-4:
The ADX indicator applied to shares of WFR.

Recognizing Major Trending Indicators

The number of trending indicators out there is mind-boggling, but all trending indicators are based on price, volume, or both. So using several trending indicators on a single chart doesn't give you an advantage. To get the most benefit from trending indicators, never use more than two or three.

Unlike non-trending indicators, trending indicators tend to have no upper or lower limits. The higher an indicator's reading, the stronger the underlying trend. You should only apply trending indicators after you've determined that a security is in fact trending either by eyeballing the chart or by using the ADX indicator, which I explain in the earlier section, "Determining Whether a Security Is Trending."

The last item you want to remember about trending indicators is that they can be applied to all securities: stocks, commodities, mutual funds, ETFs, and so on. You can even apply them to price derivatives, such as the ratio between two securities. How you interpret trending indicators is the same regardless of whether you apply the indicators to prices or to some derivative of prices.

The following sections help you get up close and personal with three major trending indicators:

- ✔ Directional Movement Index (DMI)
- ✔ Moving averages
- ✔ Moving Average Convergence/Divergence (MACD)

The compass of indicators: Directional Movement Index (DMI)

The *Directional Movement Index* (DMI) is a powerful technical indicator. Not only does it reveal whether a security is trending, but it also reveals the direction of that trend, whether it's increasing in strength, and when it ends.

DMI is composed of three plots:

- ✔ **+DMI:** The positive directional movement index (+DMI) plot indicates how effective bulls were in pushing prices above the previous day's high. +DMI ranges between 0 and 100. The higher the reading, the stronger the bulls.

- ✔ **–DMI:** The negative directional movement index (–DMI) plot shows how efficient bears were in pushing prices below the previous day's low. –DMI ranges between 0 and 100. The higher the reading, the stronger the bears.

- ✔ **ADX:** ADX measures the difference between +DMI and –DMI. So basically it measures the strength — or lack thereof — of a trend. (For more on ADX, see "Determining Whether a Security Is Trending," earlier in this chapter.)

Swing traders use crossovers in +DMI and –DMI as trading signals. When +DMI crosses above –DMI, buyers have wrestled control of shares. When –DMI crosses above +DMI, on the other hand, sellers have wrestled control of shares. Frequent crossovers between +DMI and –DMI signify that neither bulls nor bears have control of shares, a fact that's reflected in an ADX reading below 20.

Most charting software calculates DMI over 14 days and uses 25 as the standard ADX average. Both settings are worthwhile.

Figure 5-5 provides a sample of what DMI looks like in shares of Alvarion (symbol: ALVR). When –DMI crosses above +DMI, as it did on October 8, a sell signal is generated. Notice that ADX remains above 20 throughout the crossover.

Figure 5-5:
A chart
of ALVR
includes a
chart of the
DMI.

I don't trade off of the crossovers of +DMI and –DMI, nor do I recommend you do so. Although practically every uptrend and downtrend is preceded by the corresponding +DMI or –DMI crossing above the other, whipsaws occur frequently. It's difficult to tell when a crossover occurs whether the security's still trending or is entering a trading range. That's why I find DMI to be of more value when used as an exit indicator than when used as an entry indicator. While I'm long shares of XYZ Corp., for example, I don't want to see –DMI cross over +DMI — ever. If it does, I exit as quickly as possible. The reverse is true if I'm short shares of ABC Corp.

Use DMI in the following manner to get the most bang for your investing buck:

1. **Confirm that a trend is in place by using the ADX plot in the DMI.**

2. **If a trend exists, enter a trade using moving averages or MACD.**

   For more on either of these trend-following indicators, check out the following sections in this chapter.

3. **Enter in the direction of +DMI or –DMI.**

   If +DMI is above –DMI, enter on the long side. If –DMI is above +DMI, enter on the short side.

4. **Exit when +DMI or –DMI crosses above its counterpart.**

A mean, lean revelation machine: Moving averages

Moving averages — rolling averages of price data designed to reveal the underlying trend in that data — are the most widely used technical indicators. When you use them, understand that the shorter the average, the more frequently the average generates signals.

A ten-day moving average, for example, averages the last ten days of price history. On the eleventh day, the moving average drops the oldest day and uses the new day in its formula. (**Note:** The simple moving average equally weights all bars in its calculation.)

You'll encounter two types of moving averages in your swing-trading ventures, and whether you use one more than the other is entirely up to you:

- **Simple moving averages:** This indicator reveals the consensus price agreement over X number of days, where X represents the length of the moving average. When prices rise above their ten-day moving average, for example, you can conclude that market participants believe the security's value is rising above the average of the last ten days. Conversely, when a security's price falls below its ten-day moving average, the security's value is falling below the consensus price over the last ten days.

- **Exponential moving averages (EMA):** This indicator also shows consensus price agreement over a certain time frame, but it weights historical prices differently. Exponential moving averages respond faster than simple moving averages because they weight recent price action more heavily than older price action. The downside to this responsiveness is an increase in the number of false signals.

Figure 5-6 provides a comparison of the two moving averages using a chart with a nine-day simple moving average and a nine-day EMA. This chart shows shares of Smith International (symbol: SII) in late 2007 and early 2008. The slope of the EMA changes before the slope of the simple moving average, as highlighted on January 3, 2008, and February 7, 2008. On both days, the EMA gave a signal one day before the simple moving average. But this quickness came at the cost of whipsaws. Notice that on December 17, 2007, the slope of the EMA turned negative prematurely, whereas the slope of the simple moving average remained positive. A swing trader relying on the EMA may have exited too early and missed out on a price gain of 10 percent in 10 days.

The most important part of both moving averages is slope. The slope can be positive (the moving average is rising), negative (the moving average is falling), or zero (the moving average is flat).

You should *always* trade in the direction of the slope. If you're looking to buy a security, the slope of that security's moving average must be positive — no exceptions. If you're looking to short a security, the slope of that security's moving average must be negative — no exceptions. You can trade a security either when the slope of the moving average turns positive or negative — depending on whether you're buying or shorting — or when multiple moving averages cross.

Figure 5-6: A comparison of the simple moving average and the EMA using shares of SII.

Swing trading securities based on a moving average isn't a complete trading system. The moving average is simply an entry signal. It doesn't tell you how much of your capital to allocate to the position, where you should place your stop loss, or when you'll take profits. For more on these topics, flip to Chapter 10.

In the next couple of sections, I show you how to swing trade using slope changes and moving average crossovers.

Riding the roller coaster: Trading slope changes

The first question you must consider when trading securities based on the slope changes of moving averages is what *moving-average length,* or the number of days, to use. Assuming you're using daily charts, stick to a moving-average length of 18 days or fewer. (I'm partial to the nine-day moving average myself.)

After you've determined the number of days you're looking at, follow these steps to buy a desired security using slope changes:

1. Find a security that's trending, as shown by the ADX indicator.

When the ADX indicator is above 20, the security's trending. But you still don't know the direction of that trend. You can figure it out by simply examining the chart and determining whether prices are forming a series of higher lows and higher highs or a series of lower highs and lower lows. Or you can use the DMI indicator described previously in this chapter.

Trade only in the direction of the trend. If the trend is up and the nine-day moving average slope turns negative, don't short the security. While the slope of the moving average is negative, the overall trend is positive; shorting in these situations can be like swimming against the tide.

2. **After you've determined that a trend is in place and that the direction is up, buy when the slope of the moving average changes from flat or negative to positive.**

If you trade during market hours, the slope may change to positive at 10 a.m., only to be reversed by closing time at 4 p.m. If you can watch the market intraday, I recommend trading in the last half hour, when it's likely the slope change won't be reversed. Wait to trade on the day following the slope change if you can't watch the market intraday.

3. **Place the stop loss level below a recent low.**

Some swing traders place their stop loss order below the low of the day when the buy signal occurred, which represents the exit in the event of loss.

4. **Exit after the moving average turns flat or negative.**

In the event of profit, you may exit when the slope of the moving average turns from positive to negative, when a certain return objective is met, or after a certain period of days. However, I prefer the method recommended in this step.

The process for shorting securities based on slope changes isn't all that different from the process for buying. Follow these steps:

1. **Identify that a trend exists by using ADX or the eyeball approach.**

2. **Confirm that the direction of the trend is down by using DMI or the eyeball approach.**

3. **Short when the moving average slope turns negative after being flat or positive.**

4. **Place a stop loss above a recent peak.**

5. **Exit based on time, return objective, or the slope turning positive.**

Figure 5-7 highlights buying shares of a security on the upswing of the slope of a nine-day simple moving average in shares of Axsys Technologies (symbol: AXYS). With the ADX above 30, you can see that shares of Axsys

Technologies are trending, so trending indicators are appropriate. In this case, you'd wait for the slope to turn positive (if the slope is already positive, you've missed the opportunity and should pass on the trade). After the slope turns positive, buy the security with a stop loss below a recent trough (in this scenario, $19.95 marks a recent trough). Your exit would depend on your trading strategy.

Figure 5-7:
Shares of
AXYS in
mid-2007
plotted with
a nine-day
moving
average and
ADX.

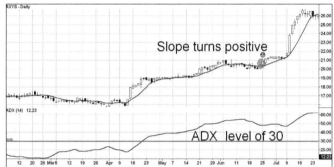

Crissing and crossing: Trading moving average crossovers

Another way to use a moving average is by trading crossovers. Moving average crossovers occur more frequently than slope changes, which means swing traders using crossovers may enter or exit a trade earlier than traders relying on changes in the slope of a moving average. But nothing in this world is free — that added earliness comes at the cost of increased whipsaws.

Multiple moving averages convey information on the value of a security over several time periods. When a short-term moving average crosses above a moving average of longer length, market participants are beginning to change their opinion of the security. Specifically, the company's short-term value is increasing over its long-term value, a move that may signal the beginning of a new trend or the continuation of a previous trend.

When a short-term moving average crosses below a long-term moving average, the security's value is declining relative to price consensus established over the long-term moving average, which may precede a price decline.

The basic method of trading moving average crossovers on the buy side is as follows:

1. **Determine whether a trend exists by using ADX or the eyeball approach.**

2. **Confirm that a moving average crossover occurs in the direction of the trend by using DMI or the eyeball approach.**

3. **Buy when the short-term moving average crosses above the long-term moving average.**

4. **Place a stop loss order below a recent trough.**

5. **Exit based on time, return objective, or when the short-term moving average crosses below the long-term moving average.**

Stick to moving averages that are 18 days in length or fewer. Although longer-term moving averages — such as the 50-day moving average — are more meaningful than shorter-term moving averages, they generate signals too infrequently for swing traders.

I recommend you use the crossover of the four-day moving average and nine-day moving average. When the four-day moving average crosses

✔ Above the nine-day moving average in an established uptrend, you should buy the underlying security

✔ Below the nine-day moving average in an established downtrend, you should short the underlying security

Figure 5-8 highlights a long trade in shares of Western Digital (symbol: WDC) based on the crossover of the four-day moving average above the nine-day moving average. If you'd found this potential trade when the four-day moving average had already crossed above the nine-day moving average, you'd be too late to buy it.

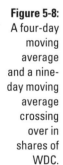

Figure 5-8:
A four-day moving average and a nine-day moving average crossing over in shares of WDC.

A meeting of the means: MACD

Moving Average Convergence/Divergence (MACD), a variation on the moving average crossover covered in the preceding section, is a third popular trending indicator. Unlike standard trending indicators, MACD shows the direction of a trend as well as its intensity and measures the strength of buyers and sellers.

MACD is a plot of the difference between two exponential moving averages: the 12-day exponential moving average (EMA) and the 26-day EMA. The MACD line rises and falls as the difference between the 12-day EMA and the 26-day EMA expands and contracts. When the 12-day EMA crosses above the 26-day EMA, the MACD line crosses above 0. When the 12-day EMA crosses below the 26-day EMA, the MACD line crosses below 0.

But the difference of these two exponential moving averages isn't the only plot in the MACD indicator. Believe it or not, the MACD line has a moving average applied to it — an average of an average, if you will. And the difference between the MACD line and its moving average is plotted as a *histogram* — a graphical representation of this difference. A rising histogram is a sign that buyers are increasing in strength. A falling histogram is a sign that sellers are increasing in strength.

The standard settings for the MACD indicator are to use the 12-day and 26-day exponential moving averages and to smooth out the MACD line using a 9-day moving average. Go with 'em.

To see MACD in action and to fully understand its moving parts, take a look at Figure 5-9, which shows MACD applied to shares of First Solar (symbol: FSLR). The MACD line plot is shown along with the nine-day moving average of the MACD line. The difference between these two plots is represented graphically in the form of a histogram below the two lines.

Figure 5-9: This chart shows shares of FSLR with the MACD indicator applied.

MACD can generate trading signals in three ways:

- Positive and negative divergences
- MACD crossover above or below its nine-day moving average
- MACD line crossing above or below the 0 line

I don't recommend trading securities based off of the MACD line's crossing of the 0 line. Doing so is identical to trading a security based off of the crossover of the 12-day and 26-day exponential moving averages. (For a refresher on EMAs, see "A lean, mean revelation machine: Moving averages," earlier in this chapter.)

The following sections delve into the ins and outs of trading using MACD.

Marking highs and lows: Positive and negative divergences in MACD

A positive divergence in MACD occurs when a security makes a new low but the MACD histogram fails to confirm that low, indicating that sellers are weakening in strength and that a trend change is imminent. A negative divergence develops when a security's price reaches a new high but the MACD histogram fails to confirm that high, indicating that buyers are weakening and that a trend change is looming.

Figure 5-10 depicts a positive divergence in the MACD histogram on a mid-2007 chart of streetTRACKS Gold (symbol: GLD), an exchange traded fund that tracks the prices of gold bullion. The positive divergence developed in late June as the price of streetTRACKS Gold fell to new lows while the MACD histogram made higher lows. The chart also shows an opportunity to trade off of the crossover in the MACD line. In late April, this line fell below its nine-day moving average, generating a sell signal.

Figure 5-10: This chart of GLD in mid-2007 shows the different ways you can use MACD.

If you use divergences, you must use a stop loss order after entering your orders. Also, enter the position only after the MACD histogram turns in the direction of the trade. If you're looking to buy a positive divergence in MACD, wait for the histogram to stop falling and turn up — that's your signal to enter the trade. If you're looking to short a negative divergence in MACD, do the opposite — wait for the histogram to stop rising and turn down.

Crossing the line: MACD crossover of its nine-day moving average

The MACD line often crosses over its nine-day moving average. When the MACD line crosses above this moving average, you have a buy signal (assuming trending markets). When the MACD line crosses below it, you have a sell signal (again, assuming trending markets). You can interpret a moving average crossover the same as you would a standard moving average crossover (see the earlier section, "Crissing and crossing: Trading moving average crossovers," for details).

Follow these steps to enter your trade:

1. **Verify whether a trend is in place by using ADX or the eyeball approach.**

2. **Wait for an MACD line to cross above (if you're buying) or below (if you're shorting) its nine-day moving average.**

3. **Enter the day of the crossover (if you watch markets intraday) or the day after the crossover (if you trade using end-of-day figures).**

4. **Place a stop loss below a recent low (if you're buying) or above a recent high (if you're shorting).**

5. **Exit when the MACD line crosses back below (if you're long) or above (if you're short) the nine-day moving average.**

Refer to Figure 5-9 to see a moving average crossover signal highlighted in shares of streetTRACKS Gold. Notice that in late April, the MACD line crossed below its nine-day moving average, generating a sell signal.

Spotting Major Non-Trending Indicators

Non-trending indicators, also called *oscillators,* are designed to track swings in trading ranges. Securities are in trading ranges more often than they trend. Trading ranges represent a stalemate. Neither bulls nor bears can meaningfully push prices past the battle lines. The bulls' home front is the support zone. The bears' home front is the resistance zone. Both groups are struggling to push prices deep into the other's territory. And yet, every attempt is rebuffed.

Non-trending indicators are banded between two extreme values: one over-bought and the other oversold. When bulls push prices to the area of resistance, the security is overbought and is likely to reverse (otherwise, a trend would begin and non-trending indicators wouldn't be appropriate). The key to determining whether a trend exists is to use the tried-and-true method of the ADX indicator or the eyeball approach (see "Determining Whether a Security Is Trending" for how to use the eyeball approach).

When ADX is below a value of 20, a trading range is in force, so you want to use non-trending indicators to stay on the right side of the trade as you attempt to profit from the back-and-forth swings in the trading range. The wider the trading range, the more potential profit you can extract. A range between $50 and $60 is more lucrative than one between $55 and $60 because you have an opportunity to profit off of $10 in the range versus only $5 in the narrower range.

The non-trending indicators you should get to know are stochastics and the Relative Strength Index, both of which I cover in the next two sections.

Stochastics: A study of change over time

The most popular non-trending indicator is *stochastics,* which calculates the position of today's close relative to a range established over a time period specified by the user. The higher the close today relative to the range, the more overbought the security. An overbought security is expected to revert to its mean. The best way to explain this phenomenon is to imagine stretch-ing a rubber band as far as you can. If you let go, the rubber band snaps back into place. Stochastics measures how far the rubber band stretches.

This particular indicator also points out when the rubber band is beginning to contract and return to its starting position. Just because a security is over-bought doesn't mean it must immediately turn around and march back to the oversold territory. Oh how easy trading would be if things were that simple!

Following are the two major components of the stochastics indicator:

- **%K plot:** This plot measures where the current close of the security's price relates to the highest high and lowest low over a period.

- **%D plot:** This plot is simply a three-day average of the %K plot.

Common swing trading practice calls for traders to use a 14-day stochastics period. I see no reason to disagree.

The stochastics indicator generates two main signals (which I explain further in the following sections):

✔ Positive and negative divergences between stochastics and the security's price pattern

✔ Crossovers of %K and %D from above the overbought level or below the oversold level

Positive and negative divergences

A positive divergence in stochastics forms when a security's price falls to a new low while the stochastics indicator traces a higher trough, signaling that sellers are exhausted and buyers are preparing to turn prices around. A negative divergence in stochastics can be seen when prices reach a new high while the stochastics indicator traces a lower high, signaling that buyers are exhausted and sellers are preparing to turn prices lower.

Figure 5-11 illustrates how a divergence, in this case between the price of Best Buy (symbol: BBY) common stock and the stochastics indicator, can flash an important signal about an imminent change in a security's price direction. While shares of Best Buy rallied to the $51 to $52 level twice in December 2007, the stochastics indicator formed a lower peak on the second rally. This movement signaled that buyers were exhausted and sellers were gaining the upper hand. Shortly thereafter, shares of Best Buy fell 15 percent in two weeks.

Figure 5-11: This chart illustrates the effectiveness of divergence as an important signal of impending change.

Follow these steps to use stochastics in your trading program:

1. **Confirm whether a trading range exists by using ADX or the eyeball approach.**

2. **If a trading range exists, buy or short after stochastics forms a positive or negative divergence, respectively.**

   Enter the position on the long side only when %K turns up over %D. Enter the position on the short side only when %K turns down under %D.

Crossovers from overbought and oversold levels

The more popular use of stochastics trading signals occurs when the %K plot crosses over the %D plot and exits an overbought or oversold territory. Charting programs peg *overbought* and *oversold* territories as 80 and 20, respectively. This measurement simply means that when prices move to an extreme, within 20 percent of the upper or lower boundaries of a historical price range, you can expect a reversal of the extreme.

Amateur swing traders often buy a security in a trading range simply because stochastics is overbought or oversold. This move is a recipe for whipsaws galore. Instead, wait for stochastics to enter the overbought or oversold territory. After it has, consider your rifle aimed, but don't pull the trigger just yet. Wait for stochastics to exit the overbought or oversold area. By being patient, you save yourself the heartache that can come when an overbought or oversold security decides to exit its range and enter a trend. When that occurs, stochastics remains overbought or oversold for several days or weeks.

Figure 5-12 demonstrates several profitable trades of ImClone Systems (symbol: IMCL) shares that could've been achieved by using the overbought and oversold ranges in the stochastics indicator. With ADX below 20, shares of ImClone were clearly in a trading range. In this type of scenario, you'd wait for stochastics to enter the overbought territory (represented by the upper horizontal line) and short when %K crosses below %D and below the overbought zone of 80. Alternatively, you'd wait for stochastics to enter the oversold territory and buy when %K crosses above %D and above the oversold zone of 20.

To trade using stochastics and the overbought and oversold levels, follow these steps:

1. **Identify whether a trading range exists by using ADX (preferably below 20) or the eyeball approach.**

2. **Wait for %K to enter the overbought or oversold territory.**

   Short the security when %K crosses down through %D and below the overbought zone. Buy the security when %K crosses up through %D and above the oversold zone.

Figure 5-12:
This chart
shows how
observing
overbought
and over-
sold levels
can help
you profit
from short-
term swings
in a trading
range.

3. **Exit after stochastics reaches the opposite zone.**

   Alternatively, you can exit after a return target is achieved or a certain number of days have passed.

Relative Strength Index (RSI): A comparison of apples and oranges

The *Relative Strength Index (RSI)* is an underused non-trending oscillator that compares a security to itself. Not only does it tell you when a security's price is overbought or oversold, but it can also form chart patterns that are useful for determining the likely direction of a breakout.

RSI isn't relative strength in the traditional sense of the term. *Relative strength,* as explained in Chapter 6, usually refers to comparing the strength of one security to another. For example, shares of Microsoft may be advancing while the market is falling — a classic sign of relative strength.

RSI actually examines the price history of a security over a certain number of days (14 is the standard setting, which I recommend). It compares the average gain achieved on up days with the average loss realized on down days. An average of the gains on up days and the losses on down days is computed, and the ratio between the two (average gains over average losses) yields the indicator.

Like most oscillators, the RSI is range-bound between 0 and 100. Unlike stochastics (covered in the previous section), a reading below 30 indicates an oversold level, whereas a reading above 70 indicates an overbought region. RSI is particularly helpful, because chart patterns like the head-and-shoulders or cup-and-handle patterns (explained in Chapter 4) form from time to time. These chart patterns can be interpreted in the same way as if they'd occurred in the price chart.

The next few sections cover the three major ways of using the RSI indicator to trade by using

- ✔ Positive and negative divergences
- ✔ Chart patterns that develop in the RSI
- ✔ The indicator's turn down from an overbought region or turn up from an oversold territory

Making use of positive and negative divergences in RSI

A positive or negative divergence develops when RSI fails to confirm a new high or new low in a security's price. You should trade divergences only after RSI turns down (if the divergence is negative) or turns up (if the divergence is positive). And of course, always use stop losses to protect your capital.

Follow these steps to trade divergences in the Relative Strength Index:

1. **Determine whether a trading range exists by using ADX or the eyeball approach.**

2. **Identify a divergence when the security makes a new high or new low while the RSI fails to confirm the new peak or trough.**

3. **Wait for the RSI to turn up (in the case of positive divergences) or turn down (in the case of negative divergences) before entering a position.**

4. **Keep a tight stop loss above a recent peak if you're shorting or below a recent trough if you're buying.**

   You want to take this step in case the divergence fails or the security traces multiple divergences.

Figure 5-13 shows a chart of Regeneron Pharmaceuticals (symbol: REGN) that demonstrates a negative divergence in RSI. Shares of REGN rally to new highs while RSI traces lower troughs — a warning of underlying weakness.

Observing RSI chart patterns

Seeing chart patterns in RSI is uncommon. Yet these patterns are more reliable than trading based off of overbought or oversold zones. RSI chart patterns may form at the same time as a chart pattern in the actual price of the security.

Figure 5-13:
This chart demonstrates a negative divergence in RSI.

Figure 5-14 demonstrates a classic head-and-shoulders chart pattern occurring in the RSI indicator in shares of BioMimetic Therapeutics (symbol: BMTI). Despite prices rallying to the $18 range, RSI signaled that an underlying weakness was brewing when it formed a lower peak in early January 2008. The actual signal to short didn't occur until the head-and-shoulders pattern was completed by the breakdown of RSI through the neckline. In a situation like this, you should short on the breakdown of RSI through the right shoulder, also known as its turn down from the overbought region (above 70).

Figure 5-14:
This chart shows a formed head-and-shoulders pattern in the RSI indicator.

Trading the RSI indicator's overbought and oversold zones

The process of trading the RSI indicator's turn up from the oversold region and turn down from the overbought region is nearly identical to the process of trading overbought and oversold regions using stochastics, covered earlier in this chapter. Here's how you do it:

1. **Figure out whether a trading range exists by using ADX (preferably below 20) or the eyeball approach.**

2. **Wait for the RSI indicator to enter the overbought or oversold territory (above 70 or below 30 on most charting programs).**

    Short the security when RSI turns down from an overbought reading and through the overbought zone. Buy when RSI turns up from an oversold reading and through the oversold zone.

3. **Exit after RSI reaches the opposite zone.**

    Alternatively, you can exit after a return target is achieved or a certain number of days have passed.

Combining Technical Indicators with Chart Patterns

Using technical indicators with chart patterns helps you increase your swing trading accuracy. To combine the two, you need to evaluate trades based on what the chart is saying and what the technical indicators are saying, and only take those trades where both chart and indicators communicate the same message. Perhaps the chart pattern is a cup-and-handle formation or a potential breakaway gap to the upside — both positive developments. If your technical indicator — say the DMI indicator — flashes a buy at that same time, you may have good reason to believe a buy is profitable.

Figure 5-15 demonstrates this point beautifully. Shares of ManTech International (symbol: MANT) develop what appears to be a classic cup-and-handle formation. Cup-and-handle formations are bullish, and swing traders normally buy a security after it crosses above its handle, as ManTech International did on December 19, 2007. However, the trade failed a few days later.

To spot the brewing trouble in a case like this, you can't use chart patterns alone. You need to use the RSI indicator in conjunction with a chart pattern to avoid a loss on your trade. In this example, the RSI flagged a troubling divergence forming during the cup-and-handle pattern. While prices of ManTech International moved to new highs, the RSI failed to confirm that strength.

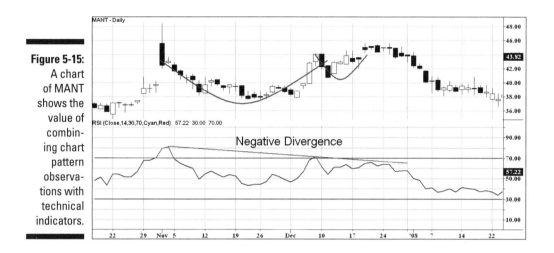

Figure 5-15:
A chart
of MANT
shows the
value of
combin-
ing chart
pattern
observa-
tions with
technical
indicators.

Using Technical Indicators to Determine Net Long or Net Short Positioning

One of the key questions you face as a swing trader is whether to be net long or net short at any given time (*net long* simply means the value of your portfolio's long positions is higher than the value of your portfolio's short positions; *net short* means the opposite).

When markets are roaring higher, you want the majority of your positions to be on the long side. Any short positions you hold are likely to result in losses or small profits, and it's tough to fight the trend. When the markets are falling, being net short is the way to go. Markets fall faster than they rise because fear is a stronger emotion than greed. Long positions held in a bear market are likely to result in losses.

Technical indicators are useful tools to assist you in determining whether to be net long or net short. You may apply an indicator to a market index and go net long or net short based on the signals you receive from that indicator. But if you choose this route, make sure your indicator provides few and accurate signals. You don't want to be changing your net exposure weekly — or worse, daily.

Your indicator or mechanism for determining when to be net long or net short should respond quickly enough when a trend turns down. Test your indicator on past market cycles to determine whether it caught downturns quickly or slowly. Also make sure your indicator doesn't generate so many signals that whipsaws abound. Always strive for balance.

I recommend using the nine-week moving average. When the slope of the nine-week moving average is negative, expect more trading opportunities to be on the short side of the market. When the slope of the nine-week moving average is positive, expect more trading opportunities to be on the long side of the market. Figure 5-16 shows a chart of the S&P 500 Index with a nine-week moving average.

Figure 5-16:
The S&P 500 Index with a nine-week moving average.

You may rely on basic chart analysis to signal the changes between being net long or net short. Remember that the long-term trend in the equity markets is up, and therefore you're likely to be net long far more often than you are net short. This rule of thumb also holds true if you trade international stocks.

Chapter 6

Analyzing Charts to Trade Trends, Ranges, or Both

In This Chapter

▶ Understanding the differences between trading trends and ranges

▶ Making the most of a strong trend

▶ Working with an identified trading range

▶ Conducting intermarket and relative strength analysis

*M*ost swing traders make their money in one of three ways: trading strong trends, trading ranges, or both. A *trend* is the persistent up or down movement of a security's price. Trends can last anywhere from a few days to a few years, but generally, a security must rise to new highs or fall to new lows every few weeks to be considered trending (for a swing trader, that is; long-term investors define trends in a different time frame). If you choose to accept trading trends, your job is to find the strongest trends — up or down — and ride them until you exit for a profit or are forced out for a loss (a small one, hopefully!).

Many markets and securities are neither trending upward nor downward, though. Instead, they're oscillating up and down between clearly defined price levels called *ranges*. As with trends, trading ranges can occur over short periods or long periods. The longer a trading range has been in place, the more likely it is to continue. For example, if Dummies Corporation stock has been trading between $50 and $60 for the last three months, it's safe to assume that the stock is in a trading range. Your job is to buy near $50 and sell near $60.

But just what makes a trend strong or weak? And how do you know whether to trade trends or ranges (or a mixture of both)? I help you figure out your answers to these questions in this chapter. Please note, though, that in order to fully understand the guidance in this chapter, you need to have a solid understanding of chart patterns and technical indicators, which I cover in Chapters 4 and 5 — head to those chapters first if you need a refresher.

Trading Trends versus Trading Ranges: A Quick Rundown

Most swing traders focus primarily on trading trends simply because the profits tend to be bigger than when trading ranges. The added beauty of trends is that they require little or no work on your part to manage. In an uptrend, the security's price rises consistently and doesn't fall much from its highs — say 5 percent to 10 percent at the most. Entering a trend early (in the first few days of the start of a new trend) allows you to enter when the risk is lowest. Entering a trend that has been in place for several weeks or (gulp!) months raises the chance that you're getting on just when you should be getting off.

The difficulty in riding trends arises from identifying when a trend has begun and exiting quickly when it's clear the trend is over. The latter problem is the biggest concern for you as a swing trader. Trends aren't difficult to find and enter, but when a security moves counter to its trend, you have to decide whether that move is simply a normal part of the trend development or something more sinister (the end of that trend).

Although trading ranges isn't as popular among swing traders as trading trends, don't be fooled by the ranges' small profits. Swing traders tend to have a higher win ratio when trading ranges than when trading trends. In other words, you may make smaller profits per trade if you trade ranges, but you'll also tend to be right more often than if you were trading trends.

One of the advantages of trading ranges versus trading trends is that with ranges your profit and risk objectives are easily identified. Your profit objective is simply the other side of the range; for example, if you're shorting a stock at $60 per share, your goal is to cover that short near $50 per share. Similarly, your risk is clearly defined: If you buy near $50 per share, you're going to exit your trade if the stock trades below $49 or $48. Such a move outside the established trading range likely signals the beginning of a new trend.

When trading ranges, the biggest risk you face is a security beginning a new trend. Because your trade depends on the continuation of the range, you're unlikely to be on the right side of the trade should a trend develop. For example, you could lose a bundle on a stock if you short shares near $60 (with a range between $50 and $60) and the stock proceeds to break out above its upper trading range of $60 per share and run to $70 or higher. If the stock falls from $60 to $40, you miss the move from $50 to $40 because your profit objective calls for exiting at the lower bound of the range. Therefore, you're unlikely to ever be on the right side of a trend if you focus on trading ranges.

So should you trade trends, ranges, or both?

Unfortunately, as with many aspects of swing trading, you won't find a one-size-fits-all answer. Some traders are looking for those big moves — that 10 percent or 20 percent move that will happen over a few days. They're willing to tolerate being wrong some (or even most) of the time in their quest for home runs. Such swing traders should focus on trends. Other traders are patient and are content with hitting singles and doubles each inning. They're fine with 3 percent or 5 percent returns on each trade. They're right 50 percent or more of the time, and they cut losses fast. Such swing traders are best suited for trading ranges. If you're not sure which method fits your personality, read about the methods outlined in this chapter and pick the one you feel most comfortable with.

A brief explanation of the conception of ranges

Trends occur for obvious reasons: A security is either undervalued or overvalued and begins to trend when investors take notice and correct that mispricing. But just why do trading ranges exist? Understanding the psychology should help you with trading ranges.

As with all technical analysis, trading ranges represent the psychology of market participants. Generally, investors — if given perfect information — can assess the true value of company within a 5 percent to 10 percent range. No two investors will assess the value of a company at exactly the same price, but they'll have values that are close to one another.

A trading range develops when investors arrive at the *correct* value of a company. The lower part of the trading range represents the consensus low estimate of the company's value, and the upper part of the trading range represents the consensus high estimate of the company's value.

✔ **When shares fall to the lower part of the range,** market participants buy shares because they perceive that value to be too low for the company. When this occurs en masse, shares form a lower support level that represents the cheapest level investors believe shares are worth at that time.

✔ **When shares rise to the upper part of the range,** investors holding that security begin to sell because they believe this to be a best-case scenario value of the company. Meanwhile, investors buying at the upper range are likely to sell at the same level to break even should shares decline.

Trading ranges are likely to continue until some new piece of news or event serves as a catalyst to propel shares higher or lower from their ranges. In other words, securities break trading ranges when investors watching and/or holding those securities realize that the underlying value has changed. This change often marks the beginning of a trend that lasts until a new trading range develops where market participants peg the value of a company between two extremes.

If you understand how ranges work, you're more likely to recognize a range that represents true consensus and not simply a small pause in a security's move upward or downward. Also, you're attuned to how news or events may affect a security breaking out of its range.

Advanced traders may use both methods to take advantage of both ranges and trends. That's because the overall market may determine whether range trading or trend trading is easier at any given moment. A zooming bull market pushes the majority of stocks higher, and trading ranges is difficult. A tough bear market pushes the majority of stocks down, regardless of their fundamentals, and trends are few and far between when a market is gridlocked in a trading range.

Trading on Trends

Trend trading is swinging for that home run and occasional grand slam. Swing traders focusing on trends are looking for big returns in short periods. They're looking to enter a trend that has clearly established itself. Because trends move fast and furious, they have to keep stop loss orders tight to exit on a moment's notice if the wave they're riding crests.

So first things first: How exactly do you find strong enough trends to trade? And when you find a strong trend, how do you know whether the time is right to enter on that trend?

Finding a strong trend

You can find trending securities in multiple ways. You can do a *bottom-up search,* where you're looking up close at individual stocks, or you can do a *top-down search,* where you're scoping out industry groups and then narrowing your view to individual stocks. You then can determine trend strength through a variety of ways. One way is the eyeball approach, in which you size up a chart by simply looking at it. Or you can use technical indicators that tell you — with little interpretation — whether the security you want to trade is trending and whether that trend is up or down. The *ADX indicator* is often used to measure whether a security is trending or non-trending without regard to whether the trend is upward or downward. Most popular charting programs include the ADX or include it as part of the *DMI indicator.* You can find out more about ADX and DMI indicators in Chapter 5.

An ADX reading above 20 signals a trend. The higher above 20 the ADX reading is, the stronger the trend. But excessive values (for example, readings above 40) may indicate an overheated trend that's about to reverse.

Here's a quick look at how you can use both search methods:

  ✔ **Bottom-up search:** Trending stocks can be found daily in popular newspapers like *The Wall Street Journal* or *Investor's Business Daily.* For example, each day both newspapers publish which stocks are making new 52-week highs or new 52-week lows. These stocks are often trending up or down, depending on whether the security is making a new high or a new low. What you want to see is a stock that hasn't made a new high or a new low in a long time and then bursts onto the scene. These stocks are often just beginning their trends.

Another bottom-up method of identifying trending stocks is through research services. *High Growth Stock (HGS) Investor* software, for example, allows users to screen stocks in particular groups, markets, and so on by those making new highs or new lows over any chosen time period. The period you choose should be long enough to signal a meaningful trend, but not so short as to capture stocks moving normally up and down. After all, a stock making a new one-day high isn't very meaningful.

✔ **Top-down search:** You can locate strongly trending stocks by looking at strongly trending industry groups. Popular research services like Daily Graphs, *HGS Investor,* and Morningstar provide data on which industry groups are the top performers over the last several months. Just because a group is hot right now, however, doesn't mean it will be hot forever; industries fall out of favor just as individual securities do.

Begin your search by looking at the top ten performing industry groups and drilling down to find securities that may be trending. Again, you want stocks just making new highs after a period of moving sideways. Examine the chart and see if the security is clearly rising. You get more tools on measuring trends using indicators in Chapter 5.

To find candidates to short, examine industry groups that fall in the bottom 10 percent of performance. Then drill down into those groups to locate individual stocks that are just breaking into new lows. These are the prime candidates to short.

Just because a stock belongs to an industry group that's in an uptrend doesn't necessarily mean that the stock is also trending or that it's trending upward. It's possible to find stocks that belong to a hot industry but that are falling on hard times. So make sure you're only buying stocks in strong trends in groups that are trending upward and shorting stocks in strong trends in groups that are trending downward.

Figure 6-1 highlights shares of Mosaic Company (symbol: MOS), which is ripe for trading a trending stock. On February 13, 2007, shares hit a 52-week high and appeared in *The Wall Street Journal* on February 14, 2007.

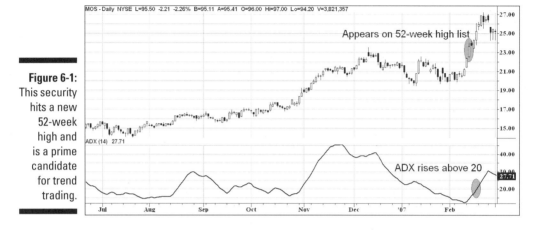

MOS - Daily NYSE L=95.50 -2.21 -2.26% B=95.11 A=95.41 O=96.00 HI=97.00 Lo=94.20 V=3,821,357

Appears on 52-week high list

ADX (14) 27.71

ADX rises above 20

Figure 6-1:
This security
hits a new
52-week
high and
is a prime
candidate
for trend
trading.

Knowing when to enter a trend

The biggest risk swing traders who focus on trends face is the possibility of buying or shorting a trend that's just about to end. Ian Woodward, a professional trader, equates buying or shorting stocks late in their trends to acting like an unruly dog chasing speeding cars. Sure, it may be fun for the dog, but sooner or later he's going to get run over.

To minimize your risk of riding a crashing wave, you must follow some system that only enters at the right time. The ideal setup is a security making a fresh, new high or low over the last 26 days.

So how do you know if the trend you're riding is just beginning or winding down? If you don't have access to a security program that can identify such new highs or new lows, then rely on *The Wall Street Journal*'s daily list of stocks hitting 52-week highs or 52-week lows. Additionally, you want to see an ADX reading above 20 to indicate the presence of a trend.

As with all aspects of trading, you can never be 100 percent sure about a trade. The best you can do is put the odds in your favor by only entering on some type of signal. If the trend is genuine and is going to continue, you've entered early. If the trend is failing, you'll know shortly because your signal will likely reverse itself if the trend ends or breaks down.

The signal you use can be based on chart patterns or technical signals. Generally, chart patterns give traders earlier warning than technical signals, but technical indicators require little interpretation, which makes your job easier. For example, a stock rising above its 50-day moving average could be a signal to buy, or a MACD crossover (covered in Chapter 5) could be a signal to short (depending on the direction of the crossover). Many swing traders only enter trends on the long or short side when a security first makes a new high or new low of X number of days, provided this is the first new high or new low in the last month or two. Otherwise, you run the risk of buying or shorting a stock that's extended or has been making new highs and new lows for a long time.

Another approach to entering swing trade orders is to wait for a pause in the trend and enter on a *day of strength* or *day of weakness.*

- ✔ **To enter on a day of strength,** you must wait for the stock to form three consecutive bars of declining highs. Then you enter on the next bar that trades higher than the previous bar's high.

- ✔ **To enter on a day of weakness,** you must wait for the stock to form three consecutive bars of rising lows. Then you enter on the next bar that trades lower than the previous bar's low.

In Figure 6-2, the chart of Apple Inc. (symbol: AAPL) shows a strong uptrend that began in late July 2007 on a strong gap up in share prices. After rising 40 percent, shares retraced their steps and made three consecutive lower highs marked by the numbers 1, 2, and 3. (Notice that the day prior to number 1 doesn't count because its high exceeds the previous bar.) After making four lower highs, the stock moved higher and exceeded the high of the fourth bar, signaling the continuation of the uptrend and an ideal entry point.

Whatever signal method you use, make sure to *only* enter the trade on that actual signal. You'll find dozens of trending stocks that gave signals 5, 10, or 20 days ago — ignore them. You can't be disciplined if you're entering trends late. Only enter on a signal you choose.

Figure 6-2:
A day of strength is often a good opportunity to enter a strong trend.

If you look back at Figure 6-1, you'll notice that the 52-week high registered on February 13, 2007, was the first in two months. Remember, you want to avoid buying a strong trending stock that has been making new 52-week highs every other day. An extended period of time between 52-week highs is a means of protecting yourself from buying an extended stock. Enter either on the sign of a new high or on a day of strength (the day of strength approach will help you avoid getting run over by speeding cars).

Figure 6-3 highlights the day of strength for Mosaic and the ADX reading above 20 on that day. In this example, the day of strength allows ADX time to give a clear signal on whether the stock is trending or not. Should you have entered on February 14, 2007, the day of the 52-week high? That depends on what your trading strategy calls for: If you buy new highs immediately, then the answer is yes. However, I recommend using ADX as a means of weeding out weak trends from strong trends. In this case, the ADX was below 20 on the day the stock made a new high. The ADX indicator didn't register a reading over 20 until February 20, 2007.

Figure 6-3: ADX above 20 signals the existence of a trend — enter on a day of strength.

Managing your risk by setting your exit level

Setting your exit level will depend on when you enter the security. I cover exit levels in more detail in Chapter 10, but in short, your exit price (think of it as your emergency exit) will either be based off a technical-indicator signal, a price level, or a time exit (that is, exiting after a certain number of days have elapsed). Your target likely will be based off a technical indicator or price level because of the ease of establishing the exit rules. Following is an explanation of each of these exit-setting mechanisms:

- ✔ **Technical-indicator exit signal:** This includes exiting on the break down below a moving average or on a crossover of MACD (both of which are covered in Chapter 5).

- ✔ **Price-level exit level:** Entering on a new, 52-week high will require an exit level right in the trading range that the stock is emerging from. If you bought shares of Mosaic as they made a new high on February 13, you would set an exit level between $21 and $22 per share. If the trend is real, the stock shouldn't fall back into its original base.

- ✔ **Time-based exit level:** Because the target exit price isn't important to demonstrate how to enter and manage the Mosaic trade, I assume a simple time-based target of 20 days.

If you enter on the day of strength that I recommend in the preceding section, your exit level is easier to compute than it would be using the other methods identified here. In this case, your exit should be based off the low directly preceding the day of strength.

Trading Ranges: Perhaps Stasis Is Bliss?

Finding a security in a trading range can be more difficult than a finding a trending stock. Screening for securities making new highs or new lows is much easier.

Technical indicators (which I cover in Chapter 5) can be useful in identifying when a security is in a trading range and when to enter or exit a trade. However, not all technical indicators are applicable to trading ranges. Trending indicators, as the name suggests, are useful when a security is in a trend. Non-trending indicators (often called *oscillators*), on the other hand, should be used when securities are in a trading range. You should choose one or two oscillators (at most) to use in a trading system.

Finding a security in a strong trading range

When swing traders want to determine if a security is in a trading range, they often use an ADX indicator. The calculator methodology is beyond the scope of this book, but I can tell you that most popular charting programs include ADX (or include ADX as part of the DMI indicator). What you need to know is that an ADX value below 20 signals a non-trending market, and an ADX value above 20 often signals a trending market.

A range must be wide enough to allow for meaningful profits. For example, if a stock trades between $56 and $60, the range would be so tight that profits would be eaten up by commissions, taxes, and so on. No hard and fast rule exists for how wide is wide enough, but $5 to $7 on a stock trading below $100 is a good range to target.

The strength of trading ranges depends on a few factors:

- **Time:** The longer a trading range has been in force, the more likely it is to continue.

- **Touches of support and resistance:** The more times a security touches its support and/or resistance level (see Chapter 4), the more powerful that support or resistance level is. Look for trading ranges with several touches or tests of support and resistance.

- **Flat ranges:** When I refer to *flat ranges,* I mean how much a trading range resembles a rectangle. Some trading ranges have resistance levels that rise or support levels that fall; these ranges are suspect because they don't clearly identify true areas of support or resistance. In fact, they may be some other chart formation entirely. The flatter the support and resistance levels, the stronger your conviction should be that the trading range is genuine.

Figure 6-4 shows a chart of MEMC Electronics Materials (symbol: WFR). You can see the trading range by eyeballing the chart and identifying clear support and resistance levels. Notice also that the ADX level is below 20 on the chart, signaling a non-trending market.

Figure 6-4:
This chart shows a trading range with resistance at $65 and support at $52.

Entering on a range and setting your exit level

Your entry is likely to be driven by either a day of strength (defined earlier in this chapter) or a technical signal. For the MEMC Electronics example, I assume you're using stochastics (an indicator useful in measuring strength or weakness in trendless markets; see Chapter 5 for more on stochastics) to signal a buy order.

Stochastics flashes a buy signal when the signal line crosses above the moving average from an oversold level. That area is highlighted in Figure 6-5. In the case of MEMC Electronics, the buy signal from stochastics occurs when shares are around $55.

Figure 6-5:
This chart shows a buy signal from stochastics and a profit objective near the upper end of the trading range.

The target profit in trading ranges is just the opposite side of the trading range. In this case, resistance was solid around $65 per share, so a reasonable profit target is $64. Shares of WFR hit that level roughly six weeks after the buy signal was generated.

The risk level of this trading range is located slightly below the support level. A meaningful movement in share price below the support level signals the trading range has ended, but don't be strict on what you consider meaningful. For example, if the support level is at $52, a risk level of $51 may be unreasonable given the volatility in the chart.

I prefer to set risk levels right below major, whole, round numbers. Traders often fall into the trap of putting stop loss orders or buy stop orders at round number levels. The problem with setting risk levels or buy orders at round numbers is that hundreds of other traders may be the doing the exact same thing, meaning that you're likely to get a bad execution or get whipsawed (shaken out of the trade by a rapid price movement).

For the example shown in Figure 6-5, with support at $52 and an upper resistance level at $65, I recommend placing a stop loss order right below $50 per share. In my view, a trade below $50 is a good indication that the trading range has ended and the stock is beginning a downtrend.

Note: Right after the buy signal from stochastics is generated, shares of WFR trade down sharply, touching a low of $49.70. (Notice, though, that shares never close below $53.) If you had set your risk level exit at $50, you would have been exited from this trade early.

Comparing Markets to One Another: Intermarket Analysis

Intermarket analysis is an underutilized technique in technical analysis. Intermarket technicians analyze currencies, equity markets, bonds, and commodities to determine which market holds the most promise. Often, an upturn in one market signals an upturn or downturn in another market, and intermarket analysis can give you an early lead on a rally or decline in that sector or market. Rising bond prices often precede equity market rallies. Rising commodity prices, on the other hand, can lead to a downturn in stock prices. Knowing the relationships among the four major markets — bonds, currencies, commodities, and stocks — means that you can anticipate changes in market leadership.

I begin this review of intermarket analysis by taking a bird's-eye view of the investment landscape. Currencies (specifically, the U.S. dollar) analysis is helpful as investors seek to profit from strength or weakness in an investor's domestic currency. Then I cover commodities (for example, oil, gold, and copper) because commodity prices have been in a major bull market in the last few years. I also get into bond prices and interest rates. Bonds are the biggest competitor to the equity markets, so strength or weakness in bonds can lead to strength or weakness in equity prices.

Passing the buck: The U.S. dollar

The U.S. dollar is the world's reserve currency, or the most widely used currency. The dollar is affected by a host of factors, including the interest rates the Federal Reserve sets (known as *monetary policy*), the national debt, and the current budget deficit or surplus. As you may have learned in your economics course, the value of a currency (assuming it freely floats on the world markets) is determined by the supply and demand for that currency.

The Federal Reserve controls short-term interest rates in the United States, and short-term interest rates, in turn, have a significant impact on the value (or demand) for U.S. dollars. If the Federal Reserve raises interest rates, the dollar is likely to strengthen because investors seek out high yields on their investments. A government that pays 10 percent interest on short-term investments will attract a flood of investors from the outside world, prompting strength in that country's currency. However, if that government cuts interest rates to 2 percent, fewer investors will be willing to loan their money to the government or banks in that country (assuming other world yields are higher than 2 percent), thus weakening that nation's currency.

Fiscal policies affect the dollar but usually take longer to materialize. If the U.S. government spends more than it has (that is, it generates budget deficits), the dollar's value may decrease because a budget deficit represents borrowing money today at the expense of paying it back in the future. The larger the deficit or national debt, the more pressure on the dollar. Think of it this way: The more the government spends, the more available U.S. dollars are. By increasing the supply, you decrease prices.

So how can you make money with this knowledge? Here's how you may benefit when the dollar strengthens or weakens:

- **Dollar strengthening:** When the U.S. dollar strengthens, it usually bodes well for U.S. stocks and U.S. bonds. International investors are attracted to strong currencies because the investors can increase their potential return by profiting from the rise in a U.S. stock and a rise in the U.S. currency.

- **Dollar weakening:** Weakness in the U.S. dollar can translate into higher commodity prices. Look for gold, crude oil, and other world commodities to benefit from a weak dollar.

The chart in Figure 6-6, which shows the U.S. dollar (top) and gold prices (bottom), illustrates how intermarket analysis can boost your returns. The U.S. dollar began a major decline in August 2007 while gold prices began a major advance. If you see the U.S. dollar weaken, look for swing trading opportunities on the long side in commodities or commodity-related securities (like gold miners or oil explorers). A weak U.S. dollar tends to lead to higher commodity prices (in U.S. dollars), and a strong U.S. dollar tends to lead to lower commodity prices (in U.S. dollars).

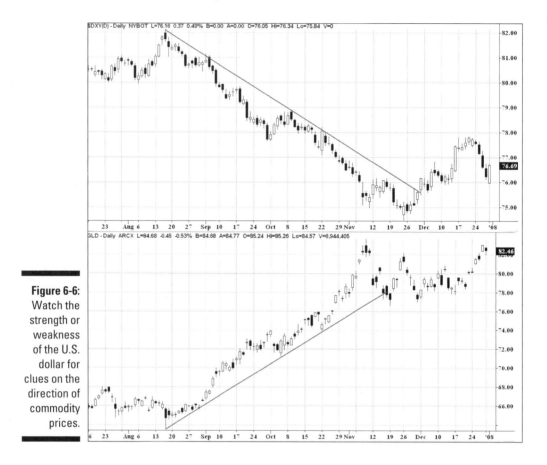

Figure 6-6:
Watch the strength or weakness of the U.S. dollar for clues on the direction of commodity prices.

Tracking commodities

Commodities come in different flavors:

- **Energy commodities** include items like crude oil, heating oil, and natural gas.
- **Metal commodities** include gold, silver, and platinum.
- **Livestock and meat commodities** include live cattle and lean hogs.
- **Agricultural commodities** include corn and soybeans.

Between the 1980s and early 2000, commodities didn't get much respect and were considered unimportant in the so-called new economy. Many traders underweighted or divested altogether investments in the commodity space.

All that changed in 2000. With the equity market top in 2000, investors sought out new investment opportunities, and gold, oil, and other commodities benefited from the interest. Later, at the turn of the 21st century, demand for commodities from emerging markets like China and India rose markedly. Because commodity prices in general had been poor investment options in prior years, commodity producers hadn't invested in sourcing new supplies. For example, because crude oil prices had been range-bound during much of the 1990s, energy firms didn't invest in new equipment or search for new oil discoveries. As a result, prices of these commodities shot up when demand increased.

Most individual investors never buy commodities directly because of the sophistication needed to trade futures contracts. But recent innovations have allowed equity investors to take advantage of movements in commodity prices. For example, a trader wanting to take advantage of a bull market in gold prices can purchase shares of GLD, the streetTRACKS Gold shares, which trade on the New York Stock Exchange.

You can track the prices of commodities in many ways, but the most popular baskets are the Commodity Research Bureau Index and the Goldman Sachs Commodity Index.

Although commodities can make you a pretty penny (made out of copper, I might add), they also give important signals on the direction of other asset classes. Commodities represent goods that you and I buy day-to-day — whether we realize it or not. When prices of commodities rise, inflation can result. Inflation is a principal risk of bond investors because interest payments aren't adjusted for the value of the dollar.

Therefore, commodity prices *tend* to correlate negatively to bond prices (and thus, positively correlate with interest rates because bond yields move inversely to bond prices). Rising commodity prices usually occur with falling bond prices and rising yields. Conversely, falling commodity prices usually occur with rising bond prices and falling yields.

No relationship is guaranteed in the financial market, and it's possible for commodity prices to trend in the same direction as bond prices. But such action is unlikely to last long. Bond investors eventually sell bonds if they believe the risks of inflation are rising. A small move in the prices of commodities may not convince them that such a risk is imminent, but a sustained rally or decline in commodity prices affects the strength or weakness in bond prices.

Figure 6-7 shows just how that relationship played out in 2006. Commodity prices, as measured by the CRB Index, began rallying in late March. Shortly thereafter, bond prices fell (and bond yields rose). The bottom chart shows the yield on the 30-Year Treasury Bond. As you can see, commodity prices and bond yields move in the same direction. As a swing trader, you can use this knowledge to your advantage — a sustained rally in commodity prices leads to higher bond yields and trading opportunities for bond traders.

Figure 6-7:
Bond
yields and
commod-
ity prices
tend to be
positively
correlated.

Commodity price performance relative to bonds can help you pinpoint market sectors to target for investments. Here are some guidelines:

- ✔ If the ratio between commodity prices and bond prices is rising (meaning that commodity prices are outperforming bond prices), you should look for investment in sectors that are inflation-sensitive, like basic material manufacturers (aluminum manufacturers, copper producers, energy companies, and so on).

- ✔ If the ratio between commodity prices and bond prices is falling (meaning that bond prices are outperforming commodity prices), then look for investment opportunities in interest rate-sensitive sectors such as home builders, real estate, and utilities.

Watching how bond price and stock price movements correlate

Stocks and bonds are major investment vehicles for millions of people and institutions the world over. The interest rates that bonds pay are principal competitors to stock investments. The higher the interest rate offered, the less investors will allocate to stocks. The lower the interest rate bonds pay, the more investors will allocate to stocks.

 Bond prices are extremely sensitive to inflation. As inflation rises, the value of the series of payments that bonds pay decreases. A poor Consumer Price Index reading from the government will cause bond prices to fall. A low inflation report, on the other hand, tends to push bond prices higher.

Many valuation models of the U.S. stock market compare the yield on government or corporate bonds to the earnings yield of equity securities. For example, the Fed Model (covered in detail in chapter 8) compares the yield on the 10-Year Treasury Bond to the earnings yield of the S&P 500 Index. If the 10-Year Treasury Bond currently yields 5 percent and the S&P 500 Index forward P/E ratio is 15 times earnings, investors using this model would conclude that equity prices are undervalued when compared to bonds. (To get the earnings yield of the S&P 500 Index, you simply calculate 1 divided by the P/E ratio. In this example, 1 divided by 15 equals 6.67 percent, which is higher than the 5 percent the 10-Year Treasury Bond paid.)

Bond prices tend to lead stock price movements. As bond prices rally, bond yields fall, making stocks an attractive alternative. Conversely, falling bond prices (and thus, rising bond yields) tend to lead stock price weakness. This relationship doesn't hold in deflationary environments where bond prices rise while stock prices fall. However, deflationary environments are the exception in U.S. economic history.

Figure 6-8 highlights an example of the typical relationship between equity prices and bond prices. The figure compares bond *yields* for the 30-Year Treasury Bond (top) and the S&P 500 Index (bottom) in 1996–1997. Notice that a peak in the yield of the 30-Year Bond in July 1996 corresponds with a bottom in equity prices. A similar peak/bottom occurs in April 1997. A sustained decline in bond yields corresponds with a rallying equity market. But correlation doesn't imply causation. In other words, although there's a relationship between these markets, you can't say that the rally in equity prices was caused by the declining yield of the 30-Year Treasury Bond.

As a swing trader, you should watch the relationship between bond yields and stock prices. When yields enjoy a sustained rally, be on the lookout for a pullback in stock prices. You may enter short trades, for example, in securities breaking down to new 52-week lows. If you see yields falling, it may precede a rally in stock prices. Be on the lookout for stocks hitting 52-week highs or exhibiting strength via breakouts from trading ranges.

Figure 6-8:
Equity prices and bond yields tend to be negatively correlated.

Putting Securities in a Market Head-to-Head: Relative Strength Analysis

A twist on *inter*market analysis is *intra*market analysis, often called *relative strength analysis.* In addition to comparing markets to one another, swing traders should use intramarket analysis to compare securities within one market. Relative strength analysis is like having your own pair of X-ray vision goggles that allow you to see which securities are truly strong and which are totally faking it.

Relative strength analysis involves charting one security or index relative to another. The ratio generated from the two can be analyzed like any stock chart. Most charting programs calculate such ratios for you with the click of a mouse. You can compare all sorts of things against each other: Apple Inc. versus Google, or Clorox versus the overall market. You can even compare markets against each other to get an idea of when leadership switches from one market to the other.

Suppose you want to buy a strong stock. Should you be focusing on large cap, mid cap, or small cap stocks? Relative strength analysis can answer that question. By comparing one group to another, you can detect when one group is strengthening relative to the other.

But be careful — you want to make meaningful comparisons. Comparing General Motors to Ford or General Motors to the auto industry in general makes perfect sense, but I'm not sure what you could gain from comparing General Motors to Google.

I like to begin my analysis with a macro view of the world. I want to know which equity markets are hot and therefore worthy of my dollars. One advantage swing traders have these days is the ease of accessing equity markets from all over the world. Many exchange-traded funds and American Depository Receipts allow swing traders to gain profits from almost anywhere on earth.

Treating the world as your oyster: The global scope

Because this book is targeted to swing traders, who frequently trade stocks, the first step that I address in intramarket analysis is to explore which equity markets are exhibiting strength globally. If you trade commodities, you replace this step with an analysis of the major commodities versus each other.

The following are the major equity markets you should be familiar with and can compare to one another:

- **Developed world**
  - The United States (S&P 500 Index)
  - Western Europe (use iShares S&P 350 Index, symbol: IEV)
  - Japan (use iShares MSCI Japan Index, symbol: EWJ)
- **Emerging markets**
  - Latin America (use iShares S&P Latin American 40 Index, symbol: ILF)
  - China (use iShares FTSE/Xinhua China 25 Index, symbol: FXI)
  - Asia (use iShares MSCI Pacific Index, excluding Japan, symbol: EPP)

You can analyze dozens of other individual markets using proxies such as the iShares mentioned here (you can find proxies for the markets in Austria, Belgium, Australia, South Africa, Brazil, and so on). But I like to keep things simple and present only the major developed markets and the key emerging markets.

The second step in analyzing relative strength between equity markets is to construct a ratio chart between two different markets. When analyzing ratio charts, apply the technical tools you pick up in Chapters 4 and 5. Look for support and resistance ranges. Also, determine whether the ratio is trending (which indicates that one market is dominating the other) or in a trading range (which indicates that both markets are achieving similar returns).

Make sure you read your ratio chart correctly. The first thing you should do when you examine a ratio chart is determine whether a rising ratio means market A or market B is performing well. Most charting programs clearly designate which market is in the numerator of the fraction and which market is in the denominator of the fraction. (In the example shown in Figure 6-9, the numerator market is designated by being charted above the denominator market.)

A simple rule of thumb is that a rising ratio means the market index in the numerator of the fraction is outperforming the market index in the denominator of the fraction.

Talk of numerators and denominators may bring back unpleasant memories from grade school, so take a look at an example that helps bring the analysis home.

Figure 6-9 shows the ratio of the S&P 500 Index to the FTSE/Xinhua China 25 Index as measured by the iShares security. This figure shows three charts. The first chart is the actual ratio between the two indexes (S&P 500 divided by the FTSE/Xinhua China 25 Index). The second and third charts are just plots of the actual indexes used in the computation of the first chart. (Most charting programs provide the underlying indexes used in the computation of a ratio chart.)

This chart covers the two equity markets from March 2007 through June 2007. Notice that the ratio chart is declining in March (signaling strength of China or relative underperformance of the U.S. equity market) but stabilizing in May and June. However, a break below that support level on June 11 signals the resumed outperformance of the Chinese stock market over the U.S. equity market. That break is a strong signal to buy the iShares FTSE/Xinhua China 25 Index.

Intramarket analysis isn't confined to equities. As a swing trader, you can compare gold prices to the Commodity Research Bureau Index, for example, to determine whether gold prices are outperforming other major commodities. Or you can compare the relative strength of the 10-Year Treasury Bond to the 30-Year Treasury Bond. The combinations are endless.

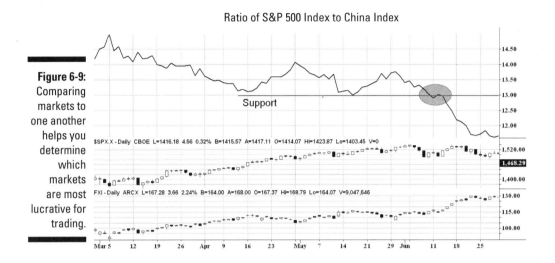

Figure 6-9:
Comparing
markets to
one another
helps you
determine
which
markets
are most
lucrative for
trading.

Ratio of S&P 500 Index to China Index

Holding industry groups to the market standard

Another application of relative strength analysis is to compare industry groups to the overall market. According to William J. O'Neil, founder of *Investor's Business Daily* newspaper, industry group performance can explain between 30 percent and 40 percent of a stock's performance. When oil service company stocks are hot, for example, shares of companies in the industry will rise together. When Internet retailer stocks are out of favor, look out below! These stocks will tend to go down together.

Why do stocks sometimes behave like a herd of animals? Well, think of it on a simple level: If you operate a shoe store in Run of the Mill City, USA, you probably experience sales increases or decreases in line with other shoe retailers. If a hot brand comes out one year and propels your sales higher, don't you expect other shoe retailers to experience similar success? The reason stocks in industry groups tend to behave in a similar fashion is they face many of the same market forces in their industry: both the benefits and risks. When the U.S. government spends more on defense, all defense companies benefit together. One company may get a bigger slice of the pie than another, but the entire pie is bigger, so other companies benefit. On the other hand, when the government tightens its purse strings, expect to see shares of most defense companies fall on hard times.

Industry group intramarket analysis (that's a tongue twister!) compares industry groups to the overall market. When the ratio between the two is rising or falling, you can expect to find promising long or short opportunities from that industry group.

You use the normal technical analysis tools from Chapters 4 and 5 on the ratio. Figure 6-10 highlights an alternative energy index (clean energy) as compared to the S&P 500 Index in 2007. A rising ratio in this chart means that the alternative energy index is outperforming the general market. On the other hand, a declining ratio implies the opposite — that the S&P 500 Index is outperforming the clean energy index.

From late 2005 through mid-2006, the ratio of the clean energy index to the S&P 500 Index was steadily rising. However, it experienced a sharp break in May. This break of the trendline signaled that clean energy was no longer outperforming the overall market. Instead, the break heralded the beginning of underperformance relative to the general market that lasted for approximately eight months (not shown on this chart).

After you identify a turning point among an industry group and the market, you can take advantage of that difference by either trading the index itself (via a proxy such as an iShare) or drilling down into the industry group to find trading candidates.

In the case of the example in Figure 6-10, you know that the clean energy sector is underperforming the market. So now compare each stock in the sector to the sector itself to find out which stocks are underperforming the sector. This comparison will uncover a weak stock in a weak group, heavily pushing the odds into your favor.

Figure 6-10:
Comparing industry groups to the broader market can help you identify promising industries to trade.

Clean Energy Index vs. S&P 500 Index

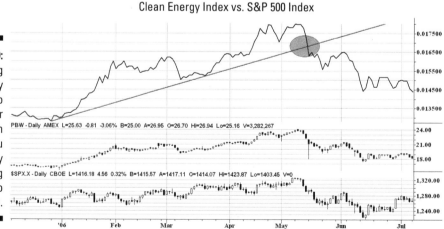

One company that fits the bill is FuelCell Energy (symbol: FCEL). Figure 6-11 shows a ratio chart of FuelCell Energy compared to the clean energy index. The breakdown of the ratio in late May signals a period of underperformance in the stock in relation to the industry. The industry was already beginning to underperform the market at this point, so FuelCell is a prime candidate to short: a weak stock in a weak group.

Ratio of FuelCell Energy to Sector

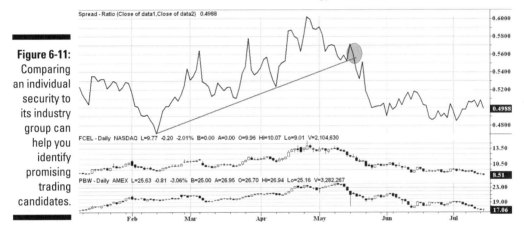

Figure 6-11: Comparing an individual security to its industry group can help you identify promising trading candidates.

Part III

Digging Deeper into the Market: Fundamental Analysis

The 5th Wave   By Rich Tennant

"I read about investing in a company called Unihandle Ohio, but I'm uneasy about a stock that's listed on the NASDAQ as UhOh."

In this part . . .

Having another tool at your disposal can increase your swing trading success rate, so in this part, I take you up close and personal with fundamental analysis. Then I describe how to gauge a security's value by either starting with an examination of its overall industry or a closer look at the security itself. Finally, I show you how to pull out useful trading insights by zeroing in on a target company's financial statements through the Six Step Dance. Although some swing traders shy away from fundamental analysis, practicing it takes you a step ahead of the competition.

Chapter 7

Understanding a Company, Inside and Out

In This Chapter

▶ Conducting fundamental analysis through financial statements

▶ Breaking down the key elements of financial statements

▶ Considering qualitative data

▶ Comparing a company to its peers with relative valuation

*T*o begin at the beginning (yes, I like things to be logical), 100 years ago — if you're reading this sentence before 2034 — Benjamin Graham and David Dodd published a seminal work in the development of fundamental analysis: a book called *Security Analysis.* It argues for determining the value of a company by using its financial statements (specifically the *balance sheet,* which shows assets and liabilities, and the *income statement,* which shows profit and loss over a specified period of time). Later, John Burr Williams wrote *The Theory of Investment Value,* which argues for determining a company's worth by discounting future dividends, or simply putting a future value in today's dollars. For example, $200,000 one year from now may be worth $181,818 today, assuming the "discount rate" is 10 percent (that is, investing $181,818 today and earning a 10 percent return yields $200,000 after one year).

Today's investment models incorporate concepts from both these works to assess corporate value. *Valuation* nowadays is the process of using data from financial statements or comparable firms to assign a value for a company. This chapter introduces you to the important concepts in equity valuation — namely, what to look for in the companies you buy or short. I strongly believe that it's possible to estimate a company's value within 10 to 15 percent of its actual value in little time. The extra hours that Wall Street analysts put into forecasting is largely to improve the precision of their estimates.

Whether you're analyzing equities or another market, remember that you don't need an MBA or CFA designation to intelligently use fundamental analysis. Following some rules of thumb and taking some time to understand a company can go a long way toward improving your swing trading profits.

Getting Your Hands on a Company's Financial Statements

Financial statements can be pretty daunting documents. They don't have any pictures, and they're written in pretty boring language (not like the hilarity of this book). Financial statements really should carry some type of warning label that says, "Do not operate heavy machinery while reading."

To help you avoid the pain of reading minutiae that you're unlikely to ever need, I've broken down the financial statement puzzle into three broad categories:

- What to look for
- When to look
- Where to look

What to look for

Public companies are required by law to file reports with the U.S. Securities and Exchange Commission (SEC) — a government agency that enforces securities laws — at least on a quarterly basis and sometimes more frequently.

The SEC filings you should be aware of, including filings that cover a firm's financial statements, are listed here. Even if you never visit the SEC Web site (www.sec.gov) in your life — and that may not be such a bad thing — you should be familiar with the nomenclature (fancy word for "words") of the industry:

- **10K:** Yes, at first glance the "10K" sounds like a marathon or perhaps $10,000. But in fact, the *10K* in this context refers to an annual report companies must file with the SEC that contains a wealth of information. The 10K contains audited financial statements, information on a company's history, lines of business, competitive information, management's expectations, and more. A company must file its 10K 60 days after the end of its fiscal year. (A fiscal year usually begins January 1 and ends December 31, but some companies have fiscal years ending in June, September, or other months.)

- **10Q:** The *10Q* is a quarterly report companies must file with the SEC. It's shorter than the 10K and contains, most importantly, a firm's financial statements. Firms also may break out details on quarterly performance and the reasons for an increase or decrease in earnings or sales. A company is required to file a 10Q 35 days after the end of its quarter.

✔ **8K:** Companies file *8K* statements after some material event occurs in their business that they must alert shareholders to. These events can be positive or negative, such as being acquired, entering bankruptcy, acquiring another company, or failing to meet an exchange's listing requirements. 8K filings are very timely because public companies must file them four days after the event occurs.

Concurrent with the release of earnings, companies conduct conference calls to discuss the prior quarter. These conference calls also provide the opportunity for listeners to ask questions of the CEO, CFO, and other executives. If you've never listened to this kind of conference call, don't worry. You're not missing out on much. It isn't a party, the jokes are dry, and the executives are anxious to wrap it up. Listening to these calls is a necessity for long-term investors, but not for swing traders (though it is useful). The time commitment required to listen to several companies' conference calls makes doing so impractical.

When to look

As a swing trader, you must know when a company is slated to release its earnings. You can call the company directly to find out its earnings release date, or you can review its historical earnings releases (which typically go out three months apart) to know when to expect the next announcement. Typing a company's stock symbol into Yahoo! Finance shows you historical news items, including earnings announcements.

If you're considering trading shares of a company, wait until after it releases its earnings report because earnings announcements can cause major movements in a stock price — up or down. Consequently, predicting whether a company's results will please Wall Street is difficult. Often a company may report robust earnings with an unimpressive outlook that sends shares spiraling downward. (Don't forget that stocks tend to fall much faster than they appreciate. Commodities, on the other hand, tend to rise much faster than they fall.)

Fundamental data, unlike technical data, doesn't change on a day-to-day basis. Financial statements are at least one month stale, meaning a lag exists between when a company files its report and the date the financial data is reported. So some financial statements may be three months old, depending on when you view the data. Corporate press releases come out on a more frequent basis but are often immaterial. The big fundamental news days are when a company releases its quarterly earnings.

Quarterly earnings provide traders with an update on the company's operations. Often they include selected information from financial statements (full financial data often isn't disclosed until the company files its 10Q with the SEC; see the preceding section). Quarterly earnings reports also update traders on whether management feels comfortable with its targets or benchmarks (assuming the company set such benchmarks in the past).

Where to look

Many moons ago, getting a company's financial statements was a hassle that involved finding the number for the company's investor relations department, calling to request an investor's packet, and waiting for it to arrive via snail mail. People often had to do a lot of legwork to get the information they needed, so imagine how much work went into analyzing just ten potential prospects! Back in those days, swing trading wasn't really popular because of steep commissions. Waiting days to receive financial information was yet another barrier.

Fortunately, the Internet has changed all that. With the click of a mouse, you have access to thousands of companies' financial statements. The time it takes to bring up a new firm's financial statements depends only on how long it takes you to type in that firm's ticker symbol.

You can access a company's financial statements by visiting the SEC Web site (www.sec.gov), but it's not especially user-friendly. A better option is to visit Web sites that provide the information for free — and there are plenty of them. The screen shots used in the financial statements throughout this chapter come from Google Finance (finance.google.com), which provides basic quote information, recent and historical news releases, charts, financial statements, and corporate summaries. Yahoo! Finance also has excellent data on a company, its industry, its expected growth rates, and more. Just point your browser to finance.yahoo.com and type a symbol in the quote box. You can get quotes, charts, corporate information, analyst coverage, ownership, and financials on most any publicly traded company.

Assessing a Company's Financial Statements

So what should you be looking for when a company reports earnings? The most common question to ask yourself is: "Did the company meet or beat expectations?" This guideline applies to both sales and earnings. The larger the percentage beat, the better.

Expectations drive Wall Street. A big surprise can be a signal that analysts aren't accurately projecting a company's earnings. A company that shows a trend of rising earnings surprises (for example, a 10 percent earnings surprise, followed by a 15 percent earnings surprise and a 20 percent earnings surprise) often has superior price performance relative to the market. Conversely, companies with negative earnings surprises have poor price performance. Look for a surprise in the direction you're trading. Consider the case of Southwestern Energy Company, which exhibited a positive earnings surprise of 7.1 percent in September 2007, 16.7 percent in December 2007, and 24 percent in March 2008. Between December 31, 2007, and April 30, 2008, shares of Southwestern Energy rose 51.87 percent. The earnings surprise momentum wasn't the sole reason for the rise, but it provided a clue that something positive was brewing.

Read over the quarterly earnings reports for hints on future performance. Management may hint at problematic times ahead with words such as "challenging" and "competitive environment." These are signals that earnings may not meet consensus expectations, and therefore you should carefully examine major changes in debt levels, cash levels, cash flows (if disclosed), and inventory levels.

The first step in analyzing financial statements is to understand their components. Granted, financial statements may seem frightening, not to mention boring. In my opinion, watching paint dry is more exciting than looking at a financial statement. And that's why this section isn't an academic lesson in accounting. Rather, I give you a basic understanding of what makes up financial statements and, even better, how you can view summaries on the Internet. Wall Street analysts read through hundreds of pages of financial statements before writing up reports on companies. Fortunately, you don't need to do anything close to that to be a profitable swing trader.

Public companies must issue four main financial statements each quarter. As a swing trader, you need concern yourself with only three of them.

Balance sheet

A *balance sheet* is a snapshot of a firm's financial health. Does the company have a lot of debt? Does it have a lot of cash on hand? You can answer these questions and more by viewing its balance sheet.

The balance sheet breakdown

The balance sheet is separated into assets (usually the first half of the balance sheet) and liabilities and shareholders' equity (usually the second half). These two sides must equal each other. Academic textbooks often present assets on the left-hand side of a page and liabilities and shareholders' equity on the right-hand side. In real life, expect to see liabilities and shareholders' equity below the assets section.

Assets are items a company owns that provide some future benefits — like cash, inventory, and plants or equipment. They're further divided into *current* and *long-term* assets.

- ✔ **Current assets** are those assets that are expected to be converted into cash within one year. Items you'll find in the current assets section of a balance sheet include cash, inventory, and *accounts receivable* (credit the company is expecting to convert into cash). You want to see that a company has a good amount of current assets relative to its current liabilities (which I get to shortly).

- ✔ **Long-term assets** refer to items that are expected to be used for more than one year. Expect to see items such as land, plants and equipment, and long-term investments. There's no good absolute number you want to see in this arena. Some industries are capital intensive and require lots of long-term assets. Others, like software firms, have few long-term assets. Within the same industry, a firm that achieves more profits per total assets is often valued higher than a firm that achieves fewer profits per total assets.

On the *liabilities* portion of the balance sheet, you find items the company owes others. Like assets, liabilities are divided into two categories: *current* and *long-term.*

- ✔ **Current liabilities** are expenses or accounts the company is expected to pay over the next year (short-term debt, salaries, expenses, and the like). You want a firm's current assets to be at least 1.5 times its current liabilities if you're interested in buying stock in the company, and below 1.0 times current liabilities if you're looking for a shorting opportunity.

- ✔ **Long-term liabilities** are those items the company is expected to pay back but aren't due for 12 months or longer. Long-term debt is usually the most important long-term liability. Compare long-term debt to shareholders' equity. Ideally, a company should have little long-term debt relative to equity — say less than 30 percent. The more debt a company has, the riskier the company is.

Finally, shareholders' equity (sometimes presented as owners' equity) is the difference between total assets and total liabilities. This is what's left over for stock shareholders after meeting the obligations of debt holders. Shareholders' equity includes stock and the amount of earnings the company has accumulated over time.

How to properly assess a balance sheet

You can develop a feel for a company's financial health by looking at balance sheets and surmising whether the company is in good, average, or poor shape. Use these guidelines to help you:

- ✔ **Cash is king.** The more cash a company has relative to its debts, the better. The less cash a company has relative to its debts, the worse off it is.

- ✔ **Compare current assets to current liabilities.** A ratio of 1.5 or higher is usually a sign that the company isn't going bankrupt in the next 12 months. A ratio below 1 may signal real problems ahead.

- ✔ **Compare long-term debt to shareholders' equity.** The higher the percentage, the more leveraged a company is. Stick to buying companies with debt levels below 30 percent.

- ✔ **Large increases in accounts receivable are a red flag.** If a company's accounts receivable grow faster than sales, it may mean the company is extending loose credit terms to increase sales. And that can spell trouble if the company is unable to recover all amounts owed to it.

- ✔ **Large increases in inventory levels are a red flag.** If inventories rise faster than sales, the company may be on the cusp of a slowdown as it works to sell off inventory. This problem is more pronounced in the technology sector where inventory values quickly decline due to industry advancements.

Figure 7-1 brings these concepts to life with the balance sheet of a publicly traded company, Marvel Entertainment (symbol: MVL). Marvel owns the rights to such popular comic book characters as Spider-Man, X-Men, Ghost Rider, and the Incredible Hulk. Identify the key parts of the balance sheet: current assets, long-term assets, current liabilities, and long-term liabilities. (You won't know every line item that appears in this example. Further research can help you understand those items that I don't cover.)

Glancing quickly over the balance sheet, you should notice that Marvel has more current liabilities than current assets for the period ending September 30, 2007: $117.91 million versus $218.88 million. This fact is an immediate red flag. If you were looking at Marvel as a buying opportunity, you might stop here. The company has significant short-term debt relative to its cash levels, and the situation is deteriorating as evidenced by the current assets to current liabilities in the prior quarter: $165.89 million versus $195.50 million.

Something else that should jump out at you is the leverage Marvel employs. Long-term debt ($218.56 million) relative to shareholders' equity ($150.54 million) is an astounding 145 percent. This company is beyond leveraged!

Financial Statements

Marvel Entertainment, Inc. (NYSE:MVL)

Income Statement | **Balance Sheet** | Cash Flow

In Millions of USD (except for per share items)	As of 2007-09-30	As of 2007-06-30
Cash & Equivalents	11.61	14.16
Short Term Investments	10.00	30.38
Cash and Short Term Investments	21.61	44.54
Accounts Receivable - Trade, Net	37.71	36.38
Receivables - Other	-	-
Total Receivables, Net	42.35	63.74
Total Inventory	10.08	11.51
Prepaid Expenses	5.02	4.71
Other Current Assets, Total	38.86	41.40
Total Current Assets	**117.91**	**165.89**
Property/Plant/Equipment, Total - Gross	-	-
Goodwill, Net	346.15	346.15
Intangibles, Net	0.36	0.70
Long Term Investments	-	-
Other Long Term Assets, Total	260.86	186.28
Total Assets	**728.57**	**703.04**
Accounts Payable	1.93	2.26
Accrued Expenses	111.55	104.90
Notes Payable/Short Term Debt	0.00	0.00
Current Port. of LT Debt/Capital Leases	-	-
Other Current liabilities, Total	105.39	88.34
Total Current Liabilities	**218.88**	**195.50**
Long Term Debt	218.56	133.20
Capital Lease Obligations	-	-
Total Long Term Debt	**218.56**	**133.20**
Total Debt	**218.56**	**133.20**
Deferred Income Tax	-	-
Minority Interest	-	-
Other Liabilities, Total	140.59	136.34
Total Liabilities	**578.03**	**465.04**
Redeemable Preferred Stock, Total	-	-
Preferred Stock - Non Redeemable, Net	0.00	-
Common Stock, Total	1.31	1.31
Additional Paid-In Capital	725.24	723.12
Retained Earnings (Accumulated Deficit)	322.05	285.78
Treasury Stock - Common	-894.84	-768.75
Other Equity, Total	-3.21	-3.46
Total Equity	**150.54**	**238.00**
Total Liabilities & Shareholders' Equity	**728.57**	**703.04**
Shares Outs - Common Stock Primary Issue	-	-
Total Common Shares Outstanding	**75.55**	**80.79**

Figure 7-1:
The balance sheet of MVL for the quarters ending September 30, 2007, and June 30, 2007.

Source: Google Finance

REMEMBER

The amount of research you conduct beyond the cursory examination presented here depends on the type of swing trader you are. More work can help you make better decisions, but there isn't enough time in one day to closely examine several companies. For example, further research into Marvel Entertainment would've revealed that the company has become so highly leveraged because of its push into making its own films rather than licensing its characters. But you can't pore over hundreds of pages of SEC filings to learn details that may, or may not, influence your decision to swing trade the stock.

Income statement

The *income statement* shows a company's profit and losses over a period of time. That time is usually reported as 3 months and 12 months. The main parts of the income statement are the revenues, gross profit, operating income, and net income.

The income statement breakdown

"Revenues" is a fancy way of saying "sales." In Europe, revenues are often called "turnover." Whatever term you use, this financial statement represents a company's lifeline. Without sales, you can't make profits. Growth-oriented companies can grow sales at double (and even triple) digit rates in times of economic expansion.

After revenues, an income statement lists a firm's *gross profit* (the amount of profit left over after a company subtracts all direct costs related to the products it sells — called *cost of goods sold*). An example best illustrates these terms: If Dummies Corporation reports sales of $10 million in 2008 (due, no doubt, to the success of *Swing Trading For Dummies*), the firm's cost of goods sold would include the cost of printing the book, hiring yours truly to write it, paying editors to proofread it, and more. These are all direct costs. You wouldn't include any indirect costs, like the salary of the CEO, in the calculation of the cost of goods sold because they aren't directly attributable to the cost of the book.

Gross profit is often calculated as a percentage of sales. The higher the ratio, the more profitable the firm. Often companies receive higher valuations because of higher gross profit margins.

After gross profit, the next main heading in the income statement is the *operating income.* Operating income is what's left over after taking out all indirect costs from the gross profit figure. Indirect costs include selling, general, and administrative costs. Marketing, for example, is considered an indirect cost. The costs of electricity and office desks are also indirect. Subtracting these items from gross profit yields operating income.

Finally, a few more subtractions are made from operating income to arrive at *net income* — the bottom line. Subtract interest expense (like interest payments on debt) and taxes and you get net income. Net income is usually presented in dollars and as a per share figure. That is, companies divide net profit by the number of shares the company has outstanding in order to calculate income per share.

How to properly assess an income statement

Keep these suggestions in mind to stay on your game and spot strength and weakness in income statements:

- ✔ **Compare sales growth rates (year over year) to net income growth rates (year over year).** Ideally, you want to see net income rise at a faster pace than sales.

- ✔ **Keep an eye on the trend of gross profit as a percentage of sales.** A rising ratio is a healthy sign, whereas a declining ratio is a red flag.

- ✔ **Keep an eye on the trend of operating income as a percentage of sales.** Again, a rising ratio is a healthy sign and a declining ratio is a red flag.

- ✔ **Compare sales and earnings to year-ago periods.** Comparing either figure to prior quarters rather than the prior year may lead you to incorrect conclusions regarding the company's health.

- ✔ **Watch for growth in outstanding shares.** This growth can be a red flag that the company is issuing more shares and thereby diluting existing ones.

Figure 7-2 shows the income statement of Marvel Entertainment for the three months ending September 30, 2007, and the three months ending June 30, 2007. Identify the key parts of the income statement: revenues, gross profit, operating income, net profit, and net income per share (*earnings per share, or EPS*).

Marvel posted revenues of $123.64 million in the quarter ending September 30, 2007. Now, you may be tempted to say that number represents impressive growth over the previous quarter, when Marvel posted revenues of $101.47 million. However, you shouldn't compare quarters to previous quarters because seasonality can wreak havoc. For example, a toy manufacturer will experience a steep drop in sales after the holiday shopping season. To maintain consistency, compare quarterly results with the results from the year-ago period.

Gross profit as a percentage of sales basically remained unchanged from the June quarter (at 85.7 percent) to the September quarter (85.8 percent). (Comparing items that are a percentage of sales across quarters isn't as problematic as comparing sales or earnings across quarters.) Gross profits as a percentage of sales are rarely this high, but Marvel receives licensing fees, which have little cost directly associated with them.

Operating income as a percentage of sales also remained largely unchanged (going from 53 percent to 52.7 percent). Marvel reported net income of $29.09 million in the June quarter, equivalent to 34 cents per share, and $36.27 million in the September quarter, equivalent to 45 cents per share. Marvel has 80.52 million shares outstanding.

Financial Statements

Marvel Entertainment, Inc. (NYSE:MVL)

Income Statement | Balance Sheet | Cash Flow

In Millions of USD (except for per share items)	3 months Ending 2007-09-30	3 months Ending 2007-06-30
Revenue	123.64	101.47
Other Revenue, Total	-	-
Total Revenue	**123.64**	**101.47**
Cost of Revenue, Total	17.53	14.50
Gross Profit	**106.11**	**86.98**
Selling/General/Admin. Expenses, Total	39.50	31.86
Research & Development	-	-
Depreciation/Amortization	1.44	1.39
Interest Expense(Income) - Net Operating	-	-
Unusual Expense (Income)	-	-
Other Operating Expenses, Total	-	-
Total Operating Expense	**58.47**	**47.75**
Operating Income	**65.18**	**53.73**
Interest Income(Expense), Net Non-Operating	-3.09	-2.32
Gain (Loss) on Sale of Assets	-	-
Other, Net	0.53	2.31
Income Before Tax	**62.62**	**53.72**
Income After Tax	**41.55**	**33.50**
Minority Interest	-5.29	-4.42
Equity In Affiliates	-	-
Net Income Before Extra. Items	**36.27**	**29.09**
Accounting Change	-	-
Discontinued Operations	-	-
Extraordinary Item	-	-
Net Income	**36.27**	**29.09**
Preferred Dividends	-	-
Income Available to Common Excl. Extra Items	**36.27**	**29.09**
Income Available to Common Incl. Extra Items	**36.27**	**29.09**
Basic Weighted Average Shares	-	-
Basic EPS Excluding Extraordinary Items	-	-
Basic EPS Including Extraordinary Items	-	-
Dilution Adjustment	-	-
Diluted Weighted Average Shares	80.52	84.91
Diluted EPS Excluding Extraordinary Items	0.45	0.34

Figure 7-2: MVL's income statement for the quarters ending September 30, 2007, and June 30, 2007.

Source: Google Finance

Cash flow statement

The *cash flow statement* tells you how much cash the company generated (cash flows from operating activities), what it did with its cash (cash flows used in/generated from investing activities), and whether it borrowed money or paid out cash (cash flows from financing activities).

The cash flow statement breakdown

The first section of this financial statement details cash flows used in or generated from operating activities. It starts with net income and makes various adjustments to tally up how much cash was generated or used during the period — ending with cash flow from operating activities. What kinds of adjustments are made? An increase in inventories reflects a use of cash and therefore should be subtracted from net income. On the other hand, a company adds back *non-cash expenses* taken out of net income in the income statement. Non-cash expenses are costs a company recognizes on its income statement that aren't actually paid out. For example, if a company owns a car used for business, it may recognize a $5,000 non-cash expense in one year to reflect the car's loss of value.

As a swing trader, don't get too caught up in the details. The most important item of this section is *cash flow from operating activities* — the bottom line. This shows whether the company actually generated cash from its business during the period. A company can report strong net income and have negative cash flow if a majority of sales are on credit, for example. Look for cash flow from operations to be consistent with net income (that is, they should rise together and fall together).

The second section of the cash flow statement is the cash flow from investing section. The most important item here is usually *capital expenditures,* or the costs incurred to maintain, upgrade, or acquire physical assets. Generally, the smaller the level of capital expenditures relative to sales, the better.

The third and final section of the cash flow statement is the *cash flow from financing activities* section. This part of the statement shows any dividends paid and any issuance or payment of debt or stock. Ideally, a company can sustain its operations from the cash it generates internally, but sometimes a company looks outside itself to fund growth. It may issue debt or stock for that reason. Issuing stock dilutes the value of other shareholders' equity, and issuing debt may saddle the company with a debt burden that's difficult to bear.

How to properly assess a cash flow statement

Always look at a cash flow statement with these points in mind so you can more easily spot a company's strengths and weaknesses:

- ✔ **Compare cash flow from operations to net income.** Net income rising with cash flows declining is a negative sign. Falling net income with rising cash flows may reflect a high level of non-cash expenses.

- ✔ **Keep an eye on capital expenditures (in the cash flows from investing activities) relative to sales.** The higher the ratio, the worse off the company.

✔ **Look at the methods the company depends on for its cash.** Does it generate its own cash from operations and not need to borrow money? Or is the company issuing stock and heavily borrowing to make ends meet? Answering "yes" to the first question is a good thing; "yes" to the second question isn't a good sign.

✔ **Look for major changes in the cash flow from the financing activities section.** A large amount of debt issuance may be a red flag. Payment of debt, on the other hand, is a good sign that a company is deleveraging itself.

✔ **Watch for large items or breaks in historical levels of cash flows.** Both can signal major events like an acquisition or payment of debt. Paying down debt is generally a good thing, whereas acquisitions can be good or bad. Unless acquisitions are a part of a firm's strategy, I'm often weary of them.

Check out Figure 7-3, the cash flow statement of Marvel Entertainment.

Notice that Marvel reported net income of $36.27 million in the quarter ending September 30, 2007, but actually used cash in operations of –$8.68 million. Film production costs used up cash generated in the quarter. Marvel is spending cash today in hopes of blockbuster films tomorrow.

Fortunately, capital expenditures were extremely low ($0.37 million) because film companies don't have a lot of physical assets that need to be upgraded, maintained, or purchased.

Figure 7-3:
The cash flow statement of MVL for the quarters ending September 30, 2007, and June 30, 2007.

Financial Statements

Marvel Entertainment, Inc. (NYSE:MVL)
Income Statement | Balance Sheet | **Cash Flow**

In Millions of USD (except for per share items)	3 months Ending 2007-09-30	3 months Ending 2007-06-30
Net Income/Starting Line	36.27	29.09
Depreciation/Depletion	1.44	1.39
Amortization	-	-
Deferred Taxes	-7.42	-1.05
Non-Cash Items	-0.60	2.38
Changes in Working Capital	-38.36	-31.12
Cash from Operating Activities	**-8.68**	**0.69**
Capital Expenditures	-0.37	-0.45
Other Investing Cash Flow Items, Total	26.06	-30.58
Cash from Investing Activities	**25.70**	**-31.04**
Financing Cash Flow Items	-	85.15
Total Cash Dividends Paid	-	-
Issuance (Retirement) of Stock, Net	-127.37	-52.17
Issuance (Retirement) of Debt, Net	107.84	0.00
Cash from Financing Activities	**-19.53**	**32.98**
Foreign Exchange Effects	-0.04	0.17
Net Change in Cash	**-2.55**	**2.81**

Source: Google Finance

Low capex may mean higher profits

Capital expenditures (affectionately shortened to *capex*) represent investments by firms into their businesses. So you may think that the more a company invests in itself, the better the performance of its stock. In reality, high capex isn't correlated with strong stock price performance. Jeremy Siegel, a professor of finance at the Wharton School of Business (and former teacher of mine) writes in his book *The Future for Investors* (Crown Business, 2005):

> *There is strong evidence that firms with the highest level of capital expenditures suffer the worst performance across the entire stock market. Five portfolios are formed, ranging from the firms with the lowest to the firms with the highest capex to sales*

ratios. The portfolios are rebalanced each December 31 using the last twelve months' sales and capital expenditures . . . those firms that engaged in the most capital expenditures provided investors with the worst returns, while those that had the lowest expenditures had overwhelming better returns — more than 3.5 percent per year higher than the S&P 500 Index over almost half a century.

The two sectors Siegel identifies as having the lowest capex to sales are the healthcare sector at 0.07 and the consumer staples sector at 0.044. Interestingly, the healthcare sector posted the best return of all sectors in the market between 1957 and 2003.

Finally, the investing activities section of the cash flow statement shows a large amount of borrowing: $107.84 million. The company purchased (or retired) $127.37 million worth of existing stock, a positive sign for shareholders because fewer shares on the market tends to lead to higher stock prices.

Not Just Numbers: Qualitative Data

Fundamental analysis isn't just based on numbers. A company is more than its earnings, sales, and so on. Would you value a company led by a well-known investor the same as a company led by your neighbor? Qualitative factors also determine whether a company's stock is a value or not.

Some qualitative factors that great performing stocks often share are

- **High management ownership:** Insider ownership is a sign that the executives who run the company are putting their money where their mouths are. The financial ownership also aligns shareholder interests with management's interests. A CEO is likely to think twice about taking an action that may depress the stock price if he or she owns a good chunk of company stock in a 401(k) plan. The rule of thumb here is that insider ownership of at least 10 percent of outstanding shares is a bullish sign.

✔ **A wide moat:** Hundreds of years ago, castles often used moats as a defense mechanism to prevent would-be attackers from successfully penetrating the castle walls. An economic moat is similar: It's the degree of competitive advantage a company has that prevents competition from taking market share.

Warren Buffett, a well-respected investor and head of Berkshire Hathaway, is a major proponent of the idea of economic moats. He looks for companies that would be difficult to displace because of brand loyalty or cost advantages. Moats are often established in the pharmaceutical business because of drug patents that ensure the developer of a new drug will be the sole provider of that drug for a number of years.

You can see the world, to some extent, as consisting of companies with wide moats and those with more narrow moats (called *commodities*) — a product you can buy from anywhere and don't care much about who manufactures it is a commodity. Think of things like salt, sugar, or — increasingly today — computers. Contrast the businesses that provide these products with companies that have wide moats and are difficult to displace. Starbucks — which Jerry Seinfeld jokingly calls "Five Bucks" — is able to charge premium pricing for cups of coffee. Sometimes the moat may be a result of some technological advantage. Google, for example, was a tiny technology company in 1996 but developed a search technology that dwarfed the behemoths at Microsoft and Yahoo! In a short time, Google gained a major foothold in the search engine field and was able to translate that market share into advertising dollars.

Ask yourself when reviewing companies how difficult it would be for a company to displace the firm you're examining. The more difficult it is to displace, the wider the moat.

✔ **Positive catalysts:** Catalysts help investors revalue shares upward. Successful new products (like Apple's iPhone) and new management (like Hewlett-Packard's Mark Hurd) are both catalysts that cause investors to revalue shares.

A catalyst can also originate from outside the company. When one company is acquired or bought out in an industry, competitors of that company often see share price increases as investors revalue shares based on the purchase price multiple used in the acquisition. Investors also often hope that another buyout will occur in the industry.

Negative catalysts that may propel shares of a firm downward can include an earnings miss, a competitor's introduction of a new product, and the resignation of key management.

Valuing a Company Based on Data You've Gathered

You may feel like you can charge people for advice on analyzing financial statements, reviewing earnings reports, and evaluating qualitative data, but just how much is this darn company worth? There's no line on the financial statements that says, "This company is worth $5 billion. Please do not pay more than this amount. Thank you."

If you get ten different analysts in one room and ask them to analyze one company, you're likely to get ten different answers (ideally they're at least close to one another). So there are differences in how investors value firms.

Understanding the two main methods of valuation

The two main ways stocks are valued today are relative valuation models and absolute valuation models:

- A **relative valuation model** is likely the model you'll use most often as a swing trader. *Relative valuation* is estimating a company's value based on what its peers in the marketplace are trading at. The model may be based on earnings (using the price to earnings ratio, for example), sales (price to sales ratio), book value (price to book value), or a dozen other ratios.

  By far, the price to earnings ratio (P/E) is the most common method of relative valuation. For example, if Macy's and Dillard's trade for 12 times earnings, then gosh darn it, maybe J.C. Penney should too. Maybe it even deserves to trade at a premium to Macy's because its earnings are expected to grow faster in coming years than its competitors. Or perhaps J.C. Penney deserves to trade at a discount to its competitors because it has a lower net profit margin (net income divided by sales) than its competitors. You get the idea.

- An **absolute valuation model** is calculated independently of the valuations of a company's peers. Instead of drawing conclusions based on what Macy's or Dillard's are trading, an analyst valuing shares of J. C. Penney determines a value based on the company's earnings, cash flows, or dividends. Corporate valuation differences arise primarily out of disagreements over expectations of future earnings. If it were possible to know with certainty how much a company would make in the next ten years, there would be little disagreement on the value of the company today.

Relative valuation models are easier and faster to calculate than absolute valuation models. Swing traders usually rely on relative valuation models because of the complexity and time commitment inherent in absolute valuation models. I address both here so you know that two basic methods of analysis exist, but because this book is targeted to swing traders, I don't go into more detail on how to construct an absolute valuation model.

Implementing the swing trader's preferred model

Using the relative valuation model is the quick and dirty way of getting you close to the actual value of a company you're considering. All it takes are two easy steps:

1. **Choose your price multiple.**

   This metric can be P/E, price to sales ratio (P/S), or any of the other metrics highlighted in Chapter 8.

2. **Figure out what multiple your security should trade at for that multiple.**

   Determining what's a "correct" P/E ratio (or any ratio) is no easy task. The best way to start is to look at the average P/E of the industry. Then, decide whether the company you're assessing deserves to trade at a premium or discount to the industry. A company that can grow earnings faster than its industry is generally awarded a higher P/E than its competitors.

Figure 7-4 shows financial statistics of major drug manufacturers and the average statistics for the entire industry. Merck (symbol: MRK) trades at a premium to its industry on a P/E basis (24.58 times versus 21.31 times). But that may be justified given Merck's operating margins (operating income/ sales) of 25.22 percent versus the industry average of 14.53 percent. In addition to Merck, this figure shows statistics for Bristol-Myers Squibb (symbol: BMY), Pfizer (symbol: PFE), and sanofi-aventis (symbol: SNY). *Note:* The acronym TTM stands for "trailing twelve months."

A swing trader looking at Merck may determine that a premium valuation is justified given the strength of operating margins and the recent quarterly revenues growth versus the average industry. Coming up with an appropriate multiple is more art than science. First determine whether the company should trade at a premium, discount, or in-line multiple versus its industry. If the company should trade at a premium or discount (because earnings growth or operating margins or return on equity are higher or lower than the industry average), determine an approximate size to the premium or discount by measuring how much higher or lower the company's growth or margins are versus the industry. For example, a company growing twice the rate of its industry may be worth a price multiple twice its industry average. Alternatively, a company that's growing at half the rate of its industry may deserve to trade at a discount that's half the industry average.

You can use other financial ratios to estimate the value of a company relative to its peers. Remember to make higher or lower allowances for things like profit margins, earnings growth rates, and efficiency ratios. Chapter 9 provides more details on how to determine a fair multiple. You may need to award a company (with a higher multiple and, hence, higher valuation) if it has strong earnings growth rates. Alternatively, a company with poor growth rates or poor efficiency ratios may need to trade at a discount to its peers.

Competitors

DIRECT COMPETITOR COMPARISON

	MRK	BMY	PFE	SNY	Industry
Market Cap:	131.62B	53.13B	164.46B	130.29B	772.66M
Employees:	60,000	43,000	98,000	100,289	336
Qtrly Rev Growth (yoy):	12.30%	21.60%	-2.40%	2.50%	11.40%
Revenue (ttm):	24.00B	18.67B	48.15B	43.50B	318.28M
Gross Margin (ttm):	76.10%	67.31%	84.01%	74.42%	71.06%
EBITDA (ttm):	8.08B	3.90B	19.67B	15.82B	17.32M
Oper Margins (ttm):	25.22%	16.23%	29.74%	19.65%	14.53%
Net Income (ttm):	5.38B	2.12B	6.99B	5.87B	-904.54K
EPS (ttm):	2.460	1.076	2.113	2.15	N/A
P/E (ttm):	24.58	25.03	11.40	22.46	21.31
PEG (5 yr expected):	1.82	1.4	2.07	3.09	1.81
P/S (ttm):	5.49	2.86	3.39	3.03	3.65

BMY = Bristol-Myers Squibb Co.
PFE = Pfizer Inc.
SNY = Sanofi-Aventis
Industry = Drug Manufacturers - Major

Figure 7-4: Key statistics of several large drug manufacturers relative to the industry.

Source: Yahoo! Finance

Don't let analysts do your thinking for you!

If your head is swirling with the idea of valuing a company, you may be asking, "Can't an analyst just tell me what to think? Analysts make big bucks to look at firms inside and out and tell me whether to buy or sell them, right?" Wrong! Well, not about the big bucks part. Analysts are well compensated (maybe too well compensated) to form opinions on companies, and they provide a valuable service. They spend their time looking at a handful of companies, usually in one industry, and issue buy or sell recommendations for the masses. But there's something you should know about Wall Street: It's largely a big boy's club. (There, I said it.) And because it's a club, firms don't always have your best interest in mind.

Because analysts can sell a buy recommendation to anyone with money (and you can only shop around sell recommendations to people who actually hold the stock already), the number of buy recommendations out there far outnumber the number of sell recommendations. So if you issue an opinion to buy a stock, you can shop that opinion to literally anyone with money. But issue a sell recommendation and your target audience shrinks dramatically.

In the late 1990s, major investment banks like Morgan Stanley or Merrill Lynch often issued a buy recommendation right after selling the company's stock to the public. This worked like clockwork, day in and day out, as investors rode stocks down into the pennies (literally!) after being assured by those smart Wall Street analysts that all was well. The market collapse in 2000 brought calls for reforms, and the public learned that analysts often privately ridicule the very companies they publicly endorse.

The reform of Wall Street is a good thing, but analysts still may have unknown conflicts. Moreover, as a group, analysts are often wrong about the timing of buys and sells. In 2005, Zacks Investment Research conducted a survey to find out whether buy-recommended stocks outperform sell-recommended stocks. You may guess that the demarcation between these two extremes is wide enough that this question doesn't need to be asked, but you'd be wrong. A 2005 *Wall Street Journal* article entitled "Analysts Keep Misfiring with 'Sell' Ratings" found that stocks with a large proportion of sell ratings (that is, with more sell ratings than buy or hold ratings) performed better than stocks with no sell ratings and only buy or hold ratings.

So don't rely on an analyst's buy or sell recommendation to help you determine whether a swing trade is good or not. You need to use your own judgment. This recommendation also extends to the area of TV, specifically the various stock-picking programs on CNBC or Fox News. I'm amazed at how many traders and investors get stock picks from these programs. Don't they realize that millions of others are watching, too? And the mass is often wrong when it comes to the market — even when it includes top Wall Street analysts.

Chapter 8

Finding Companies Based on Their Fundamentals

In This Chapter

▶ Working your way down the ladder by assessing the market and the industry

▶ Employing screens to discover swing trading candidates

▶ Figuring out which method works for you

*Y*ou can identify fundamentals-based trades (and technical-based trades for that matter) in two ways: by beginning with the security's market and drilling down into the promising industries or by identifying candidates with promising characteristics on a grassroots level. One approach is top down, whereas the other is bottom up. Both ways have merit.

This chapter outlines how to identify promising candidates to buy or short using a fundamentally driven top-down or bottom-up approach — and how to determine which approach is right for you.

Seeing the Forest for the Trees: The Top-Down Approach

The *top-down approach* identifies promising swing trading candidates by starting with market analysis (looking at stock markets, commodity markets, currency markets, and the like). Then it drills down into specific industries before finally examining individual securities. This approach implicitly argues for greater weight on markets and industries over the merits of an individual company because these big-picture items are more important in determining a security's return than company-level factors. A top-down trader cares less whether he or she swing trades XYZ Oil Company or ABC Oil Company (based on the individual characteristics of each company) and more about whether he or she is trading an energy stock or a drug stock.

The top-down approach allows you to understand the condition of the overall market, which is valuable because the majority of securities follow trends in the overall market. For example, if the stock market is dreadful and hits new lows every few weeks, you're probably going to come up short on your long trades. On the other hand, if you avidly short every stock that moves while the market hits new highs, you'd best be prepared to take some nasty losses.

Using this approach, you begin evaluating whether the overall market is overvalued, undervalued, or just right. Then you question whether the industry is likely to outperform or underperform the market. Finally, you look at the individual security to see whether its statistics are impressive enough to warrant investment.

Top-down analysis involves two specific steps:

1. **Determine whether the overall market is correctly priced.**

   This step allows you to determine whether the overall market is cheap or dear so that you know whether you should trade the long or short side. As a swing trader, you don't have time to call analysts, survey government data, and build an economic model that perfectly captures all information that may influence an overall market. Even if you did have the time for all that, I've never seen proof that such complexities improve forecasting abilities (my apologies to my econometrics professor).

2. **Assess the prospects of different industries in the market.**

   This step helps you focus on the promising industries or lagging ones so that the wind is at your back when you buy or short securities within that industry. If the market is overvalued, for example, which industries present the most opportunity on the downside? Being right on the overall market and wrong on the industry may leave you with losses.

The following sections break down the details of how to dig into market and industry analysis to benefit from the top-down approach.

Sizing up the market

You can't identify good swing trading candidates with the top-down approach without first evaluating the overall market. Fortunately you can choose from three measures to determine whether the overall market is cheap, fairly priced, or expensive.

Just because a market is cheap or expensive according to these measures doesn't mean you should ignore price action. Ideally, price action should confirm the findings of these measures. When it doesn't, you know something's wrong and that the current trend may end. For instance, these measures would've told you that the stock market was expensive or overvalued at the beginning of 1999. But that didn't stop the Nasdaq Composite Index from nearly doubling during that year. The smart swing trader would've followed the upward price action. But he or she would've kept tight stops in light of the findings of these three valuation measures and, as a result, would've been better prepared for the ensuing collapse of the Nasdaq in 2000 that took prices lower by nearly 80 percent through 2002.

The models I present in the following sections are all yardsticks. They aren't to be taken as fact. Stock markets can be over- and undervalued for long periods of time. But as a swing trader, you should know where value is. Even if you trade in the near term on the other side of value, you'll know whether a trend has legs based on whether it goes against or with the direction of value. For example, the bull market in technology stocks in 1998 and 1999 was incredible and powerful. But it didn't last long. Knowing that the market was overvalued — as all three of these indicators would've told you — would have prepared you for the major bear market that began in 2000 and ended in late 2002.

Taking the easy path: Long-term P/E ratio

The long-term P/E ratio method of determining whether a market is over- or undervalued is the crudest and simplest method you can use. It simply compares the market's current P/E to its long-term average. The real question is: Do you look at the P/E based on the last 12 months of earnings, or do you look at it based on the expected earnings in the coming 12 months?

Reviewing the expected earnings over the next 12 months makes more sense than relying on historical earnings. After all, companies are valued based on their future, not their past. Historical earnings are especially unhelpful at *points of inflection,* where a major turn happens in the economy. The recent past looks very little like the coming future.

Fortunately, Standard & Poor's (S&P) publishes the P/E of the S&P 500 Index based on both historical and future earnings. The S&P Web site (www.standardandpoors.com) provides spreadsheets that show the P/E for the S&P 500 Index (large companies), the S&P 400 Index (mid cap companies), the S&P 600 Index (small cap companies), and the S&P 1500 Index (the entire market). To download these spreadsheets, go to the S&P Web site and click on these items in the following order: "Indices," "Equity Indices," "United States," "S&P 500," and finally "Operating Earnings & Estimates by GICS Sector."

From 1936 through 2007, the average P/E of the S&P 500 Index — which represents a large part of the market — has been 15.50 (see Figure 8-1). When the market trades significantly above this level (say 20 times earnings), that can indicate the market is overvalued. When the market trades well below this level, that may signal that the market is undervalued.

Historical P/E Ratio of S&P 500 Index

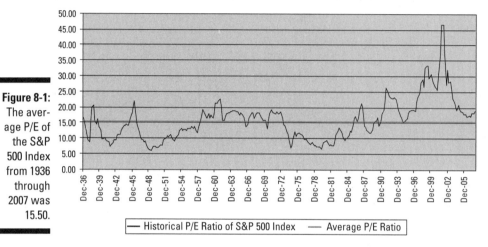

Figure 8-1:
The aver-
age P/E of
the S&P
500 Index
from 1936
through
2007 was
15.50.

Historical P/E Ratio of S&P 500 Index —— Average P/E Ratio

The S&P Web site breaks out data into two segments: as reported earnings and operating earnings. I recommend you use the operating earnings spread-sheet, because reported earnings can be distorted by one-time events that aren't reflective of a company's underlying fundamentals. One-time events that aren't part of a company's operations — like the gain generated from selling land or the loss suffered due to a hurricane — can distort a firm's underlying strength or weakness. The operating earnings category ignores these one-time effects and examines only those earnings generated from a firm's operations.

The long-term P/E ratio method has the following downsides when it comes to valuing a market:

✔ **It ignores the other investment opportunities you can acquire.** Stocks are one asset class and compete with other asset classes, most often bonds, for investors' dollars. When bonds offer investors low returns — say 1 or 2 percent — stocks tend to be valued at a higher premium to their historical average. A P/E of 15 may be cheap when bonds are offering investors a return of 1 percent. You can address this issue by combining the long-term P/E ratio with a method that looks at other types of securities, such as the two models addressed in the following sections.

✔ **It may yield a result that won't be reached for many months, or even years.** Take a look again at Figure 8-1. Between 1996 and 2000, the market was overvalued based on long-term P/E but didn't suffer a major correction for a few years. However, the eventual correction was swift and painful. That's why you must use the long-term P/E ratio method in conjunction with price action (that is, technical analysis) when deter-mining how to swing trade in a specific market.

✔ **It isn't useful as a short-term timing vehicle.** The P/E model isn't a short-term trading model and hence may hurt swing traders that depend on short-term price movements. It tells you the direction the wind is blowing, but sometimes the market ignores reality and marches the wrong way. Eventually, the market gets it right. But in the near term, this gap in accuracy may cost you a lot of money.

Solve this lag by incorporating charts with the P/E model. If the P/E model indicates that the market is undervalued but the trend is down according to the charts, don't fight the tape. Instead, short the security in question. However, be alert for signals of a trend change. The near-term weakness may not be sustainable, and the market may be due for a rebound. Similarly, if the P/E model indicates the market is overvalued but the trend is definitively up, don't argue with the market. Go long, but keep tight stop loss orders to protect yourself when the fundamentals prove out and the market takes a swoon. Be on the lookout for divergences in technical indicators.

The major indexes may be going in one direction while the majority of stocks are heading in a different direction. Believe it or not, the market indexes can be led by a small number of securities. Indicators such as the Advance/Decline Line or the New High/New Low Index can tip you off to a deteriorating or strengthening market when they diverge from the major averages. (The Advance/Decline Line and the New High/New Low Index can be plotted in most major charting programs, such as *TradeStation* and *High Growth Stock Investor.*)

Computing a "fair value" estimate: The Fed Model

The *Fed Model* compares the yield of the market to the yield of the 10-year U.S. Treasury Note. So essentially it compares the return you may expect to earn in stocks with a major competing asset class so that you aren't examining stocks in a vacuum. As a result, you have a reference point from which to base your estimation of the market's current value. For example, when the stock market is offering a higher yield than bonds, this model assumes that investors will migrate to stocks. When bonds are offering a higher yield than stocks, the model presumes that investors will flock there.

Here's how to reach the point of comparison:

1. **Determine the market's P/E and calculate its inverse.**

   This number isn't reported by most research providers. Fortunately, you can find the market's P/E on the S&P 500 Web site.

2. **Calculate the inverse of the market's P/E to determine the market's earnings yield.**

   The math is easy here. If the P/E is 12, calculate the inverse by taking 1 and dividing it by 12 (that is, 8.33 percent). If the P/E is 20, the inverse is 5 percent.

Estimating the S&P 500 Index's fair value

To estimate where the S&P 500 Index should be trading at — according to the Fed Model — translate the yield on the 10-year U.S. Treasury Note and then multiply that implied P/E by the expected earnings of the S&P 500 Index.

Say that the yield on the 10-year Treasury Note is 4.50 percent. Translate that yield into a P/E ratio by dividing 1 by 0.045 to get 22.22. Multiply that P/E by the expected earnings of the S&P

500 Index (see the earlier section, "Taking the easy path: Long-term P/E ratio," for where to find this info). If the Index's expected earnings for the coming year are $80, then its fair value is 1,777.60.

I don't put much stock in this method of computing an index level because yields change daily. I prefer instead to simply know whether the market is over- or undervalued.

---

3. Find the yield on the 10-year Treasury Note.

You can locate this number online (try `www.bloomberg.com/markets/rates/`) or you can look it up in *The Wall Street Journal*.

Suppose the P/E of the S&P 500 Index today is 15. That means the earnings yield is 1 divided by 15, or 6.67 percent. For purposes of this example, say the yield on the 10-year Treasury Note is 4.50 percent. Based on the Fed Model, stocks are undervalued relative to bonds because the yield on the S&P 500 Index is higher than the yield on the Treasury Note.

Some swing traders take this model one step further to calculate what the S&P 500 Index should be trading at. The math is simple, but you don't have to do it to know whether the equity market is over- or undervalued. But if you want to know anyway, check out the nearby sidebar.

One criticism of the Fed Model is that U.S. Treasury government bonds provide lower yields than other bonds. (The lower the yield, the more attractive stocks look when compared to bonds.) U.S. Treasury government bonds are considered "risk free" because the U.S. government has the power to print dollars. Therefore, the U.S. government is unlikely to default on bonds it issues. The *yield,* or return, on these bonds is lower than bonds issued by states or corporations, which can default.

Improving the ol' standard: The adjusted Fed Model

The *adjusted Fed Model* compares the earnings yield on stocks to corporate bonds. But you can't compare yields to just any bonds; different types of bonds carry different levels of default. The higher the potential default, the higher the yield the bond pays. It's unfair to compare buying shares of Coca-Cola to buying a bond issued by a troubled home lender likely to default on its obligations.

Rating agencies, primarily Standard & Poor's (S&P) and Moody's, measure the likelihood of a company defaulting on its obligations and assign rankings to different bonds. S&P's scale ranges from AAA (representing the highest-quality bonds) to D (representing ready-to-default bonds). Moody's scale ranges from Aaa (highest) to C (lowest).

Figure 8-2 highlights a table taken from Yahoo! Finance's Bond Center that breaks down the different bond rankings assigned by S&P and Moody's. Investment-grade bonds, which many institutional investors are restricted to, have ratings between AAA and BBB on the S&P scale and Aaa and Baa on the Moody's scale. These bonds tend to be higher-quality bonds and have a low risk of default. Bonds that are below investment grade have a higher frequency of default (often higher than 1 percent).

When using the adjusted Fed Model, you should examine the yield on 10-year AA Corporate Bonds. These bonds are high quality, attract investment dollars from institutional investors, and represent a competitor to stocks. The higher the yield on corporate bonds, the less likely stocks are to be preferred over bonds. But don't just take the yield of any AA-rated Corporate Bond. Instead, use a composite or average of all AA Corporate Bonds.

So where can you get this information? Fortunately, it's provided free of charge in this Internet age. Figure 8-3 shows a snapshot from the Yahoo! Finance site that provides the yield on bonds with different ratings and *maturities* (the term of the bond). Notice that the yield on 10-year AA-rated Corporate Bonds is 5.60 percent.

Moody's	S&P	Definition	Notes
Aaa	AAA	Highest Rating Available	Investment grade bonds.
Aa	AA	Very High Quality	
A	A	High Quality	
Baa	BBB	Minimum Investment Grade	
Ba	BB	Low grade	Below investment grade.
B	B	Very speculative	
Caa	CCC	Substantial Risk	
Ca	CC	Very poor quality	
C	D	Imminent default or in default	

Figure 8-2: A comparison of bond rankings in the S&P and Moody's scales.

Source: Yahoo! Finance

CORPORATE BONDS				
MATURITY	YIELD	YESTERDAY	LAST WEEK	LAST MONTH
2YR AA	3.19	3.25	3.21	3.28
2YR A	3.16	3.12	3.11	3.32
5YR AAA	3.78	3.83	3.68	3.94
5YR AA	4.08	4.11	3.85	4.05
5YR A	4.53	4.49	4.26	4.22
10YR AAA	5.09	5.29	5.08	4.93
10YR AA	5.60	5.56	5.22	5.13
10YR A	5.94	5.92	5.41	5.46
20YR AAA	6.63	6.58	6.40	5.43
20YR AA	6.67	6.66	6.24	5.74
20YR A	6.49	6.44	6.27	5.98

Figure 8-3:
Find out the yield of corporate bonds with different maturities and S&P ratings by surfing the Internet.

Source: Yahoo! Finance

Now that you know the yield on 10-year AA Corporate Bonds, you can compare that to the yield on stocks. Suppose the P/E of the S&P 500 Index is 19 today. That means the earnings yield is 1 divided by 19, or 5.26 percent. Using the information provided in Figure 8-3, you know that the yield on 10-year AA Corporate Bonds is 5.60 percent. Based on the adjusted Fed Model, stocks are overvalued relative to bonds because the yield on 10-year AA Corporate Bonds is higher than the earnings yield on the S&P 500 Index. As a swing trader, you should be alert for weakness in stocks.

As with the regular Fed Model, you can take this model one step further and calculate a *fair value* (what the fundamental analysis measures say the index *should* be trading at) of the underlying index by converting the yield on 10-year AA Corporate Bonds into a P/E ratio. A yield of 5.60 percent converts into a P/E of 17.86. To calculate the fair value, multiply the P/E of 17.86 by the expected earnings on the S&P 500 Index.

Assessing industry potential

Industries largely determine the profits of companies. Naturally, profits differ between Dell and Hewlett-Packard, but even larger differences exist between a grocery store chain and a PC manufacturer. Therefore, take special care in determining the attractiveness of an industry using fundamental characteristics.

You can identify which industries to focus on by looking at

  ✔ **Historical performance:** Certain industries tend to shine when the overall economy's growing; others sparkle when the overall economy's contracting. Technology stocks, for example, tend to do well when the economy is in its early or middle expansion period. Financial stocks tend to perform well in late contraction (as the economy emerges from a recession). For suggestions on how to find this historical information, flip to Chapter 9.

✔ **Industry fundamentals:** Just as you determine whether a stock is cheap or expensive based on items like P/E, return on equity, and expected earnings growth rates, so too can you value industries based on these same factors. The two best places to get this information are Yahoo! Finance (free) and *HGS Investor* software (paid).

Yahoo! Finance reports the following statistics on major industry groups (data from `biz.yahoo.com/p/s_conameu.html`):

- **1-day price change:** The percentage change of a security over one day.

- **Market capitalization:** The value of a firm as determined by its market price.

- **P/E:** A security's price divided by its earnings per share.

- **Return on equity:** A company's total profits during a year divided by shareholders' equity. This figure represents shareholders' "return" on their investment.

- **Dividend yield:** Total dividends paid in a year divided by the current share price. The dividend yield tells you how much return you can expect to make from the dividend payments.

- **Long-term debt to equity:** Dividing long-term debt by shareholders' equity tells you whether a company's capital structure is heavily leveraged.

- **Price to book value:** Market capitalization divided by book value. This figure measures how expensive or cheap a security is based on its net assets.

- **Net profit margin:** The amount of profit a company can squeeze out for every dollar of sale.

- **Price to free cash flow:** A company's market capitalization divided by its free cash flow during the last 12 months — or the amount of excess cash the company generates that it can use however it wants.

Price to free cash flow, which compares a company's market price to its level of annual free cash flow, is my favorite measure on an industry-wide basis. If you're looking to buy strong securities, search for industries that have low price to free cash flow ratios — as long as they're above zero. If you want to short weak securities, seek out price to free cash flow ratios that are high or negative. Negative free cash flow identifies industries in distress. Notice that in Figure 8-4, the financial sector has the lowest P/E among the major sectors — generally a good sign — but has a price to free cash flow ratio that's negative. This low ratio is a red flag that the earnings in the P/E ratio may be inaccurate.

Figure 8-4 is a snapshot taken from Yahoo! Finance that shows various fundamental measures for the major market sectors. As a swing trader, you want to choose sectors with low P/E, low price to free cash flow ratios, and high return on equity statistics.

Additional data sources such as *HGS Investor* software and the Daily Graphs service of *Investor's Business Daily* (both paid services) provide earnings growth rates on a sector or industry basis. You should examine this information because industries experiencing the highest earnings growth rates and trading at the lowest valuation levels tend to outperform industries with low earnings growth rates and/or high valuations. These specific vendors can also assist you in identifying promising industry groups ripe for swing trading. By using these fundamental criteria in conjunction with the economic cycle chart shown in Chapter 9 (and on the Cheat Sheet), you can determine which industry group is likely to perform best.

For example, look for industries with low price to free cash flow ratios that may present compelling opportunities. Also look for industries with expanding profit margins or higher-than-average earnings growth rates. Just make sure that the price action of the industry is in harmony with the fundamental measures. Otherwise, the apparent rally or weakness may be short-lived.

After identifying the strong or weak industry group you want to swing trade, drill down into the companies that make up that industry to find the most over- or undervalued candidate based on the Six Step Dance explained in Chapter 9

Figure 8-4:
This snapshot shows various fundamental measures on all major sectors.

Sector	1 Day Price Change %	Market Cap	P/E	ROE %	Div. Yield %	Long-Term Debt to Equity	Price to Book Value	Net Profit Margin % (mrq)	Price to Free Cash Flow (mrq)
Basic Materials	-2.15	5546.7B	16.69	22.83	2.04	0.48	4.49	12.93	-11.54
Conglomerates	-1.88	539.3B	17.40	19.70	3.00	2.98	13.95	11.00	590.90
Consumer Goods	-0.76	2479.1B	17.16	19.35	2.50	1.55	-51.94	7.85	14.34
Financial	-1.60	100175.6B	10.89	17.06	0.34	3.02	2.48	11.65	-17.51
Healthcare	-0.82	2190.1B	36.65	14.31	2.26	1.13	10.75	11.79	41.14
Industrial Goods	-1.62	1069.1B	18.79	17.87	1.60	0.83	13.57	6.35	31.42
Services	-0.76	2763.6B	25.84	13.97	1.81	1.68	-0.11	6.20	-26.83
Technology	-0.52	5004.7B	20.03	13.32	2.25	0.66	7.17	8.24	2.38
Utilities	-1.05	733.8B	18.15	12.88	3.39	1.56	2.78	8.24	467.30

Source: Yahoo! Finance

Starting from the Grassroots Level: The Bottom-Up Approach

The bottom-up approach is starkly different from the top-down approach, which I describe earlier in this chapter. Instead of beginning with the overall stock market and moving to the industry group, the *bottom-up approach* places less emphasis on overall economic cycles by beginning at the company level and working its way up. If you favor fundamental analysis over technical analysis or are trying to find promising long candidates in a weak market (or weak candidates in a strong market), you may favor the bottom-up approach over the top-down one.

The bottom-up approach usually begins with some type of screen, which you use to identify promising long and short candidates. Some screens are very liberal — they generate dozens of possible candidates, diluting the amount of time you can spend on any one. Other screens are very conservative — the criteria used are so stringent that you may have only five or six possible candidates to evaluate. Think of using a fundamentals-based screen as sifting for gold. A lot of garbage surrounds those valuable nuggets, and your job is to find them amid all the trash. In the following sections, I show you how to do just that.

Using screens to filter information

Fundamental screens can consider everything from earnings growth rates to average daily volume to analyst estimate changes. Sometimes this variety leads to information overflow, which may be discouraging if you're using a fundamental screen for the first time. Fortunately, because you create your own screen using the criteria *you* want to focus on, you don't need to bother with the premade, too-much-information batches vendors peddle to the public.

In addition to covering the general screening criteria to use, I delve into two screens on the long side: a growth-oriented screen and a value-oriented screen. I show you which criteria you really need to examine for each type of screen in order to sift effectively. **Note:** These screens are for illustrative purposes only to guide your development of your own screens.

Take advantage of both value and growth screens in your swing trading. When growth is outperforming value stocks, use the growth screen. And when value is what's in, focus on the value screen. Determine which is in the lead by plotting a ratio chart (explained in Chapter 6) of a growth and value index.

Figure 8-5 highlights the one-year and five-year returns for growth and value stocks in the large (Russell 1000), mid (Russell Mid Cap), and small (Russell 2000) cap arenas.

Notice the striking differences in returns. Over the five-year period ending December 31, 2006, the Russell 1000 Value Index (large cap value) generated an annualized return of 10.86 percent versus the Russell 1000 Growth Index's (large cap growth) 2.69 percent return. If you convert the annualized return (which is like an average return over the period) into a total return (how much the index rose in total over the five-year period), the figures look even more astonishing: The large cap value index rose 67.45 percent during the five years while the large cap growth index rose 14.19 percent.

Figure 8-5:
The one-year and five-year returns for growth and value stock indexes.

Periods ending: December 31, 2006		
Index Name	1 Year	5 Years
Large-Cap Indexes		
Russell 1000® Growth Index	9.07	2.69
Russell 1000® Value Index	22.25	10.86
Mid-Cap Indexes		
Russell Midcap® Growth Index	10.66	8.22
Russell Midcap® Value Index	20.22	15.88
Small-Cap Indexes		
Russell 2000® Growth Index	13.35	6.93
Russell 2000® Value Index	23.48	15.37

Source: Russell.com

You can see why knowing which horse is in the lead matters. When value's in favor, as it clearly was during these time periods, swing trading value stocks is like flying a plane with strong tailwinds. Swing trading growth stocks can be profitable as well, but the headwinds lower your overall return.

In 2007, for the first time in seven years, the winds blew in the other direction and growth stocks began to outperform value (see Figure 8-6). Whether this change is the beginning of a trend or a one-off event tied largely to the melt-down in the financial services sector (financial services make up the largest industry weighting in the value indexes) remains to be seen. But keeping tabs on these changes will place you in the right stocks.

Figure 8-6:
In 2007, growth stocks began to outperform value stocks for the first time in several years.

Periods ending: December 31, 2007	
Index Name	1 Year
Large-Cap Indexes	
Russell 1000® Growth Index	11.81
Russell 1000® Value Index	-0.17
Mid-Cap Indexes	
Russell Midcap® Growth Index	11.43
Russell Midcap® Value Index	-1.42
Small-Cap Indexes	
Russell 2000® Growth Index	7.05
Russell 2000® Value Index	-9.78

Source: Russell.com

What you should know about basic screening criteria

Before you start working with screens, you should note that value and growth screens tend to have similar characteristics. For example, both screens should exclude low-priced securities and securities that trade infrequently. When looking for candidates on the long side, they should both include a field for high return on equity.

A major difference between value and growth screens is that growth screens tend to focus on earnings growth rate fields, whereas value stocks focus on valuation metrics like P/E ratios. Additionally, some fields differ between the two. For example, low-priced stocks are often identified using the price to sales ratio. Growth stocks are rarely found using that measure.

Don't be surprised if you see the same fields in both growth and value stocks with different filter values. For instance, the return on equity criteria is present in both the value and growth screens, because return on equity is an important measure in all companies you buy or sell. The higher this statistic, the more profit the company is able to squeeze out from every dollar of equity.

When inputting your screening criteria, take care not to be on either the liberal or conservative extreme. You want your screen to capture companies from several industries, not just one that happens to be on hard times. If members of one industry group dominate a screen, one of your criteria is likely too strict. But you don't need every industry to be represented to have a good screen. When one industry is on hard times, then it may be understandable that few, if any, members of that group appear in screens identifying potential buy candidates.

When growth is on the rise

The important criteria to include in a growth screen include:

- **A share price measure:** This number allows you to exclude stocks trading below some value you input, such as $5 per share.

- **Average daily volume:** This part of the screen helps you avoid securities that trade a few hundred shares a day and are thus difficult to enter or exit. No doubt these securities hold opportunities, but I don't believe the potential return makes up for the risk.

Growth stocks typically reside in the technology, healthcare, and consumer discretionary sectors, but they can reside in other parts of the market as well. Following are the factors that characterize growth companies:

- Earnings growth rates above the market average (for example, above 25 percent)

- Sales growth rates above the market average (such as above 10 percent)

✔ New products and new management

✔ Low or no-dividend payment

✔ High price to book ratios

✔ Higher-than-average P/E

Use the growth screen when growth is outperforming value stocks. In constructing your growth screen, be restrictive enough that you have just a handful of companies to work from, but not so restrictive that you exclude potential opportunities.

Using a growth screen to find fast-growing companies

Growth stocks exhibit high earnings growth rates. Therefore, the following growth screen, which can be implemented with most popular screening programs, focuses on earnings growth recently and historically. Although the method of inputting these screening functions is largely dependent on the screening program you use, I recommend you always input these numbers:

✔ **Last closing share price ≥ $5:** I consider stocks below $5 to be penny stocks.

✔ **Average daily volume (last 50 days) ≥ 100,000 shares:** Unless you're trading $5 million or more, average daily volume of 100,000 shares with securities priced $5 or higher should allow you to get in and out without too much trouble.

✔ **Earnings per share (EPS) growth (most recent quarter versus year-ago quarter) ≥ 25 percent:** This is the figure recommended by William J. O'Neil, founder of *Investor's Business Daily.*

✔ **Annualized five-year historical EPS growth rate ≥ 10 percent:** O'Neil recommends this number as well.

✔ **Relative strength rating ≥ 80:** Another recommended figure from the *Investor's Business Daily* founder.

✔ **Return on equity ≥ 18 percent:** Based on my experience, 18 percent is the minimum return on equity I'd look for in companies I want to swing trade on the long side.

I consider these criteria to be important in growth stocks. The first two fields ensure that you're looking at liquid stocks that trade above $5 per share, which excludes penny stocks from your analysis. The next two focus on earnings growth rates: the lifeblood of the growth stock. The fifth field examines price performance relative to the overall market. (Growth stocks that you buy should be performing in the top 20 percent of the overall market.) The final criterion, the return on equity field, limits your analysis universe to companies that are being run well, meaning their earnings growth is driven by management effectiveness and not necessarily by overall industry fundamentals.

You may notice that valuation metrics aren't used in this screen. That's because growth stocks appear overvalued using traditional metrics like P/E or price to sales ratio (P/S). These metrics can be incorporated, if you want, to identify supposedly cheap growth stocks. For example, the previous screen can be amended to add a criterion that the P/E of a screened security is less than or equal to the P/E of the overall market.

Applying a growth screen when you want to short

If you're looking for high-priced stocks that exhibit poor price performance, consider using this type of screen. Many of the same criteria used in the preceding screen are the same. This one differs in that it looks for securities exhibiting strong negative earnings growth rates rather than positive ones. It also looks for companies with poor price performance (via the relative strength rating). Finally, this screen introduces a new field called "Earnings Surprise" to help you find companies that are disappointing Wall Street. Companies often release poor news slowly, which creates a "drip drop" effect. This is often found in companies with negative earnings surprises.

Following are the figures to use in a growth screen when you want to short:

- Last closing share price ≥ $5

- Average daily volume (last 50 days) ≥ 100,000 shares

- EPS growth (most recent quarter versus year-ago quarter) ≤ –25 percent

- P/E ≥ industry average

- Last quarter earnings surprise ≤ –10%

- Relative strength rating ≤ 20

The first two fields identify "tradable" securities trading above $5 per share with average daily volume of 100,000 shares or higher. The third criterion focuses on companies that have stubbed their feet — earnings growth was negative in the recent quarter, potentially signaling a worsening profit picture for coming quarters. But you want to short overvalued companies — and that's why the fourth criterion restricts your search to companies with P/E ratios above their industry average. The earnings surprise criterion helps you identify companies that aren't managing Wall Street expectations well. The final criterion indicates companies with poor price performance — a prerequisite for identifying shares of companies that are likely to fall.

When value is in vogue

Value stocks are characterized by low valuations, first and foremost. Value screens must home in on the valuation metric via popular statistics like P/E, PEG ratio, or the price to sales ratio (P/S). You don't emphasize earnings growth rates or sales growth in value stocks. Although finding a company with strong earnings growth rates makes a value stock that much more attractive, don't exclude a company for consideration (on the long side of the market) just because earnings may not be growing rapidly and, in fact, may be declining.

Using a value screen to find leading value stocks

A value screen is most helpful when value stocks are outperforming the market. Value stocks are characterized by their industries and their valuations relative to the overall market.

Here's a value screen you may use to focus on promising candidates by using the P/S valuation metric (remember, this is just one example, and one I recommend — you should experiment and develop your own screen for selecting securities):

- ✔ Last closing share price ≥ $5

- ✔ Average daily volume (last 50 days) ≥ 100,000 shares

- ✔ P/S ≤ 1.25

- ✔ Dividend yield ≥ 1.0%

- ✔ Return on equity ≥ 18%

- ✔ Relative strength rating ≥ 80

The first two fields restrict you to an investment universe that trades often and above $5 per share. The next ranking restricts you to so-called cheap securities, as measured by P/S. Value stocks often pay dividends, so I like to see some dividend payout. But beware of companies that pay dividends of 10 percent or more. These companies are often distressed and about to cut their dividend payments. Finally, the relative strength ranking helps ensure you concern yourself only with securities performing in the top 20 percent of the market. These securities tend to outperform the market in the near term.

Applying a value screen when you want to short

If you want to short value stocks, you can make some tweaks to the preceding screen. Now, you're looking for poor price performance rather than strong price performance. You're also searching for negative earnings surprises — a sign that the company is disappointing Wall Street and may continue to do so.

Following is the value screen to use when you want to short:

- ✔ Last closing share price ≥ $5

- ✔ Average daily volume (last 50 days) ≥ 100,000 shares

- ✔ P/S ≤ 1.25

✔ Dividend yield ≥ 1.0%

✔ Relative strength rating ≤ 20

✔ Last quarter earnings surprise ≤ –10%

The first four fields are unchanged from the value screen on the long side. These criteria narrow the universe of securities to actively traded value stocks. The final two criteria, however, identify value stocks that have faltered. A stock that sports a weak price rank (in the bottom 20 percent of the market) is a sign that the firm has fallen on hard times or that the valuation has gotten too extreme. A negative earnings surprise is another sign that the company is no longer able to meet Wall Street's expectations.

Assessing your screening results

After completing your screen, you need to have some kind of ranking system so you can focus on the most promising candidates first and work your way down. You can rank securities by their P/E ratios, for example, from lowest to highest if you're looking for swing trading candidates on the long side of the market. Or you can rank securities by their return on equity or price to free cash flow ratios. Ranking helps you push the cream to the top.

HGS Investor allows users to create "combo rankings," which allow ranking based on two or more measures (like 30 percent weight on EPS rank and 70 percent weight on P/E).

When identifying a promising swing trading candidate using a fundamental screen, the right security should jump out at you. You shouldn't have to do a lot of equivocating or questioning. Here's how to analyze your results:

✔ If the security is one you want to go long in, verify that it exhibits strong earnings, has a low valuation, and is in a well-performing industry.

✔ If you'd rather short the security, make sure it shows declining earnings growth, has a high valuation, and is in a poor-performing industry.

Deciding Which Approach to Use

Which approach should you use? As much as you may hate to hear it, this question doesn't have a right answer. The approach you choose is solely dependent on your style of trading. Do you prefer to identify the ripe industries that are poised to take off? If so, use the top-down approach. Do you enjoy developing screens and then examining the filtered results for promising candidates? In that case, use the bottom-up approach.

Fundamentals-based investors are usually bottom-up oriented. Swing traders and technical traders are often top-down oriented. However, a fundamentals-based trader can be top-down, and a technical swing trader can be bottom-up. *Remember:* There's no right or wrong way. The promising candidates are the ones that you find regardless of whether you begin with a top-down or bottom-up approach.

Ideally, a security you find by using the bottom-up approach can also be found by using a top-down approach. But employing both approaches simultaneously is complex and time consuming. Choose one and stick to it so that you perfect identifying promising industries (if you're a top-down type) or securities that are under- or overvalued on the grassroots level (if you're a bottom-up type).

Chapter 9

Six Tried-and-True Steps for Analyzing a Company's Stock

In This Chapter

▶ Getting familiar with the company you want to swing trade

▶ Examining its financial stability and earnings and sales data for clues to the bigger picture

▶ Seeing how the competition's share price measures up — relatively speaking

*A*nalyzing a company is kind of like going grocery shopping without a shopping list. You can go to the store and look around for what you want, but without having something in mind, you spend a great deal of time walking through aisles trying to think whether you need more of this or more of that. Taking a list along is much more efficient. You know what you need to get and are less likely to be swayed by impulse buys scattered throughout the store. (Why exactly are grocery stores selling DVDs en masse, anyway? Are Americans now buying their favorite movies and their deli meats at the same time?)

In this chapter, I clue you in to the Six Step Dance. Consider it your grocery list of what to look for when analyzing a stock you want to buy or sell. These six efficient, reliable steps aren't set in stone. I didn't pick them up from some secret society that holds the keys to the "right" way to evaluate companies. Instead, I offer you the process I use when looking at a potential investment and how to tell whether this method of analysis is right for you.

The Six Step Dance: Analyzing a Company

Forget the salsa or polka. The Six Step Dance isn't a real dance. It's actually a way to look at a company's fundamentals to quickly determine whether shares are over- or undervalued. Table 9-1 shows you how the Six Step Dance compares to three other analysis methods — forgoing fundamental analysis, analyzing stocks via EPS ranking, and using extensive modeling in *Microsoft Excel* — in terms of time efficiency, accuracy, and appropriateness for swing trading.

Note: Time isn't a luxury for a swing trader. Hence, the list in Table 9-1 isn't exhaustive. You're not going to have to call a company's suppliers or customers and inquire about their business operations. (I'm not even sure how much outperformance such an exercise would really add to an investment portfolio in the long run!)

Table 9-1	Comparing Fundamental Analysis Tactics		
Analysis Method	**Time Efficiency**	**Accuracy Level**	**Appropriate for**
No fundamental analysis	Very time-efficient	No accuracy	Day traders
EPS ranking	Very time-efficient	Average	Day and swing traders
Six Step Dance	Time-efficient	Above average	Swing traders
Extensive modeling	Not time-efficient	Most accurate	Long-term investors

If fundamental analysis isn't your cup of tea, you can forgo it at your own peril. Forgoing fundamental analysis entirely is time-efficient because it requires no time on your part with regard to studying what makes a company tick. But because you have no yardstick to measure with, you've no idea whether the shares of a company you buy are expensive or cheap. This approach is most appropriate for day traders. Day traders trade on news, volume, and momentum. They pay little attention to a company's earnings, balance sheet, or competitive position in the industry.

Earnings per share (EPS) ranking is also time-efficient but with the added benefit of being somewhat accurate when it comes to selecting securities. Day and swing traders can benefit from incorporating EPS ranks into their trading.

Extensive modeling is what Wall Street analysts do. They spend hours poring over 10Ks, 10Qs, and other SEC filings and use *Microsoft Excel* to forecast financial statements three to five years into the future. They call competitors, suppliers, and end customers to understand how a company's products are selling in the marketplace. They even visit the company and speak with management. The accuracy level's high here. But as I show you in Chapter 7, that doesn't mean analysts draw the right conclusions in their recommendations.

The Six Step Dance falls somewhere in the middle of the bunch shown in Table 9-1. It's time-efficient after you get up to speed on how to do it. The analysis of your first few companies using this method is a slow process, but you should be able to quickly review a company by using the Six Step Dance before too long.

You don't need to run through all six steps for every company that crosses your desk. Many companies will fail one or two of the steps and be thrown out of your trading idea box. You're not an analyst with a deadline to meet for your portfolio manager; you *are* the portfolio manager. Use your time wisely and address all the key points before you enter a trade, and you'll be able to quickly go through a list of companies and exclude those that just don't have promising fundamentals.

Taking a Company's Industry into Account

A company's potential profits depend on the nature of its industry. For example, some companies require significant start-up costs to launch. Think about how expensive it'd be to enter the commercial airline market. Today, Boeing and Airbus make nearly all commercial aircraft. To launch your own commercial airline business, you'd have to have billions of dollars to research, design, produce, and market planes. The costs of entering the food service business, on the other hand, are much lower. That's why Tommy from down the street can have a lemonade stand. These cost considerations play into the economics of a sector, which determine how much profit potential companies within that sector have.

The first step in your stock analysis is to understand the nature of the industry in which a company operates. Peter Lynch, the legendary Fidelity fund manager, quips in his book that he'd never invest in a company that can't be explained by a child with crayons. Similarly, Warren Buffett never invests in a company he can't understand, which is one reason he didn't participate in the technology boom of the 1990s. (Then again, he didn't participate in the crash of 2000, either. In fact, Buffett's company, Berkshire Hathaway, actually bottomed the same month the Nasdaq peaked in March of 2000.)

Swing traders don't have to be so strict. I'm not asking you to buy crayon kits or swear off technology investments. But understanding or having insight into an industry can help you better trade stocks in that market.

The bottom line in analyzing the nature of a company's industry is to follow four steps:

1. **Understand how the company makes profits.**

   Does it profit by selling a commodity or by selling business services? The former is tied to the economy, whereas the latter may be growth-oriented.

2. **Determine whether the industry is growth- or value-oriented.**

   This way, you have an idea of whether valuations are average, above average, or below average.

3. **Find out what rate of earnings growth is expected for the industry as a whole in the coming three to five years.**

4. **Determine which stage the economy is in.**

Economic cycles affect sector performance, so recognizing the relative strength or weakness of the economy at any given time is essential.

Scoping out markets you're familiar with

Swing trading companies in industries you know can pay off handsomely. For example, if you're an avid gamer or have a child who plays video games, then you probably know that the Nintendo Wii is scoring massive success and out-selling its rivals. Shares of Nintendo rose 500 percent between 2006 and 2007 on the success of that console.

Not convinced? Consider the portable music player industry and then look at Apple's iPod. These puppies flew off the shelves from 2003 through 2007. As a result, shares of Apple rose 1,700 percent between 2004 and 2007.

Don't think that just because your time horizon's measured in days or weeks that you can't benefit from trends that last years. A savvy swing trader buys the dips of shares of super-successful companies like Nintendo or Apple and sells the mania.

Identifying what type of sector a company is in

Every company caters to a specific market sector. As part of the Six Step Dance, you want to first identify whether the company you're looking at falls into the *growth sector* (characterized by above-average valuations and growth rates relative to the overall market) or the *value sector* (characterized by below-average valuations and growth rates relative to the overall market). Following are the industries I classify as growth industries:

- **Consumer cyclical:** This sector includes retailers, homebuilders, auto and clothing manufacturers, cable companies, and other businesses that cater to the general consumer.

- **Healthcare:** Pharmaceutical and biotech companies, HMOs, and medical instrument manufacturers are just some of the businesses that fall within this niche sector.

✔ **Information technology:** This market area is composed of software developers and computer and semiconductor manufacturers, among others.

✔ **Telecommunications:** Cellular service providers, fiber optic wire/cable manufacturers, and cellphone manufacturers are just some of the telecom companies you may encounter.

And here are the industries that I group into the value sector:

✔ **Consumer staples:** This category is made up of businesses such as grocery stores, food producers, beverage manufacturers, and cosmetic companies.

✔ **Energy:** Drilling companies, integrated energy firms, explorers and producers, and equipment manufacturers all work within the energy industry.

✔ **Financials:** This market area includes banking companies, Real Estate Investment Trusts (REITs), investment banks, insurance companies, mortgage lenders, and so on.

✔ **Capital goods:** Aerospace and defense companies, railroad businesses, farming product and heavy equipment manufacturers, and others meet the needs of this category.

✔ **Basic materials:** This industry involves chemical specialty companies, paper and steel manufacturers, and related businesses.

✔ **Utilities:** The electric and gas utilities you use daily belong in this group.

Sectors perform differently depending on the economic cycle. Figure 9-1 shows the sectors that tend to perform best depending on the stage the economy is in.

Figure 9-1: Market sectors perform differently depending on the stage of the economic cycle.

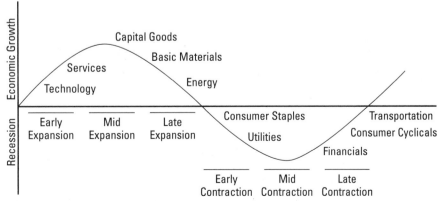

Companies in growth sectors usually earn higher P/E ratios than companies in value sectors. Value sectors often feature companies that pay higher dividend yields than companies in growth sectors. There's no right sector to be in. If anything, different sectors are right to be in at different times.

Be aware that market sectors determine firms' valuations. For example, electric utilities aren't known for their earnings growth potential. So don't exclude an electric utility from consideration simply because it doesn't meet some absolute level of earnings growth you specify. Analyze companies on a curve based on their industry. Otherwise, you may be comparing apples and oranges. A 15 percent growth rate for a technology firm can look amazing when compared to a grocery store chain, but such a comparison isn't fair.

Just because a sector is a value sector doesn't necessarily mean that sector can't grow earnings at eye-popping rates. Consider the energy sector. For much of the '90s, the energy sector was a classic value sector with companies priced at below-average P/E ratios when compared to the market index. But when energy prices began a magnificent climb early in the 21st century, the energy sector transformed — temporarily — into a growth sector. So seeing energy companies trading at 25 times earnings (a P/E ratio usually reserved for high-growth technology companies) isn't unreasonable, because earnings growth rates are up significantly. But in the long term, the energy sector is a value sector.

Just because a sector is marked as value doesn't mean profits in that sector will be less than profits in a growth sector. When growth is out of favor, value sectors shine.

Quick and dirty analysis for fundamental-analysis-phobes

Don't like the idea of fundamental analysis? Are you a chart reader at heart? If you answer yes to either question, then get excited because this sidebar's going to brighten your day.

Some swing traders care about just one factor: the ticker tape. They don't care about what a company does, what it sells, how it makes its money, and the like. That knowledge, they may argue, isn't going to make them more money when their time horizon's measured in days.

Such an argument is half-right. The shorter your time horizon, the more noise inherent in the movement of a security's price. So a company with amazing fundamentals may still see stock-price depreciation in the short term. The returns of such companies may be realized only by holding for months or — gulp — years. However, this argument ignores the fact that strong, sustained moves in security prices are fundamentally driven. And having a working knowledge of the fundamentals means you're more likely to catch these strong moves with legs. If you only focus on the ticker tape, you aren't able to distinguish short-term blips from a strong trend that's likely to take prices higher quickly.

The solution to this quandary is the earnings per share (EPS) rank, which tells you how a particular company's earnings compare to the rest of the market's earnings. The ranking appears each day for all stocks that trade on the Nasdaq and both the New York and American Stock Exchanges. It can be found in a second (so it's not time consuming to incorporate into your analysis), but still provides a yardstick to measure a firm's fundamentals relative to the overall market.

Created by *Investor's Business Daily* founder William J. O'Neil, EPS rank compares a company's earnings per share growth in the last two quarters and over the last three to five years with all publicly traded companies in the William O'Neil database. Another company that publishes an EPS ranking is *High Growth Stock Investor (HGS Investor),* a top-down software product that provides quantitative and fundamental data on publicly traded stocks. Like *Investor's Business Daily,* the EPS ranking of *HGS Investor* compares a firm's earnings to all other publicly traded companies in the market. *HGS Investor* computes its EPS ranking by analyzing improvement in a firm's earnings (by looking at the slope or rate of change of earnings) over the past three years.

The EPS ranking system isn't perfect, but it provides a quick snapshot of a company's financial health. Earnings ultimately drive stock prices, and the stronger a company's earnings growth, the faster its shares will appreciate. EPS rank is standardized on a 99-point scale, so the higher, the better. A ranking of 99 means that the security's earnings per share growth outperformed 99 percent of all publicly traded companies. Conversely, a ranking of 1 means that the company's earnings per share growth outperformed just 1 percent of all publicly traded companies.

Look for companies with EPS rankings of 80 or more, which allows you to home in on the top 20 percent of the securities in the market. If you're looking for securities with falling stock prices that you'd like to short, then focus on stocks with EPS rankings of 20 or less. These stocks are the scum of the market, so to speak, and are likely to see poor share-price performance.

If push comes to shove and you find yourself uninterested in analyzing companies from a fundamental level, then at the very least use the EPS ranking. This single number conveys a lot of useful information about a company and can help guide you in your trades. Just don't think of it as a silver bullet.

An innate disadvantage of EPS ranking compared to more in-depth analysis methods is that it naturally favors growth-oriented securities over value-oriented securities. It says a lot about how well a company has grown its earnings relative to the entire market but not much about whether the shares of that company are under- or overvalued.

EPS ranking also ignores some key financial measures that are important to determining whether shares of a company are worth buying or avoiding. For example, a company's *return on equity* (an important statistic that says how effective management is, which I cover in Chapter 8) isn't directly reflected in an EPS ranking.

Determining a Company's Financial Stability

A financially stable company generates cash from its operations, which it can use to fund its own growth. This type of company has little or no debt on its balance sheet and pays little interest to creditors. Without the burden of debt on its shoulders, a fiscally sound company can seize investment opportunities more readily than a company dealing with massive debt.

But if you're looking for companies that depreciate in value, financial *instability* is your ticket. Such companies struggle to meet interest payments on debt and may only make in profits a few times what their interest expense is for the period. For example, Struggling Inc. may have such a major debt burden that the interest on its debt is 25 or 50 percent of its total profits. If it makes $5 million, it may pay out $2.5 million in interest on debt. This is the type of company most likely to fail if business turns sour.

Whether you're looking for long or short ideas, financial stability plays an important role in selecting candidates. In the next few sections, I break down the three ratios that can give you a quick feel for whether a company is financially stable.

Current ratio

The *current ratio* compares short-term assets to short-term debts and measures how well a company can meet its near-term liabilities with its near-term assets. This commonly used ratio helps answer the question, "Will this company have any difficulty surviving over the next 12 months?" Just because a company has more near-term liabilities than near-term assets doesn't mean it has to file for bankruptcy. It can instead take out a long-term loan to meet its near-term obligations, for example.

Financially sound companies have current ratios of 1.5 or higher. You can't draw any significance from a very large number, say 5 or 6. But when swing trading on the long side, home in on current ratios above 1.5. On the short side, consider companies with current ratios below that, because these companies may be facing near-term pressures.

Debt to shareholders' equity ratio

The *debt to shareholders' equity ratio* (or *debt to equity ratio* for short) gives you insight on how a company finances assets via equity and debt — referred to as capital structure. The higher the debt to equity ratio, the more leveraged the company is. Two firms generating identical profits have different efficiency ratios (such as return on equity, covered in Chapter 8) if they use different amounts of debt.

Think of the matter this way: Two traders, Salma and Allen, begin the year with a $50,000 swing-trading account. Salma trades throughout the year and earns a 20 percent return on her account to end the year with $60,000. Allen, on the other hand, decides to use a margin account, borrowing $50,000 from his broker. He too earns 20 percent on his account. However, he ends the year at $70,000 rather than $60,000. A 20 percent return on $100,000 yields him $10,000 more than Salma's 20 percent return on her $50,000 account.

Such a benefit can turn into heartache because *leverage,* the amount of debt a company uses, can distort financial ratios. When all's well, one company may look more efficient than another. But when the situation turns sour, your sunshine-filled day can turn cloudy fast. Had that 20 percent return in the preceding example been a 20 percent loss, Salma would be at $40,000 at year-end. Allen, on the other hand, would be staring at a $30,000 account, a $20,000 loss from his initial investment.

When you swing trade on the long side, look for companies that aren't highly leveraged. I prefer to see a debt to equity ratio no higher than 30 percent. Some swing traders disagree with my viewpoint; they see highly leveraged companies as having high profit potential. Although that may be true, such traders are also exposing themselves to bigger potential losers.

Whichever view you take, realize that restricting yourself to low-leverage companies may exclude some industries from investment. For example, homebuilders are typically highly leveraged. I personally forgo such industries so I can sleep better at night.

Conversely, look for highly leveraged companies when you want to swing trade short. Losses can multiply for such companies when business turns down. I view a company as being highly leveraged when it has a debt to equity ratio above 50 percent.

Interest coverage ratio

The *interest coverage ratio* measures how well a company covers the interest payments on its outstanding debt. The quickest way to bankruptcy is to stop meeting the terms of your outstanding debts, and the interest coverage ratio tells you whether a company is in danger of falling behind on its interest payments by comparing two figures:

- A company's *earnings before interest and taxes* (EBIT)
- A company's interest expense

You compare EBIT because interest expense is viewed as part of the cost of doing business. Hence, a company can use pretax money to make interest payments. Check out the formula for the interest coverage ratio:

$$\text{Interest Coverage Ratio} = \frac{\text{Earnings Before Interest and Taxes (EBIT)}}{\text{Interest Expense}}$$

Financially healthy companies should have an interest coverage ratio of 5 or higher, depending on the industry. Again, the exact "healthy" figure depends on the industry. But requiring a high ratio (when you're trading the long side) protects you if conditions turn sour. Financially unhealthy companies have an interest coverage ratio of 2 or less.

You can pull both items in the interest coverage ratio from a company's income statement, but more often than not, you can obtain the ratio for free from a Web site. I recommend the finance section of Reuters for a summary of key ratios on thousands of publicly traded stocks (see www.reuters.com/finance). This site also compares the financial ratios of one company to its industry's ratios to help you determine whether a company's interest coverage or debt levels are in line with its industry.

Want an example of how you can use the interest coverage ratio? As you can see in Figure 9-2, Toll Brothers, a homebuilder, has an interest coverage ratio of 3.55, below my threshold of 5. Notice also that Toll Brothers's interest coverage ratio is well below its industry and sector. These factors reinforce the view that the company is experiencing near-term difficulties. If you were looking to swing trade Toll Brothers on the long side, this chart should convince you to consider other companies. Alternatively, this chart may be a sign that Toll Brothers is worth pursuing if you're looking for a short candidate.

Figure 9-2:
A low interest coverage ratio is a red flag for Toll Brothers.

Ratios

Toll Brothers Inc TOL (NYSE)

FINANCIAL STRENGTH

	Company	Industry	Sector	S&P 500
Quick Ratio (MRQ)	NM	1.40	0.98	1.23
Current Ratio (MRQ)	NM	1.73	1.66	1.74
LT Debt to Equity (MRQ)	0.64	0.39	0.73	0.56
Total Debt to Equity (MRQ)	0.64	0.43	0.97	0.72
Interest Coverage (TTM)	3.55	16.45	14.81	13.46

Source: Reuters Finance

Looking Back at Historical Earnings and Sales Growth

You've heard it a dozen times: Past performance isn't indicative of future results. But don't tell that to Patrick Henry, the American revolutionary remembered for crying, "Give me liberty or give me death!" As far as I know, Patrick Henry wasn't a swing trader. But he did say something that can apply to analyzing companies' fundamentals: "I have no way of judging the future but by the past."

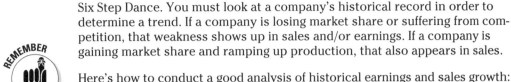

Analyzing a company's historical sales and earnings is the third part of the Six Step Dance. You must look at a company's historical record in order to determine a trend. If a company is losing market share or suffering from competition, that weakness shows up in sales and/or earnings. If a company is gaining market share and ramping up production, that also appears in sales.

Here's how to conduct a good analysis of historical earnings and sales growth:

1. **Examine a company's sales and earnings growth over the last several years.**

2. **Get a feel for whether the company is mature (growing sales and earnings at a low rate) or growing (increasing both sales and earnings at double digits).**

3. **Compare growth rates across the industry so you know whether the company deserves to be awarded a higher multiple than its competition.**

   Avoid companies with negative sales or earnings growth if you're going long. Steer clear of companies with positive sales or earnings growth if you're going short.

Fortunately, this analysis can be done visually (after all, a picture's worth a thousand words) or quantitatively. Relax, you don't have to acquaint yourself with another formula on what constitutes good or poor results. Regardless of the direction of growth, a company may be over- or undervalued depending on what market multiple it trades at or what cash flow it generates.

If a company's experiencing growth, you need to figure out whether that growth is accelerating, slowing down, or holding steady. A company undergoing accelerated growth is often awarded a market multiple above its industry — as long as that growth outpaces the industry average. On the other hand, a company facing declining earnings or sales — at a time when the industry is growing — is often awarded a market multiple below its industry.

Be sure to review at least three years' worth of sales and earnings growth. William J. O'Neil of *Investor's Business Daily* recommends looking for companies with an earnings growth rate of at least 25 percent in the previous two quarters (when compared to the year-ago periods) and an annual earnings growth rate of 25 percent throughout the last three years.

I certainly like to see such growth in the companies I'm looking to swing trade on the long side. But I don't exclude a company solely because it doesn't have that minimum 25 percent earnings growth rate. My yardstick is to find companies growing earnings at a faster pace than the industry.

Earnings growth can't continue indefinitely if sales remain constant. The type of sales growth I look for depends on a company's size. The larger the company, the more I allow for lower levels of sales growth. Growing sales 25 percent when total sales are $10 million is much easier to do than growing sales 25 percent when total sales are $10 billion.

On the short side, you want to see deterioration in both sales and earnings. A company losing market share is often reluctant to admit its position until after everyone knows. Accelerating weakness is especially bearish because the extent of the decline is unknown until it flattens out. And even then, there's no guarantee it'll rise again.

Examining both sales and earnings pays off. Consider the income statement of Vonage (symbol: VG) from 2002 through 2006. During that period, Vonage grew sales from $1 million to $607 million — now that's remarkable growth! So surely Vonage was a steal to buy, right? Not when you look at the bottom line: net income. During that same period, Vonage's losses increased from $13 million to $339 million, and the company's stock price fell from $17 per share when the stock was issued in 2006 to $2 per share by the end of 2007, as shown in Figure 9-3.

Income Statement

Vonage Holdings Corp VG (NYSE)

Annual Income Statement					View: Income Statement ⊙ Annual ○ Quarterly
In Millions of U.S. Dollars (except for per share items)	**2006** 12/31/06	**2005** 12/31/05	**2004** 12/31/04	**2003** 12/31/03	**2002** 12/31/02
Total Revenue	607	269	80	19	1
Cost of Revenue, Total	286	124	42	13	2
Sell/General/Admin. Expenses,Total	638	398	105	31	10
Depreciation/Amortization	24	11	4	2	1
Total Operating Expense	948	534	151	47	13
Operating Income	(340)	(265)	(72)	(28)	(12)
Interest Expense, Net Non-Operating	(20)	(1)	0	(1)	0
Inter/Invest Inc, Non-Oper	21	4	1	0	0
Interest Income (Exp), Net Non-Operating	2	3	1	(1)	0
Other, Net	0	0	0	(2)	0
Net Income Before Taxes	(339)	(262)	(70)	(30)	(13)
Provision for Income Taxes	0	0	0	0	0
Net Income After Taxes	(339)	(261)	(70)	(30)	(13)
Net Income Before Extra. Items	(339)	(261)	(70)	(30)	(13)
Net Income	(339)	(261)	(70)	(30)	(13)

Figure 9-3: Snapshot of VG's income statement from 2002 through 2006.

Source: Reuters Finance

Understanding Earnings and Sales Expectations

Wall Street values companies based on future income projections, not past income results. So another critical step in your stock analysis is examining what a company is likely to earn in the future.

The good news is that a "right" figure for future growth simply doesn't exist. A company can report an earnings growth rate of 100 percent during a quarter versus the year-ago period and still see its stock price tumble like there's no tomorrow — if Wall Street expected 150 percent earnings growth.

For better or worse, Wall Street analysts estimate a company's future earnings and sales by meeting with management, talking to competitors, building elaborate models only they can understand, and flipping a coin. (I'm only half joking.) Analysts often estimate earnings in the same range to avoid the embarrassment that comes if an estimate's far off the market. After all, if they're wrong together, they have an excuse. But if one analyst is way off and everyone else is on target, that analyst may have some explaining to do. But you don't have to go through all that trouble. Instead, you can let the analysts do the heavy lifting to give you a ballpark figure from which you can work. Talk about a home run!

Whenever you use analysts' estimates, you want to know whether they can give you an idea of a company's sales or earnings trend. (Is it rising or falling? Is it increasing or decreasing?) That's why I recommend using these so-called expert estimates in conjunction with the history of a company's earnings surprises.

The *earnings surprise history* helps you determine whether the analysts over-anchored their analysis. *Anchoring* is a behavioral finance term that refers to an individual's tendency to anchor beliefs on some reference point. For example, analyst Martha may believe that Dell is the undisputed PC seller in the world. But when Dell announces a lousy quarter and Hewlett-Packard — a chief rival to Dell — reports an excellent one, analyst Martha may be tempted to retain her old belief that Dell is still the leader and may have just stumbled temporarily. It may take three or four quarters of results before analyst Martha finally catches onto the trend and adjusts her models to reflect the new reality — perhaps just before the trend changes again!

An earnings surprise history table compares a firm's actual reported earnings to the *consensus* (or average) estimate of Wall Street. A company that reports earnings of $1.10 per share when Wall Street expected earnings of $1.00 per share surprises Wall Street by 10 cents per share, or 10 percent. Some Web sites (like the finance section of Reuters) report the absolute difference between the actual results and the estimates, whereas others (like Yahoo! Finance) report the actual and percentage difference.

Earnings surprise histories are extremely important in swing trading. Because earnings estimates represent Wall Street's consensus estimates on sales and earnings going forward, the consistent over- or underestimating of sales or earnings is very telling. An inconsistent pattern has little significance.

When analyzing Wall Street's estimates of earnings and sales, practice the following:

1. Determine the trend and the slope of the trend.

For example, is the slope increasing or decreasing?

2. Examine the earnings surprise history.

You want to see whether analysts are consistently underestimating (positive surprises) or overestimating (negative surprises) a company's sales and earnings.

Although seeing increasing or decreasing surprises (depending on whether you want to go long or short) is great, don't place that requirement on the earnings surprise history, because doing so is somewhat burdensome.

Figure 9-4 shows the earnings and sales surprise history of Merck Company (symbol: MRK) over five quarters: September 2006 through September 2007. Notice how analysts consistently underestimated sales (and earnings, to a lesser extent) throughout the five quarters. This consistent underestimation is a clue that shares of Merck are probably mispriced. Shares of Merck returned more than 32 percent in 2007.

Estimates

Merck & Co Inc MRK (NYSE)

HISTORICAL SURPRISES

Estimates vs. Actual

In USD	Estimates	Actual	Difference	
Revenue (in Millions)				
Q3: 09/2007	6,032.74	6,074.10	41.36	Consistent
Q2: 06/2007	5,794.47	6,111.40	316.93	positive
Q1: 03/2007	5,440.76	5,769.40	328.64	surprises
Q4: 12/2006	5,351.23	6,044.20	692.97	
Q3: 09/2006	4,957.88	5,410.40	452.53	
EPS				
Q3: 09/2007	0.69	0.75	0.06	
Q2: 06/2007	0.72	0.82	0.10	
Q1: 03/2007	0.84	0.84	0.00	
Q4: 12/2006	0.51	0.50	-0.01	
Q3: 09/2006	0.50	0.51	0.01	

Figure 9-4: A quarterly earnings and sales surprise history of MRK.

Source: Reuters Finance

Checking Out the Competition

No company is an island. It competes with other firms in its industry. Understanding who the other players are and their fundamentals gives you insight on whether shares you're trading are cheap or dear. That's why you always want to examine a company's competitors and understand how they differ from it.

Companies in the same industry tend to benefit and suffer together, because the forces that affect all firms in an industry are usually the same. The key is understanding how the firms within the industry differ.

This essential part of the Six Step Dance is all about classifying the way in which the company you're swing trading is distinguishing itself. You can generally sort a company's stand-out-from-the-pack strategy into one of these four bins:

- **Cost-leadership strategy:** The cost-leadership company strives to be the lowest-cost producer in the industry. Often, it achieves this status by employing economies of scale or by being large enough to spread costs across a broad number of items in order to lower prices. Of course, the cost leader's products must be similar to higher-priced products in the market. No cost leader can simply offer cheap items that are clearly inferior to what consumers can purchase elsewhere. Good examples of cost leaders are Wal-Mart and Southwest Airlines.

- **Differentiator strategy:** A differentiator strives to offer a better product than others in its industry and usually charges a premium price for that product. Tiffany & Co. is a classic differentiator company.

- **Cost-focus strategy:** A company pursuing a cost-focus strategy tries to offer the lowest prices on a narrow part of the industry. A company that manufactures cheap memory for PCs, for example, practices cost focus.

- **Differentiator-focus strategy:** A company pursuing a differentiator focus attempts to offer a superior product in some aspect of quality for a narrow subset of the market. NVIDIA, a premium graphics chip maker, employs the differentiator-focus strategy by offering graphics cards aimed at gamers and graphic designers.

You can sometimes tell which strategy a company is pursuing by examining three key profit margins: gross profit margins, operating margins, and net profit margins. If a company can charge a premium price for its products, it tends to earn higher margins (on all three measures) than its competitors. (Flip to Chapter 7 for a refresher on profit margins.)

Figure 9-5 shows a competitor analysis of four companies in the computer industry: Apple Inc. (symbol: AAPL), Dell Computer (symbol: DELL), Hewlett-Packard (symbol: HPQ), and Microsoft (symbol: MSFT). Because Microsoft isn't a computer manufacturer, its comparisons aren't as meaningful as the other three companies. But I'm going to take a look at the following anyway to determine which strategy each company is following:

- **Gross margins:** Apple and Microsoft have the highest gross margins of the lot at 33.97 percent and 78.41 percent, respectively. Microsoft is a software firm with lower production costs, which is why its gross margin is so much higher than the rest of the companies in this analysis. But you can immediately tell that both Apple and Microsoft are charging more for their products than Dell or Hewlett-Packard. This move is consistent with a differentiator strategy.

✔ **Operating margins:** Apple and Microsoft also have higher operating margins than the other competitors at 18.37 percent and 37.87 percent, respectively.

✔ **Net profit margins:** This table doesn't explicitly list the net profit margins of the four companies, but it does provide sufficient data to calculate these margins. (***Remember:*** Net profit margins are equal to net income divided by sales. Of the three margins listed here, net profit margins are the most important.) If you calculate the net profit margins for the four companies, you find that Apple and Microsoft have the highest of the bunch at 14.58 percent and 27.52 percent, respectively.

Pay close attention to profit margins, especially relative profit margins. The Motley Fool Web site (www.fool.com) recommends buying stocks of companies with net profit margins of 10 percent or more. I agree with this rule as a generality, but you should recognize that different industries have different forces that may inhibit a company from realizing such high margins.

Competitors in the PC Industry

DIRECT COMPETITOR COMPARISON	AAPL	DELL	HPQ	MSFT	Industry
Market Cap:	151.20B	46.52B	115.82B	317.24B	46.52B
Employees:	21,600	83,300	172,000	79,000	21.60K
Qtrly Rev Growth (yoy):	28.50%	8.50%	15.20%	27.30%	2.70%
Revenue (ttm):	24.01B	59.61B	104.29B	54.07B	24.01B
Gross Margin (ttm):	33.97%	18.75%	24.36%	78.41%	33.97%
EBITDA (ttm):	4.73B	4.11B	11.48B	22.07B	4.11B
Oper Margins (ttm):	18.37%	5.97%	8.42%	37.87%	5.62%
Net Income (ttm):	3.50B	2.99B	7.26B	14.88B	2.99B
EPS (ttm):	3.931	1.325	2.677	1.524	1.33
P/E (ttm):	43.93	15.67	16.81	22.25	34.34
PEG (5 yr expected):	1.53	1.18	0.94	1.49	1.53
P/S (ttm):	6.49	0.79	1.12	5.94	0.78

DELL = Dell Inc.
HPQ = Hewlett-Packard Co.
MSFT = Microsoft Corporation
Industry = Personal Computers

Figure 9-5:
Snapshot of the fundamentals for AAPL, DELL, HPQ, and MSFT.

Source: Yahoo! Finance

Valuing a Company's Shares

Valuing a company's shares may be the single most important part of the Six Step Dance. Although you can value a company in several extensive ways, this step focuses on relative valuation models, which are the poor man's valuation choice (perhaps that's a poor choice of words — oops! that too). A relative model doesn't answer the question, "How much is this company worth to the penny?" Instead, it answers the question, "Relative to its competitors, are shares of this company properly valued?"

So to end your stock analysis dance with high marks (and a wealth of knowledge to make the right decision for your swing trading), here's what to do:

1. **Gauge whether shares of the company you want to swing trade are cheap or expensive relative to that company's competitors.**

2. **Analyze whether the relative cheapness or expensiveness is justified by reviewing expected earnings growth rates.**

I break down the nitty-gritty of these two essential steps in the next couple sections.

Gauging shares' relative cheapness or expensiveness

Determining whether the shares of a company you're looking to swing trade are cheap or expensive relative to its competitors is essential. Realize that this question is different than asking what the market capitalization of the company is. Just because a company's worth $10 billion doesn't mean it's more expensive, on a relative basis, than a company worth $1 billion. The $10 billion company may be cheaper, for example, when earnings are compared at market value.

So how do you go about figuring out this relative value? By using the most accessible valuation metric — the price to earnings ratio (P/E) — in combination with other popular ratio metrics such as price to sales (P/S), price to cash flow, and *PEG* (P/E divided by the expected earnings growth rate). Each ratio has its pros and cons, which is why you need to use more than one when valuing a company.

Time to meet the ratio tools in your valuation toolbox:

- ✔ **P/E:** Calculate P/E by dividing a firm's share price by the trailing 12 months of earnings per share. A forward P/E is a firm's share price divided by the expected earnings per share in the coming 12 months. P/E is a popular metric because earnings drive market prices.

  P/E can easily be distorted on the positive or negative side. For example, a company may take a large one-time charge, which lowers its earnings per share temporarily. If you don't back that charge out, you may value shares of the company incorrectly. That's why you should always try multiple valuation techniques.

- ✔ **Price to cash flow:** I consider this ratio the most important one after P/E. Cash flow, like sales, is difficult to manipulate through accounting shenanigans. This ratio divides the market capitalization of a company by trailing 12 month cash flows (taken from the cash flow statement, which I cover in Chapter 7).

- ✔ **PEG:** Also known as the price/earnings to growth ratio, this is the only ratio that incorporates a firm's growth rate into its calculation. I rank PEG closely behind the price to cash flow measure. You can calculate it by dividing a firm's P/E by its annual EPS growth rate. A company trading at 20 times earnings but growing earnings at 30 percent per year would sport a PEG of 0.67.

- ✔ **P/S:** The P/S helps you value a company that doesn't have earnings. This ratio is equal to a company's market capitalization divided by total sales. Like P/E, P/S is widely reported. Sales are more difficult to manipulate than earnings (U.S. accounting rules notwithstanding), but they aren't a helpful metric if a company's unable to translate them into earnings. For example, Vonage Holdings (look back at Figure 9-3) had a superb P/S that kept on getting better because the company grew sales while it bled losses.

Use P/S sparingly and always within a single industry.

For all four ratios, know that the lower the number, the cheaper the stock.

Figuring out whether the comparative share-price difference is justified

After you know how cheap or expensive a company's stock is based on the four common valuation metrics (see the preceding section for details), you're ready to determine whether that relative cheapness or expensiveness is justified. Peter Lynch, the legendary fund manager, posits that a company should trade for a similar rate as its P/E. A company growing earnings 15 percent, for example, deserves to trade at 15 times earnings.

I agree with this postulation. You can determine a company's growth rate by examining expected earnings growth rates. Just consider the case of popular search engine company Google (symbol: GOOG), which has been one of the hardest companies to value. Every new high it made was followed by calls from analysts saying that shares simply couldn't go any higher. But guess what? Shares of Google rose some more!

Could you have swing traded Google shares on the long side using a valuation technique that called for shares of Google to trade at roughly the same level of its growth rate? At the end of 2007, Google's shares traded for 50 times earnings. Meanwhile, the industry traded at 40 times earnings. With such a premium, shares of Google must be overvalued, right?

Not necessarily. Figure 9-6 provides a snapshot of Google's fundamentals at the end of 2007 (all data used in this description has been circled). Although Google's P/E is 24.6 percent higher than the industry's P/E, Google's historical sales growth is 45.8 percent higher than the industry's. Also, Google's historical EPS growth is 23 percent higher than its industry. By those measures, Google doesn't look expensive relative to its industry. Analysts estimate that Google's earnings per share will grow 33 percent annually throughout the next five years. If that's true, Google's shares should trade at 33 times earnings, all else being equal.

Ratios

Google Inc GOOG.O (NASDAQ)

VALUATION RATIOS

	Company	Industry	Sector	S&P 500
P/E Ratio (TTM)	49.93	40.08	26.95	19.70
P/E High - Last 5 Yrs.	NM	38.17	47.86	33.19
P/E Low - Last 5 Yrs.	NM	15.74	18.05	15.45
Beta	1.36	1.27	1.44	1.00
Price to Sales (TTM)	13.34	9.37	5.42	2.83
Price to Book (MRQ)	9.46	7.15	5.87	4.28
Price to Tangible Book (MRQ)	10.93	10.83	9.03	8.47
Price to Cash Flow (TTM)	40.79	31.43	21.20	14.10
Price to Free Cash Flow (TTM)	68.81	53.21	29.00	30.65
% Owned Institutions	61.49	37.62	50.85	71.57

GROWTH RATES

	Company	Industry	Sector	S&P 500
Sales (MRQ) vs Qtr. 1 Yr. Ago	57.32	38.79	20.51	15.17
Sales (TTM) vs TTM 1 Yr. Ago	60.68	41.61	8.05	14.66
Sales - 5 Yr. Growth Rate	161.68	102.64	27.79	14.65
EPS (MRQ) vs Qtr. 1 Yr. Ago	43.14	37.69	32.94	11.97
EPS (TTM) vs TTM 1 Yr. Ago	62.66	50.95	28.63	14.95
EPS - 5 Yr. Growth Rate	205.43	16.24	35.12	23.45

CONSENSUS ESTIMATES ANALYSIS

EPS						P/E
Q4: 12/2007	31	4.45	4.78	4.04	0.16	--
Q1: 03/2008	15	4.89	5.35	4.53	0.21	--
FY: 2007	32	15.61	16.05	15.19	0.17	40.88
FY: 2008	31	20.78	22.43	18.67	0.86	30.72
LT Growth Rate (%)	15	33.17	61.80	18.00	11.55	--

Figure 9-6: Snapshot of Google's fundamentals at the end of 2007.

Source: Reuters Finance

See, that's not so hard! But you don't have to go on earnings or sales estimates alone to peg a company's relative value. You should also look at a company's financial position, net profit margins, and return on equity relative to its industry. If a company trades for the average P/E or price to cash flow ratio of its industry but is achieving

- ✔ Higher profit margins or higher returns on equity, perhaps it should trade at a premium to its industry.

- ✔ Lower profit margins or lower returns on equity than its peers, perhaps it should trade at a discount to its industry.

Always keep relativity in mind when comparing the share prices of a company you want to swing trade with the prices of its competitors. Be sure you're on the right side of the trade when you enter a long position. You want to buy shares of a company that's at a discount to its industry or not enough of a premium given expected growth rates.

Handling hazy conditions

The best scenario for a swing trader is when a company exhibits superior growth rates and superior profit margins to its competitors but trades at some discount. That's a no-brainer. But that doesn't always happen. Sometimes, a company's shares exhibit higher margins but lower growth rates than its peers. Or a company may have higher growth rates but lower returns on equity than its peers. What are you to do in these circumstances?

Skip that company and move on to another if major ambiguity is a factor. Or use the expected earnings and sales growth rates as a guide for what the "right" market multiple should be. If you still need some guidance, rank the importance of the three measures mentioned here in the following order:

1. Earnings growth rate

2. Return on equity

3. Profit margin

All else being equal, a company with a higher earnings growth rate than its competitors should trade at a premium to a competitor. If both companies have the same expected earnings growth rate, then the company with the higher return on equity ratio should trade at a premium to its peer. If that's also equal, then the company with the higher profit margin should trade at a premium to its peer.

These yardsticks can help you value companies — relatively speaking, of course. But relativity is all you need as a swing trader.

Part IV
Developing and Implementing Your Trading Plan

The 5th Wave   By Rich Tennant

Defining your investment risk with the:
TOAST RETRIEVING RISK TOLERANCE TEST

LOW RISK | Waits for toast to pop up even though it's burning.

MODERATE RISK | Goes after toast with wooden toast prongs.

HIGH RISK | Goes after toast with all metal butter knife.

ULTRA HIGH RISK | Goes after toast with metal butter knife wearing a wet swim suit and a stainless steel colander on head.

In this part . . .

Surprisingly, your success as a swing trader isn't driven by your skill at reading price charts or financial statements. Your risk management system and trading plan are far more important factors. Some of the greatest swing traders have even gone so far as to say that entering trades at random can be profitable if your risk management system allows you to let profits run and cut losses quickly. Kind of inspiring, huh?

Here, you find out how to build a first-rate risk management system. But just to make sure you're feeling comfortable with your newfound skills, I walk you right through the swing trading process (from finding trading candidates to entering orders to evaluating your performance) so that you can develop a complete swing trading plan. With that said, full speed ahead!

Chapter 10

Strengthening Your Defense: Managing Risk

In This Chapter

▶ Getting the scoop on risk measurement and management

▶ Avoiding losses at the individual stock and portfolio levels

▶ Crafting your exit game plan

*I*f you've ever seen the popular 1984 film *The Karate Kid* starring Ralph Macchio and Pat Morita, you may already know why this chapter is the most important in this book. In the film, karate master Mr. Miyagi teaches the timid teenager Daniel Larusso martial arts. But instead of beginning Larusso's training with how to throw a right hook or how to do a round kick, Miyagi stresses defensive techniques. "Wax on, wax off," he tells his student. The lesson is that you must block your opponents' punches and kicks or you won't last very long in a fight.

Believe it or not, swing trading isn't that different (fortunately, there's no need to train by waxing cars). I believe that the biggest determining factor of whether you'll be successful as a swing trader is how well you're able to implement your own risk management system. All too often, managing risk gets relegated to one or two simple rules of thumb: diversify your holdings and limit your investment in a single security, and all should be merry. Au contraire — although diversification and position sizing are important parts of risk management, they don't encompass all features of it. Moreover, traders often fail to fully implement diversification and position sizing correctly.

Managing risk is threefold: limiting the risk from a single position, limiting the risk on the portfolio level, and executing the orders your risk system tells you to execute. The first two can be taught to a five-year-old, but the practice of following your risk system is more difficult. As a swing trader, you have no one behind you making sure you follow these rules, and that means you're literally your worst enemy. If you get sloppy and ignore a rule here or there, you may get away with it a few times, but eventually the market will punish you.

Two tales of foolish woe

Not convinced of the importance of risk management? Consider the following hotshots who managed hundreds of millions of dollars and posted amazing returns . . . only to lose it all under difficult market environments when you can differentiate the skilled from the amateurs.

Victor Niederhoffer: Dr. Victor Niederhoffer is a well-known hedge fund manager and statistician with an impressive resume: Harvard undergrad with a PhD from the University of Chicago. He taught finance at the University of California, Berkeley, in the 1970s. You'd think that if anyone knew about risk, it'd be Niederhoffer.

Niederhoffer launched his own hedge fund and did quite well: He posted annual returns of 35 percent per year for several years. One popular magazine even named his hedge fund the number one fund in the world in 1996. But remember that trading can be deceptive, and the appearance of success can be illusory.

Niederhoffer's party came to a crashing end in 1997. His wrong bet on Thai bank stocks coupled with a major decline in the Dow Jones Industrial Average caused Niederhoffer major losses and forced him to shut down the fund. All those glorious gains in prior years were wiped out. Had Niederhoffer better diversified, invested in more liquid assets, and not used heavy leverage, he may have walked away with a few bruises but the ability to fight another day.

Despite his major setback, Niederhoffer launched a new hedge fund in 2002 and, remarkably, was awarded a prize for the best performing fund in 2004 and 2005. But — and I kid you not — his fund was closed in September 2007 after suffering a decline of more than 75 percent following the sub-prime market collapse and credit crunch. "He is his own worst enemy," Nassim Taleb, the author and derivatives trader, says of Niederhoffer. "One of the most brilliant men I have ever met, and he wastes his time selling options — something nobody can have any skill in — and it leaves him vulnerable to blowing up."

Long Term Capital Management: Long Term Capital Management (LTCM) was a hedge fund founded in 1994 with two — count 'em, two — Nobel Prize winners in economics on its board of directors. With people that smart steering the ship, there was no way anything negative could happen . . . or so it would seem. (As you may be catching on, portfolio returns and intelligence seem to be negatively correlated.)

In the early years, LTCM posted incredible returns: 40 percent on average. But the firm used extensive leverage (borrowing money to amplify possible returns — for example, using $1,000 to buy $2,000 worth of stocks). A crisis in Russia sparked major losses in LTCM's positions, and the firm went bust. LTCM failed because it took on extraordinary leverage and because its risk management system assumed markets would become *efficient,* meaning security mispricings wouldn't persist or widen. Markets aren't always rational, and during periods of panic, they become very irrational.

The point of these examples isn't to convince you that a Nobel Prize in economics or a degree from Harvard won't save you from the possibility of blowing up. In fact, it's nearly the opposite: These things may be a greater hindrance than a benefit! Why? Perhaps degrees from top schools or Nobel Prizes make individuals arrogant of the risks that are present in the market. After all, if I know everything and the market is moving in a direction contrary to my thoughts, then clearly the market is wrong. That kind of thinking can kill your stock portfolios.

Risk Measurement and Management in a Nutshell

Trading in general can be very deceptive — things aren't always as they appear. A hotshot trader or portfolio manager may post tremendous returns year-in and year-out, but if that trader or manager doesn't manage risk well, he or she may be one day away from blowing up and losing everything.

Risk management is the science (and sometimes the art) of limiting the losses your portfolio may suffer. This chapter breaks down limiting risk into two components: limiting the risk of an individual security and limiting risk at a portfolio level.

Fortunately, you can limit the potential losses of your portfolios by following several rules, which this chapter discusses in detail:

- ✔ Limit the amount of capital you invest in a position (position sizing)
- ✔ Invest in securities that trade frequently (liquidity)
- ✔ Spread out your capital over several positions (diversification)
- ✔ Spread out your capital over different sectors (diversification)

Risk management is how you put these various methods together into a coherent strategy. Before you buy or sell a stock, you must have written rules on how you'll respond should that trade go sour. That's your risk strategy. But that doesn't mean you won't experience losses. All professional (and great) traders lose money. What separates the successful ones from the burnouts are those who manage their risk well.

You have to be humble when you invest in the financial markets; you can't ever think you're smarter than the market. The minute you think that is the same minute your proverbial head will be handed to you on a silver platter.

First Things First: Measuring the Riskiness of Stocks before You Buy

Before you can manage the riskiness of your portfolio, you need to measure the riskiness of the stocks you're considering. So just how can you measure the riskiness of an individual stock? There are a number of factors to consider, all of which can give you an idea how much a security's share price may move in the near term:

- ✔ **The stock's *beta,* which is the risk of a stock compared to a market:** Beta is often overlooked by individual traders and has more weight with institutional traders. Although beta is backward-looking (that is, the historical volatility doesn't necessarily mean a stock or security will be as volatile in the future), you should know a security's beta in order to get an idea of how it has historically traded relative to the market.

- ✔ **The stock's *liquidity,* or how frequently traders exchange the security's shares:** Liquidity refers to the ease of entering and exiting a security, and you shouldn't overlook it. Liquidity may not seem important when you're entering a security because you can be patient and enter over time, but its importance becomes paramount when you need to exit and can't find a buyer (or seller, if you're short).

- ✔ **The size of the company:** Institutional traders care more about size than individual traders. Over the long term, small company stocks have out-performed large company stocks. But because small company stocks are more volatile, traders must take extra precautions when investing in "tiddlers." (Seriously, that's what they're often called.) For example, you may have a tighter stop loss on a small cap security than a large cap security.

- ✔ **The company's share price:** I usually don't trade stocks below $10 per share. Many major institutional buyers can't even trade in stocks in the single digits. Hence, these stocks are more susceptible to manipulation (for example, via rumors in trading chat rooms).

Assessing the beta: One security compared to the market

Beta is one way to measure how risky a position is. In plain English, beta tells you how volatile a security is relative to the market. Unfortunately, beta isn't always right. Its calculation (which is beyond the scope of this book) is based on historical data. There's no guarantee that the beta of a stock may not change — say from 2 today to 1 tomorrow. Therefore, you should know the beta of a security to get a general idea of how volatile that security is, but don't bet your life on it.

Take a gander at some information on the shares of Microsoft Corporation as an example:

Symbol: MSFT	**Share Price:** $30.26
Beta: 1.16	**Volume:** 56.29 million

Microsoft Corporation has a beta of 1.16, which means that, on average, Microsoft shares tend to rise or fall 1.16 times the general market. If the S&P 500 Index rose 1 percent in a day, you may expect to see Microsoft shares rise 1.16 percent.

There's no "right" beta for a security. A security that may move up a lot *is* desirable, but not if it can also cause you losses significant enough to take you out of trading. That doesn't mean you have to pass up a security that has a very high beta. But it does mean you may have to allocate less to that security because of its inherent volatility.

Looking at liquidity: Trade frequency

To understand liquidity, it helps to understand how the market works. The market is composed of millions of buyers and millions of sellers. The big companies — like Dell Computer or Coca-Cola — almost always have thousands of traders wanting to buy or sell stocks. But what about other companies? Some securities may not have that many traders interested in buying or selling stock on a particular day. The problem with that scenario is that the fewer the shares that trade, the more expensive it is to get into and out of a position.

In general, you should avoid at all costs companies with low liquidity. Although there may be some excellent opportunities in stocks that trade 500 shares a day, there are also ample opportunities in stocks that trade 500,000 shares a day. Why expose yourself to the risk of being unable to find a buyer for your shares if you need to exit in a hurry? You shouldn't.

So how liquid should shares of a security be before you purchase stock in it? That depends on your account size. If you're investing $25,000, you probably need to stick to stocks that trade at least 100,000 shares per day. If you're investing $1,000,000, you may be looking for stocks that trade at least 250,000 shares per day.

As a rule of thumb, your position size shouldn't represent more than 5 percent of the average daily volume of the shares.

Suppose you're interested in buying shares of LowLiquid Corporation, which trades (in this hypothetical world) on the New York Stock Exchange under symbol LL. Table 10-1 shows the current orders outstanding for the purchase and sale of shares in LowLiquid Corporation.

Table 10-1		Hypothetical Order Book	
		Sell 100 Shares	$36
		Sell 100 Shares	$26
Buy 100 Shares	$25		
Buy 100 Shares	$24		
Buy 100 Shares	$23		

An *order book* shows what the market maker sees: the current orders outstanding for a security. In this example, you see that buyers are interested in purchasing shares of LowLiquid Corporation for $25, $24, and $23 per share. However, the only sellers available at this time are selling shares for $36 and $26.

If you want to buy shares of LowLiquid Corporation, it may be a difficult proposition. Enter a market order for 200 shares, for example, and you'll buy 100 shares at $26 and 100 shares at $36 — giving you an average cost basis of $31. With the current bid at $25, you're already down almost 20 percent!

The *spread,* or difference in share prices, may not be always so large, but this example is intentionally exaggerated to illustrate the high cost that illiquidity can have on your portfolio.

Sizing up the company: The smaller, the riskier

Another factor to consider when determining how risky shares of a company are is the size of that company. Large company stocks (often called *large capitalization stocks* or *large cap* for short) are often less volatile — and therefore less risky — than small company stocks. But what is "large" and what is "small?" Ask Mr. Market Cap. *Market cap* tells you the value of a company — or more accurately, the value that Wall Street gives it today. The calculation of market cap is simple, but you're unlikely to need to calculate the figure because most Web sites and research services provide it for free. Yahoo! Finance (http://finance.yahoo.com) and Google Finance (http://finance.google.com/finance) are two popular sources for this information.

Market cap is defined as

Total shares outstanding × Price per share = Market capitalization

Generally, companies are classified into one of four market cap categories based on market capitalization:

Market Cap Category	*Market Capitalization*
Large cap	$15 billion or higher
Mid cap	Between $1 billion and $15 billion
Small cap	Between $300 million and $1 billion
Micro cap	Below $300 million

Micro cap companies tend to have low liquidity. Moreover, they're susceptible to market manipulation. For example, a trader may start a rumor in online chat rooms or via e-mail that a particular company has a cancer drug break-through. That kind of unsubstantiated rumor won't cause a large cap's shares to blink, but it may send a micro cap's stocks through the roof (or the floor, if the rumor isn't true or isn't good!). Although swing traders trade all these securities, you're best off avoiding micro cap stocks whenever possible.

Avoiding low-priced shares: As simple as it sounds

Low-priced shares reflect higher risk than high-priced securities. As a swing trader, you want to ride quick and strong trends up or down (whether you're buying or shorting). Low-price stocks can interfere with that plan because they introduce new risks.

Cheap stocks are generally defined as those that trade below $5 per share. Many institutional asset managers can't even purchase stocks below $5 because they're widely seen as high-risk gambles. Stocks that trade below $5 often have low liquidity, which means one trade can heavily influence the price action in one day. So buying the breakout of a stock priced at $3 may turn out to be nothing more than a flash in the pan.

To stay ahead of the game, avoid stocks below $5 per share that trade fewer than 250,000 shares per day and have market capitalizations below $300 million.

Limiting Losses at the Individual Stock Level

When you know how to determine how risky a stock is, you can use that information to guide how you manage its risk in the context of your portfolio. Managing risk at the individual stock level means making sure that no single position destroys your portfolio. Managing risk at the portfolio level means preventing several small losses from destroying your portfolio.

The way you manage risk at the individual stock level is through position sizing. And to set your position size, you have to know how much you're will-ing to lose. That loss potential is directly related to the purpose of a stop loss order, which ensures that should you be wrong — and you will be, many times — you can exit the position with (ideally) just a small loss.

Manipulation can even happen in large company stocks

Larger companies generally aren't subject to wild swings resulting from rumors. However, in August 2000, an elaborate hoax sent one large company's stock plummeting. In the evening of August 24, a press release from Emulex Corporation was issued with the following headline: "Emulex Announces Revised Earnings; SEC Launches Investigation into Accounting Practices. Paul Folino Steps Down as CEO." Good grief! You don't need to be a stock wizard to realize that's one piece of bad news.

The next morning, Emulex's stock, predictably, tanked. Within the first hour of trading, the stock was off 62 percent from its previous close. During that horrific decline, traders and investors scrambled to get comments from the company on why the CEO was stepping down, what caused the earnings miss, and why the SEC was investigating the firm's accounting practices. But poor Emulex: It's based on the West Coast, and 10:30 a.m. on the East Coast meant it was 7:30 a.m. on the West Coast.

Emulex eventually opened for business and quickly shot off press releases stating that the CEO had no intention of leaving, earnings weren't being restated, and the SEC wasn't conducting an investigation. So where did the press release come from? Turns out a former employee of a small Internet wire service sent the false press release to his former employer. He held a short position in the stock and drove its price down to make a tidy profit — $250,000 or so. Bloomberg, Marketwatch, and other reputable news services picked up the story without checking its accuracy. And before long, all of Wall Street thought the press release was genuine. The perpetrator of this elaborate scheme was later caught and prosecuted criminally.

The story of Emulex is a major exception to the rule that large company stocks generally aren't manipulated by news items. What occurred in Emulex is far more likely to occur in *penny stocks* (U.S. stocks that trade below $5) than in other companies' stocks. In the case of penny stocks, a market newsletter recommendation or a posting on a message board, rather than a false press release, may cause a spike or fall in price. Yet Emulex's story does reveal how costly trading can be when a stock — be it penny or large cap — is manipulated.

Figuring out how much you're willing to lose

Most professional swing traders limit the amount of loss they'll tolerate from a single position to 0.25 percent to 2 percent of total capital. *Remember:* Your loss will be affected by commissions, slippage, and *market impact* (the possibility of your trade moving the stock price up or down). Therefore, it may be best to stick to a yardstick of 0.75 percent of your capital, anticipating that these other costs will likely push your total loss to 1.25 percent or so of your capital.

Before you even determine how much to invest in a security, you must first determine how much you're willing to lose. If you agree with the 0.75 percent loss threshold that I recommend, simply take out a handy dandy calculator and compute:

0.75% × Your capital = Tolerable loss

If your portfolio is $50,000, the most you should be willing to lose on a single position is $375.

The amount you risk on a single position is different than the amount you buy or sell of that security. You may risk 1 percent or $1,000 (if your account value is $100,000) on a single position but end up buying $8,000 worth of that security. To achieve the risk of 1 percent, you must exit the position if the loss on the $8,000 reaches $1,000.

Setting your position size

You can position size either by applying a percent of capital approach (a constant rate of capital, say 5 percent) or by allocating new positions by a risk level you identify. Regardless of which strategy you pursue, make sure you include some discussion in your trading plan on how you determine the risk level.

By percent of capital

Setting your position size based on a percent of capital is the simplest way to allocate capital to new positions. For example, if you have an account worth $50,000 and select a 3 percent level of capital to invest in each security, you allocate $1,500 to each trade.

Many position traders (individuals with time horizons measured in months) invest an equal percentage of capital to each of their investments. As their capital base grows, they can invest more in each position. Conversely, as their capital base shrinks, they invest less in each position.

Ultimately, you should invest in ways you feel most comfortable with. However, I strongly advise against varying the percent of capital invested in new securities instead of using a constant percent of capital approach, because setting different percentages can result in random performance. Having a higher conviction in one trade (and thus allocating a higher percentage to it) may interfere with the success of your strategy if you're a poor predictor of your own success. Trading doesn't have to be complicated to be fun and profitable. Adding complexity where none is needed can lead to sub-par returns. If you want to vary your position size based on the attractiveness of the risk/reward present in the trading opportunity, skip to the next section.

You won't find a hard and fast rule when it comes to selecting a specific percentage level to use in setting position size. Choose a percentage level that's too small (such as 0.5 percent), and hitting a home run won't do much to boost your bottom line. But select a level that's too large (such as 10 percent), and you could lose your shirt if the stock gaps down hard. Your stop loss levels can only limit risk so much, and a security that gaps down will result in a loss larger than the 0.25 percent to 2 percent limit described earlier.

Use the following rules to help you set your percent of capital position sizing level if you decide to use this method (as opposed to the risk level approach described in the next section).

- ✔ Set a small percent of capital level (2 percent to 4 percent) if you trade securities that exhibit

  - Illiquidity (remember, what's liquid to you may not be liquid to a $1 billion hedge fund; in other words, size matters)

  - Low share prices ($10 or less is low)

  - High betas (anything above 2.0)

  - Small capitalization size (below $300 million)

- ✔ Set a large percent of capital level (4 percent to 8 percent) if you trade securities that exhibit

  - Liquidity

  - High share prices

  - Low betas

  - Mid and large capitalization sizes

After setting the percent of capital you want to allocate to your trades, you have to set your stop loss level. This part is easy given that you've already calculated your threshold of tolerable loss (refer to the earlier section "Figuring out how much you're willing to lose"). Set your stop loss level at the price that would cause the loss on your position to equal 0.75 percent of your total capital.

Here's an example of this process at work: Assuming an account value of $50,000 and a loss threshold level of 0.75 percent, the maximum loss you can tolerate on any one position is $375. You determine the time is right to buy shares in Dummies Corporation at $40 per share. You also decide to use a 6 percent of capital allocation approach to your swing trading. Where do you place your stop loss?

Your stop loss should be set at a price that yields a loss of $375. Investing 6 percent of your assets in Dummies Corporation means you'll buy 75 shares:

$6\% \times \$50,000 = \$3,000 \div \$40$ per share = 75 shares

To arrive at your stop loss level, divide your loss threshold by the number of shares you buy; then subtract the result from your purchase price to get your stop loss level:

$375 ÷ 75 shares = $5

$40 – $5 = $35 stop loss level

By risk level

Setting your position size using a percent of capital method may seem arbitrary. After all, isn't that saying that you have no idea which trade will be profitable and which one won't be?

Technically, the answer to your astute question is yes; in effect, you're saying that you have no idea which trade will be profitable. But then again, you wouldn't be trading in the first place if you knew the trade wouldn't be profitable.

A smarter method of setting your position size is varying it according to your desired exit level. In the example that I set up in the previous section, you compute an exit level strictly based on the price that would produce a loss of 0.75 percent of your capital. Alternatively, you can determine a key level at which you want to exit and then determine a position size based on that level. This is how most professionals swing trade. An arbitrary price may have no meaning ($35 in the previous example), whereas a specific price level may signal the end or beginning of a trend. I use a chart to illustrate how a specific level can help you determine a position size.

Figure 10-1 shows a chart of Google (symbol: GOOG), the search engine giant. Google's shares have been consolidating and look ready to break out. In your infinite wisdom (hey, why not build yourself up?), you decide to purchase shares.

Figure 10-1:
Assessing a chart can help you calculate how large a position to take.

Before you calculate how large a position to take, assess the chart. This daily chart shows Google's stock price from early April 2007 through mid-September 2007. Google's stock rose strongly from mid-May 2007 through late July 2007 — up 22 percent in two months. However, a poor earnings report sent Google's stock sharply down (and serves as a reminder that trading around earnings reports can be hazardous).

Pretend today is September 18, 2007, and you've decided Google is worth a swing trade. How much of your capital should you invest?

Setting your position size based on a risk level requires you to determine a price that, if reached, indicates that the trade has gone sour. Obviously, if shares fall to $460, you have a hint that something isn't right. But that's far too late — you need a more immediate warning sign.

Try using a previous swing low as a line in the sand for your stop loss level. In this example, assume that the recent swing low highlighted in the chart is the level that, if reached, indicates that you're wrong about the trade. That level is $505.

Google's stock is trading at $545, and you're willing to risk 0.75 percent of your capital on each trade. (***Remember:*** 0.75 percent represents the loss you're willing to tolerate from a position, not the maximum amount you're willing to allocate to a single position.) To calculate how many shares of Google to buy, use this formula and plug in your numbers:

Amount of capital at risk ÷ (Entry price – Stop loss level)

$375 (or 0.75% of $50,000) ÷ ($545 – $505) = 9.375 shares, or 9 shares

Thus, setting your position size based on your risk level means purchasing 9 shares of Google. (Round down when you have a fraction. Rounding up may mean adding more risk, whereas rounding down always keeps you below your specified loss threshold.)

This example brings to light one weakness of this approach: The closer the exit price is to your entry price, the larger the implied position. In fact, if your exit price is $1 or less than your entry price, the preceding formula may tell you to invest more than your total capital in one stock, which makes no sense!

The solution to this weakness is to put a ceiling on the amount you invest in any security. Colin Nicholson, a popular trader from Australia, places a 6 percent ceiling on his trades. In the example, if you purchase 9 shares of Google at $545, you're investing 9.81 percent of your total capital in one stock.

Although *technically* only 0.75 percent of your capital is at risk (if you place your stop loss), there's *always* a chance that the stock will gap down or up and cause your loss to be much greater than your limit. Stop loss orders don't guarantee an exit at the price specified because there's always the chance a security may gap lower or higher, depending on whether you're long or short.

Building a Portfolio with Minimal Risk

When you know the maximum amount of capital you want to allocate to a single position — based on the percent of capital approach or the risk level approach, covered in the previous sections — you're ready to take a step back and see the forest for the trees.

The risk of focusing on individual securities at the expense of your portfolio is a simultaneous breakdown of several positions. If you have 25 positions in your portfolio, for example, and the amount at risk for each position is 1 percent, it's conceivable (and almost anything can happen in financial markets) that all 25 positions will go against you at the same time and cause a major loss of 25 percent of your portfolio.

Don't believe it can happen? Consider that the markets dropped 22.6 percent on October 19, 1987. Few believed a move of that magnitude could happen in a single day. That loss actually exceeded any single-day loss experienced during the Great Depression.

External factors beyond anyone's control can impact markets day to day. And it's possible for a short position you hold to get bought out (sending its stock price through the roof) at the same time that the markets tumble, sending your long positions through the floor. To combat this risk, you should monitor the risk not only at the individual stock level but also at the total portfolio level. This idea is no more complicated than others covered in this chapter. It just requires good record-keeping to execute fully.

Limit all position losses to 7 percent

The prudent approach to limit the losses from all your positions is to place a ceiling on the amount of capital you risk at any one time. Determine how much to risk on any single position — I recommend between 0.25 percent and 2 percent of total capital. The cumulative total of the amount at risk for each position is considered your *total capital at risk*.

I recommend limiting your total capital at risk to 7 percent. Doing so means that the most you could lose in a single day if everything were to go wrong is 7 percent. Of course, you shouldn't set stop losses so close to your entry prices that they're triggered frequently; that may be a sign you aren't giving your stock room to fluctuate. A 7 percent level should rarely (if ever) be triggered because it would require all position stop losses to be executed on the same day.

The maximum amount you should risk in a single position, in my opinion, is 0.5 percent. This amount allows you to have at least 14 positions ($0.5\% \times 14 = 7\%$). The larger the amount you risk on a single position, the fewer positions you can hold. And the fewer positions you hold, the higher the risk of your portfolio and the greater chance of a major account value swing that may be difficult to recover from.

To help you understand how this 7 percent rule works, consider an example: Trader Bob has constructed a portfolio of seven different positions that's worth $50,609. Figure 10-2 shows, from left to right, the symbol of each of his positions, the current stock price for each of his positions, his entry price, the number of shares he owns, his stop loss level (exit level), and his total amount at risk based on the specified exit level.

Symbol	Current Price	Entry Price	Shares	Exit Level	Amount at Risk
GOOG	$545.30	$535.27	7	$499.12	0.50%
AAPL	$152.25	$140.92	28	$140.92	0.00%
PTR	$149.50	$154.12	26	$139.52	0.75%
PBR	$65.78	$70.60	56	$61.56	1.00%
KMB	$73.85	$69.40	57	$62.74	0.75%
MRK	$59.65	$50.57	79	$44.16	1.00%
KO	$48.25	$56.41	71	$47.50	1.25%
Cash		$1.00	$23,000		
Total Portfolio value				$50,609.31 **Total At Risk**	5.25%

Figure 10-2: Information from Trader Bob's hypothetical portfolio.

The total amount of capital that Trader Bob has at risk based on this portfolio is 5.25 percent, found by summing up the Amount at Risk column. So Trader Bob can risk an additional 1.75 percent of his portfolio on new positions before he hits the 7 percent ceiling that I recommend. That 1.75 percent may be spread across five or more positions.

If you enjoy finding Waldo, you may have noticed that the amount of risk listed for shares of AAPL, or Apple Inc., is 0.00 percent. What gives? As a position moves in your favor, you can adjust the stop loss price higher or lower, depending on the direction you're trading. In this case, shares of AAPL were purchased at $140.92 and promptly began rising. After a nice gain,

Trader Bob decided to raise his stop loss level to his entry price level. Doing so meant he could risk more capital in other positions he owns. The assumed worse outcome from his position in AAPL is to break even (barring the stock price gapping down).

The amount at risk can never be a negative value, so don't use negative risk amounts when you can raise your stop loss order to a price that locks in a profit. If Trader Bob raises his stop loss to $150 in the future, his amount at risk isn't –0.5 percent. Raising your stop loss order ensures your portfolio doesn't swing trade too aggressively and compensates for the inherent limits of stop loss orders. After all, you may or may not get executed at your stop loss price. So if a security gaps down below your stop loss price (assuming you're trading on the long side), your stop loss order will be executed at a much lower price than you anticipated.

Diversify your allocations

Another method of limiting losses on a portfolio level is diversification. No doubt you've heard the term thrown around on financial news networks. It seems every expert often recommends avoiding "putting your eggs in one basket." Fortunately for you, this section gives you a bit more to go on than a farm analogy.

Diversification is one of the shining gems mined from academia. In a nutshell, investing in more than one security, sector, or trading vehicle helps protect you in the event that a problem befalls one or more of those securities. The aim is to have a portfolio in which some securities' gains offset other securities' losses. The best scenario is simply a portfolio with all gainers, but in reality, some positions make money while others lose money.

At its simplest level, diversification can be seen as a tool of avoiding the problems of a single company. For example, you may buy shares in General Motors and Ford so that, if Ford takes a tumble, your shares in General Motors can offset your losses.

But what happens if an autoworkers strike brings down *both* General Motors and Ford? In that scenario, owning securities not in the auto business may be prudent. So you pick up shares of Nike and Dell Computer. But when the United States goes into recessions, shares of all your U.S.-based companies are likely to fall. That means you may want to be investing in Asia or Europe as well.

These examples give you an idea of the benefits of diversification. The simplest form of diversification is investing in several securities, but you also can diversify according to industry exposure and asset class. I cover all three of these options in the following sections.

By number of securities

The most elementary way of diversifying your portfolio is simply to spread your assets across several securities. The more, the better — the thinking goes. But how many securities constitute a diversified portfolio?

The benefits of diversification can be realized with 10 to 20 securities, but I should warn you: This number assumes the companies are in different industries and countries. Investing in 10 semiconductor manufacturers doesn't expose a portfolio to businesses outside of a small niche of the market.

Your trading plan should indicate a target number of positions you trade. The more positions you have, the less time you'll have to devote to each single one and the more likely your returns will mirror the market. So keep your number below 20 or 25.

Following the position sizing guidelines outlined earlier in this chapter (see "Setting your position size") largely takes care of this first point of diversification by number because the risk guidelines ensure that you have several positions. But if you're going to brave the market without these guidelines, try to construct a portfolio of at least ten different positions and securities in different industries (see the following section for tips).

By industry exposure

According to William J. O'Neil, founder of *Investor's Business Daily,* an industry group roughly determines 30 to 40 percent of a security's return. So being exposed to only one or two industry groups is extremely risky because the returns of your securities will be very similar. Think about it in terms of the auto example from earlier in this chapter: Are the factors affecting General Motors and Ford all that different? Or Dell Computer and Hewlett-Packard? Exxon Mobil and Chevron?

Following is an outline of the major industry sectors (as defined by the Global Industry Classification Standard, or GICS). Fortunately, the software services you use should break down the industry or economic sector that your securities belong to.

- Energy
- Materials

    - Industrials
    - Capital goods
    - Commercial services
    - Transportation

- Consumer discretionary
  - Automobiles
  - Retailers
- Consumer staples
  - Food and drug retailing
  - Household products
- Healthcare
- Financials
- Information technology
- Telecommunications services
- Utilities

There's nothing wrong with concentrating in a few sectors — say four or five. But beware of investing in only one or two sectors because you won't benefit from the diversification benefits inherent in investing in different parts of the economy.

Be sure to set a minimum number of industry groups that you trade in. I recommend identifying at least three different sectors and trading a minimum of six different *industry groups,* smaller classification groupings than sectors. For example, energy drilling, energy services, and energy integrated are all industry groups in the energy sector.

By asset class

Another way to diversify your portfolio is to invest in different investment vehicles. The asset classes you trade decrease your overall portfolio risk, so if you're using this approach, you should shoot to trade two to three different asset classes. Two primary vehicles for achieving diversification by asset class are exchange traded funds (ETFs) and American Depository Receipts (ADRs):

- **Exchange traded funds (ETFs):** These funds are a growing segment of the market. They represent baskets of stocks in a sector, style (such as growth or value), country, and even short positions of major indexes. ETFs now also provide exposure to commodities and currencies. Trading ETFs helps diversify your portfolio across several stocks in one sector or country. For example, you may be right on a substantial move in oil stocks, but you may select the one oil company that's having problems. Buying an energy ETF (such as the iShares Dow Jones US Energy ETF) allows you to profit from the movement of several energy stocks. Purchasing one ETF is like instant diversification across a style or sector of the market.

Sometimes there's a bull market in commodities or currencies while stock markets are lagging. So various asset classes can provide a boost of returns in addition to lower risk. Here are some of the main ETFs that offer you exposure to commodities:

- **Precious metals:** Gold can be traded via streetTRACKS Gold (symbol: GLD); silver can be traded via iShares Silver Trust (symbol: SLV). If you're interested in metals and mining, you can swing trade the SPDR S&P Metals & Mining ETF (symbol: XME).

- **Energy:** Your options for trading energy ETFs include Energy Select Sector SPDR (symbol: XLE). Or you can trade energy stocks that rise and fall with the price of oil. Energy exploration and production companies especially track changes in crude oil and natural gas prices.

- **Agricultural commodities:** The Dow Jones-AIG Agriculture Total Return ETF (symbol: JJA) provides exposure to agricultural commodities.

You can obtain exposure to currencies (such as the Euro or Canadian Dollar) through the various Currency Shares ETFs found at www. currencyshares.com.

✔ **American Depository Receipts (ADRs):** ADRs allow you to take advantage of strength (or weakness) in a company based outside the U.S without ever leaving home. Currently, the fastest growing markets are in China, India, and Latin America.

Mixing international securities into your portfolio offers greater diversification benefits than having strictly U.S. stocks because international markets may zig when the U.S. market zags. The more technical explanation of the benefit of ADRs is that foreign securities have lower correlation ratios to the U.S. market than domestic securities. Of course, the currency of those foreign markets may also improve (or hurt) your returns. To find a list of international equities, check out www.adr.com.

Combine long and short positions

You can reduce the risk for your total portfolio by combining long and short positions. Having long and short positions gives you a lower standard deviation of returns than if you have a portfolio that's 100 percent long or 100 percent short (which means its returns vary less than the overall market). Translating that into English: A swing trader who combines long and short positions is protected in the event of a major rally or decline in the market. Gains off of shorts/longs can offset losses from longs/shorts.

When the overall market is in a heavy bull advance, a portfolio with short positions is likely to be stopped out of those positions often (meaning your stop loss orders will be executed). Alternatively, when the overall market is in a heavy bear decline, a portfolio with long positions is likely to be stopped out of those positions frequently. In other words, profitably shorting in a strong bull market or profitably going long in a strong bear market is difficult.

The conundrum of having too many long or short positions has two possible solutions:

- ✔ **Limit the amount of your portfolio that's short or long, depending on the strength or weakness of the market.** For example, in a strong bull market, you may hold short positions not exceeding 20 percent of your entire portfolio. Alternatively in a strong bear market, you may hold long positions not exceeding 20 percent of your entire portfolio.

- ✔ **Trade different asset classes that may be trending in a different direction than the stock market.** If stocks are in a raging bull market, perhaps your short positions can come from the commodities or currency markets (see the preceding section for ideas of how to gain exposure to these markets).

Whichever method you choose, make sure your trading plan outlines how you determine when you're net long (that is, when you hold more long positions than short) or net short (when you hold more short positions than long).

Planning Your Exit Strategies

Your *exit strategy* dictates when you'll exit a security. Some swing traders believe that an exit strategy is more important than an entry strategy, and I agree wholeheartedly.

Believe it or not, a trader can generate healthy profits by randomly entering securities if he or she has an exit strategy that lets winners run and cuts losers fast.

Sometimes you'll exit for profits, and other times you'll exit for losses. Of course, the most desirable exit strategy is exiting for profits. The next desirable option is exiting because of the passage of time. The least desirable exit strategy is exiting for losses. Most trades, however, fall into the profit or loss category. Rarely will you exit because of time.

Exiting for profitable trades

Stop loss rules are your way out when a trade goes bad (more on that topic later in this chapter). But what should you do when a trade turns out right?

There are three major ways to exit profitable trades: by a predetermined profit target, by a predetermined price target, or by swing lows/highs.

Predetermined profit target

A predetermined profit target is the easiest method of taking profits off the table. When you enter your trade, you set a specific gain (usually expressed in percentage terms) that you seek and then take your money off the table after that gain has been achieved.

Swing traders shouldn't set unreasonable profit targets; your profit target is a function of your time horizon. Because swing traders' horizons can vary from a few days to a few weeks, your profit target may range from the low single digits to the low double digits. If you're active in the markets and trade often, then your profit target should be modest — closer to 5 percent. However, if you prefer to hold your swing trades for a few weeks, then a 10 percent or 15 percent profit target is attainable.

Some professional swing traders exit in stages. For example, they may sell 50 percent of their position after a security has risen 10 percent in price. Then they may ride the rest of the position until there's a technical breakdown or change in fundamentals. The advantage of exiting in stages is that you lock in profits early. A security that rises 10 percent and then falls back to your entry price results in a 0 percent return if you failed to take profits on its way up.

Exiting in stages may improve your returns, but it also requires more work. There's more record-keeping, for example, if you exit in stages versus exiting in one go. You also generate more commissions, more taxes, and so on. Make sure that your strategy fits your work ethic and time commitment to the market.

Predetermined price target

A predetermined price target is an alternative way to take money off the table. In this case, you set a specific target based on the chart or the fundamentals of the company.

In the case of technical alert criteria, you may set your profit target equal to a prior swing high or swing low. Securities tend to find resistance and support at price levels achieved in the past, so you may set your target on the basis that the security will reach that prior peak. (I cover how to determine technical alert criteria in Chapters 4 and 5.)

In the case of fundamental criteria, you may set your profit target equal to a price multiple of the security — a price multiple based on earnings, sales, and so on (see Chapter 9 for more on the different price multiples). For example, if you suspect that Dell's shares should be trading for a price to earnings

(P/E) ratio equal to Hewlett-Packard's shares, then your price target would be equal to Hewlett-Packard's P/E ratio multiplied by Dell's trailing earnings. (I cover fundamental analysis in detail in Part III.)

One word of caution: Don't set price targets equal to round numbers or whole dollar amounts (like $35, $80, or $120). Many novice traders set their price levels in the same area, which may prevent the security from reaching that price. For example, if you buy a security and expect the stock to face some headwind when it reaches $50, place your limit order to sell shares at $49.83 or a level nearby. Traders who place their limit orders right at the level of resistance and at a round number often are left with unfilled orders.

Swing lows/highs

Swing traders often use prior swing lows and highs as reference points on when to jump ship from a profitable investment. A breakdown below a low or above a high may signal the beginning of a new downtrend or uptrend, respectively.

This strategy differs somewhat from the predetermined price target I explain in the preceding section. In that strategy, you set a price target of when to take profits off the table. In this case, however, you use prior swing lows and highs as reference points for when to exit. If you're long shares of a security, this strategy calls for putting a stop loss order below a recent swing low. In contrast, a predetermined price target calls for placing a limit sell order when the security reaches the area you expected.

Figure 10-3 shows Exxon Mobil (symbol: XOM) from July 2007 through October 2007. It illustrates how a predetermined price target differs from exiting on a swing low or high.

Figure 10-3: This chart of XOM shows how you can plan your exit based on previous swing highs.

In the case of buying shares of Exxon Mobil, you may have set a sell limit order near the prior high of $94 (but not *at* $94 — use a price below that and not a round number).

Contrast the Exxon Mobil exit to the strategy of placing a stop sell order below prior swing lows in the chart of Sigma Designs, Inc. (symbol: SIGM), shown in Figure 10-4. It shows that by placing a sell stop order below prior swing lows, you can stay in a strong trend longer and reap a larger percentage of the move.

Figure 10-4:
Placing stop loss orders below swing lows helps you stay in strong trends and get out of lagging ones.

Taking cues from technical signals

In addition to taking profits based off of swing lows and swing highs, you can take profits based off of technical signals. When using technical signals (flip back to Chapter 5 for a refresher on the various technical indicators), ensure that some crystal clear trigger or catalyst is present that leads you to take profits.

Some examples of selling strategies for profits include:

- ✔ Exiting when shares close below a moving average (for example, a nine-day moving average)
- ✔ Exiting when the MACD line crosses below (or above, if you're short) the signal line
- ✔ Exiting when –DMI crosses above +DMI (if you're long)
- ✔ Exiting when prices break an uptrend line (or downtrend line)

Consider Figure 10-5, which highlights how a swing trader may have taken profits in a trade of shares of W&T Offshore (symbol: WTI) on the turn-up of the nine-day moving average. The profit-taking exit in this example is based on the share price closing below the nine-day moving average. The potential

profit — assuming entry and exits near the closing prices on the days highlighted, and exclusive of commissions, taxes, and slippage — is 19.18 percent
over 18 days. The stop loss level (which I delve into in the later section,
"Exiting based on a stop loss level") should be placed below a recent swing
low but not exactly at the low or exactly at a round number.

Figure 10-5:
Taking
profits
based off of
a technical
signal in
shares of
WTI.

Exiting based on the passage of time

A time trigger exit is sometimes necessary when a position you trade meets
neither its profit target nor its stop loss exit. But because your capital
shouldn't be tied up in a position that isn't generating profits, I must cover
the rare but possible exit based on the passage of time.

Perhaps you bought or shorted at the wrong time, or an event you expected
to occur didn't materialize. In any case, a security that meanders sideways is
tying up your capital. You're better off exiting the security and having cash at
your disposal should an opportunity present itself.

As with other aspects of swing trading, there's no hard and fast rule on what
constitutes sufficient time for a position to make a move. If you trade often
with a time horizon measured in days, you should give a position up to a week
to make a move. However, if you're a swing trader who goes for larger moves
that unfold over a few weeks, you may give a position more time.

Exiting based on a stop loss level

Wouldn't it be nice if your only decision was when to take a profit off the
table? "Hmm . . . should I leave with a 10 percent gain or wait for a 15 percent
gain?" Alas, you don't always have this luxury.

Many times you'll be faced with the prospect of exiting a position at a loss. Although it may be difficult to admit you were wrong, you have to get used to it if you're going to be a swing trader. The most common way you'll exit losing positions is through a stop loss level.

Technically, a stop loss can be mental or physical:

✔ A *mental stop loss level* is a price level you keep in your own records but only submit to your broker when the security has reached that price level. The advantage of using a mental stop loss level is that you may avoid a whipsaw — being forced out of a position due to a short but violent move up or down.

✔ A *physical stop loss order* is an order you submit to your broker the second your entry is executed. When you enter a stop loss order (which should be submitted "Good till cancelled" so that it doesn't expire after one day), your order is visible to other traders, so it's possible for them to move prices to take out your order.

Although this risk exists, I can't stress enough the importance of using physical stop loss orders entered with your broker for the first few years you swing trade. You expose yourself to the risk of a whipsaw, but you also avoid the risk of failing to exit when a security's price moves fast and furious (furiously, for all you English majors).

Stop loss orders should be entered around some major support/resistance level or technical level. If you're long shares of a position, your stop loss order should be below the entry price and entered as a sell order. If you're short shares of a position, your stop loss order should be above the entry price and be entered as a buy to cover order.

The following techniques for setting stop losses only apply to swing traders who set their positions based on a risk level. Swing traders who set their position sizes based on a percent of capital approach automatically determine a stop loss level based on their loss threshold level. Swing traders who set their position sizes based on a risk level, however, should understand the different methods of selecting a risk level.

Stop loss based on a support/resistance level

This first approach to setting your stop loss level is straightforward. By examining a chart, you should be able to determine levels of support and resistance that, if broken, would signal the end or beginning of a trend. Your job, should you choose to accept it, is to identify a level that's most applicable to you.

To simplify matters, suppose you're interested in buying a security. In that case, your stop loss level should be based around a major support level (preferably, right below that support level). A three-year-old support level isn't going to have significant relevance most of the time (an exception being if the support level was tested several times during those three years).

In general, a support level is significant the

- ✔ More recent it is
- ✔ More often it has been tested
- ✔ Closer it is to a significant price level ($100, $10, $50, and so on)
- ✔ Heavier the volume is on the formation of the support level

Choose important support levels so that you only exit a position when a trend change is most likely. Choosing a weak support level may cause you to exit a position prematurely.

Stop loss based on a technical level

You may exit a position based on the breaking of a significant technical level. Dozens of technical indicators can be plotted on a chart, and when one of those indicators gives a signal, an informed swing trader exits.

Technical indicators can be tricky. Just because your technical charting program may have 101 different technical indicators developed by individuals I won't name here (because I don't know their names) doesn't mean you need to use all 101 indicators in your strategy. In fact, professionals often use only two or three to make their decisions. Why not use all the bounty with which you've been bestowed?

As it turns out, all technical indicators are based on one or two inputs: price and volume. Consequently, there are only so many ways you can peel an onion before you realize those tears are coming out no matter what you do. You don't get a performance boost from using ten indicators; instead, you get ten people telling you largely the same thing.

Stop loss orders are sometimes used in conjunction with moving averages. Some swing traders place stop loss orders right below a major moving average and adjust the order every day or two. Others who use mental stop loss orders may wait for a security to close below a moving average before taking action to enter an order with their broker.

Figure 10-6 shows a stop loss order executed based on the nine-day moving average (DMA). A gap up in shares of Yahoo! (symbol: YHOO) in early 2006 seemed to be a prelude to a strong uptrend. However, shares of Yahoo! quickly reversed. Setting a stop loss based on a support level may have exposed you to the violent fall, whereas a stop loss based on the moving average would've given you an earlier exit.

A stop loss order can be based on actual signals from a technical indicator (such as MACD). The downside to using such orders is that delays can result. You don't know for sure what price a security must reach before an indicator will signal its flashing red lights. Using an indicator like a moving average, which is actually plotted on the chart, is helpful because you can identify a specific price before the signal is given.

Figure 10-6:
A stop loss order for YHOO, based on the nine-day moving average.

Responding wisely when you take a hit

The only thing worse than exiting a position for a loss is doing nothing. If you break your rules and decide to pass on a sell signal, you'll be run over by a fast-moving car. Maybe not today and maybe not tomorrow, but the market exacts painful penalties from traders who think rules don't apply to them.

Interestingly, women tend to be better at this aspect of trading than men. For the same reason that men are prone to drive around in circles before they ask for directions, male traders often refuse to recognize their mistakes. Cutting a loss is admitting you're wrong — admitting you're lost and need help. Female swing traders often have less ego — and smaller losses to show for it.

To make this topic more palpable, think of your stop loss orders as insurance policies (that's masculine, right?). When a position falls to your stop loss level, you have to exercise your policy and get out. (Your insurance policy returns your original capital minus the small loss.) By ignoring your sell order, you're effectively relying on hope. If you turn out to be right, you've only reinforced a negative behavior.

This is one reason many swing traders fail outside of a supervised office. In a corporate atmosphere, someone is looking over your shoulder to make sure you're doing your job right. Take a shortcut or two, and you'll be called out for it. In trading, you have to look over your own shoulder. No one will punish you for ignoring the rules except "Mr. Market." And he isn't forgiving.

So how can you respond wisely to losses? Remember that all traders face losses, and the only poor way to respond is to not respond at all. Keep the following points in mind:

- **All traders experience losses.** You may take comfort in exiting a position for a loss if you know that all professional traders experience them. No matter how good you become, you'll always have losing positions. The key is to limit those losses, exit them, and move on. Does Michael Jordan make every shot he takes? No. Did Pele score a goal each time he touched the soccer ball? No. What you'll find as a swing trader is that most of your positions will produce average gains — in line with the market. A few will do tremendously well, and a few will do tremendously poorly.

To rise to the top of your game, you need to allow those superstar positions to run as much as possible and stop as quickly as possible a position that's a drag on your portfolio. The quicker you exit, the sooner you're able to move on and find a new position that may be a home run (too many sports analogies for one sidebar?).

✔ **Failure to act can be disastrous.** Okay, I've hammered this point home, but there's good reason for it. Many swing traders start out using stop loss orders but become lazy after a string of successes. But as surely as night follows day, losses will follow profits. When markets are in a strong trend — up or down — they invite risk taking and carelessness. Investors and traders are lulled into a sense of safety. Small losses often turn into big gains if given enough time, but these are temporary illusions. Good times and easy money eventually end — and

the end can be violent. (Yes, I'm trying to scare you.)

Consider shares of Akamai Technology Inc. (symbol: AKAM). In mid-2007, shares made a strong move upward to $50 (remember what I said about round numbers acting as resistance?). You may have bought on a breakout above $50 per share, expecting the trend to continue. However, shares began to falter and fell back to the $46–$47 price range. Note that this was right below the prior swing low — a level that may've been specified as point of exit. During this period, the Dow Jones Industrial Average was at a new all-time high. So why worry about a short-term decline? Why not wait it out for a rally back to the $50 level? As it happened, shares of Akamai fell 46 percent following that small initial decline. A swing trader who exited quickly when the prior swing low was violated would've left with a small loss. A swing trader who waited to see what happened would've been wallowing in misery.

Chapter 11

Fine-Tuning Your Entries and Exits

In This Chapter

▶ Getting to know how the market works

▶ Identifying key entry and exit orders for your swing trades

▶ Figuring out how to place orders whether swing trading is your hobby or your living

*T*rade execution is the home stretch of swing trading. If you've dotted your i's and crossed your t's, then how you execute your swing trade is unlikely to spell the difference between success and failure. Still, you should perfect entering your orders as much as possible so that you aren't burned by a security that's in the process of reversing direction. Perfecting your order entry largely means knowing what type of order to enter, a factor that's mainly dependent on whether you're a full- or part-time swing trader. If you've done your homework, though, your execution strategy should emphasize entry with the flow of the market.

If you're a full-time swing trader or you execute trades during market hours, you have more order types at your disposal than if you're trading part-time. You also have the opportunity to use a couple of helpful tools to refine your trades: intraday charting and Nasdaq Level II quotes. In this chapter, I outline the major order types and tell you which ones you should use most, depending on your situation. I also explain how to make the most of intraday tools to refine your swing trading.

If you're a part-time swing trader, you should follow a different entry strategy than your full-time counterparts. But never fear! This chapter outlines the unique considerations you face when entering and exiting positions.

Understanding Market Mechanics

Understanding the mechanics of the underlying markets is essential to knowing when to enter or exit an order. On a basic level, I'm guessing you understand that securities have bid prices (where you can sell) and ask prices (where you can buy). Both the bid and ask have a number of shares associated with them. For example, the bid may have 100 shares associated with it, indicating you can sell 100 shares at that price. But who's buying and selling these securities to you?

Dealers who make markets in certain securities are called *market makers*. Market makers are often decried as evil geniuses who control security prices. In all honesty, they aren't geniuses . . . or evil creatures. They're just ordinary folks who can push prices to clear your limit orders or stop orders aggregated around a certain price.

From the market maker's perspective, a bid is where he or she is willing to buy the security, and an ask is his or her offer to sell the security at that price. Market makers offer a certain amount of stock on the buy and sell sides. So if a market maker is offering 2,000 shares of Danaher at $75.23 and you enter a market order for 2,500 shares, your first 2,000 will be executed at $75.23. However, the remaining 500 shares may be executed at a higher price. A thinly traded stock may have 2,000 shares available at $75 per share and 500 shares available at $76. A 2,500 share market order in such a stock would fill at $75 and $76.

When a security has great *market depth* (many orders on the buy and sell side), plenty of shares are available for buying or selling. When a security has little depth, few shares are available. Certain order types (such as a market order; see "Living life in the fast lane: Market orders," later in this chapter for more on this type) in a security with little depth may move it significantly — at least for a little while.

Because certain order types can move prices significantly in thinly traded securities, you want to stick to actively traded securities. You don't want to expose yourself to significant liquidity risk. Swing traders normally generate *alpha,* or outperformance, in the quality of their buys and sells, not in their ability to correctly estimate the mispricing of liquidity risk.

If a security has a wide spread, you can enter a certain order type (specifically a limit order, explained later in this chapter) to buy or sell at a price between the bid and the ask. When market makers receive your order, they have two options: They can execute the trade at the specified price (or a better one), or they can place your order as the best bid or offer.

Suppose you want to buy shares of fictitious company Wide Spreads Inc., and the bid/ask spread is $17.50/$19.25. (For now, ignore the fact that as a shrewd swing trader, you'd never transact in a security with such a wide spread.) If you enter a buy limit order for $18.25 ($1 less than the current asking price), the company's market maker must either execute your order or make your order the new bid. So either you'll receive an execution or the new bid/ask spread will be $18.25 to $19.25. Someone entering a market sell order will be executed at your bid, and your buy order will be filled.

When I first learned that I could affect bid/ask spreads, I entered orders left and right just to see my order come up on top. I don't recommend this tactic, because your orders may actually be executed.

Surveying the Major Order Types

In order to efficiently enter or exit a long or short position on a security you want to swing trade, you need to get acquainted with the major types of orders. These order types are available to anyone buying securities — whether you're a long-term investor, day trader, or swing trader. But swing traders may use certain order types more than other kinds of traders or investors do.

Orders can be *good until cancelled* (GTC), which means the orders stay open until you execute or cancel them, or *good until the day* (GTD), which means the orders remain open until the market closes.

The following sections describe the four major types of orders and when you want to use them.

Living life in the fast lane: Market orders

Get me in and get me in now. That's the mantra of the *market order,* an order that instructs your broker to buy or sell a security immediately, regardless of price. Market orders are useful when urgency to enter a security based on a particular chart pattern or technical indicator abounds (turn to Chapters 4 and 5 for a refresher on how to read charts and indicator signals). You may also want to use them when a security is very liquid, and there are so many shares on the bid and ask sides that you're unlikely to receive an execution price starkly different than where the security's currently trading.

I caution you against using market orders when entering a position. I'm more likely to use one to exit a position instead. Never, ever enter a market order when the markets are closed, because a security may gap higher or lower at the next day's open and result in an execution you don't want.

Market orders should only be used by full-time swing traders.

Knowing your boundaries: Limit orders

Limit orders instruct your broker to buy, sell, or short a security at a specific price or a better one. Better, of course, depends on the direction of the trade. The better price is lower when you're buying and higher when you're selling.

I'm a big proponent of limit orders. Even when the current price of a security is agreeable to you, and a market order may make sense, a limit order protects you from being on the receiving end of a price execution that's significantly above or below the current market price.

Part-time traders can analyze markets after the close and enter limit orders for the following day. After you receive confirmation that the limit order has been executed, you should enter a stop loss order.

Calling a halt: Stop orders

A *stop order* specifies that you enter or exit a position after the security's price reaches a predefined level. Two types of stop orders exist:

- ✔ **Sell stop orders:** This type of order instructs your broker to sell shares of a security at a preset price if the security reaches that price or a lower one. Sell stop orders are useful to protect your capital or enter a short position.

- ✔ **Buy stop orders:** A buy stop order instructs the broker to buy a security if its shares trade at or above a predefined price level. Consider employing buy stop orders when entering a position on the long side or attempting to protect your capital on a short position.

Both types of stop orders become market orders when the price in question is reached. Note, however, that because they become market orders (which instruct a broker to execute a trade immediately), you may receive a price that's worse or better than the price you specify.

Mixing the best of both worlds: Stop limit orders

Think of a *stop limit order* as a combination of a stop order and a limit order. When your predefined price is reached, the stop limit order becomes a limit order to ensure you don't execute at a price that's significantly different than what you expected. You shouldn't mind not getting filled if you haven't entered the security yet or if you're simply trying to maximize profit. But when matters are growing ugly, you can't afford for an order not to execute because it became a limit order.

Only go on green lights

When I first started trading, I often sized up charts based on my limited knowledge. I had no formal trading plan. Instead, I brought up a security price chart that I'd identified as being undervalued on some fundamental basis and looked for chart patterns I recognized while applying technical indicators. If I saw that the Moving Average Convergence/Divergence indicator was officially on a buy, I'd take the plunge.

I later discovered that this method is suboptimal trading. Why? Because such an approach often leads to entering a trade well after a signal was generated. If you wait until a signal is generated and then enter your order shortly thereafter, you're less likely to enter a trend late.

A better swing trading approach is to only execute when you see clear-cut signals in a security's price movement and only execute on the day (or the day after) that signal appears. For this method to work, you need to make sure you don't have multiple signals firing off every second. If you go through 50 securities, only a few should have conditions that meet your entry criteria. Otherwise, your criteria may be too loose.

Suppose your trading plan calls for entering a security when its nine-day moving average turns positive. Does that allow you to enter any time the moving average is rising? The answer depends on whether the nine-day moving average has just turned up or has been rising for several days.

This chart shows a late entry on December 19, when the nine-day moving average was rising (and had been rising for nine days). Entering late in a case like this is riskier and allows you to take less profit than you could have if the execution were timed to the day the actual signal appeared.

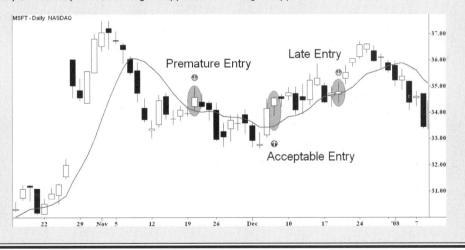

MSFT - Daily NASDAQ

Premature Entry

Late Entry

Acceptable Entry

You should only use a stop limit order when entering a security or for entering an order to take profits. Don't use a stop limit order as a stop loss order, because the limit part of the order may prevent a timely exit when things are turning sour.

Just for kicks, say you decide to buy shares of THQ Inc. that have been in a range between $15 and $20. Suppose you enter a buy stop order of 1,000 shares at $20.29 — so you can enter a position after shares break above their trading range. If THQ reports blockbuster earnings one day and shares open at $30 per share, you'll own 1,000 shares at $30 or so. However, you'll have increased your position size by 50 percent because of the gap. The original order would've bought $20,290 worth of stock. The actual order buys $30,000 worth of stock.

The solution to this conundrum is a stop limit order. Had you entered a stop limit order of $20.29, the stop order would've become a limit order after shares traded at or above $20.29. A buy limit order at $20.29 wouldn't have been executed if shares were trading at $30.

Placing Orders as a Part-Time Swing Trader

Having a full-time job doesn't preclude you from swing trading. You just need to carefully craft your order-entry system to account for the uncertainty of how security prices will perform when the market opens the following day.

One of the keys to mastering order entries and exits is to execute *only* on the day after a trading signal — likely a chart pattern of some kind or a technical indicator. Never initiate just because an entry signal exists today but was generated a few days or weeks back. If your entry method calls for buying stocks when the nine-day moving average turns up, don't buy a security with a nine-day moving average that turned up last week.

The next two sections break down how you can enter and exit a security as a part-time swing trader.

Entering the fray

A limit order is your primary entry weapon as a part-time swing trader. If a buy signal appears on a particular day, you can review the day's price behavior and determine where to place a reasonable limit buy order. Be choosy. If your limit order isn't filled, no big deal. There are plenty of fish in the sea — just wait for the next one. By not desperately chasing after the security, you can enter trades on *your* terms when prices come to you.

You don't want to trade the opening of a market. This is a chaotic time when news that emerged after the market closed the previous day is reflected in opening share prices. There can be major swings, both positive and negative.

Never, never, never — did I say never? — enter a market order when the market is closed. Doing so can only cause grief and heartache. A market order entered after the market closes is executed at the following day's opening price — regardless of what that price is. Because movements can be fierce at the opening, you can't enter market orders the previous day due to the uncertainty of where the price executions will occur. Even if you want to buy shares at the price they closed at the prior day, a market order may be executed significantly above or below that price, depending on prevailing market conditions (that is, how many market orders exist, the distribution of buys and sells, and the market maker's own share inventory). Always keep in mind the ol' Wall Street saying concerning order entry when the market opens versus when the market closes: "Amateurs trade the open. Professionals trade the close."

Exiting to cut your losses (or make a profit)

Exiting a swing trade is another matter. Unlike entering, where patience can pay dividends, exiting should be done quickly and judiciously. Why? Because you usually exit a position for one of two reasons — either your profit target was hit or an indicator flashed an exit signal. When either of these scenarios occurs, don't sit around to see what other traders will do.

When you exit for a loss, you want out at the available price. That's why I recommend that part-time swing traders use stop loss orders, which automatically convert into a market order when the specified price level is reached. As a part-time swing trader, you should also use trailing stop loss orders. These are stop loss orders that are raised or lowered (depending on whether you're long or short the security) over time as the trade goes in your favor. Raising these orders protects your profits (unless the security gaps through the stop loss area).

Placing Orders if Swing Trading's Your Full-Time Gig

If you're a full-time swing trader, you have more tools at your disposal. Because you can watch the market during the day, you can enter market orders when appropriate and monitor short-term buying and selling activity.

The following sections lay out how to set up your trading system as a full-time swing trader and how to put various tools to use to make your job easier.

Considering the best order types for you

Like your part-time counterparts, you can plan to rely on limit orders for entries and stop loss orders for exits if you're a full-time swing trader. However, because you spend more time swing trading, you have the luxury of choosing how you enter trades depending on the overall market environment. Rarely is a security so hot that you absolutely need to execute a market order. More often than not, you can size up the market and enter a limit order near a recent intraday support or resistance level.

You want to execute an order entry or exit *only* on the day of a trading signal, which pops out at you with the help of chart patterns or technical indicators. Always react to current trading signals, not signals that first appeared on your radar a while back.

Taking advantage of intraday charting to time your entries and exits

As a full-time swing trader, you can improve your trading results by applying an *intraday trading overlay,* which is a system of entry based on intraday charting, to your existing entry plan. After a trading signal is generated on a daily chart, you can zoom in on a 30-minute or 1-hour chart and time your entry based on some technical indicator (see more on that later in this chapter). Sometimes, this trading overlay can help you avoid buying or shorting securities that are about to reverse course. Other times, the intraday trading overlay helps you receive better prices on your trades. Of course, it's also possible that the trading overlay could result in paying worse prices if a security is in a strong trend. There are no free lunches in trading.

For example, you may enter securities on the day (or the day after) their nine-day moving average turns higher, provided that certain intraday charting signals are also met. This second step filters out securities that may be showing strength on a daily chart but weakness on an hourly or 30-minute chart.

I don't think an intraday trading overlay is absolutely essential to swing trade successfully, but it can improve your returns if used intelligently. The system's intention is to improve your entry or exit price by analyzing the prior days' support and resistance levels and reading the signals generated by the technical indicators. If a buy signal is generated on a daily chart but you see weakness in the intraday chart, then the prudent course of action is to wait for the intraday chart to stabilize and rebound before entering. Occasionally, the intraday trading overlay keeps you out of a security that's in the process of tanking or rising, depending on whether you're buying or shorting.

Intraday trading overlay saved the day

Want some proof as to how using intraday trading overlay can help improve your swing trading results? Consider the following figure that provides an example of a daily chart buy signal that wasn't confirmed by the intraday chart.

This figure shows Toll Brothers in April 2008 (with a daily chart on the top and an hourly chart on the bottom). A swing trader entering a short position based on the nine-day moving average's slope could've avoided a whipsaw (when shares rallied shortly after falling) by using an hourly chart. The nine-day moving average turned negative on April 11. However, the hourly chart showed an MACD indicator divergence: As prices moved lower, the MACD histogram traced higher troughs. (See Chapter 5 for more on this and other technical indicators.) This movement preceded a rally in shares of Toll Brothers and a reversal of the nine-day moving average slope.

So although the daily chart generated a sell signal based on that moving average, the hourly chart showed the bulls gaining strength — knowledge that helped save the swing trader using this system some heartache and loss.

Selecting the appropriate time frame

Most real-time charting programs allow you to analyze 1-minute, 5-minute, 10-minute, 30-minute, and 1-hour charts. That's an awful lot of time frames. If a technical indicator looks negative on one intraday time frame, a naïve swing trader may turn to a different intraday time frame to see whether that indicator gives the signal he or she wants. After all, charts, like statistics, can be tortured into telling you what you want to hear.

Always be consistent in the time frames you use (such as daily and hourly, or daily and 30 minutes). I recommend sticking to one intraday time frame because doing so simplifies matters and avoids the temptation of flipping through time frames to see which one is giving you the signals you want to see.

Personally, I prefer a 30-minute or hourly chart. I feel that charts covering shorter periods of time belong in the day trader's arena, because the shorter the time period, the noisier the market. You want to trade short but powerful trends that are driven by some fundamental reason — not by the fact that some pension fund's liquidating shares to deliver a retiree a lump-sum payment.

Choosing your entry criteria

Intraday charting systems can be as varied as systems based on daily price data. An hourly or 30-minute chart may call for entry based on one of the following criteria:

- ✔ A moving average crossover
- ✔ An MACD buy signal
- ✔ A breakout out of a consolidation phase
- ✔ A new hourly bar high

You may base your entry signals on a technical criterion identified above or on some different technical criteria of your choosing. Just don't base your entry criteria on chart patterns. I've found that chart patterns formed over a few hours aren't as reliable as those formed over several weeks or months.

Balancing the advantages and disadvantages of intraday trading signals

Your biggest advantage as a full-time swing trader over a trader who can't watch the markets throughout the day is the ability to enter an order as soon as a trading signal appears. This advantage is even greater in securities that tend to be volatile. By paying attention to the signals generated through your intraday charting system, you can enter earlier than traders who rely on end-of-day data.

Yet this blessing can easily become a curse, because trading signals gener-ated intraday can be reversed intraday. In such cases, you may need to exit your position because the original reason for entering was reversed.

One way to mitigate the risk of an intraday trading signal reversal is to execute orders in the last hour of the trading day.

Investigating who's behind the bidding: Nasdaq Level II quotes

Nasdaq Level II quotes, posted prices that show you who's bidding for and offering shares of the security you're about to enter, are more of a staple for day traders, but they may be helpful in your full-time swing trading arsenal. They allow you to quickly see the relative positioning of orders by market makers. Generally, Nasdaq Level II quotes are only available for securities trading on Nasdaq and can be obtained from most brokers and real-time charting programs.

The following sections help you dive into the nitty-gritty of Nasdaq Level II quotes.

Contrasting Level I and Level II quotes

Level I quotes (think of them as the standard quotes you receive from Yahoo! Finance or Google) report what the current bid and ask prices are. They also include how many shares are being bid and how many shares are being offered. But don't expect any bells or whistles. A Level I quote, like that shown in Figure 11-1 of shares of Warnaco Group (symbol: WRNC), shows top-level data that can be helpful as a snapshot.

Figure 11-1: A Level I quote of WRNC.

Warnaco Group Inc. (WRNC)		At 4:00PM ET: 44.68 ↑1.49 (3.45%)

WARNACO GROUP INC (NasdaqGS: WRNC)

Last Trade:	44.68	Day's Range:	43.32 - 45.19
Trade Time:	4:00PM ET	52wk Range:	26.90 - 45.19
Change:	↑1.49 (3.45%)	Volume:	826,558
Prev Close:	43.19	Avg Vol (3m):	998,270
Open:	44.09	Market Cap:	2.02B
Bid:	42.89 x 800	P/E (ttm):	26.33
Ask:	45.70 x 400	EPS (ttm):	1.70
1y Target Est:	49.57	Div & Yield:	N/A (N/A)

More On WRNC
Quotes
▶ Summary
Options
Historical Prices
Charts
Interactive
Basic Chart
Basic Tech. Analysis
News & Info
Headlines
Financial Blogs
Company Events
Message Board

WRNC 18-Apr 3:55pm (C)Yahoo!
Add WRNC to Your Portfolio
Set Alert for WRNC
Download Data
Add Quotes to Your Web Site

Source: Yahoo! Finance

Nasdaq Level II quotes give traders a wealth of information on order and trading activity in Nasdaq-listed securities. Whereas a Level I quote tells you what the best bids and offers are, Level II quotes tell you who else is bidding or offering shares away from the market (that is, at prices above the best offer and below the best bid). This information can be valuable in discerning short-term price movements.

Figure 11-2 shows a typical Level II quote. You can see that different market makers are offering to buy (left side) and sell (right side) shares of Microsoft (symbol: MSFT). Notice that at each price, a market maker offers a certain amount of shares (shown here as size). The number of market makers offering shares on both the buy and sell sides at very close prices indicates that this security has significant market depth.

Avoid thinking that Level II quotes confer some type of trading advantage. Other swing traders, day traders, and the like have Level II quotes. The key is how you *use* the quotes. As a swing trader, you must recognize that you won't derive a significant source of *alpha,* or outperformance, from your near-term trading by using Level II quotes. You can, however, improve your entry and exit prices and add a small amount of return during the course of a year.

Your intraday trading overlay may rely on Level II quotes as opposed to technical signals generated on an hourly or 30-minute chart. In that case, you may enter on pullbacks in price action. Alternatively, you may wait to see strong buying or selling activity, depending on whether you're looking to open a long or short position.

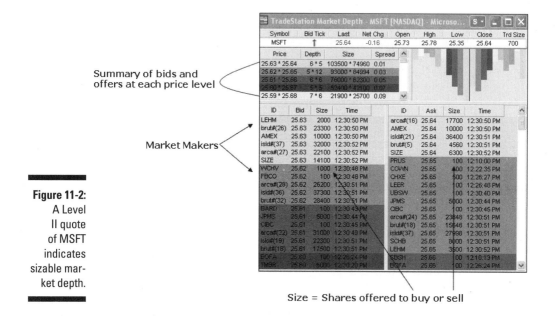

Figure 11-2:
A Level II quote of MSFT indicates sizable market depth.

Summary of bids and offers at each price level

Market Makers

Size = Shares offered to buy or sell

The ups and downs of intraday trading

Intraday trading certainly has its ups and downs. Just take a look at these examples.

If shares of Southwestern Energy move higher and trigger a moving average crossover or MACD buy signal at 10 a.m., when shares are at $25.37, a full-time swing trader is able to execute a limit order near or at $25.37. Southwestern Energy may move higher and close above $26 by the end of the day. The swing trader who trades on after-market data has to enter a limit order for the following trading day — and Southwestern Energy may rise further the next morning. So the full-time swing trader may enter a position at a significant discount or premium (depending on whether said swing trader is buying or shorting) compared to a part-time swing trader relying on after-market data.

But this blessing can be a curse because trading signals generated intraday can be reversed intraday. In other words, Southwestern Energy shares may trade at a certain price level to generate an MACD buy signal at 10 a.m. A swing trader may then buy shares of the company on that signal. However, a late day sell-off may send shares lower, reversing the original signal. The part-time swing trader who relies on after-market data to trade won't be whipsawed like the full-time swing trader. Because the part-time trader relies on data based on closing prices, the false signal generated intraday never shows up on his or her screen.

I used to think that having Level II quotes somehow gave me an advantage over the common man — like I was going to improve my trading game with a tool akin to X-ray vision. Don't buy into that idea like I did. Level II quotes are a short-term guide — and I mean short. Day traders derive more value from Level II quotes than swing traders because their time horizons are measured in minutes. Of course, I don't mean you should ignore the Level II quote screen. Just consider placing more emphasis on intraday charting (covered earlier in this chapter).

Evaluating the quotes

Level II quotes have a couple of salient features. First, bids and offers for securities are separated into two panes. The left pane displays various market makers' bids to buy at various prices, and the right pane displays the offers to sell by various market markers at various prices. Confused? Take a look back at Figure 11-2.

The left side of the pane shows that LEHM is offering to buy 2,000 shares of security MSFT at $25.63. LEHM is the market maker and is the four-letter abbreviation of Lehman Brothers. (All market makers are identified by four-letter symbols.) Directly below LEHM is BRUT, who's offering to buy 23,300 shares at $25.63. If you look at the right pane, you can see that ARCA is offering to sell 17,700 shares of MSFT at $25.64. (Unlike Lehman Brothers, which is a market maker, BRUT and ARCA are electronic communication networks

[ECNs] and are likely representing customer orders and *not* market maker activities. You can read more about ECNs in Chapter 1.) The bid/ask spread is only one cent, and the number of shares offered at the bid and ask are large. This security has significant depth. A swing trader placing a market order is unlikely to move the security an inch.

Verifying the accuracy of quotes with the Time & Sales report

Market makers play games to cover their true intentions on how many shares they're bidding on or offering for sale. They realize that if they show their hand too much, then traders will react to that information and make their lives more difficult. Your task is to determine whether their stated intentions are consistent with their actions.

The *Time & Sales report* (shown in Figure 11-3 and available from most brokers and real-time charting packages) shows the actual buys and sells that occur during the trading day. Sometimes market makers try to deceive other traders on what their intentions are and whether they're aggressive buyers or sellers in the market — or whether they're indifferent. So keep an eye on the Time & Sales report, and monitor whether trades are being executed at the asking price, the bid price, in between the bid and ask, or outside of the bid or ask.

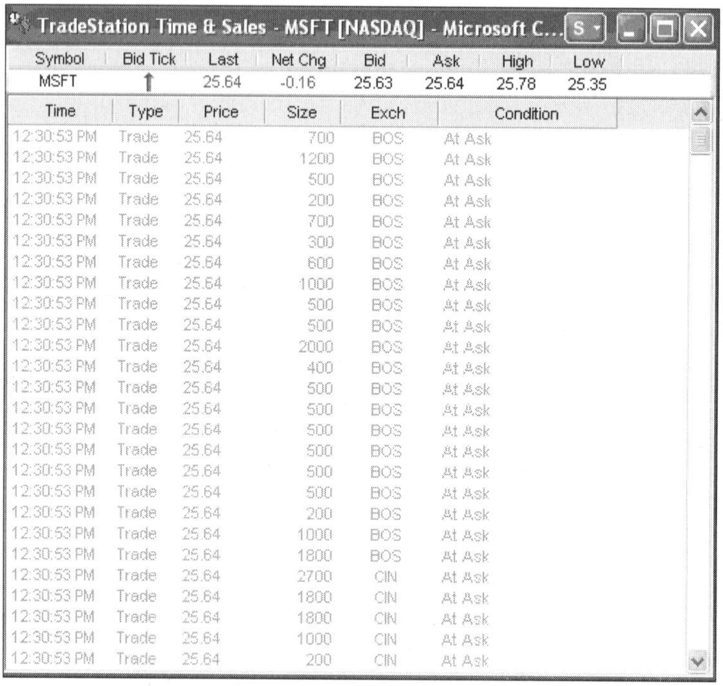

Figure 11-3: Use the Time & Sales report to compare actual trades to market makers' supposed intentions.

Getting the lay of the market-maker land for direct-access trading

If your broker offers you direct-access trading (the ability to trade directly with market makers or specialists), you may be able to direct your orders to specific market makers. (For further explanation of direct-access trading and help deciding whether it's appropriate for you, please refer to Chapter 2.) Therefore, you should have an idea of who the major market makers are. Following are the top ten market makers and their four-letter abbreviations for Nasdaq-listed and NYSE-listed securities. For a complete, up-to-date list of both, visit www.nasdaqtrader.com and click on "Market Statistics" at the top of the page. Then click on "Top Liquidity Providers."

Top Ten Liquidity Providers (at press time): Nasdaq-Listed Securities

- Wedbush Morgan Securities Inc.: WEDB
- Lehman Brothers Inc.: LEHM
- Morgan Stanley & Co., Incorporated: MSCO
- UBS Securities LLC: UBSS
- Merrill Lynch, Pierce, Fenner & Smith Incorporated: MLCO
- Citadel Derivatives Group LLC: CDRG
- Goldman, Sachs & Co.: GSCO
- J. P. Morgan Securities Inc.: JPMS
- Credit Suisse Securities (USA) LLC: FBCO
- Knight Capital Group Inc.: NITE

Top Ten Liquidity Providers (at press time): NYSE-Listed Securities

- Wedbush Morgan Securities Inc.: WEDB
- Morgan Stanley & Co., Incorporated: MSCO
- J.P. Morgan Securities Inc.: JPMS
- Citadel Derivatives Group LLC: CDRG
- Merrill Lynch, Pierce, Fenner & Smith Incorporated: MLCO
- Instinet LLC: INCA
- Lehman Brothers Inc.: LEHM
- UBS Securities LLC: UBSS
- Credit Suisse Securities (USA) LLC: FBCO
- Lime Brokerage LLC: LIME

The Time & Sales report is helpful when used in conjunction with the Level II quote screen, which shows posted prices by market makers, because the Time & Sales report shows actual trades. These facts help tell you whether market participants are bluffing. For example, a market maker may post a large sell order on behalf of a client so as to scare others into selling to him or her at lower prices. Using the Time & Sales report and Level II quote screens together can tell you whether

- **Buyers are more aggressive than sellers:** This scenario is likely the case if there are major buyers on the bid with large share sizes, and the shares offered on the ask side are small in comparison. If the Time & Sales report shows executions at the ask price (or above it), you have confirmation that buyers are more aggressive.

  ✔ **Near-term price pressure is coming:** This situation tends to happen if
    large share sizes are being offered on the ask by multiple market
    makers, and the share sizes offered on the bid are small. Confirm price
    weakness with the Time & Sales report where trades should be occur-
    ring at or below the bid price.

Swing traders who incorporate Level II analysis into their trading systems
often look for signs of short-term strength or weakness to improve their
timing. In such cases, the Time & Sales report must be read in conjunction
with the changing quote system.

In fast-moving markets, the report moves quickly. Trades may occur at the
bid, at the ask, in between the bid and ask, or outside the bid and ask. When
trades are executing at the ask, that's a sign of short-term price strength.
When trades are executing at the bid, that's a sign of short-term price
weakness.

Chapter 12

Walking through a Trade, Swing-Style

In This Chapter

▶ Looking for market trends and finding top industry groups

▶ Choosing the best trade candidates and limiting your losses

▶ Making the trade and recording it in your journal

▶ Watching your positions and improving your system

*R*emember those times in high school or college when your teacher explained some pretty technical concepts that seemed to fly right over your head? (If this doesn't apply to you, congratulations, you're a genius in my book.) I can recall several subjects, both boring and exciting, that I never fully understood, even as the concepts were being explained.

However, when I heard the teacher say, "Let's walk through an example," my eyes lit up. Examples bring color to concepts. They elucidate fine points that can't really be fully understood without practical application.

Consider this chapter your own "Let's walk through an example" moment. Here, I take the view of the swing trader looking for a trading opportunity, and this chapter provides an example of identifying a potential trade by going through the eight major steps. These steps show you how to integrate concepts covered in other parts of this book. I use the top-down analysis framework (see Chapters 6 and 8) to identify and execute the trade, and all the data I use is actual market data. If you see how I approach and research potential candidates to swing trade, you can build on the techniques I present or incorporate aspects you agree with.

Step 1: Sizing Up the Market

Mr. Market is where all things start for the swing trader. You have to know the state of the equity, commodity, fixed income, and even currency markets to be a savvy trader. Why? Because these markets are related. For example, if you notice that currency prices are rising, you should be prepared for a bear market in bond prices. Or if you see bond prices falling rapidly, you're likely to see weakness in equities. Rising oil prices positively affect shares of energy companies; the weakening dollar helps boost commodity prices; and so on. Watching all major markets improves your trading ability by giving you an indication of the likely direction of other markets.

Because you're likely to trade equities, you may want to closely examine U.S. equity markets to determine which style (growth or value) is performing well and which market cap ranges (large cap, mid cap, or small cap) lead the market. The best way to achieve this analysis is through relative strength charts, which plot one index versus another (see Chapter 6).

Looking for short-term trends on the daily chart

At the time I'm writing this, the date is April 4, 2008. I want to analyze how the equity markets look. Figure 12-1 shows a snapshot of a daily chart of the S&P 500 Index in late 2007 and early 2008. Also plotted are the MACD indicator and the 17-day moving average. The 17-day moving average smoothes out price changes and helps determine short-term market direction.

When I examine any market, I ask myself whether the market is in a trading range or trend. Figure 12-1 shows a market that's in a trading range. However, it looks to be entering a trend. Notice any familiar chart patterns on the far right of the screen? (Check out Chapter 4 for a refresher on popular chart patterns.)

Figure 12-1:
The daily chart of the S&P 500 Index in late 2007 and early 2008.

I see a potential inverse head-and-shoulders pattern (I've listed the left shoulder as "LS," the right shoulder as "RS," and the head as "Head"). This formation is bullish and is near completion, which argues for higher prices near-term. Also notice that the slope of the 17-day moving average is positive. Finally, the MACD plot is above the 0 line, indicating that the 12-day exponential moving average is above the 26-day exponential moving average (see Chapter 5 for more information). All these factors argue for short-term price strength.

Analyzing the weekly chart for longer-term trends

One chart's time frame isn't sufficient for your analysis. You must also look at the weekly chart to determine whether the longer trend is up or down.

The weekly chart in Figure 12-2 shows the S&P 500 Index in late 2006 through early 2008, along with the 17-week moving average and the weekly MACD. The intermediate trend is down, as measured by the 17-week moving average's negative slope. However, the short-term trend is up, as indicated by the rising MACD histogram (a facet of the MACD indicator explained in Chapter 5).

The weekly chart shows conflicting data. The daily chart shows a market with a rising 17-day moving average, a rising MACD signal line, and a potential inverse head-and-shoulders pattern — all bullish items. The weekly chart, on the other hand, shows a falling 17-week moving average, meaning that the intermediate trend is down.

Figure 12-2:
The weekly chart of the S&P 500 Index from late 2006 through early 2008.

But the weekly MACD histogram is rising, which indicates short-term price strength. Because swing traders have short-term time horizons, they should trade in the direction of the short-term trend. You can always adjust quickly to the other side of the market should the short-term trend turn down and be consistent with the intermediate trend. But the weekly chart indicates that caution is warranted. The intermediate trend can exert itself at any time. Keep stop loss orders tight.

If you're primarily trading stocks, then analyzing other asset classes may help you identify which sectors to focus on and whether to trade the long or short side of the market. For example, when the yields on government bonds become significantly higher than the earnings yield of the S&P 500 Index (see Chapter 8 for a full explanation of how to calculate this), stock prices may come under pressure as money flows into higher yielding assets.

This first step shows a mixed market. The short-term trend is up, but the intermediate trend is down. You should focus on trading candidates on the long side. The market is in rally mode, and you want to ride the wave. Perform a similar type of analysis in the bond, currency, and commodity markets.

Step 2: Identifying the Top Industry Groups

In the example I began in the previous section, the short-term trend is up, so you should look for new positions on the long side of the market. To do so, you need to examine the leading industry groups. Buying stocks in leading groups increases the chances your stock will rise with the overall market.

You can identify leading industry groups in several ways. *Investor's Business Daily* publishes a ranking of all industry groups in the market. You can focus on that list's top 10 percent to identify stocks on the long side of the market. *High Growth Stock Investor (HGS Investor)* is a software program that provides a ranking of the leading/lagging industry groups and allows users to plot each industry group. Analyzing industry group charts is a step up from simply focusing on the top 10 percent because you can apply the technical analysis tools I cover in Chapters 4 and 5.

Figure 12-3 shows a chart of the top-performing industry groups from early February through late April 2008. The groups are ranked in order of performance. For example, the Construction Residential/Commercial Index is ranked 99 for the week of April 4, which means it outperformed 99 percent of all industry groups. Put another way, it performed in the top 1 percent among all groups.

Name	Symbol	4/4/08	3/28/08	3/21/08	3/14/08	3/7/08	2/29/08
1. Constr-Resid/Cml Index	INDEX	99	99	99	90	86	86
2. Steel-Producers Index	INDEX	99	99	95	98	99	98
3. Retail-Home Products Index	INDEX	98	98	98	68	79	56
4. Energy-Drilling Index	INDEX	98	95	88	96	95	98
5. Retail-Discount Index	INDEX	97	96	99	71	69	40
6. Energy-Explor&Prod Index	INDEX	96	97	96	98	98	99
7. Transpt-Railroads Index	INDEX	96	99	97	96	94	94
8. Machine-Farm Index	INDEX	95	94	92	82	94	90
9. Retail-Bldg Prods Index	INDEX	94	94	96	85	78	72
10. Machine-Const/Mining Index	INDEX	94	80	58	89	90	87
11. Energy-Royalty Tr Index	INDEX	93	96	99	99	98	97
12. Machine-General Index	INDEX	92	77	75	73	74	61
13. Transpt-Air Freight Index	INDEX	92	92	91	83	88	81
14. Energy-Alternatives Index	INDEX	91	57	3	41	82	92
15. Retail-Auto Parts Index	INDEX	90	74	84	59	56	18
16. Container Prod Index	INDEX	90	91	80	79	82	67
17. Trvl&Leisr-Game/Hobby Index	INDEX	89	88	82	51	31	28
18. Metal Products Index	INDEX	88	73	54	65	77	69
19. Retail-Apparel/Shoe Index	INDEX	88	71	72	35	30	46
20. Chem-Speciality Index	INDEX	87	85	71	94	97	96
21. Elec-Parts Distrib Index	INDEX	86	53	37	47	59	48
22. Elec-Connect&MiscPrt Index	INDEX	86	43	41	48	40	38
23. Comp-Educ/Enter Index	INDEX	85	85	87	84	80	79
24. Bev-Brewer&Distiller Index	INDEX	84	88	90	92	88	90
25. Transpt-Trucking&Parts Index	INDEX	84	82	69	58	56	34
26. Comp-Financial Index	INDEX	83	80	68	74	68	65
27. Conglomerate Index	INDEX	82	75	74	84	86	86
28. Retail-Mail Order Index	INDEX	82	67	85	73	40	33
29. Machine-Mtl Hdlg Index	INDEX	81	82	64	69	75	79
30. Pollution Equip&Svc Index	INDEX	80	84	80	77	92	89
31. Elec-Military Index	INDEX	80	83	86	87	89	88
32. Retail-Office Supl Index	INDEX	79	63	57	56	52	14
33. Auto-Parts & Equip Index	INDEX	79	76	63	57	76	73
34. Banking-NE Index	INDEX	78	90	93	88	80	82

Figure 12-3: The top-performing industry groups from early February through late April 2008.

So what this step tells you is that you should start your search for promising swing trades in the industry groups ranking in the top 10 percent for long candidates and the bottom 10 percent for short candidates.

Now that you know which groups are leading, look for candidates in the top two industry groups: Construction Residential/Commercial and Steel Producers. The following section takes you through that step.

Step 3: Selecting Promising Candidates

Knowing which industry groups to focus on is really half the battle, so you cover most of your assessment in just the first two steps. Your success is driven more by which side of the market you trade and the industry groups you select than by which company you select in an industry.

So how do you choose promising candidates on the long side of the market in the two industry groups cited in the preceding section? Most swing traders primarily use technical analysis to select a security. I recommend you use fundamental analysis first to select the most promising candidates. Then use technical analysis to time your entries and exits.

I want to stress the importance of considering a company's fundamentals: Even if it's simply ranking companies in an industry by their PEG ratios (the lower the better, as explained in Chapter 9) or taking the Earnings Rank provided by *Investor's Business Daily, HGS Investor,* and other products, you're better off incorporating some type of fundamental approach in your swing trading versus no fundamental analysis at all.

Screening securities

Before you select a company to trade, be sure to apply some filter to the security both on the long and short side of the market within the industry group you're analyzing. This screen (see Chapter 8 for more on how to use screens) is primarily designed to filter out thinly traded securities (those that carry significant liquidity risk) and penny stocks (which I define as stock trading below $5 per share). I recommend the following simple screen, which I use regularly:

- ✔ Stock price ≥ $5
- ✔ Average daily volume ≥ 100,000 shares
- ✔ Market capitalization ≥ $250 million

Applying this screen to the Construction Residential/Commercial industry group narrows the list down to 17 companies, whereas applying the filter to the Steel Producers group leaves 14 companies.

Ranking the filtered securities and assessing chart patterns

After applying a filter to the securities on both sides of the leading and lagging industry groups, rank the remaining securities by some measure — a fundamental one (such as return on equity) or a technical one (such as days since last DMI crossover, covered in Chapter 5). Then review the securities in that industry and isolate the ones that meet your entry criteria (which should be simple and clear, free of subjective interpretations).

In general, I prefer to rank securities by price to cash flow ratio or earnings rank. Then I go through the stock charts of the leading securities and look for the stocks with the most promising chart patterns. I find that this two-step process works best because it begins with fundamentally strong companies and then looks for attractive charts. If you begin with attractive charts, you're going to have a tougher time finding fundamentally promising companies among the strongest charts because you'll be unable to quickly rank the fundamentals of any prospects to other candidates. (In other words, it's easier to find strong charts among undervalued companies than it is to find undervalued companies among strong charts.)

So that's how I go about ranking securities, but your method may vary. You can approach this process in literally an endless number of ways, and no one way is right. The important thing is that your method is based on principles that you agree with and that lead to strong performance.

Chapters 4 and 5 take you through finding securities from the technical side of the market, whereas Chapters 7, 8, and 9 take you through the fundamental steps. In this section, though, I walk you through the process I'd follow if I were trading these securities.

Narrowing your list of prospects

Ranking securities pushes the cream to the top. For this trade, I've ranked the securities in both industry groups by return on equity (which is covered in Chapter 8). The results are shown in Figure 12-4.

Constr-Resid/Cml

	Name	Symb	ROE
1	NVR INC.	NVR	29.28%
2	DESARROLLADORA HOMEX S A DE	HXM	21.24%
3	BROOKFIELD HOMES CORP	BHS	4.16%
4	D R HORTON INC	DHI	0.00%
5	GAFISA S.A.	GFA	0.00%
6	TOLL BROS INC	TOL	-3.32%
7	BEAZER HOMES USA INC	BZH	-8.56%
8	Constr-Resid/Cml Index	INDEX	-24.47%
9	RYLAND GROUP INC	RYL	-25.31%
10	MERITAGE HOMES CORP	MTH	-33.26%
11	M D C HLDGS INC	MDC	-35.02%
12	PULTE HOMES INC	PHM	-41.74%
13	CENTEX CORP	CTX	-43.78%
14	LENNAR CORP	LEN	-44.37%
15	STANDARD PAC CORP NEW	SPF	-50.39%
16	HOVNANIAN ENTERPRISES INC	HOV	-50.93%
17	KB HOME	KBH	-75.33%

Steel-Producers

	Name	Symb	ROE
1	AK STL HLDG CORP	AKS	60.03%
2	COMPANHIA SIDERURGICA NACL	SID	52.83%
3	GERDAU S A	GGB	48.67%
4	TENARIS S A	TS	33.80%
5	MECHEL OAO	MTL	31.76%
6	NUCOR CORP	NUE	29.53%
7	STEEL DYNAMICS INC	STLD	28.59%
8	Steel-Producers Index	INDEX	27.09%
9	AMPCO-PITTSBURG CORP	AP	23.93%
10	POSCO	PKX	23.07%
11	ARCELOR MITTAL	MT	20.98%
12	TERNIUM SA	TX	19.28%
13	UNITED STATES STL CORP NEW	X	17.76%
14	GRUPO SIMEC S.A.B. DE C.V.	SIM	12.76%

Figure 12-4:
A ranking of stocks by return on equity in two industry groups.

Handpicking the lucky ones

After you rank the securities you zone in on, go through the stock charts to identify criteria that meet your trading strategy. What you look for depends on what you've decided to incorporate into your trading plan. Perhaps you're looking for moving average crossovers in the presence of strong volume. Or maybe you're looking for cup-and-handle formations. Your trading rules need not be complex.

In fact, simple entry rules trump more complex ones. Buying when the moving average slope turns positive, for example, can be an effective entry criterion. Or you can buy when the MACD line crosses the 0 line. But more complex entry techniques can also work well. Perhaps you implement a trading indicator you read about in a trade magazine, or you wait to trade on divergences between an indicator and the share price. Whatever the method, make sure your entry criteria are clear and not subjective. You don't want an entry method that gives ambiguous signals or relies on someone's interpretation to determine whether to buy. Subjective analysis is risky because it opens up trading to inconsistent behavior.

For the purposes of this example, I'll buy a security when the MACD line crosses above its signal line, and I'll exit when the security closes below its nine-day moving average. To be more precise, I'm not looking for securities where the MACD line is simply above its signal line — several securities meet that rather loose criterion. No, I'm looking only for those securities with MACD lines above signal lines *today*. (You should only go on green. Never jump the gun by buying before a signal is generated and never wait and buy a few days after a signal is given.)

After reviewing the securities listed in Figure 12-4, I find two stocks that meet my entry criteria: Gafisa S.A. (symbol: GFA) in the Construction Residential/Commercial group, and Companhia Siderurgica Nacional (symbol: SID) in the Steel Producers group.

I never trade a security that's due to report earnings in the next two weeks, and I strongly advise you to follow this rule. As trading expert Ian Woodward said: "You don't have your hand on the steering wheel when you trade securities right before earnings dates." (If you're wondering, I confirmed that GFA and SID aren't due to report earnings in the next two weeks.)

GFA's chart, shown in Figure 12-5, reveals a security that's been in a trading range. On the far right side of the chart, notice that the MACD line has crossed above its signal line, meeting the entry criterion I outlined earlier. Also notice that volume on the day of the crossover was above average. The nine-day moving average has turned higher, but it has generated several whipsaw signals, a sign that the stock is in a trading range.

Figure 12-6 shows a chart of SID. SID has been consolidating for a few weeks and is breaking out of its consolidation. The MACD line is crossing over its signal line, but volume is below average. The nine-day moving average recently turned higher. Both are signs that the short-term trend is turning up.

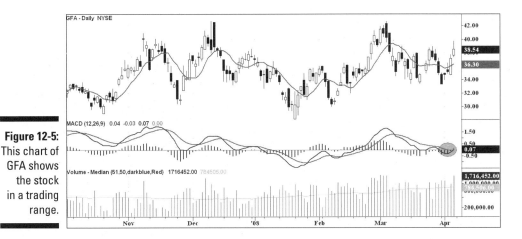

Figure 12-5:
This chart of GFA shows the stock in a trading range.

Figure 12-6:
This chart of SID shows the stock moving out of a consolidation phase.

Step 4: Determining Position Size

Okay, so I've found my trade, but how much do I allocate to it? Not all of it — nobody's that certain about a trade unless they have inside information, and even then, there's never a 100 percent guarantee that things will turn out the way you want.

Chapter 10 outlines two different ways to set your position size: by percent of capital (not recommended) or by risk level. Determine your position size by identifying your stop loss level and limiting losses between 0.25 percent and 2.0 percent of your account value should the security reach that stop loss level. For these two trades, I'm setting my position size based on a risk level. Specifically, I'm going to calculate how many shares I can buy of GFA and SID, assuming I place stop loss orders below a recent support level.

Keeping an eye on dollar fluctuations

Both swing trade candidates in this chapter are foreign firms, as is probably evident by the companies' names. Foreign companies that generate profits in foreign currencies are more valuable in U.S. dollars if the dollar weakens relative to those foreign currencies.

As you can see from the nearby graph, the U.S. dollar index hit major peaks in July 2001 and February 2002, but it's been in a strong downtrend since then because budget deficits and current account deficits have made the dollar less attractive to foreign investors. Should the U.S. continue to run major current account deficits (driven by balance of trade deficits), the dollar may continue to weaken. That's why reviewing the strength or weakness of the U.S. dollar should be a routine part of your market analysis. A declining dollar should heighten your awareness of foreign firms (often traded as American Depository Receipts) or U.S. firms with significant sources of foreign income. A complete listing of ADRs can be found at www. adr.com.

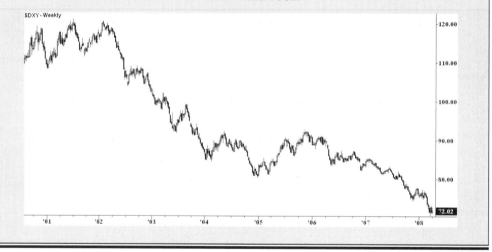

Setting your stop loss level

Your stop loss level is your emergency exit. Trading without one is akin to suicide. You need to know where to get out if things turn sour.

The GFA chart (refer to Figure 12-5) has a clear support level of $33.50. If the stock were to trade below $33.50, I believe it would be a sign that the trade had failed. But of course, I never place stop loss orders at predictable price levels where others may also place their orders. So I've decided to set my risk level at $33.18.

The SID chart (refer to Figure 12-6) has a clear support level of $35. If the stock were to trade below $35, I believe it would be a sign that the trade had failed. But again, I avoid placing stop loss orders at predictable price levels. So I've decided to set my risk level at $34.59.

Limiting your losses to a certain percentage

Your losses should be limited to some percentage of your total assets. Your position size is based on that percentage. If you limit losses to 2 percent of your total assets (an amount I consider aggressive), you should be able to take larger trades than swing traders who limit losses to 0.5 percent of their account values.

I'm assuming that my investment account is $100,000 and I want to limit my risk to 1 percent of my account. Also, I'm using the closing share price on April 4, 2008 — $38.54 — as my purchase price.

So how many shares of GFA can I buy? Here's how the math goes:

1. **Subtract the stop loss level from the purchase price.**

   $38.54 − $33.18 = $5.36

2. **Multiply the maximum allowable risk by the investment account total.**

   1% × $100,000 = $1,000

3. **Divide the number in Step 2 by the number in Step 1.**

   $1,000 ÷ $5.36 = 186 (rounded down)

Hence, I can buy 186 shares of GFA. (I recommend rounding down so you don't increase your risk beyond the 1 percent level).

Assuming the same account total, risk level, and purchase date as GFA, how many shares of SID can I buy? To get the answer, I go through the same mathematical procedure as I did with GFA:

1. **Subtract the stop loss level from the purchase price:**

   $39.22 − $34.59 = $4.63

2. **Multiply the maximum allowable risk by the investment account total:**

   1% × $100,000 = $1,000

3. **Divide the number in Step 2 by the number in Step 1:**

   $1,000 ÷ $4.63 = 215 (rounded down)

Hence, I can buy 215 shares of SID.

Step 5: Executing Your Order

Your order entry strategy should be consistent with your swing trading time commitment. Full-time swing traders can add an intraday trading overlay strategy to attempt to buy at a better price (flip to Chapter 11 for more on using this approach). Part-time swing traders should use limit orders to enter near the closing price on the day the signal was generated.

Personally, I don't use a secondary trading overlay for the simple reason that I'm not looking to add value on such a micro level. My outperformance (or *alpha*) should come over holding the trade for a few days or a few weeks. Hence, I'm not as concerned about what the security is doing minute to minute — as long as it holds above my stop loss level.

Whether you're a full- or part-time swing trader, entering stop loss orders (as *good until cancelled* so they aren't cancelled after one day) as soon as you execute your trades is critically important.

The only exception to this rule is for full-time traders who watch their positions during market hours, every day. Such traders can, if they so choose, enter price alerts on their positions at levels where a stop loss order would be entered. Using shares of SID from earlier in this chapter as an example, a full-time swing trader may enter the stop loss level $34.59 as the level when he or she receives an alert from *TradeStation* in the form of an e-mail or a message box. After that alert is hit, the trader can execute the order, perhaps using a Level II quote to assist in the timing of the trade.

But using such mental stop loss orders has its downsides, the biggest of which is that exiting losing positions isn't automated. Entering a position isn't as laced with emotions as exiting for a loss is. When you have to sell a losing position (or cover a losing short position), you may start to second-guess yourself. You may look at the chart to see whether the stop loss level was set too aggressively. Perhaps there's a support level a few points below the current price and you'd prefer to nudge down the stop loss level. And then perhaps while you're thinking about this, you notice that the price has temporarily recovered above the stop loss level. "See, I knew this was probably going to turn around." Before you know it, you've come up with perfect excuses on why you should let it run farther and cut losses at some other level.

That's why I prefer automated stop loss levels. Yes, entering a stop loss level does officially post my order for all to see. But I'll take that cost over the possibility of letting my emotions influence my exit from a losing position. The stop loss order does its job, no emotions involved. It executes, and you're notified after it happens.

Step 6: Recording Your Trade

Now that I've executed my trades, my next job is to record them in my trading journal. The more detailed your journal, the more helpful it is. On the other hand, if you enter so much detail that you come to dread recording your trades, you may fail to keep your journal up to date and the work will eventually pile up. So always try to strike a balance.

In Chapter 3, I highlight the information your journal should contain — you want to keep it simple but provide enough detail to make the journal useful. Figure 12-7 shows a snapshot of a journal entry for SID.

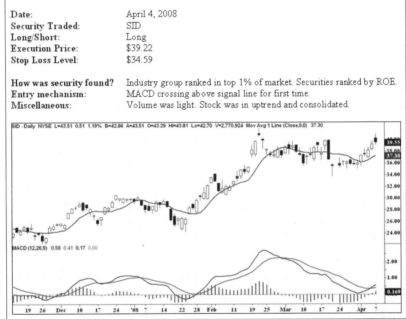

Figure 12-7: Your trading journal should include enough details to make it useful.

Step 7: Monitoring Your Shares' Motion and Exiting When the Time is Right

After you enter your positions and record them in your trading journal, you should monitor them and focus on your exit strategy, which should tell you when to exit in three scenarios:

- ✔ When the position is profitable

- ✔ When the position is unprofitable

- ✔ When the position meanders sideways

My exit strategy in this example, like my entry strategy, is simple:

- ✔ Ideally, I exit on a close below the nine-day moving average. If shares rally, the close below the nine-day average will keep me on an uptrend.

- ✔ If and when shares hit their stop loss level, I exit, pronto.

- ✔ If shares meander and do nothing, I exit after ten days so I can deploy the capital elsewhere.

Going back to the examples from earlier in this chapter, right after I purchased shares of GFA, the stock began declining (see Figure 12-8). Within four days, it was trading below its nine-day moving average, triggering an exit based on the strategy I outlined. I purchased shares at $38.54 and exited around $35.92, a loss of 6.8 percent. However, the position sizing step of my strategy (remember, I only purchased 186 shares) limited the extent to which this position affected my account — I lost only 0.5 percent of my entire portfolio, which is an acceptable loss.

The SID trading position turned out differently (see Figure 12-9). Shares of SID rose right after my entry and, as of the date of this writing, haven't triggered one of my established sell rules. The position has gained 10.66 percent since my entry, or 0.9 percent for my total portfolio.

Figure 12-8: Shares of GFA fell below their nine-day moving average on April 10, 2008.

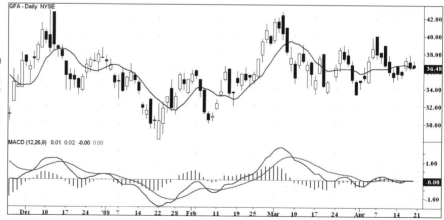

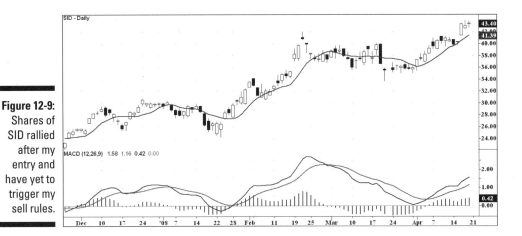

Figure 12-9:
Shares of
SID rallied
after my
entry and
have yet to
trigger my
sell rules.

Step 8: Improving Your Swing Trading Skills

No swing trader is perfect, and no trading system works 100 percent of the time. You'll always suffer losses — they're unavoidable. You must expect losses and work them into your swing trading strategy. Many a good system has been corrupted by an ambitious swing trader tinkering with this and that, trying to achieve a success rate that's simply unrealistic.

But that doesn't mean you can't improve your system. One way to refine your system and become a better trader is to review your journal entries monthly to detect patterns in your winning or losing positions. But don't change your trading plan often or because of one or two losing trades. Alter your plan only in response to a pattern of losses that you think can be improved upon, or in response to a significant — or potentially significant — loss (such as 5 percent or more of your total account value). For instance, if your losses are large, you likely need to adjust your risk management strategy as opposed to your entry and exit strategy.

Returning to the example from earlier in this chapter, I'm going to review the losing GFA trade with an eye on improving my trading strategy. When I look at the GFA position (see Figure 12-10), I see that shares are in a trading range. Notice that the daily ADX indicator is at 11.27 on entry, signaling a non-trending market (for more on the ADX indicator, check out Chapter 5). The weekly ADX (not shown in the chart) is even worse: 12.19 at entry. When the ADX rises above 20, a trend is in place. The ADX indicator in shares of GFA is communicating something very different.

Figure 12-10:
Shares of GFA were in a trading range when my buy order was executed.

My trading strategy is based on riding trends. As a result, I may improve my trading plan by filtering out securities that aren't clearly trending. Perhaps I could improve my strategy by filtering out securities where the weekly ADX indicator is below 20.

Why did I choose to use the weekly ADX versus the daily ADX to filter out non-trending stocks in my trading plan? Technically, this is just a preference. Either strategy will work. But I noticed that shares of SID had an ADX value of 16 on entry. Filtering out stocks with *daily* ADX values below 20 excludes SID as well as GFA. However, filtering out stocks with *weekly* ADX values below 20 excludes GFA but not SID, the profitable trade. That's why reviewing not only your losing positions but also your profitable ones is important.

Chapter 13

Evaluating Your Performance

- -

In This Chapter

▶ Calculating simple returns

▶ Computing annualized returns

▶ Using the time-weighted return method

▶ Measuring up to the benchmarks

▶ Making changes to your trading plan

- -

*A*re you a swing trading star or a work in progress? The only way to know is by calculating your portfolio's returns. Admittedly, doing so isn't the most exciting task. But as a swing trader, you must compute your returns to find out whether you're doing an amazing job or a lousy one.

Performance calculation can be complicated by several factors, including taxes, commissions, SEC fees, and other expenses. Cash deposits or withdrawals, which I cover later in this chapter, also complicate the process of figuring your returns. Your job is to account for such complications accurately so that your return figures solely reflect your skill. Return miscalculations can lead to unskilled traders thinking they're hot stuff (see a real-life example of this embarrassment in the Beardstown Ladies sidebar later in this chapter) or skilled traders thinking they aren't making the grade.

Although some brokers offer performance calculation, far too many simply report the account balances at month's end, which fails to remove the distorting effects of cash flows. If your broker computes performance, find out whether the performance figures are time weighted. If they are, you can use them.

No Additions, No Withdrawals? No Problem!

The simplest return calculation occurs when an account begins at a certain asset level, experiences no withdrawals or deposits, and appreciates or depreciates over time solely due to trading in the account. To calculate your returns in this situation, use the following formula:

$$\text{Total Return} = \frac{\text{Ending Market Value} - \text{Beginning Market Value}}{\text{Beginning Market Value}}$$

Here's a quick example to illustrate this performance calculation.

On December 31, 2009, Trader Claire's account value is $86,430. Trader Claire swing trades in the first three months of 2010, buying and selling different stocks every few days. By March 31, 2010, Trader Claire's account value has reached $92,872. During the first three months, Trader Claire made no deposits or withdrawals from her account. The ending account value reflects all commissions Trader Claire paid in the first three months, but it doesn't reflect taxes because she's trading in an Individual Retirement Account (IRA), a tax-deferred investment account. What is Trader Claire's total return during the period? If you plug these account values into the preceding equation, you find that her return was 7.45 percent:

$$7.45\% = \frac{\$92,872 - \$86,430}{\$86,430}$$

Although this equation is the simplest return calculation equation, swing traders may be depositing and withdrawing assets periodically, which requires adjustments to the formula. To figure out how to calculate your return in such a situation, see the later section "Accounting for Deposits and Withdrawals: The Time-Weighted Return Method."

Comparing Returns over Different Time Periods: Annualizing Returns

The return calculated in the preceding section represents a return over a specified time period. The return calculation remains the same whether the beginning and ending values are three months apart or three years apart.

However, you can't really compare a return achieved over three years to one achieved over three months. That's why the investment management industry usually calculates *annualized returns,* or returns converted to an annual basis. You can think of annualized returns as an average return. For example, a 50 percent return over a five-year period is roughly equivalent to an annual return of 10 percent.

I say *roughly* because the actual annualized return is less than 10 percent due to compounding — or generating earnings on reinvested earnings. I'm just using an average to illustrate the concept. I show you how to calculate the actual annualized return with a tale of two traders who are arguing about who has superior investment skills.

Trader Hot Stuff is convinced his return of 76.23 percent achieved over a five-year period is superior to the return of his friend, Trader Humble, who achieved a return of 52.09 percent over a three-year period. So who's right? To find out, you must convert both traders' returns into annual returns, which you can do by completing the following steps:

1. **Compute the return over the specified time period.**

   Assuming no withdrawals or deposits were made, calculate the return over the time period using the equation shown in the preceding section. (If deposits or withdrawals did occur, use the time-weighted return calculation method I describe in the later section "Accounting for Deposits and Withdrawals: The Time-Weighted Return Method.")

   In the case of Trader Hot Stuff and Trader Humble, the return has already been calculated over the time period for both traders. The returns are 76.23 percent over five years and 52.09 percent over three years.

2. **Add 1 to the return calculated in Step 1.**

   Returns are expressed in percentages, so if you want to add 1 to a percentage, you have to convert the percentage into decimal form. Trader Hot Stuff had a return of 76.23 percent, which equals 0.7623 in decimal form. Trader Humble had a return of 52.09 percent, which equals 0.5209 in decimal form. Adding 1 to both returns yields 1.7623 for Trader Hot Stuff and 1.5209 for Trader Humble.

3. **Determine what time-period conversion fraction you should use to convert the return into an annual return.**

   Use the following equation to calculate the fraction:

   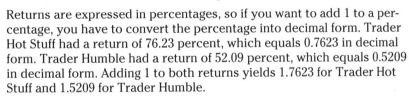

   $$\text{Time-Period Conversion Fraction} = \frac{\substack{\text{Time period you want to convert return into} \\ \text{(Usually expressed in months or years)}}}{\substack{\text{Time period return is currently expressed in} \\ \text{(Must use same unit of measurement as numerator)}}}$$

   - The numerator in this fraction will always be either 12 (months), 1 (year), or 4 (quarters). Whether you use 12, 1, or 4 in the numerator depends on what time period the return you computed in Step 1 is measured in.

   - The denominator is equal to the time period covered by the return in Step 1. Make sure that the denominator's unit of measurement (months, years, or quarters) is equal to the numerator's unit of measurement.

For Trader Hot Stuff, the numerator is 1 because the return is in years, and the denominator is 5 because the time period is five years. So Trader Hot Stuff's time-period conversion fraction is $1/5$. For Trader Humble, the numerator is 1 because the return is in years, and the denominator is 3 because the time period is three years. So Trader Humble's time-period conversion fraction is $1/3$.

4. **Raise the figure computed in Step 2 to the fraction calculated in Step 3.**

   You need a scientific calculator for this computation. (If you don't own one but have access to a PC, the computer's built-in calculator, which is under "Accessories," can be used as a scientific calculator by clicking on "View" and selecting "Scientific.") For Trader Hot Stuff, raising the answer from Step 2 to the fraction from Step 3, you get $1.7623^{1/5} = 1.11999$. For Trader Humble, you get $1.5209^{1/3} = 1.15000$.

5. **Subtract 1 from the figures in Step 4 and convert the result into a percentage.**

   The final step produces the annualized return that you're looking for. After you subtract 1, convert the result into a percentage by moving the decimal point two places to the right.

   For Trader Hot Stuff, the calculation looks like this: $1.11999 - 1 = 0.11999$ = approximately 12 percent when you move the decimal. For Trader Humble, $1.15000 - 1 = 0.15000 = 15$ percent.

So Trader Hot Stuff achieved an annualized return of 12 percent over the five-year period, whereas Trader Humble achieved an annualized return of 15 percent over the three-year period. Trader Humble's annualized return is 3 percent greater, on an annualized basis, than Trader Hot Stuff's return.

Now that you know how to compute annualized returns, I must throw out this word of caution. Never — ever — annualize a return that spans a time period of less than a year. Doing so can lead to ridiculous returns that don't reflect what can normally be achieved in a year. For example, a return of 10 percent in a month is equivalent to an annualized return of 214 percent. That's not exactly a realistic objective.

Accounting for Deposits and Withdrawals: The Time-Weighted Return Method

If you don't make any deposits to or withdrawals from your investment account, the return calculation is straightforward. Simply determine the positive or negative change in account value and divide that by the initial account value, as I show you in the equation in "No Additions, No Withdrawals? No Problem!" earlier in this chapter. But if you do make deposits and/or withdrawals, the returns on that account are more difficult to measure and require a few more steps to calculate.

For example, if you start with $100,000 in capital, swing trade for a few months, and then deposit an additional $50,000, how do you account for the growth in assets? Part of the growth may be due to your swing trading profits. But part of the growth is also attributable to the additional deposit. If you end the year with an account value of $200,000, you can't calculate your return simply by backing out the $50,000 deposit and then plugging the other numbers into the formula. Remember, that $50,000 may have grown or declined in value, and that change in value has to be reflected in your return calculation. The nearby Beardstown Ladies sidebar illustrates the perils of failing to properly account for these cash additions.

When deposits and withdrawals occur in an account, you can calculate returns in two ways:

- ✔ **The time-weighted return method:** This method calculates the account's return independent of any cash flows. Because time-weighted returns are computed irrespective of the timing of cash flows, they're a better measure of a manager's skill than money-weighted returns.

- ✔ **The money-weighted return method:** This method figures the return based on the return of the account *and* the value added due to the timing of cash flows.

In the investment management industry, the time-weighted return method is more widely accepted because it removes the distorting effects that can arise when large cash flows come into or out of an account. For that reason, I devote this section to using that method.

One way of calculating time-weighted returns is to break a portfolio out by the dates of withdrawals and deposits and then calculate the returns for each time period in between these cash flow events using the formula shown in this chapter's first section. To do this, you need to know the value of the portfolio right before each deposit or withdrawal occurs. After computing the returns for the smaller time periods, you can string together the returns through a process known as *geometrically chain-linking the returns.* That sounds much worse than it actually is — I promise. I break it all down in the following sections.

The Beardstown Ladies

The Beardstown Ladies were a group of women from Beardstown, Illinois, who started an investment club to buy and sell stocks. Sixteen women started the club in 1983, and the average age of the women was 70 years. They apparently were sick and tired of being told how to invest their own money and decided to try it out for themselves. Each woman contributed $100 and added $25 every month. They relied on common sense in selecting their investments. For example, they purchased shares of Wal-Mart after seeing the retail giant land in their backyard and fill its parking lot much more often than rival K-Mart. They bought shares of medical device maker Medtronic after one of the investment club members had a pacemaker implanted.

The outside world took notice of the club after the women posted some impressive returns. Between 1984 and 1993, their annualized returns were 23.4 percent, almost double the return the Dow Jones Industrial Average achieved in that same period. Soon, the media were in hot pursuit. The Beardstown Ladies were featured on CBS's *This Morning* television show. They also appeared on *Good Morning America* and *Today*. The women saw tremendous interest from investors, both in the U.S. and abroad, and were invited to share their investment insights at events in Brazil, Germany, and England.

By 1994, public interest had grown to the point that the Beardstown Ladies decided to publish a book on their investment strategy — with cooking recipes to boot. The book was called "The Beardstown Ladies' Common-Sense Investment Guide." The story was easy to sell: The prospect of the average Joe (or Joan) beating the Wall Street "experts" appealed to people as a David versus Goliath tale.

But this tale ended somewhat sadly. In 1998, after the book had sold some 800,000 copies and been translated into seven languages, a Chicago magazine noticed that the women used a faulty return calculation method. Specifically, the women included their monthly contributions of $25 as part of their gains. After adjusting for these cash flows, the actual return from 1984 to 1993 fell from 23.4 percent to 9 percent — a return well below the Dow Jones Industrial Average's return in that period. The Beardstown Ladies, upon learning of the Chicago magazine's find, hired an outside auditor to compute the returns. That auditor found the same results as the Chicago magazine.

Today, the Beardstown Ladies still meet to discuss stocks and positions. Some of the original members have died or retired from the club, but the same common sense approach to investing remains. For 15 minutes, the ladies of Beardstown had their fame.

Breaking the time period into chunks

The number of deposits and withdrawals you make in an account determines the number of time periods for which you need to calculate returns. You simply take the number of these cash flow events and add 1. So if you have four different deposits and withdrawals, you need to calculate returns for five discrete time periods, as the following example illustrates.

Time really is money: Why one method is better

The simplest way to illustrate the difference between the time-weighted return method and the money-weighted return method is through an example.

Portfolio manager Laura oversees a stock portfolio valued at $100 million. Today is January 1, 2009. Laura swing trades the portfolio for the first four months of the year and earns a return of 12 percent, leaving her portfolio valued at $112 million. On May 1, Laura's portfolio receives a deposit of $200 million, pushing its total value to $312 million. Between May 1 and December 31 of that year, Laura's portfolio loses 6 percent.

Okay, do you think Laura's return for the full year was positive or negative? That depends on whether you use a time-weighted or money-weighted return methodology. A time-weighted return ignores the major cash flow that occurs midyear and instead asks, "How much would a single dollar appreciate or depreciate had it been invested on day 1?" The money-weighted return asks, "Did the portfolio actually make or lose dollars?" The two questions may sound similar, but the difference is that the money-weighted return takes into account the effect of cash flows.

In this example, Laura's skills should leave her with a positive return for the year because she gained 12 percent in the first four months and only lost 6 percent in the next eight months. A time-weighted return calculation shows that Laura gained 5.28 percent for the year. However, on a dollar basis, Laura actually lost more money than she gained. In the first four months of the year, Laura's 12 percent return generated profits of $12 million. However, she lost 6 percent on $312 million, or $18.72 million. That swamps the gains of $12 million and leaves Laura with a deficit of $6.72 million. Laura's money-weighted return is negative.

How negative? Money-weighted returns differ depending on whether the deposit occurred at the beginning, midpoint, or end of the year. Here are Laura's returns for those three scenarios:

- **If the $200 million came at the beginning of the year:** Laura's return is –$6.72 million/$300 million, or –2.24 percent.

- **If the $200 million came at the midpoint of the year:** Laura's return is –$6.72 million/$200 million, or –3.36 percent.

- **If the $200 million came at the end of the year:** Laura's return is –$6.72 million/$100 million, or –6.72 percent.

This example shows the extreme difference between the two return calculation methods. Laura's return may have been as high as 5.28 percent under the time-weighted return method versus as low as –6.72 percent under the end-of-year money-weighted return method.

Swing Trader Singh begins the year with $50,000 in his brokerage account. He makes the following deposits and withdrawals from this account:

- $5,000 deposit on February 16 (account value before deposit: $58,500)

- $3,000 withdrawal on April 19 (account value before withdrawal: $61,300)

- $9,000 deposit on June 9 (account value before deposit: $63,780)

✔ $7,000 withdrawal on December 16 (account value before withdrawal: $72,290)

✔ Ending value on December 31: $68,350

So what's the return of this swing trader's account for the year?

First, split the year into distinct periods in between each deposit and withdrawal, as shown in Figure 13-1. Because the account experienced four different cash flow events, you should come up with five distinct time periods:

✔ **Time Period 1:** January 1–February 15

✔ **Time Period 2:** February 16–April 18

✔ **Time Period 3:** April 19–June 8

✔ **Time Period 4:** June 9–December 15

✔ **Time Period 5:** December 16–December 31

Figure 13-1:
Break the year into subperiods to use the time-weighted return method.

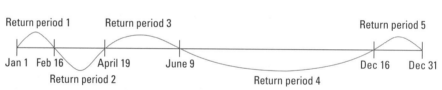

Calculating the return for each time period

Next, calculate the return for each subperiod by using the formula shown earlier in this chapter. Here's the computed return for each subperiod for Swing Trader Singh's account:

✔ **Return for Subperiod 1:** ($58,500 − $50,000)/$50,000 = 17 percent

✔ **Return for Subperiod 2:** ($61,300 − $63,500)/$63,500 = −3.46 percent (Add the deposit of $5,000 on February 16 to the account value right before the deposit to get the starting value for Subperiod 2.)

✔ **Return for Subperiod 3:** ($63,780 − $58,300)/$58,300 = 9.40 percent (Subtract the withdrawal of $3,000 on April 19 from the account value right before the withdrawal to get the starting value for Subperiod 3.)

✔ **Return for Subperiod 4:** ($72,290 – $72,780)/$72,780 = –0.67 percent (Add the deposit of $9,000 on June 9 to the account value right before the deposit to get the starting value for Subperiod 4.)

✔ **Return for Subperiod 5:** ($68,350 – $65,290)/$65,290 = 4.69 percent (Subtract the withdrawal of $7,000 on December 16 from the account value right before the withdrawal to get the starting value for Subperiod 5.)

Now that you have the returns for the subperiods, all that's left to get the return for the entire period is to chain-link the subperiod returns together.

Chain-linking time period returns to calculate a total return

Despite what you may've been told growing up, it's okay to geometrically chain-link returns together to determine the total return for an entire period. *Chain-linking returns* means combining individual returns through multiplication.

Chain-linking returns is actually a wonderful concept. It works regardless of whether the different subperiods are of equal length. One subperiod may cover three days and another may cover three months. As long as they're separate time periods and are adjoining (that is, they cover the entire time but don't overlap), then you can chain-link returns to get the total return during the period — all while ignoring the effects of cash flows.

For example, if you have the daily returns of the stock market for every single day of the year (roughly 250 days the market is open), you can chain-link them together to get the return for the whole year. Or if you have the return for 11 months and 30 days of the year, you can chain-link those 41 returns together to get the return for the entire year.

Here's the formula for calculating chain-linked returns:

Total Return = $(1 + R1) \times (1 + R2) \times \ldots (1 + RN) - 1$

R1 = Return in Subperiod 1

R2 = Return in Subperiod 2

RN = Return in Subperiod N

You can now return to the Swing Trader Singh example and use this formula to calculate his total return over the time period. Recall that Swing Trader Singh achieved the following returns in the five subperiods: 17 percent, –3.46 percent, 9.40 percent, –0.67 percent, and 4.69 percent.

Note: You must convert percentages into decimals when adding, subtracting, or multiplying. Your final return in decimal format can then be converted back into a percentage by moving the decimal point over two places to the right (that is, 0.05 is equal to 5 percent).

Swing Trader Singh's Total Return (found by chain-linking subperiod returns)

Total Return = $(1 + .17) \times (1 - .0346) \times (1 + .0940) \times (1 - .0067) \times (1 + .0469)$
$- 1 = 1.17 \times 0.9654 \times 1.094 \times 0.9933 \times 1.0469 - 1 = 0.285 = 28.5$ percent

Comparing Your Returns to an Appropriate Benchmark

After you know how to compute your returns, you should compare them to some benchmark to determine whether you're outperforming the market. But which benchmark should you use?

If you're trading stocks, you can look at nine major benchmarks:

- Large Cap Growth (Russell 1000 Growth Index)
- Large Cap Core (Russell 1000 Index)
- Large Cap Value (Russell 1000 Value Index)
- Mid Cap Growth (Russell Mid Cap Growth Index)
- Mid Cap Core (Russell Mid Cap Index)
- Mid Cap Value (Russell Mid Cap Value Index)
- Small Cap Growth (Russell 2000 Growth Index)
- Small Cap Core (Russell 2000 Index)
- Small Cap Value (Russell 2000 Value Index)

You can also compare your returns to international benchmarks. Bank of New York maintains an excellent compilation of indexes covering international stocks that trade on U.S. markets. Visit www.adrbny.com/adr_index.jsp to find out more.

Where do you find the returns for these indexes? The best Web site I've found, hands down, is the Russell return calculator (www.russell.com/indexes/performance/calculator/calculator.asp). It shows you the returns for indexes covering the aforementioned nine major classes. It's free to use and lets you compute returns over specific time periods. The Web site also annualizes returns automatically when you select time periods that extend beyond one year.

Figure 13-2 shows the output from this return calculator for several Russell indexes.

If you short securities in addition to buying them, you don't want to use the nine major benchmarks. Instead, you should focus on an absolute level of return — such as 15 percent annually — as your benchmark. Don't use an unrealistic level of absolute return, like 35 percent annually. Very few swing traders achieve such results.

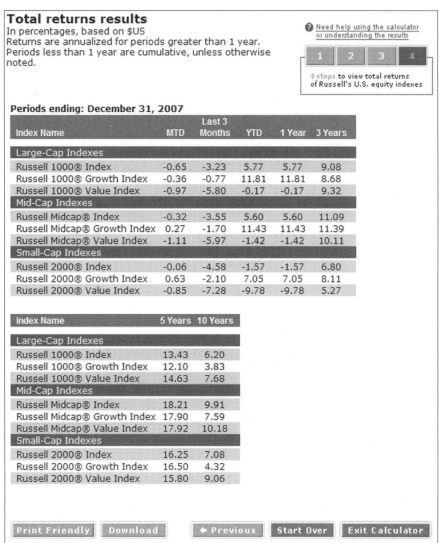

Total returns results
In percentages, based on $US
Returns are annualized for periods greater than 1 year.
Periods less than 1 year are cumulative, unless otherwise noted.

? Need help using the calculator or understanding the results

| 1 | 2 | 3 | 4 |

4 steps to view total returns of Russell's U.S. equity indexes

Periods ending: December 31, 2007

Index Name	MTD	Last 3 Months	YTD	1 Year	3 Years
Large-Cap Indexes					
Russell 1000® Index	-0.65	-3.23	5.77	5.77	9.08
Russell 1000® Growth Index	-0.36	-0.77	11.81	11.81	8.68
Russell 1000® Value Index	-0.97	-5.80	-0.17	-0.17	9.32
Mid-Cap Indexes					
Russell Midcap® Index	-0.32	-3.55	5.60	5.60	11.09
Russell Midcap® Growth Index	0.27	-1.70	11.43	11.43	11.39
Russell Midcap® Value Index	-1.11	-5.97	-1.42	-1.42	10.11
Small-Cap Indexes					
Russell 2000® Index	-0.06	-4.58	-1.57	-1.57	6.80
Russell 2000® Growth Index	0.63	-2.10	7.05	7.05	8.11
Russell 2000® Value Index	-0.85	-7.28	-9.78	-9.78	5.27

Index Name	5 Years	10 Years
Large-Cap Indexes		
Russell 1000® Index	13.43	6.20
Russell 1000® Growth Index	12.10	3.83
Russell 1000® Value Index	14.63	7.68
Mid-Cap Indexes		
Russell Midcap® Index	18.21	9.91
Russell Midcap® Growth Index	17.90	7.59
Russell Midcap® Value Index	17.92	10.18
Small-Cap Indexes		
Russell 2000® Index	16.25	7.08
Russell 2000® Growth Index	16.50	4.32
Russell 2000® Value Index	15.80	9.06

| Print Friendly | Download | ← Previous | Start Over | Exit Calculator |

Figure 13-2:
The return calculator on the Russell Web site provides returns for all the major indexes.

Source: Russell Investments

Excel can lend a helping hand

Doing these return calculations by hand can be tedious. You may also be prone to making an error if you're punching these returns into a calculator.

Microsoft Excel provides an alternative. You can set up the formula in *Excel* to calculate returns for each subperiod based on what account values you enter. Then *Excel* can chain-link the returns in a flash. Setting up this structure in *Excel* does require some *Excel* know-how that's unfortunately beyond the scope of this book. But it's not too difficult to

figure out if you have some spare time on your hands.

The following figure shows an *Excel* spreadsheet that's been set up to calculate the time-weighted return of Swing Trader Singh's portfolio. The boxed cells are the only cells that have formulas in them. The account value cells are entered manually by the user. If you set up a spreadsheet similar to this one, you can simply enter the account value figures and have *Excel* compute your time-weighted return.

Subperiod 1

Beginning Account Value	Ending Account Value		
$50,000	$58,500	Return	17.00%

Subperiod 2

Beginning Account Value	Ending Account Value		
$63,500	$61,300	Return	−3.46%

Subperiod 3

Beginning Account Value	Ending Account Value		
$58,300	$63,780	Return	9.40%

Subperiod 4

Beginning Account Value	Ending Account Value		
$72,780	$72,290	Return	−0.67%

Subperiod 5

Beginning Account Value	Ending Account Value		
$65,290	$68,350	Return	4.69%

Chain Linked Returns

Total Return	28.48%

Although I can't give an *Excel* primer in this limited space, I can give you the formula for each shaded cell to assist you in setting up this spreadsheet at home.

✔ **Cell K5:** The formula is: = (G5 − C5)/C5

✔ **Cell K8:** The formula is: = (G8 − C8)/C8

✔ **Cell K12:** The formula is: = (G12 − C12)/C12

✔ **Cell K16:** The formula is: = (G16 − C16)/C16

✔ **Cell K20:** The formula is: = (G20 − C20)/C20

✔ **Cell E23:** The formula is: = (1 + K5) * (1 + K8) * (1 + K12) * (1 + K16) * (1 + K20) −1

> **Remember:** Set the format of the cells to the appropriate units of measurement. For example, if the data you're entering into a cell is a dollar amount, you should right-click on that cell, go to "Format Cells," and select "Currency." If the data you're entering into a cell is a percentage, then right-click on that cell, go to "Format Cells," and select "Percentage."

After you identify the appropriate benchmark to use, compare your annual return to the benchmark's annual return. If you don't have an annual return, compare monthly returns (you can convert a 15 percent annual absolute return level into a monthly benchmark by dividing 15 percent by 12 and arriving at 1.25 percent).

If your return is greater than the benchmark, you're outperforming the average return achieved in your category. This outperformance may be due to leverage (that is, using margin), trading higher beta securities than your benchmark (see Chapter 10), using cash well (in situations where the market is going down) or adding real value (that is, being a skilled swing trader). Some traders would group the last two categories together, arguing that a skilled trader uses cash to his or her advantage.

To determine whether your outperformance is due to trading higher beta securities, you need to compute a "risk adjusted return" and compare that figure to the risk adjusted return of the benchmark. Common risk adjusted returns include the Sharpe Ratio and the Information Ratio. A simple risk adjusted return ratio can be computed by dividing your total return (during a month or year) by the standard deviation of returns. You must have at least 30 days of returns (that is, 30 different returns on a daily basis) or 12 months of returns for your strategy and for the benchmark in order to calculate a simple risk adjusted return. Please note: If your benchmark is an absolute return, there is no standard deviation associated with it.

Calculating standard deviation is outside the scope of this book, but it can be done in *Microsoft Excel* using the function "=stdev(returns)". (The "returns" should be replaced by the actual cells containing the 12 monthly returns or 30 daily returns. For example, if your returns were in cells A1 through A30, the function above would read "=stdev(A1:A30)" without the quotation marks.

If you don't have *Excel,* you can also use the following Web site to calculate standard deviation: `invsee.asu.edu/srinivas/stdev.html`.

When you have the standard deviation of monthly or daily returns for your strategy and for your benchmark, divide each return by its standard deviation. For example, if your strategy returned 10 percent during the year with a standard deviation of returns of 5 percent, you'd arrive at a calculated ratio of 2. If the benchmark returned 11 percent with a standard deviation of returns of 6 percent, its calculated ratio is 1.83. The higher the risk adjusted return, the better. In this example, the trader has added value relative to his or her benchmark because 2 is greater than 1.83.

Evaluating Your Trading Plan

After you compute your account's return and compare it to some benchmark (see the preceding section for more info on how to do just that), you can work on improving your trading plan (assuming it needs to be improved). If your returns exceed the appropriate benchmark, great job! But that doesn't mean you shouldn't review your trades and look for ways to refine your plan.

At least monthly, examine your trading journal and review all closed trades (those that you've exited) to determine whether you need to make any adjustments to your strategy. If your plan yields subpar returns when compared to the appropriate benchmark, perhaps you can spot a common thread among the losing positions and add a trading rule to avoid similar losses. Conversely, if you're consistently beating the benchmark, maybe you can identify a common thread among your winning positions and add a trading rule to increase the chances of finding those gainers.

Don't change your plan too often. Only change it when you're sure that a tangible benefit exists and that you can address a problem you spot in several trades. If you change your trading plan frequently, you'll never know whether you have a well-functioning plan because you can't judge a plan on the basis of a few weeks of data (unless you lose half or all your money, in which case you're probably not following the risk management techniques I outline in Chapter 10). Wal-Mart and Best Buy don't change their corporate strategies weekly, or even yearly. They plan for the long term. Even though you're swing trading, your trading plan must have a long-term perspective in the sense that it should do well across changing markets and over time.

You'll never achieve 100 percent success in your trades. A great trading plan may well result in a success rate of 50 percent if the profits from your winners are multiple times larger than the losses from your losers.

Part V
The Part of Tens

By Rich Tennant

That's the Harrisons. Never have I seen an investment portfolio start so strong and go south so quickly.

In this part . . .

What *For Dummies* book is complete without the Part of Tens? In these two chapters, you receive the inside scoop on ten simple guidelines to achieving swing trading success and ten mistakes you don't want to make . . . unless of course you enjoy seeing your cash wash down the drain. Some of these do's and don'ts may seem logical based on your current investment knowledge, whereas others (like the concept of actually having fun with your trading!) may surprise you.

Chapter 14

Ten Simple Rules for Swing Trading

▶ Taking prudent steps to become a successful swing trader

▶ Controlling your emotions (but still having fun)

Swing trading can and should be enjoyable. You can actually look forward to "working" each day! But swing trading is still a business, so you must stick to certain rules designed to keep you in the game. After all, if you have no capital, you can't trade. So the most important rule is the rule of survival. Surviving means not only managing risk but also following your own plan and your own rules. If you're not careful, swing trading can quickly go from being a business about making profits to being an outlet for your emotions.

The rules in this chapter aren't novel or complex. Instead, they're simple and straightforward. In fact, they're downright boring. But they'll keep you in the game and (ideally) help you make money. Stray from these rules at your own risk.

Trade Your Plan

A cliché that I hear over and over again is, "Plan your trade, then trade your plan." I hate to regurgitate that here, but I can't phrase it any better.

Your trading plan is your road map. It answers the following questions:

✔ What is your time horizon?

✔ What do you trade?

✔ When do you trade (going long versus going short)?

✔ How much capital do you allocate to your positions?

  ✔ What are your entry signals?

  ✔ When do you exit a position for a profit?

  ✔ When do you exit a position for a loss?

Trading plans must be carefully thought through and then written down. I prefer to keep a copy of my trading plan nearby, or a digital version of the plan accessible on my computer. One tool I use to make sure I follow my trading plan is a questionnaire I developed that I always complete *before* I enter a position. I provide a sample questionnaire in Figure 14-1 to help get you started on following your trading plan.

Your trading questionnaire may be more or less complex than the sample in Figure 14-1. Either way, having such a questionnaire forces you to think through the important issues you may overlook when you're making decisions on the fly. Stick to a trading questionnaire, as silly as you may think it sounds, and you'll find the success of your trades increasing. The more errors you avoid, the more likely your trades will turn out profitable.

Trader Joe's Sample Trading Questionnaire

Date: _____

Symbol: _____

1. Was this security identified in an industry group ranking in the top 20% of the market (in the case of long positions) or in the bottom 20% of the market (in the case of short positions)?   Yes / No

2. Was this security identified after breaking out of a base lasting three months or longer?   Yes / No

3. Has volume increased in recent days in the direction of the trade? Yes / No

4. Is the overall market trending in the same direction as the direction of the trade?   Yes / No

5. Has the MACD given a buy signal in the last three days?   Yes / No

6. Is the company slated to report earnings in the next two weeks? Yes / No

7. Has the position size been determined based on the stop loss order placement?   Yes / No

Figure 14-1:
A trading questionnaire is a useful tool that helps you stick to your trading plan.

Follow the Lead of Industry Groups as Well as the Overall Market

If you're trading stocks, you want the wind at your back, meaning your trades should be in the direction of the overall market. If the market is in a strong bull, then the majority of your trades should be long positions. And if the market is in bear mode, the majority of your trades should be short positions. Markets may also be stuck in trading ranges, in which case your long and short trades will depend on whether the market is rallying within the trading range or falling within that range.

But trading with the overall market is only part of the story. The skilled swing trader recognizes that industry groups make a difference in a security's returns. When an industry group is in the top of the pack (as identified in *High Growth Stock Investor* software or *Investor's Business Daily*), the stocks in that group are likely to follow suit. Conversely, when an industry group is in the bottom of the bottom of the pack, the stocks in that group are likely to follow suit. When the homebuilder industry group was out of favor in 2007, you could've shorted practically any homebuilder and made money (see the examples in Figure 14-2).

The industry group in which you trade is more important to your success or failure than which company you pick in that industry group. So as a swing trader, always trade stocks on the long side in industry groups that are rising, and always trade stocks on the short side in industry groups that are falling. You don't need to complicate what rising or falling means. One simple rule is to only trade stocks on the long side that are part of industry groups that are above a rising 20-day moving average.

Figure 14-2: Most securities in the homebuilder industry group bottomed out in January 2008.

Don't Let Emotions Control Your Trading!

Emotions are the biggest enemy of trading. In a sense, you're your own worst enemy. Traders who lose billions of dollars at major banks often start out losing a small amount and then try to break even or prove themselves right. Their ultimate failing lies not in their analysis or their market knowledge but in their inability to control their emotions.

The markets aren't personal. When you lose money, it's not because you made money last time. Your losses and profits are a function of your trading ability and the markets in which you trade. The true, professional trader is a master of his or her emotions. Profits don't lead to extreme joy, and losses don't lead to extreme pessimism. If you sat across the table from a professional trader, you wouldn't be able to tell whether he or she were up $50,000 or down $100,000. Professional traders are calm and don't let their emotions take over their cognitive functions.

Another factor in controlling your emotions is keeping tabs on your trades. Don't brag to others about your profits. Don't tell others about any trades you're in at the moment. Do so and you become married to your positions. If you tell your best friends that you hold shares of Oracle and you believe the share price is going to skyrocket, you'll be less likely to exit if the trade turns down. "Oh no!" you may say to yourself. "Everyone knows I hold Oracle. I can't bail now. I've got to hold to prove I was right."

Controlling your emotions isn't something that just happens one day and you never have to worry about it again. Rather, it's an ongoing battle. The two strongest emotions you're going to face are greed and fear. When markets are roaring in one direction and you're riding that wave, you'll want to hold positions longer than you need to as you amass more profits. And when markets roar in the opposite direction and your profits evaporate, you'll want to take more risks to make up for those losses.

You can't battle these emotions in any scientific way (that I know of, at least). I've always imagined that a Spock-like character who's always rational and never lets emotions interfere with his trading would make a wonderful trader. Unfortunately, *Star Trek* is a fictional story, and Vulcans don't exist. So as a trader, you need to review your trades carefully and practice being calm as much as possible. Be disciplined enough to force yourself to stop trading if you detect your emotions are affecting your trading.

Diversify!

As a swing trader, you must hold a diversified portfolio of positions. You should have at least ten different positions, and they should be in different sectors. And if you can, incorporate other asset classes in your swing trading. For example, include real estate investment trusts (REITs), exchange traded funds that track international markets, or commodities such as streetTRACKS Gold.

All these positions represent different ways to diversify your portfolio. Holding more than one position reduces *idiosyncratic risk* (a fancy way of saying the risk attributable to an individual company). Having long and short positions reduces your market direction risk. And diversification allows your portfolio to withstand market volatility — the gains from a few positions can offset the losses from others.

Set Your Risk Level

Setting your risk level goes hand in hand with setting a stop loss level, which I discuss later in this chapter. Entering a stop loss level is an order entry step, but setting a risk level is an analytical part of the process. Your stop loss order will often be at the risk level you identify in this step.

Your *risk level* represents the price that, if reached, forces you to acknowledge that your original thesis for trading the security is wrong. You can set your risk level based on some automatic percent level from your entry order, but I don't recommend this because it forces a reality on the market where one may not exist. For example, say you automatically exit a position when a security declines or appreciates (depending on whether you're long or short) by 5 percent. But why should that security stay within this 5 percent range? What if the security's daily volatility is 3 percent? It may hit your risk level in a day or two just based on normal volatility.

For this reason, I recommend that you set your risk level based on support or resistance levels. If a stock finds support at $20 frequently, set your risk level at $19.73, for example. Don't use a whole number for the risk level, or you may place your stop loss order at the same price that hundreds of others place their orders. Instead, for instance, use something like $67.37 rather than $68 if you're going long.

Your stop loss level should be set at your risk level. But formulating your risk level depends on what your trading plan calls for. If you don't want to use some obvious support level, then use a moving average, but be prepared to constantly adjust your stop loss level because the moving average is constantly changing. The wider your risk level is (that is, the farther your risk level is from your entry price), the smaller your position size. This rule of thumb ensures you aren't risking more than 1 to 2 percent of your total capital because you may be entering a security that's extended.

Swing traders who focus on trading ranges have an easier job of identifying their risk levels. They're looking for a continuation of an existing trading range. Hence, a breakout above or below a resistance or support level would signal the end of the trading range. That resistance or support level is the most obvious risk level for the swing trader.

To sum up, always specify your risk level and make its placement logical (that is, near a support or resistance level). And don't exit based on some percentage decline — like selling a position when it declines 5 or 7 percent.

Set a Profit Target or Technical Exit

I stress risk management a lot in this book. The reason is simple: You can't last long without it. But when it comes to profits, you must set your profit target or technical exit.

Your profit target is often based on a previous support or resistance level. Some swing traders set predefined profit targets of selling 50 percent of a position after it achieves a 5 percent gain from entry and selling the other 50 percent after it reaches a 10 percent gain. When trading based on a trading pattern like a head-and-shoulders pattern, your profit target may be determined by the projection price implied in the chart pattern.

My preference in taking profits is to rely on a signal from a technical indicator rather than a preexisting support or resistance level. Some securities trend longer and farther than anticipated, and they can be very profitable. Hence, I prefer to exit after a security breaks below an indicator, such as a moving average, or on a sell signal from a trending indicator. Chapter 5 covers how you can exit positions based on moving averages.

Use Limit Orders

When entering a trade, you should enter on a limit order rather than a market order. A limit order ensures that your execution occurs at the price you specify, whereas a market order can be filled at any price. Rarely will you encounter such urgency to get into a trade that you'll need to enter a market order. Moreover, you're unlikely to buy at the bottom of the day or sell at the top of the day. So be patient and you may get a better price than you originally thought.

Another reason to use limit orders is to help you avoid the cost of market impact. The larger your order size is relative to the average volume that trades in the security on a typical day, the more likely your buy or sell order will move a security's price higher or lower. A market order in a thinly traded stock may leave you with an execution that's 2 to 5 percent above the price the security was when you entered the order.

You can place a limit order at a price level near where shares have traded. The intention isn't to get lucky on some downturn in shares but to control the average cost per share. Place a limit order slightly below recent trades (when you're buying) or slightly above recent trades (when you're shorting).

Recognize that there's always the possibility your order may not get filled. But remember that your job is to be patient and execute your trade only when the timing and price are right.

Use Stop Loss Orders

You may think that stop loss orders are nothing more than training wheels. "I'm an adult. I don't need these pesky stop loss orders. I can exit when I see weakness." Unfortunately, that kind of thinking may get you killed (financially speaking, of course). Financial markets aren't playgrounds or appropriate places to find out who you are. Leave that to your local sports club.

Stop loss orders are necessary for several reasons — even if you watch the market 24 hours a day, 7 days a week:

- ✔ **They help you deal with fast-moving markets.** If you swing trade ten different positions, it's quite possible that many of them may start acting up on the same day. And they can move fast and furious if negative news is in the air. Because of the speed at which markets move, you need a stop loss to save you if you're unable to act.

- ✔ **They limit your downside.** Without a stop loss order, your downside may be all of your capital (or worse, if you're shorting). Stop loss orders act as protection, because they place some upper limit on the losses you may suffer. Of course, a security could gap through your stop loss order, but your loss would be realized then regardless of whether a stop loss order existed.

- ✔ **They help take your emotions out of the game.** When you place mental stop loss orders, you may start to arbitrarily move your imaginary stop loss as the markets move against you. So you plan to exit at $49.50, but when the security trades through that price down to $49, you tell yourself that $47.50 is a more reasonable exit point given recent market action. You justify your change and you hold on. And your losses mount.

✔ **They give you time to take your eye off the ball.** If you travel or are unable to watch the markets on a day when you're sick, stop loss orders ensure that your portfolio value is preserved. If you didn't have stop loss orders, you'd probably fear ever being out of touch with your computer and the markets. One or two lousy positions can quickly change a top-performing account into a poor performer.

For these reasons, stop loss orders are essential. You'll sleep better at night if you know that someone is watching your positions, ready to take action if they start acting up.

Keep a Trading Journal

Trading journals organize your thoughts and the reasons behind your decisions. They should be updated after every trade you execute. If you delay entering a trade into your journal, the trades may eventually pile up and overwhelm you, and you may decide not to update the journal anymore.

A trading journal is your coach. By recording the reasons you enter a position, you can review whether your assumptions are correct, and you can find out whether your trading plan needs adjustment. For instance, perhaps you always enter positions prematurely and need to incorporate some indicator to prevent you from trading too soon. Or perhaps you have a tendency to buy stocks in weak industry groups. A trading journal reveals such habits and patterns, and you can adjust accordingly. The fun part of keeping a journal is reviewing the major winners and major losers. I often learn more from reviewing my losers than I do my winners. I look to replicate the winning trades in the future and avoid the circumstances surrounding the losing trades.

Chapter 3 provides more details on what to put in your journal — the more detailed, the better. Of course, the more detailed your journal is, the more time you're going to spend updating it (especially if you have trades). Sometimes using a screen capture program can cut down on the time. Screen capture programs allow you to capture a window on your computer and store it as an image that can be transferred to a *Word* document or *Excel* spreadsheet. You can take snapshots of the security's chart and its industry group with small amounts of written text indicating how the security was found and what triggered the entry. That can be sufficient for a trading journal.

Have Fun!

This last rule may strike you as a bit off kilter. After all, earlier in this chapter I recommended fighting your emotions and the joy or pain that comes from gains or losses.

Yes, yes — I did say that. But this final rule goes to the heart of whether you can be a full-time swing trader. You have to like the business. You have to enjoy spending hours on the computer looking for candidates to buy or short. You have to find pleasure in reading books about swing trading (especially this one, of course).

If you have to force yourself to research positions, then swing trading may not be for you. If logging onto your brokerage account is a painful exercise you prefer not to do because you feel ashamed, swing trading may not be for you. Even when you're down, you have to be optimistic that your profits will come soon. And that optimism helps make those profits a reality.

So enjoy swing trading and all it entails. You'll find it can be a rewarding experience — financially and otherwise.

Chapter 15

Ten Deadly Sins of Swing Trading

In This Chapter

▶ Making sure you have enough money to start investing

▶ Remembering that too much investment in one industry or too much trading can hurt you

▶ Appreciating the value of modesty and sticking to your plans

*T*o excel in swing trading, you must not only follow the rules but also avoid harming yourself. After all, just because you speed to work every morning without getting caught doesn't mean you'll get away with it today. The same principle applies to swing trading: Committing one or more of the sins in this chapter won't, necessarily, bring about immediate punishment (and by that I mean loss of account value). But you'll eventually be called to account for repeated infractions.

I've relied on my swing trading experience to develop these sins. I admit that I've committed some, if not all, of them at one point in my life. But I always regretted the actions later on. In swing trading, you are your own worst enemy. Here, I give you the tools you need to arm yourself against the common pitfalls of the swing trading game.

Starting with Too Little Capital

Swing trading requires a minimum level of capital to execute efficiently — assuming you're swing trading for a living. If you swing trade for fun, then you may be content making an average of $500 per month. But even then, you're going to be facing an uphill battle if you have too little capital. Either way, swing trading requires an investment on your part for several reasons:

  ✔ **Diversification:** Spreading a small amount of capital, say $5,000, into ten trades is tough. That means your average trade size is $500. You may not be able to buy but five or ten shares of some securities with such a small trade size. As a result, you may try to fix the problem by decreasing your number of positions, but doing so increases your risk.

- ✔ **Cost:** Starting with $5,000 and trading securities in $500 increments proves very costly. A round-trip commission charge of $20, for example, is equal to 4 percent of your trade size, meaning your position must actually rise by 4 percent before you break even!

- ✔ **Realistic target return:** Good professional swing traders can reasonably expect to make an average of 10 to 20 percent per year on their trades. The best swing traders can do even better. If you have a small account size, you may be unhappy with that target return. So you try to magnify the return by employing leverage or trading options. Whatever the case, you're setting yourself up for certain ruin.

So how much capital do you need to get started in swing trading? I've tried to provide some guidelines to fit the different types of swing traders out there. Of course, the following are just my recommendations, not hard-and-fast rules:

- ✔ **Trading for fun:** If you enjoy swing trading as a hobby, then you can swing trade a portion of your existing assets. The restrictions outlined earlier don't apply *if* the majority of your assets are being invested wisely (that is, they're diversified and professionally managed). In this case, you can trade 10 to 20 percent of your total assets as long as your swing trading portfolio is greater than or equal to $10,000 (to cover costs like commissions or research services).

- ✔ **Trading for retirement:** If you're swing trading your retirement account, you're not depending on the trades to provide you with current income. So you can probably begin with $10,000 to $20,000 and hold 8 to 12 positions.

- ✔ **Trading for a living:** If swing trading is your full-time job, then you need to start with a reasonable size nest egg to live off of. A professional swing trader can reasonably expect to make 10 to 20 percent per year, so if you need to spend $5,000 per month on living expenses, your account value needs to be between $300,000 and $600,000. (Achieving 10 percent on $600,000 equals $60,000 per year, or $5,000 per month. But if you're really good, you may achieve a return of 20 percent per year on $300,000 — equal to $60,000 per year, or $5,000 per month.)

All things considered, I find it difficult to believe that you can swing trade well on less than $10,000. The costs of commissions, taxes, slippage, and other factors work against you so much that you can't generate reasonable returns. (*Slippage* is the difference between what you expect to pay or receive from a buy or sell and what you actually pay or receive from a buy or sell. Fast-moving markets often result in increased slippage costs.)

Gambling on Earnings Dates

It's funny how chance can excite people. Gambling for the chance to win a new car, beat state lottery odds, or become the next millionaire minted by the Publishers Clearing House seems to have broad appeal.

I believe swing trading a stock one or two weeks before its earnings date is a form of gambling. My old mentor, Ian Woodward, likens trading before earnings to driving a car without your hands on the steering wheel. I've never tried driving that way, but I believe it can be dangerous.

Earnings dates are, for the most part, unknown events. Unless you have some predictive ability I lack, you can't know with certainty whether a company will miss its earnings mark or profit handsomely. No doubt, you can make educated guesses by calling a company's suppliers and customers or analyzing how its competitors are doing. But as a swing trader, your time horizons are too short to make a serious study of such practical issues. You're better off avoiding trading stocks before their earnings dates, even in the case of large cap stocks.

When you put on a new swing trade, double-check the earnings date to make sure you aren't getting in right before a major announcement that may cause a significant change in price. If you're wrong, such a loss can seriously impair your account's value. Of course, a company's stock price can gap in between earnings dates due to other issues. But you can limit your exposure to many gaps in companies' stock prices by avoiding trading before earnings dates.

If you want to discover when a company will report earnings, find out when the company's last earnings report was and add three months to that date. Alternatively, many Web sites show upcoming earnings dates for most any company on the market. I like Marketwatch's Earnings page (www. marketwatch.com/tools/calendars/earnings.asp).

After a company has reported earnings, you can generally swing trade the stock, because the bad or good news about earnings is out.

Speculating on Penny Stocks

When I first started trading, I immediately gravitated toward *penny stocks,* which I define as all U.S. stocks that trade below $5, even though other market commentators classify them as stocks trading at $1 or less. Back in 1994, I said to myself, "Holy crap! I can make 20 or 30 percent if the stock moves by 5 cents!" I used to print out reams of data on penny stocks to analyze and study, feeling if I could get a few right that I'd make untold profits.

Unfortunately, penny stocks are the fool's gold in the market. They look tempting but don't lead to riches because they exhibit low liquidity and are volatile. They're more susceptible to rumors or message board antics, which can spike shares up or down. (*Note:* An exception to this rule is international securities that may routinely trade for a small amount of money. For example, many Australian shares trade for less than 5 Australian dollars without the negative stigma that accompanies U.S. securities trading below $5.)

When the Internet was just getting started, a posting on a message board for a penny stock company could send the stock's value shooting up or down 5 or 10 percent in a matter of seconds. Hyping or pumping stocks became common. If you try to hype shares of Apple Inc., you're going to find that your posting won't make a dent in the stock's price, because the company trades millions of shares per day that are worth hundreds of millions of dollars. But a penny stock may trade only $50,000 worth of stock per day, so hyping or pumping such a stock can send shares roaring or falling — even if you were right on the trend and position sizing.

The additional risk factors associated with trading penny stocks, like the fact that penny stocks don't even trade on some days, make it more difficult for you to profit. Also, the volume on penny stocks may be light, which increases trading costs, making it that much more difficult to earn a good return on your money. You don't need exposure to these junk companies to be a successful swing trader.

Penny stocks represent companies in poor financial health. Perhaps the company in question is hemorrhaging losses. Or maybe it has a mountain of debt on its balance sheet that it can't pay off. Whatever the ailment, a security's price communicates important information about the general market's expectations for it.

Penny stocks aren't necessarily companies you've never heard of, so don't be lulled into a false sense of security about a security just because you recognize its name. Otherwise you're setting yourself up for failure. Don't believe me? In late 2007, penny stocks included such well-known companies as Vonage Holdings, E*Trade Financial Corporation, Circuit City, and Blockbuster Inc.

Changing Your Trading Destination Midflight

Imagine the problems that may arise if pilots routinely changed their minds on their intended destination midflight. Airports wouldn't be able to anticipate which planes may be landing today, passengers would likely get upset, and the Federal Aviation Administration wouldn't know where to begin a rescue operation if an emergency arose.

Swing traders sometimes commit the sin of changing trading destinations midflight, which means changing the reason you trade a security after you've initiated the trade. More often than not, a midflight change occurs because the trade hasn't gone your way. And rather than take a loss, you prefer to sock that puppy into a stocking, because you know the market's totally off in its assessment of the company's prospects. The problem with this approach is that it keeps a poor-performing security in a portfolio when it should be sold. That security's poor performance can become worse and lead to even larger losses.

For example, imagine you trade shares of XYZ Corporation on the long side (that is, you buy shares for a short-term profit). Shortly after buying shares, XYZ suffers some indigestion, and its stock price falls by 10 percent. "Hmm . . ." you think to yourself, "XYZ is an awfully good company. Why on earth should this stock not trade for 20 percent more than its current price?" After giving it some thought, you decide that your swing trade of XYZ should really be a long-term investment. No need to take that loss right now. You know it'll turn up in a few weeks or months — maybe years.

Swing traders fall prey to this sin often because it's difficult to take losses. Taking a loss means admitting loudly and clearly that you made a mistake. And no matter how many losses you take in trading, it doesn't get easier to do. Taking losses when others are looking over your shoulder is that much more difficult.

Try to mitigate the impact of this sin by framing the way you look at losses. Like me, you may not be a gardener, but try viewing your portfolio of securities as a growing shrub. When you wake up each morning, make sure your shrub is looking fine and dandy with healthy, successful trades. Be aware that occasionally a branch will grow the wrong way whenever a trade turns sour and will begin to affect your shrub's aesthetic quality. When that happens, take out your clippers and cut that branch off for the health of your overall portfolio.

Your swing trading portfolio will have branches that need to be cut; if you let them grow, you're effectively changing your trade midflight. Stay focused on growing your portfolio over time and don't change the reasoning behind a trade just because it doesn't go your way. Instead, correct the problem and move on.

Doubling Down

By doubling down, I don't mean trying to win big at blackjack. In the swing trading world, *doubling down* means doubling your investment in a trade when the trade goes against you. This strategy may sound appealing, but it's fraught with danger. So why even consider doubling down? Because if you trade that security again and put even more money into it, a slight move in your direction could lead to untold profits!

For instance, if you buy $10,000 worth of Apple Inc. for $100 per share, and the stock immediately falls to $90, you're facing a $1,000 loss. That's not pretty. But if you double down and buy another $10,000 worth of shares of Apple at $90, you can gain back that $1,000 loss to break even when shares rise to $95. By increasing your investment to the losing trade, you lower the price the stock must rise to in order for you to gain back your prior losses. But doing so isn't worth the risk.

Doubling down is a double-edged sword — if shares march down more, your losses compound because you've now exposed yourself to double your initial investment. *Never* send good money after bad. If you have a loss on a trade, then your original trade idea was wrong. Adding more money to the trade doesn't make you right (remember, though, that your trading strategy isn't necessarily to blame, because losses are a natural part of doing business). The emotional reaction to get even exists at some level in everyone. If you lose money on IBM, for example, you want to show IBM who's boss and trade that stock the right way. But odds are good that you're only shooting yourself in the foot.

My friends in the investment community may pipe up right about now to exclaim that doubling down can be an effective investment strategy for *some* people. In fact, retirement professionals often advocate a version of doubling down. Investors who have long-term time horizons don't care about short-term losses the way swing traders do, though. As a swing trader, you must follow the beat of a different drummer, because you're principally concerned with short-term gains. Consequently, you care about short-term losses. You don't have the luxury of waiting three years to find out whether you're right. If you aren't right in the first three days, then you probably need to exit and move on to another trade.

On the other side, doubling up on a winning position is acceptable as long as the new position size fits within your risk requirements. If you're reasoning was correct on entering a trade (and that was validated by price action when the position became profitable), then you may wish to add to the position to increase your profits on that trade. The opposite holds true for losing positions. Loss is a sign that something has gone awry. Adding to a swing trade that isn't working is usually an act of desperation to break even.

Swing Trading Option Securities

Options give traders the right — not the obligation — to buy or sell some security at a future date at a certain price. Options aren't for the new trader; most pros don't handle them correctly either. They miscalculate how much risk they're exposed to by using those pretty little financial models that assume the future will resemble the past.

Swing trading stocks and commodities can be profitable, but short-term trading in options is next to impossible. Options aren't meant to be swing traded — they're meant to hedge risk and provide an outlet for speculators to feel alive by leveraging their small positions. As a general rule, don't swing trade options — I recommend not touching them at all — for these reasons:

- **Options don't trade often and can be expensive to purchase or sell.** The spread between the bid and the offer of option prices is wide. So if you buy an option at the asking price, you may already be down 5 or 10 percent on your investment relative to the bid side where you could sell your option immediately.

- **Options pose significant risk.** A stock or commodity contract may fall some percentage points but rarely hit zero. Option prices, however, commonly end at zero when their expiration date arrives. Options require you to be right about three different factors regarding a price move: direction, magnitude, and timing. If you're wrong about any of these three factors, you'll end up losing money — possibly all of it.

Thinking You're Hot Stuff

If you string together several winning trades, you may start to build confidence in your strategy and skills as a swing trader. Good for you! But if your confidence turns into arrogance, you're going to cut corners and take greater risks. Regardless of how good you think you are, plenty of other traders are out there who may be better informed or better prepared. A humble trader isn't afraid to admit mistakes. An arrogant trader thinks the market's wrong and he or she's right.

One area where I've seen the hot-stuff factor exhibited is in a trader's education. Some traders falsely believe that after you know the tools of the trade, you don't need to figure out anything else. Yet the markets are a living organism. You need to keep up to speed on the news surrounding them and the books pertaining to trading.

Try setting a goal for yourself to read at least one trading-related book a month, like I do. If you're constantly taking in new information, you're less prone to thinking that you're the be-all, end-all when it comes to trading, and you can avoid the fate of smart traders who are brilliant on an IQ level but not in practice. These folks generate impressive returns for several years only to quit swing trading because they can't control risk or admit their mistakes.

Concentrating on a Single Sector

According to behavioral scientists, traders and investors sometimes exhibit a *familiarity bias,* an investor's tendency to invest in companies he or she knows or feels familiar with. Often employees of publicly traded companies have a significant portion of their retirement assets invested in their employer's stock. Although they may feel comfortable investing in a company they know a lot about, this bias can be dangerous because it increases the chances that their portfolio won't be well diversified and that their account will experience more volatility.

Many Enron employees in the 1990s had either the majority or the entirety of their retirement assets invested in the energy company's stock. Had they diversified their holdings to less-familiar parts of the market, the payoff may've meant having a nest egg versus having nothing after Enron went bust.

In swing trading, familiarity bias rears its ugly head when you focus on a sector of the market you know a lot about. A swing trader who enjoys information technology, for example, may trade shares of Microsoft, Apple Inc., Hewlett-Packard, Cisco Systems, and so on. Such swing traders may in fact build a portfolio of 10 or 12 different stocks, but they don't have diversified investments.

Following a top-down approach to swing trading (which I explain in Chapter 8) can also lead to overinvestment in a single sector if you're not careful. For instance, if energy stocks are doing well, then you may be tempted to hold a whole basket of different energy stocks, thinking your portfolio is diversified. If you buy one stock from each of the top ten industry groups and are 70 percent invested in the energy sector, your risks are high. If energy turns down violently, those positions will all fall together.

You must diversify your portfolio across sectors and, more broadly, across asset classes. If commodities are outperforming stocks, swing trade companies that benefit from a commodity boom while shorting other, unrelated companies. Having both long and short positions helps insulate you from market volatility to some extent. But you should also be careful to avoid investing in too few sectors.

Overtrading

You may find it curious that I list overtrading as a sin in a swing trading book. How can a swing trader possibly overtrade? Isn't that the whole name of the game in swing trading? Well, yes and no.

Swing trading is principally defined by the short-term nature of the price swings it attempts to capture. Obviously, those price swings require more trading than the buy-and-hold investment strategy, but you should still trade as few times as possible in order to achieve your objective. Why?

- ✔ The more often you trade, the more work you need to do.
- ✔ Trading entails costs, and costs hurt returns.
- ✔ This extra work increases administrative costs (both money- and time-based) involved with keeping track of the trades, entering them into a journal, and reviewing them at a future date.

Swing trading is supposed to fit in the happy medium between the day trader who slaves away over miniscule price movements and the buy-and-hold investor who sits on his or her hands until they become numb. The more often you trade, the more likely you're simply trading *market noise* (moves driven by nonfundamental reasons).

Buying and selling often or intraday makes your success as a swing trader that much more difficult — so get in before a major price move and get out after you capture it.

I can't give you a set number of trades to place per week or per month, but on average, your trade length should last several days to several weeks. If you're holding positions for shorter amounts of time, you need to examine that part of your trading system. Are losses that force liquidation causing you to trade this way? Or are you becoming impatient and trading in and out because you're looking for the elusive stock that'll make a major move the day after you buy it? "Keep it simple" is a saying my tenth-grade math teacher wrote on my notebook in class one day. The same advice applies to swing trading.

Violating Your Trading Plan

If you can't stick to your trading plan, you're unlikely to make it as a professional swing trader. Your trading plan is your strategy. It governs how you trade, when you trade, and how you exit. Your trading plan should impose certain restrictions, such as how much you allocate to a single position or how you respond to losses. Those restrictions are in place to protect your capital, because the markets often lull people into a sense of confidence — only to pull the rug from underneath them when they start to cut corners.

Violating your trading plan is a little like defying authority. But unlike in a traditional job setting, where defiance involves an employee and employer, trading plan violations are acts of defiance against yourself. You're literally hurting yourself, whether you know it or not.

In addition to the macro problem with violating your trading plan, the other risk is that if you violate it routinely, even in small matters, you may violate your plan in bigger areas — such as position sizing or diversification standards. In other words, you start to think you're above the law and can make decisions as you see fit. Who needs a trading plan when you're numero uno in the market? This negligence represents a mass abandonment of time-tested, necessary rules.

As a swing trader, worry about yourself and not others. Don't chase spectacular returns that competitors generate by being careless. History has shown that the race goes not to the swift nor the battle to the strong. Success comes from a disciplined application of the trading rules that have proven themselves over time.

Of course, you can always revise trading plans if you want. Just do it outside the market hours and for a good reason, like making changes only after reviewing and assessing your trading journal entries. Random acts of violation (sounds like a criminal term, I know) make deciphering the source of strengths or weaknesses in your plan rather difficult.

Appendix

Resources

In This Appendix

▶ Choosing trading and charting software

▶ Researching the market

▶ Monitoring your portfolio

▶ Sharpening your trading skills

Swing traders rely on a variety of products and services to analyze potential trades and stay sharp in their work. Throughout this book, I've used snapshots from various services and Web sites I consult on a regular basis.

This appendix provides more details on the top ten resources I recommend. These resources aren't necessities, but they do help you quickly identify securities and monitor their activity. Other resources keep you sharp on your game.

Sourcing and Charting Your Trading Ideas

Swing trading ideas typically come from bottom-up screening or top-down searches. In this section, I present a bottom-up screening Web site (Magic FormulaInvesting) and a top-down software tool *(High Growth Stock Investor)* that can also do bottom-up screening. I also turn your attention to a useful financial newspaper *(Investor's Business Daily)* that publishes a wealth of valuable data and a real-time charting system *(TradeStation)* so you can chart your trading ideas.

Trading ideas: MagicFormulaInvesting.com

Normally, I'd be turned off by a Web site that has the word "magic" in its title. But this Web site is very different from any you've visited.

MagicFormulaInvesting.com is the brainchild of Joel Greenblatt, a successful hedge fund manager. The "magic formula" that the site's title refers to is a simple quantitative ranking formula that Greenblatt developed. This formula assesses securities by two measures:

- ✔ **A cheapness measure:** Similar to the inverse of the P/E ratio
- ✔ **An efficiency measure:** Similar to the return on equity ratio I describe in Chapter 8

Greenblatt, who wrote a book about this formula titled *The Little Book That Beats the Market* (published by Wiley), found that ranking securities solely on these two criteria generated a list of candidates that mightily outperformed the overall market. The formula is geared to long-term investors who are encouraged to hold stocks appearing at the top of the formula's rankings and update holdings at least annually.

So how can a long-term investor-type formula serve any purpose for the swing trader?

Well, as it turns out, these stocks are often great places to find trading ideas. Although Greenblatt encourages his readers to be patient and wait for promising candidates to start generating healthy returns, swing traders can simply buy those candidates that are beginning their rise and avoid those that have yet to turn around.

The Web site — which is free to use — allows you to view the top-ranked securities above a certain market capitalization you specify. This makes screening for highly rated small cap stocks or highly rated large cap stocks a cinch. After registering for the site, you're asked to enter the minimum market cap of the securities you're screening for and the number of top-ranked securities you'd like to view (25, 50, or 100). After clicking on "Go!" the screen generates the top-ranked securities meeting these criteria.

MagicFormulaInvesting.com is a bottom-up screen that looks only at fundamental criteria to identify promising securities. You can start using the screen today by logging onto www.magicformulainvesting.com.

Trading software: High Growth Stock Investor

High Growth Stock Investor (HGS Investor) is a software tool that assists in identifying promising candidates to buy or short. The software incorporates both fundamental analysis data and technical analysis data. The software can be used to identify securities using both a top-down and a bottom-up approach.

What I like about *HGS Investor* is its efficiency. Inside of five minutes, I can determine the overall state of the financial markets and where the strength or weakness is, industry-group-wise. This makes my job easy because I can simply look for long or short candidates in the strongest or weakest industry groups in the market.

To assist you in identifying which industry groups to analyze, *HGS Investor* color-codes industry group rankings. Industry groups performing in the top 20 percent of the market are color-coded green. The next 20 percent of industry groups are color-coded yellow. The industry groups ranking in the bottom 60 percent of the market are color-coded red.

HGS Investor also allows you to analyze commodities, dividend-paying securities, international securities, and value investments. Though some traders use *HGS Investor* for longer-term horizons than swing traders typically would, the software can be extremely valuable for the traditional swing trader.

You can get a free trial of *HGS Investor* by visiting the firm's Web site at www. highgrowthstock.com. An annual subscription costs around $600.

Financial newspaper with stock ideas: Investor's Business Daily

Investor's Business Daily (IBD) is a financial newspaper geared toward the short-term trader. The newspaper offers stock ideas daily (primarily long) and combines fundamental and technical criteria in its quantitative ranking measures for nearly every company that trades on the NYSE, Nasdaq, and the American Stock Exchange. *IBD* has an affinity for small cap companies generating strong earnings growth and flying under the radar screen of most asset managers. Often, *IBD* highlights infant companies before they become huge.

You can use *IBD* as a source of trading ideas. Each day, the newspaper highlights companies making new highs — often ripe territory for finding promising long candidates. *IBD* also highlights securities that have just emerged from bases and may be ripe for purchase. *IBD* is built around the top-down trading philosophy and emphasizes strong industry groups and strong stocks within those groups. The newspaper favors growth-oriented securities over value-oriented securities.

IBD can also assist you in selecting companies with strong (or weak) fundamental and technical criteria. *IBD* provides a wealth of information on thousands of stocks every day, including such data as the following:

- ✔ **Earnings per Share Growth Rating:** This fundamentals-based ranking compares a firm's earnings growth history to the other companies in the market. The higher the earnings growth relative to the overall market, the higher the EPS rating. The scale runs from 1 to 99. As a swing trader, you should focus on buying companies with EPS ratings of 80 or higher.

- ✔ **Relative Price Strength Rating:** This may be viewed as a technical ranking because it compares the price performance of a security to all securities in the market. The higher the rating, the better the security has performed relative to the market. The lower the rating, the worse the security has performed relative to the market. This scale also runs from 1 to 99, but you want to focus on buying companies with RS ratings of 80 or higher.

- ✔ **Sales + Profit Margins + Return on Equity:** *IBD* attempts to simplify fundamental analysis for you by crunching these figures and generating a grade of either A, B, C, D, or E. Of course, an A rating is assigned to companies with superior sales growth, profit margins, and return on equity ratios as measured against other firms in the market. Swing traders should focus on buying companies with a rating of A or B. Avoid buying companies with a rating of D or E.

- ✔ **Accumulation/Distribution last three months:** According to *IBD*, this rating measures "relative degree of institutional buying (accumulation) and selling (distribution) in a particular stock over the last 13 weeks." Translated into English, this rating looks at whether investors are buying shares en masse or selling shares en masse. Although *IBD* doesn't disclose the actual formula, it's safe to say that the measure compares volume on days a security closes higher to volume on days a security closes lower. As with the previous rating, stick to companies on the long side of the market with Accumulation/Distribution ratings of A or B and avoid buying companies with Accumulation/Distribution ratings of D or E. Stocks rated C are showing neither strong accumulation nor strong distribution.

- ✔ *IBD* **Composite Rating:** Finally, *IBD* publishes a Composite Rating that sums up a security's score on the aforementioned criteria and adds in a security's industry group ranking. The Composite Rating ranges between 1 and 99. As with the Earnings per Share Growth Rating and the Relative Price Strength Rating, I recommend buying stocks with an *IBD* Composite Rating of 80 or higher.

You can purchase *IBD* at your local bookstore, or visit the firm's Web site to begin a free trial: www.investors.com.

Charting software: TradeStation

You can find dozens of charting programs on the market. I'm partial to *TradeStation,* the software used for the majority of charts in this book, because of its seamless integration of charting and trading.

TradeStation is more than just a trading software tool. When the company was founded, charting and indicators were its bread and butter. *TradeStation* allows users to tap one of the dozen indicators that come prepackaged in the program or design their own trading indicators. By using those indicators, you can develop and backtest your trading strategies.

TradeStation now incorporates brokerage with the charting platform. It allows users to trade futures, equities, options, and even the foreign exchange market. What I appreciate about the program is the ability to monitor positions in real time and put trading alerts on every position I hold. For example, if I'm long shares of IBM and want an alert if shares trade at a price of $110, I can automate that in *TradeStation* and have an e-mail sent or alert signaled if my criterion is met. I place such alerts on every position I hold and on candidates I'm looking to trade.

TradeStation has won broker awards from the financial newspaper *Barron's* and the trading magazine *Technical Analysis of Stocks and Commodities.* You can learn more about the program by visiting www.tradestation.com. The *TradeStation* platform is free to brokerage clients who do a minimum number of trades a month (check with *TradeStation* to find out what that minimum is).

Doing Your Market Research

Swing traders should always be sharpening their pencils. They should know what's going on in the macroeconomic environment. For example, are interest rates high or low? Is the Fed concerned about inflation or economic growth? Is the U.S. dollar strengthening or weakening? You can keep abreast of these big-picture questions by staying on top of the latest news from financial publications. I recommend the following two.

PIMCO's Bill Gross commentary

The Pacific Investment Management Company (PIMCO) is the largest fixed income investment firm in the world. As of December 31, 2007, PIMCO managed some $750 billion in assets and employed nearly 1,000 people. William H. Gross founded PIMCO in 1971 and eventually sold the company to a German-based insurance firm for a tidy profit. Today, Gross manages the largest bond fund in the world, the PIMCO Total Return Fund. Prior to entering the financial world, Gross was a professional blackjack player in Las Vegas — a profession he says helped prepare him for Wall Street because the game focuses on calculating the odds of success and spreading risk appropriately.

Each month, Gross publishes an investment outlook piece. Although this outlook is unlikely to provide short-term trading ideas, Gross does identify major themes occurring in the financial markets. These themes may play out over the coming weeks, months, or even years, but being aware of them can be profitable. Gross is a fundamentals-based investor, and knowing the "why" behind Fed decisions or economic growth patterns is useful to any trader.

Gross's commentary is humorous, enlightening, and educational, and I make it a habit to read his outlook piece every month. But I should warn you: To fully understand the high-level concepts that Gross presents, you may need to do some additional reading. I view this as a good thing because it pushes you to raise your swing trading game.

You can access Gross's commentary by visiting PIMCO's Web site and viewing the "Featured Market Commentary." You can even sign up for e-mail alerts when Gross's commentary is published — all for free. See www.pimco.com.

Barron's weekly financial newspaper

Barron's is a weekly financial newspaper that covers equities, bonds, commodities, mutual funds, and so on. I subscribe to the newspaper and review it on the weekends to keep up to speed on the major events that happened in the past week or that may be happening in the coming week. Why do I choose a weekly paper over a daily one, such as *The Wall Street Journal?* Well, plenty of random market events occur on a daily basis. But much of it is just *noise* — immaterial news used to fill pages more than to convey anything of substance — and it can cause you to lose your focus.

Weekly newspapers are less susceptible to that problem (but still susceptible, nonetheless). Although swing traders don't need a play-by-play of the financial markets to profit, an ESPN summary of the game is helpful.

Generally, I don't rely on *Barron's* for trading ideas. Your primary sources for such ideas should be *HGS Investor* and *Investor's Business Daily,* both of which I highlight earlier in this appendix, as well as other financial Web sites. But *Barron's* is a valuable educational tool. I always review "Up & Down on Wall Street" to get a humorous and satirical take on the markets and the "Commodities Corner" to review events taking place in major commodities. Other noteworthy columns include the "International Trader" and "Charting the Market."

To subscribe to *Barron's,* visit www.barrons.com. As of this writing, a year's subscription costs $99 for the print edition or $149 for the print and online editions.

Keeping Tabs on Your Portfolio and the Latest Market News

When you hold a portfolio of swing trading positions, you're going to want to stay on top of them like a hawk. But how can you do that, aside from watching their prices change during the day? Monitoring your portfolio on a day-to-day basis can be cumbersome, especially as you hold more and more securities. Although setting alerts on your securities by using technical trading software (such as *TradeStation,* which I cover earlier in this appendix) is important, you should also keep tabs on any fundamental news developments that occur.

Yahoo! Finance portfolio tool

The easiest way I've found to keep tabs on all the news on my positions is to use the portfolio tool from Yahoo! Finance. This tool allows you to quickly enter the symbols of your portfolio holdings. After the symbols are loaded, the tool pulls down any news headlines associated with those symbols, sorted by date, from such sources as *Barron's* magazine, TheStreet.com, and company press releases circulated by Reuters and the Associated Press. By checking this Web site on a daily basis, you can stay on top of company announcements (such as earnings dates) or positive/negative mentions of your securities in the popular press. I can quickly stay on top of a portfolio of 25 positions by using this portfolio monitoring service. And the best part is, it's free.

To see the portfolio tool, visit Yahoo! Finance at `finance.yahoo.com`. Then click on the tab labeled "My Portfolio." You may need to sign onto Yahoo! or create a Yahoo! ID to uniquely identify you and your holdings. After you've logged onto Yahoo!, you can edit or create portfolios on Yahoo! Finance.

Yahoo! Economic Calendar

On almost every business day, the federal government or private organizations release economic news that affects financial markets. Some of the information is very important (such as Federal Reserve Bank interest rate decisions), whereas other data points have little impact.

To keep yourself apprised of the important stuff, turn to Yahoo! Economic Calendar, which provides a listing of all major economic news scheduled to be released in any given week. The Web site shows what data is to be released, how important the data is, and what the market expects the data to be. Some data is released before the market opens, and other data is released during market hours. I check the site at least once a week to know what major news items I can expect.

Most news items on Yahoo! Economic Calendar are defined and rated a grade that indicates their level of importance. Items with low grades, like C or D, aren't critical to your trading game. The only time those reports move markets is when the numbers come in *way* too high or *way* too low. Keep your watchful eye on reports graded A or B.

But how do you know when a report helps or hurts stocks? Follow these guidelines:

- **Inflation:** Generally, higher-than-expected inflationary data (in the form of the Consumer Price Index or the Producer Price Index) is negative for both stocks and bonds.

- **Economic data:** The growth rate in the country's gross domestic product may be interpreted as bearish or bullish for stocks, depending on the stage of the economic cycle. If the economy is weak, then strong economic growth numbers are highly prized. However, if the economy is overheating, a strong economic report may send stock prices falling fast.

- **Central Bank Actions:** These actions (for example, lowering or raising short-term interest rates) tend to have the largest effects on financial markets. When the Federal Reserve lowers interest rates by more than market expectations, it generally leads to rallies in stocks and bonds. When the Federal Reserve raises interest rates by more than market expectations, it generally leads to declines in stocks and bonds.

If these financial terms make you woozy, don't worry. You don't need to become an economist to swing trade successfully. I just want you to be on top of the reasons behind market movements so you can position yourself accordingly.

You can access the Yahoo! Economic Calendar page at `biz.yahoo.com/c/e.html`.

Fine-Tuning Your Trading Techniques

In order to improve your swing trading methods, use your spare time to stay up to speed on the latest research concerning trading techniques, indicators, and other facets of your trading plan. I recommend a couple resources that will help make you a better trader — a monthly magazine to assist in refining your system and a book to help get you in the right trading state of mind.

Technical Analysis of Stocks & Commodities magazine

Technical Analysis of Stocks & Commodities is a magazine devoted to analyzing stocks and commodities from a technical perspective. The magazine is released monthly and covers charting, computer trading methods, and technical software products. The magazine also features interviews with trading professionals discussing their approach to the markets.

The magazine isn't a resource for trading ideas. Rather, it helps traders improve their trading techniques by applying existing indicators or by using new ones. When computer code is necessary to implement an indicator that the magazine discusses, the formula or code is usually included. And I like the fact that figures are interspersed with the text to make concepts easy to understand.

You shouldn't implement every strategy or indicator you read about in this magazine. Rather, look to refine your own systems by incorporating nuggets of information that arise from time to time. Your trading system shouldn't change on a day-to-day basis (or month to month, for that matter). But the techniques you use can be refined if such honing improves performance.

To subscribe to or find out more about this magazine, visit `www.traders.com` or call 800-832-4642.

The Black Swan: The Impact of the Highly Improbable

True knowledge is understanding one's ignorance. Financial markets teach that lesson to thousands every day.

Nassim Taleb's book, *The Black Swan: The Impact of the Highly Improbable*, colorfully educates readers on the risks of thinking they know more than they really do. The book's title comes from the problem of induction, or drawing generalities based on particular events. For example, a scientist in Europe who witnesses thousands and thousands of white swans may come to the conclusion that "All swans are white." However, just because the scientist never witnesses a black swan doesn't mean that black swans don't exist. (Black swans do in fact exist.) Similarly in trading, you can't assume that certain events can't happen just because they've never happened before. And you can't assume that certain relationships must continue to exist in the future simply because they've existed in the past.

_____

Though Taleb's book isn't specifically geared to swing trading per se, I consider it invaluable because it helps train traders to think differently than the masses on Wall Street. The book is also helpful in terms of a risk management perspective. You'll be better able to manage your risk if you plan for extreme events and how they may affect your positions.

Index

• *Symbols and Numerics* •

%D plot stochastics indicator, 108–111
%K plot stochastics indicator, 108–111
1-day price change, 171
7 percent rule, 23, 215–217
8K report, 145
10K report, 144
10Q report, 144
401(k) Plan, 10

• *A* •

AAPL (Apple Inc.), 123, 195
absolute valuation method, 158–159
accounts (broker), 45–46
accumulation phase, 64–66
adjusted Fed Model, 168–170
administrative tasks
  brokers
    account types, 45–46
    choosing, 42–45
    evaluating potential, 44–45
    opening accounts, 45–46
    overview, 42
    research on prospective, 43
    types of, 42–43
  service providers
    to avoid, 50–52
    buy/sell recommendation
      newsletters, 52
    fundamental analysis software, 47–48
    message boards, 50–51
    overview, 46
    technical software, 47
    types of, 46–52
  trading journal, 52–55
  winning mindset, 56

adrbny.com (Web site), 272
adr.com (Web site), 220, 245
ADX (Average Directional Index),
  96–97, 120
agricultural commodities, 130, 220
AKAM (Akamai Technology Inc.), 229
allocation diversification
  by asset class, 219–220
  by industry exposure, 218–219
  by number of securities, 218
  overview, 217
Alvarion (stock symbol: ALVR), 98
ALVR (Alvarion), 98
amenities (broker), 44
American Depository Receipts (ADRs), 220
AMEX (American Stock Exchange), 18
analysis
  of daily charts, 248–249
  disadvantages of using analysts, 161
  establishing techniques, 19–21
  fundamental
    advantages of, 20, 37
    catalysts, 39
    classifying companies, 39–40
    comparing tactics, 182
    defined, 25
    disadvantages of, 26–27, 37
    overview, 19
    principles, 34–35
    psychology, relationship with, 37
    software providers, 47–49
    technical analysis, compared to, 26–27
    why it works, 35–36
  intermarket, 128–134
  limitations of, 36
  overview, 19
  principles of, 34–35

analysis *(continued)*
  psychology related to, 37
  relative strength, 34, 134–139
  software providers, 47–49
  stock
    competition, 194–196
    earnings and sales expectations, 192–194
    financial stability, 187–190
    industry, 183–187
    overview, 181–183
    past performance, 190–192
    valuing shares, 197–200
  technical
    advantages of, 20, 26–27, 31
    defined, 25
    disadvantages of, 32
    fundamental analysis, compared to, 26–27
    how and why it works, 29–30
    indicators, 33–34, 90–95
    overview, 19
    reading charts, 33
    weekly charts, 249–250
    why it works, 35–36
"Analysts Keep Misfiring with 'Sell'
    Ratings" *(Wall Street Journal),* 161
anchoring, 37
annualizing returns, 264–266
Apache Corporation (stock symbol: APA),
    65, 66, 67
Apple Inc. (stock symbol: AAPL), 123, 195
ascending triangle chart pattern, 76
assessing
  balance sheet, 147–151
  beta, 206–207
  cash flow statement, 154–156
  chart patterns, 252–255
  company size, 208–209
  financial statements, 146–156
  income statements, 152–153
  industry potential, 170–172
  liquidity, 207–208
  screen results, 179
assets
  diversifying across classes, 219–220, 296
  overview, 148
automated stop loss level, 258

average daily volume, 175
Average Directional Index (ADX), 96–97, 120
Axsys Technologies (stock symbol: AXYS),
    102–103

• *B* •

balance sheet
  assets, 148
  components of, 147–148
  defined, 143, 147
  guidelines for assessing, 149–151
  liabilities, 148
banking services, 44
bar chart, 61–63
Barron's (newspaper), 304–305
barrons.com (Web site), 304
basic materials sector, 185
BBY (Best Buy), 109
Beardstown Ladies, 268
bearish engulfing patterns, 82–83
benchmarks, 272–276
Best Buy (stock symbol: BBY), 109
beta, 206–207
bid, 232
BioMimetic Therapeutics (stock symbol:
    BMTI), 113
biz.yahoo.com (Web site), 171, 305
*Black Swan: The Impact of the Highly
    Improbable, The* (Taleb), 307–308
bloomberg.com (Web site), 168
BMTI (BioMimetic Therapeutics), 113
BMY (Bristol-Myers Squibb), 159, 160
Body for Life (Phillips), 56
bonds
  corporate, 169–170
  overview, 17
  stocks, relationship with, 133–134
  Yahoo! Finance Bond Center, 169
bottom fishing, 69
bottom-up approach
  overview, 21, 27, 172–173
  screens
    assessing results, 179
    criteria, 175

growth, 175–177
overview, 173–174
value, 177–179
top-down approach, compared with, 179–180
for trending securities, 120–121
Bouchentouf, Amine (*Commodities For Dummies*), 18
BRCM (Broadcom), 87
breakaway gaps, 78–79
Bristol-Myers Squibb (stock symbol: BMY), 159, 160
Broadcom (stock symbol: BRCM), 87
brokers
    account type, 45–46
    choosing, 42–45
    commission rates, 42, 44
    discount, 43
    evaluating potential, 44–45
    full service, 43
    overview, 42
    research on prospective, 43
    types of, 42–43
Buffett, Warren (investor), 157
bullish engulfing patterns, 82–83
buy-and-hold investing, 1, 11–12
buying
    abundance of buy recommendations, 161
    based on slope change, 101–102
    buy/sell recommendation newsletters, 52
BVN (Compania de Minas Buenaventura), 75

• *C* •

calculating
    P/E ratio, 198
    PEG ratio, 198
    price to cash flow, 198
    P/S ratio, 198
    returns, 263–272
    Russell return calculator, 272

candidate selection
    assessing chart patterns, 252–255
    overview, 251–252
    ranking filtered securities, 252–255
    screening securities, 252
candlestick chart
    charting with, 80–85
    overview, 61–62
    patterns
        bearish engulfing, 82–83
        bullish engulfing, 82–83
        evening stars, 83–85
        hammer, 80–81
        hanging man, 82
        morning stars, 83–84
    real body, 61
    sample, 62, 63
    shadows, 61
capex (capital expenditures), 154, 156
capital
    requirements, 289–290
    setting position size by percent of, 211–213
capital goods sector, 185
cash account, 45
cash flow from financing/operating activities, 154
cash flow statement, 153–156
catalysts, 39, 157
CBOT (Chicago Board of Trade), 19
CDRG (Citadel Derivatives Group LLC), 245
Central Bank Actions, 306
chain-linking returns, 271–272
chart patterns
    assessing, 252–255
    combining with technical indicators, 114–115
    RSI (Relative Strength Index), 112–113
charting
    bar charts, 61–63
    candlestick patterns
        bearish engulfing, 82–83
        bullish engulfing, 82–83
        evening stars, 83–85
        hammers, 80–81
        hanging man, 82
        morning stars, 83–84

charting *(continued)*
  patterns
    ascending triangle, 76
    cup-and-handle, 74–76
    Darvas box, 71–72
    gaps, 77–80
    head-and-shoulders, 73–74
    triangle, 76–77
  phases
    accumulation, 64–66
    contraction, 69–70
    distribution, 67–69
    expansion, 66–67
    markdown, 69–70
  psychology, 70–71
  roles of price and volume, 60
  software, 98, 302–303
  validity, 32
charts
  daily, 248–249
  intraday, 65
  reading, 33
  types of charts, 61–64
  weekly, 249–250
cheapness measure, 300
Chicago Board of Trade (CBOT), 19
China Mobile Limited (stock symbol: CHL), 84, 85
Citadel Derivatives Group LLC (stock symbol: CDRG), 245
classifying companies, 39–40
closed end funds, 17
combining long and short positions, 220–221
commissions, 12, 42, 44, 290
commodities
  example, 131–132
  guidelines, 132
  history, 130–131
  overview, 18
  tracking, 131
  types, 18, 130, 220

Commodities For Dummies (Bouchentouf), 4, 18
common gaps, 78
Compania de Minas Buenaventura (stock symbol: BVN), 75
Companhia Siderurgica Nacional (stock symbol: SID), 254
company size, 206, 208–209
comparing
  buy-and-hold investing and swing trading, 11–12
  day trading and swing trading, 12
  discretionary and mechanical trading styles, 28
  growth screens and value screens, 175
  Level I and Level II quotes, 241–243
  margin and cash accounts, 45
  retirement account and traditional brokerage account, 46
  returns to benchmarks, 272–276
  technical and fundamental analysis, 26–27
  time-weighted return method and money-weighted return method, 269
  top-down and bottom-up approach, 179–180
  trading ranges and trading trends, 118–120
competition
  handling hazy conditions, 200
  margins, 195–196
  overview, 194–195
  strategies, 195
consolidation period, 85
consumer cyclical sector, 184
consumer staples sector, 185
Contango Oil & Gas Company (stock symbol: MCF), 78
continuation formation, 74
continuation gaps, 79
contraction phase, 69–70
contrasting
  buy-and-hold investing and swing trading, 11–12
  day trading and swing trading, 12

discretionary and mechanical trading styles, 28
growth screens and value screens, 175
Level I and Level II quotes, 241–243
margin and cash accounts, 45
retirement account and traditional brokerage account, 46
returns to benchmarks, 272–276
technical and fundamental analysis, 26–27
time-weighted return and money-weighted return method, 269
top-down and bottom-up approach, 26–27
trading ranges and trading trends, 118–120
conventions used in book, 3
corporate bonds, 169–170
corporate press releases, 145
cost
  of goods sold, 151
  of trading, 290, 295
cost-focus strategy, 195
cost-leadership strategy, 195
Cramer, Jim (TV host), 38
Credit Suisse Securities (USA) LLC (stock symbol: FBCO), 245
crossovers, 103–104
cup-and-handle chart pattern, 74–76
currency market, 18, 128–130
Currency Trading For Dummies (Galant and Dolan), 18
currencyshares.com (Web site), 220
current assets, 148
current liabilities, 148
current ratio, 188
curve fitting, 95
customer service (broker), 44–45

• D •

daily charts, 248–249
Darvas, Nicholas (trader), 71–72
Darvas box charting pattern, 71–72

day of strength, 123
day of weakness, 123
day trading, 12
debt to equity ratio, 188–189
debt to shareholders' equity ratio, 188–189
Dell (stock symbol: DELL), 195
descending triangle chart pattern, 76
Diamond Offshore (stock symbol: DO), 82, 83
Diana Shipping (stock symbol: DSX), 78
differentiator strategy, 195
differentiator-focus strategy, 195
direct-access trading, 43, 245
Directional Movement Index (DMI), 91, 98, 99,
discount brokers, 43
discretionary trading style
  defined, 25
  mechanical trading style, compared with, 28
distribution phase, 67–69
divergences
  defined, 34
  in RSI (Relative Strength Index), 112
  as technical analysis signal, 95
diversifying
  across asset classes, 296
  allocations
    with American Depository Receipts (ADRs), 220
    by asset class, 219–220
  capital requirement for, 289
  defined, 217
  with exchange traded funds (ETFs), 219–220
  importance of, 283
  by industry exposure 218–219
  by number of securities, 218
  overview, 217
  of risk, 11, 23
  sectors, 296
dividend yield, 171

DMI (Directional Movement Index), 91, 98, 99
DO (Diamond Offshore), 82, 83
Dodd, David
 (*Security Analysis*), 143
Dolan, Brian
 (*Currency Trading For Dummies*), 18
dollar fluctuations, 256
doubling down, 293–294
Dow Jones-AIG Agricultural Total Return
 ETF (stock symbol: JJA), 220
downtrend lines, 87
DSX (Diana Shipping), 78
dumb money, 30

earnings
 dates, 291
 expectations, 192–194
 historical, 190–192
 before interest and taxes, 189
 quarterly, 145–146
 surprise figures, 37
 surprise history, 193
earnings per share (EPS), 182, 186–187, 302
EBIT (earnings before interest and
 taxes), 189
ECNs (electronic communication
 networks), 19
economic cycle, 185
economic data, 306
economic moat, 157
efficiency measure, 300
8K report, 145
Elder, Alexander (trading expert), 23
electronic communication networks
 (ECNs), 19
EMA (exponential moving average),
 100–101
emotions, controlling, 282
Emulex Corporation, 210
energy commodities, 130, 220

energy sector, 185
Energy Select Sector SPDR ETF (stock
 symbol: XLE), 220
Enron, 31, 296
entry strategy
 full-time swing traders, 238–241
 part-time swing traders, 236–237
 trading ranges, 127–128
 trends, 122–124
EPS (earnings per share) ranking, 182,
 186–187
equis.com (Web site), 47
equity markets, 135
esignal.com (Web site), 47
establishing analysis techniques, 19–21
estimating fair value for S&P 500 Index, 168
ETFs (exchange traded funds), 219–220
etrade.com (Web site), 43, 47
evening stars, 83–85
Excel (Microsoft), 274–275
exchange traded funds (ETFs), 219–220
executing orders, 258. *See also* trade
 execution
exhaustion gaps, 80
exit strategy
 defined, 221
 full-time swing traders, 238–241
 overview, 21–22, 221
 part-time swing traders, 237
 passage-of-time based, 225
 for profitable trades
  overview, 221–222
  predetermined price target, 222–223
  predetermined profit target, 222
  swing lows/highs, 223–224
  technical signals, 224–225
 stop-loss-level based
  overview, 225–226
  support/resistance level, 226–227
  technical level, 227–228
 timing, 259–261
 trading ranges, 127–128
expansion phase, 66–67
expenses, non-cash, 154

exponential moving average (EMA), 100–101
extensive modeling, 182
external catalysts, 39
Exxon Mobile (stock symbol: XOM), 223

• *F* •

fair value, 170
familiarity bias, 296
FBCO (Credit Suisse Securities (USA) LLC), 245
FCEL (FuelCell Energy), 139
Fed Model
  adjusted, 168–170
  criticisms of, 168
  overview, 167–168
fidelity.com (Web site), 43, 47
finance.google.com (Web site), 48, 146, 208
finance.yahoo.com (Web site), 48, 146, 208, 305
financial stability
  current ratio, 188
  debt to shareholders' equity ratio, 188–189
  interest coverage ratio, 189–190
  overview, 187–188
financial statements
  assessing
    balance sheet, 147–151
    cash flow statement, 153–156
    income statement, 151–153
    overview, 146–147
  finding, 146
  industry terms, 144–145
  overview, 144
  release date, 145–146
financials sector, 185
finding
  securities, 21
  strong trading ranges, 125–126

First Solar (stock symbol: FSLR), 105
Fiscal policies, 129
fixed-income markets, 17
flat ranges, 126
FLS (Flowserve Corp.), 79
fool.com (Web site), 196
401(k) Plan, 10
FSLR (First Solar), 105
FuelCell Energy (stock symbol: FCEL), 139
full service brokers, 43
full-time swing traders
  entry criteria, 240
  entry/exit strategy, 238–240
  intraday charting, 238–241
  intraday trading signals, 240–241
  overview, 13–14
  recommended order types, 238
  time frame selection, 240
fundamental analysis
  advantages of, 20, 37
  catalysts, 39
  classifying companies, 39–40
  comparing tactics, 182
  defined, 25
  disadvantages of, 26–27, 36, 37
  establishing techniques, 19–21
  overview, 19
  principles, 34–35
  psychology, relationship with, 37
  software providers, 47–49
  technical analysis, compared with, 26–27
  why it works, 35–36
fundamental screens
  assessing results, 179
  basic criteria, 175
  growth, 175–177
  overview, 173–174
  value, 177–179
funds
  closed end, 17
  exchange traded funds (ETFs), 17
futures contracts, 17

• G •

Gafisa S.A. (stock symbol: GFA), 254, 255
Galant, Mark
    (*Currency Trading For Dummies*), 18
gaps
    breakaway, 78–79
    common, 78
    continuation, 79
    exhaustion, 80
    overview, 77
GFA (Gafisa S.A.), 254, 255
GICS (Global Industry Classification
        Standard), 218–219
GLD (streetTRACKS Gold), 106, 220
Global Industry Classification Standard
        (GICS), 218–219
Goldman, Sachs & Co. (stock symbol:
        GSCO), 245
good until cancelled (GTC), 233, 258
good until the day (GTD), 233
Google (stock symbol: GOOG),
        62, 63–64, 199, 213
Google Finance, 48, 146, 208
Graham, Benjamin
    (*Security Analysis*), 143
Greenblatt, Joel (hedge fund manager), 300
Gross, Bill (bond fund manager), 303–304
gross margins, 195
gross profit, 151
growth
    classifying companies according to, 39–40
    industry examples, 184–185
    screens
        finding fast-growing companies with,
            176–177
        overview, 175–176
        shorting with, 177
        value screens, compared with, 175
    sector, 184
    stocks, 39
    trading, 40
GSCO (Goldman, Sachs & Co.), 245

GTC (good until cancelled), 233, 258
GTD (good until the day), 233

• H •

hammer, 80–81
hanging man, 82
head-and-shoulders chart pattern, 73–74
healthcare sector, 184
heavy volume, 60
Henry, Patrick (revolutionary), 190
Hewlett-Packard (stock symbol: HPQ), 195
High Growth Stock (HGS) Investor software
    data source, 172
    EPS ranking, 187, 250
    overview, 48, 300–301
    screening with, 121, 179
highgrowthstock.com (Web site), 47, 301
holding period, 10
horizontal trendlines, 88
HPQ (Hewlett-Packard), 195

• I •

IBD (Investor's Business Daily), 301–302
icons used in book, 5–6
ImClone Symbols (stock symbol:
        IMCL), 110
INCA (Instinet LLC), 245
income
    operating, 151
    as primary source, 13–14
    supplementing, 14–15
income statement
    components of, 151
    defined, 143, 151
    guidelines to assessing, 152–153
indicators. *See* non-trending indicators;
        technical indicators
Individual Retirement Account (IRA), 10

industry analysis
  familiar markets, 184
  identifying sectors, 184–186
  overview, 183
  steps for, 183–184
industry exposure, 218–219
industry groups
  defined, 219
  following, 281
  growth stocks in, 175–176
  identifying, 250–251
  market standard, 137–139
  statistics, 171
industry potential, 170–172
inflation, 133, 306
information technology sector, 185
Instinet LLC (stock symbol: INCA), 245
interactivebrokers.com (Web site), 43
interest coverage ratio, 189–190
interest rates, 129
intermarket analysis
  commodities, 130–132
  overview, 128
  stocks and bonds, 133–134
  U.S. dollar, 128–130
internal catalysts, 39
Internet. *See* Web sites
intraday charting
  balancing trading signals, 240–241
  example of, 239
  overview, 65
  selecting time frames, 240
  to time entries and exits, 238–241
intramarket analysis. *See* relative strength
    analysis
Investor's Business Daily (newspaper)
  bottom-up searching with, 120–121
  EPS rank, 187, 191, 250
  industry/sector information, 172, 218
  overview, 48, 301–302
investors.com (Web site), 302
IRA (Individual Retirement Account), 10
iShares Silver Trust (stock symbol:
    SLV), 220

• J •

JJA (Dow Jones-AIG Agricultural Total
    Return ETF), 220
J.P. Morgan Securities Inc. (stock symbol:
    JPMS), 245

• K •

Knight Capital Group Inc. (stock symbol:
    NITE), 245

• L •

Lan Airlines (stock symbol: LFL), 74
large capitalization (large cap)
    stocks, 208
Lehman Brothers Inc. (stock symbol:
    LEHM), 245
Lennar (stock symbol: LEN), 73
Level I quotes. *See* Level II quotes
Level II quotes
  evaluating, 243–244
  Level I quotes, compared with,
    241–243
  overview, 241
  Time & Sales report, 244–246
  verifying accuracy, 244–246
LFL (Lan Airlines), 74
liabilities, 148
Lime Brokerage LLC (stock symbol:
    LIME), 245
limit orders, 234–235, 284–285
limiting
  losses, 209–215, 257
  position losses, 215–217
  total capital at risk, 216–217
line chart
  overview, 61
  sample, 63

liquidity
  assessing, 207–208
  defined, 206
  providers, 245
Little Book That Beats the Market, The
    (Greenblatt), 300
livestock commodities, 130
long positions, 220–221
Long Term Capital Management
    (LTCM), 204
long-term assets, 148
long-term debt to equity, 171
long-term liabilities, 148
long-term P/E (price to earnings) ratio
  disadvantages of, 166–167
  history of, 165–166
  overview, 165
long-term trends, 249–250
losses
  admitting to, 24, 293
  exiting for, 21–22
  limiting
    overview, 209
    to a percentage, 257
    position, 215–217
    setting position size, 211–215
    willingness to lose, 210–211
  responding to, 228–229
low-priced shares, avoiding, 209
LTCM (Long Term Capital
    Management), 204
Lynch, Peter (mutual fund manager), 32

• *M* •

MACD (Moving Average Convergence/
    Divergence)
  crossover of nine-day moving
    average, 107
  example, 105–106
  overview, 105
  positive and negative divergences,
    106–107

Mad Money (TV show), 38
MagicFormulaInvesting.com
    (Web site), 300
Malkiel, Burton (professor), 32
ManTech International (stock symbol:
    MANT), 114, 115
margin account, 45
margins
  gross, 195
  net profit, 196
  operating, 196
markdown phase, 69–70
market evaluation
  adjusted Fed Model, 167–170
  Fed Model, 167–168
  long-term P/E (price to earnings) ratio,
    165–167
  overview, 164–165
market makers, 232
market research
  Barron's, 304
  daily chart, 248–249
  overview, 247–248
  PIMCO, 303–304
  weekly chart, 249–250
market standard, 137–139
market(s)
  cap, 171, 208
  currency, 18, 128–130
  depth of, 232
  equity, 135
  fixed-income, 17
  impact of, 210
  mechanics, 231–233
  orders, 233
  trending, 96
  types of, 18–19
Marketwatch Earnings page, 291
marketwatch.com (Web site), 291
markup phase, 66–67
Marvel Entertainment (stock symbol:
    MVL), 149–150
MCF (Contango Oil & Gas Company), 78
measurement moves, 76

meat commodities, 130
mechanical trading style
  defined, 25–26
  discretionary trading style, compared
    with, 28
MEMC Electronics Materials (stock
    symbol: WFR), 97, 126
mental stop loss level, 226
Merck (stock symbol: MRK), 159–160, 194
Merrill Lynch, Pierce, Fenner & Smith
    Incorporated (stock symbol:
    MLCO), 245
message boards, 24, 50–51
metal commodities, 130
Microsoft (stock symbol: MSFT), 195, 242
Microsoft Excel, 274–275
MLCO (Merrill Lynch, Pierce, Fenner &
    Smith Incorporated), 245
moats, 157
money
  dumb, 30
  smart, 64
money-weighted return method, 267, 269
monitoring motion of shares, 259–261
Morgan Stanley & Co., Incorporated (stock
    symbol: MSCO), 245
morning star, 83–84
Mosaic Company (stock symbol: MOS), 121
Motley Fool Web site, 196
Moving Average Convergence/Divergence
    (MACD)
  crossover of nine-day moving
    average, 107
  example, 105–106
  overview, 105
  positive and negative divergences,
    106–107
moving averages
  crossovers, 103–104
  defined, 100
  example, 102–103
  importance of slope changes, 100–103
  length, 101
  types of, 100–101

MRK (Merck), 159–160, 194
MSCO (Morgan Stanley & Co.,
    Incorporated), 245
MSFT (Microsoft), 195, 242
MVL (Marvel Entertainment), 149–150

• *N* •

NASDAQ, 18
Nasdaq Level I quotes. *See* Nasdaq Level II
    quotes
Nasdaq Level II quotes
  evaluating, 243–244
  Level I quotes, compared with,
    241–243
  overview, 241
  Time & Sales report, 244–246
  verifying accuracy, 244–246
nasdaqtrader.com (Web site), 245
negative catalysts, 157
net asset value, 17
net income, 151
net long, 22, 115
net profit margins, 171, 196
net short, 22, 115
NEU (NewMarket), 82, 83
New York Mercantile Exchange
    (NYMEX), 19
New York Stock Exchange (NYSE), 18
NewMarket (stock symbol: NEU),
    82, 83
newsletters, 52
Nicholson, Colin (trader), 214
Niederhoffer, Victor (hedge fund
    manager), 204
nine-day moving average, 235, 238
nine-week moving average, 116
NITE (Knight Capital Group Inc.), 245
noise, 33
non-cash expenses, 154
non-trending indicators
  overview, 34, 108
  recognizing, 107–114

non-trending indicators *(continued)*
  stochastics
    crossovers, 110–111
    overview, 108–109
    positive and negative divergences, 109–110
  trading ranges, relationship with, 125
NVIDIA, 195
NYMEX (New York Mercantile Exchange), 19
NYSE (New York Stock Exchange), 18

• O •

OHLC bar chart, 61
1-day price change, 171
O'Neil, William J.
  (Investor's Business Daily), 137, 187,
    191, 218
openecry.com (Web site), 43
operating income, 151
operating margins, 196
option securities, 294–295
order book, 208
orders
  execution, 258
  limit, 234–235, 284–285
  market, 233
  stop, 234
  stop limit, 234–236
  types of, 233–236
oscillators. *See* non-trending indicators
overbought
  defined, 34
  levels, 110–111
  zone, 114
oversold
  defined, 34
  levels, 110–111
  zone, 114
overtrading, 296–297

• P •

Pacific Investment Management Company
  (PIMCO), 303–304

part-time swing trading
  entry strategy, 236–237
  exit strategy, 237
  overview, 14–15
passage of time, 225
past performance, 190–192
pattern day traders, 10
patterns (charting)
  bearish engulfing, 82–83
  bullish engulfing, 82–83
  cup-and-handle, 74–76
  Darvas box, 71–72
  gaps, 77–80
  head-and-shoulders, 73–74
  triangles, 76–77
P/E (price to earnings) ratio
  calculating, 198
  defined, 171
  market valuation with, 158, 159, 165–167
PEG (price/earnings to growth) ratio, 198
penny stocks, 291–292
%D plot stochastics indicator, 108–111
%K plot stochastics indicator, 108–111
performance evaluation
  annualizing returns, 264–266
  basic, 263–264
  benchmarking, 272–276
  overview, 263
  time-weighted return method
    calculating return for time periods,
      270–271
    chain-linking, 271–272
    overview, 266–267
    time period breakdown, 268–270
  trading plan, 276
Pfizer (stock symbol: PFE), 159, 160
Philippine Long Distance (stock symbol:
  PHI), 71, 72
Phillips, Bill
  (Body for Life), 56
physical stop loss order, 226
PIMCO (Pacific Investment Management
  Company), 303–304
pimco.com (Web site), 304
point and figure (P&F) chart, 62, 64
points of inflection, 165

portfolio analysis and reports, 45
portfolio building
  diversifying allocations
    by asset class, 219–220
    by industry exposure, 218–219
    by number of securities, 218
    overview, 217
  limiting position losses, 215–217
  management, 305–306
  overview, 215
positions
  combining long and short, 220–221
  size
    determining, 255–257
    importance of dollar fluctuations, 256
    limiting losses, 257
    overview, 255
    setting by percent of capital, 211–213
    setting by risk level, 213–215
    setting stop loss level, 256–257
positive catalysts, 157
precious metals commodity, 220
press releases (corporate), 145
price
  during bearish engulfing patterns,
    82–83
  to book value, 171
  during bullish engulfing patterns,
    82–83
  to cash flow, 198
  commodity and bond, relationship
    with, 132
  during contraction phase, 69–70
  in cup-and-handle chart pattern, 75
  in Darvas box chart pattern, 71–72
  during distribution phase, 67–68
  effect of inflation on bond, 133
  during expansion phase, 66–67
  to free cash flow, 171
  gaps in, 77–80
  during hammer, 81
  in head-and-shoulders chart pattern,
    73–74
  during markdown phase, 69–70
  during markup phase, 66–67
  reflection of volume, 92

  role in charting, 60
  share, 206
  stock and bond, relationship with,
    133–134
  support and resistance level, 65–66
  swings related to technical indicators,
    90–92
  in triangle chart patterns, 76–77
price target, 222–223
price to earnings ratio (P/E)
  calculating, 198
  defined, 171
  market valuation with, 158, 159, 165–167
price/earnings to growth (PEG)
  ratio, 198
price-level exit level, 125
profit target
  predetermined, 222
  setting, 284
profitable trades
  overview, 221–222
  predetermined price target, 222–223
  predetermined profit target, 222
  swing lows/highs, 223–224
  technical signals, 224–225
profits
  capital expenditures, relationship
    with, 156
  exiting for, 21
  gross, 151
  potential, 12
P/S ratio, 198
psychology
  charting, 70–71
  fundamental analysis related to, 37
public equity. See also stock
  American Depository Receipts
    (ADRs), 16
  exchange traded funds (ETFs), 17
  overview, 16

qualitative data, 156–157
quarterly earnings, 145–146

• *R* •

ranges, 117. *See also* trading ranges
ranking filtered securities, 252–255
ratio
  chart, 136
  current, 188
  debt to shareholders' equity, 188–189
  interest coverage, 189–190
  P/E (price to earnings), 198
  PEG (price/earnings to growth), 198
  price to cash flow, 198
  P/S, 198
reading charts, 33
recording trades, 259
Regeneron Pharmaceuticals (stock symbol: REGN), 112
regression, 94
relative price strength rating, 302
relative strength analysis
  global scope of, 135–137
  industry group market standards, 137–139
  major equity markets, 135
  overview, 34, 134–135
Relative Strength Index (RSI)
  chart patterns, 112–113
  overview, 111–112
  positive and negative divergences, 112
  trading overbought and oversold zones, 114
relative valuation method
  implementing, 159–160
  overview, 158
research
  importance of, 24
  on prospective brokers, 43
resistance level
  during accumulation phase, 64–65
  defined, 22, 30, 64
  stop loss based on, 226–227
resources. *See also* Web sites
  market research
    Barron's newspaper, 304
    PIMCO, 303–304

portfolio management
  Yahoo! Economic Calendar, 305–306
  Yahoo! Finance portfolio tool, 305
sourcing/charting
  High Growth Stock (HGS) Investor software, 300–301
  Investor's Business Daily newspaper, 301–302
  MagicFormulaInvesting.com, 299–300
  TradeStation software, 302–303
trading techniques
  Black Swan: The Impact of the Highly Improbable, The (Taleb), 307
  Technical Analysis of Stocks & Commodities (magazine), 307
retirement account, 46
retirement trading capital requirements, 290
returns
  annualizing, 264–266
  benchmark, comparing to, 272–276
  calculating, 263–272
  chain-linking, 271–272
  on equity, 171
  realistic target, 290
  Russell calculator, 272
Reuters, 48, 49
reuters.com (Web site), 48, 190
revenues, 151
risk
  diversifying, 11
  measuring
    assessing beta, 206–207
    company size, 208–209
    liquidity, 207–208
    low-priced shares, 209
    overview, 205–206
  penny stocks, 291–292
  trading options, 295
risk level
  defined, 283
  setting, 283–284
  setting position size by, 213–215

risk management
  building portfolios
    combining long and short positions, 220–221
    diversifying allocations, 217–220
    limiting position losses, 215–217
    overview, 215
  combining long and short positions, 220–221
  defined, 205
  limiting losses
    level willing to lose, 210–211
    overview, 209–210
    setting position size, 211–215
  overview, 203, 205
  real stories of, 204
  setting exit level, 124–125
  trading ranges, 127–128
RSI (Relative Strength Index)
  chart patterns, 112–113
  overview, 111–112
  positive and negative divergences, 112
  trading overbought and oversold zones, 114
rules
  avoid emotional trading, 282
  diversify, 283
  follow industry groups, 281
  have fun, 287
  limit orders, 284–285
  set profit target/technical exit, 284
  set risk level, 283–284
  stop loss orders, 285–286
  trade your plan, 279–280
  trading journal, 286
Russell return calculator, 272
russell.com (Web site), 174, 272

• S •

sales expectations, 192–194
sales growth, 190–192
Sandisk (stock symbol: SNDK), 68, 69, 70, 86
sanofi-aventis (stock symbol: SNY), 159, 160
scottrade.com (Web site), 43
screens
  assessing results, 179
  basic criteria, 175
  defined, 21
  growth, 175–177
  with *HGS Investor* software, 179
  overview, 173–174
  securities, 252
  value, 177–179
SEC (Securities and Exchange Commission), 144, 146
sectors
  diversifying, 296
  identifying, 184–186
  performance related to economic cycle, 185
securities. *See also* shares; stock
  bonds, 17
  closed end funds, 17
  commodities, 18
  currency market, 18
  diversifying by number of, 218
  finding, 21
  fixed-income markets, 17
  futures contracts, 17
  option, 294–295
  options, 18
  phases of life, 64–70
  public equity (stock), 16–17
  ranking filtered, 252–255
  screening, 252
  trending, 95–97
Securities and Exchange Commission (SEC), 144, 146
Security Analysis (Graham and Dodd), 143
selecting
  candidates, 251–255
  trading strategies, 19–23
selling
  abundance of sell recommendations, 161
  buy/sell recommendation newsletters, 52
  examples of strategies, 224

service providers
  to avoid, 50–52
  buy/sell recommendation newsletters, 52
  fundamental analysis software, 47–48
  message boards, 50–51
  overview, 46
  technical software, 47
7 percent rule, 23, 215–217
shares. *See also* securities; stock
  price
    defined, 206
    low, 209
    measure in growth screens, 175
    monitoring, 259–261
  valuation
    overview, 197
    price relative to competitors, 197–198
    share-price justification, 198–200
short sellers during contraction phase, 70
shorting
  based on slope change, 102–103
  during distribution phase, 68
  with growth screens, 177
  in head-and-shoulders chart
    pattern, 74
  overview, 11–12
  positions, 220–221
  with value screens, 178–179
short-term trends, 248–249
SID (Companhia Siderurgica Nacional), 254
Siegel, Jeremy (professor), 32
Sigma Designs, Inc. (stock symbol: SIGM),
  80, 224
SII (Smith International), 100
simple moving averages, 100–101
Six Step Dance analysis method
  competition, 194–196
  earnings and sales expectations, 192–194
  financial stability
    current ratio, 188
    debt to shareholders' equity ratio,
      188–189
    interest coverage ratio, 189–190
    overview, 187–188

industry
  familiar markets, 184
  identifying sectors, 184–186
  overview, 183–184
  justification of share-price difference,
    198–200
  overview, 181–183
  past performance, 190–192
  valuing shares, 197–198
skills, 261–262
slippage, 290
slope
  change, 101–102
  moving averages, relationship with,
    100–103
SLV (iShares Silver Trust), 220
smart money, 64
Smith International (stock symbol: SII), 100
SNDK (Sandisk), 68, 69, 70, 86
SNY (sanofi-aventis), 159, 160
software
  charting, 98, 302–303
  fundamental analysis, 47–48
  *HGS Investor. See High Growth Stock
    (HGS) Investor* software
  technical, 47
Southwestern Energy Company, 243
S&P 500 Index, 168
S&P Metals & Mining SPDR ETF
  (stock symbol: XME), 220
SPDR Energy Select Sector ETF
  (stock symbol: XLE), 220
SPDR S&P Metals & Mining ETF
  (stock symbol: XME), 220
spread, 208, 232
SPW (SPX Corporation), 91
SPX Corporation (stock symbol: SPW), 91
standard deviation Web site, 275
standardandpoors.com (Web site), 165
stochastics
  crossovers, 110–111
  examples of, 109
  overbought levels, 110–111
  oversold levels, 110–111

overview, 108–109
positive and negative divergences,
    109–110
steps for using, 110
stock
    American Depository Receipts (ADRs), 16
    analyzing
        competition, 194–196
        earnings and sales expectations, 192–194
        financial stability, 187–190
        industry, 183–187
        overview, 181–183
        past performance, 190–192
        valuing shares, 197–200
    beta, 206–207
    bonds, relationship with, 133–134
    exchange traded funds (ETFs), 17
    growth, 39–40
    high management ownership, 156–157
    large capitalization (large cap), 208
    liquidity, 206, 207–208
    manipulation in, 210
    overview, 16
    penny, 291–292
    value, 39–40
stock symbols
    AAPL (Apple Inc.), 123, 195
    AKAM (Akamai Technology Inc.), 229
    ALVR (Alvarion), 98
    APA (Apache Corporation), 65, 66, 67
    AXYS (Axsys Technologies), 102–103
    BBY (Best Buy), 109
    BMTI (BioMimetic Therapeutics), 113
    BMY (Bristol-Myers Squibb), 159, 160
    BRCM (Broadcom), 87
    BVN (Compania de Minas
        Buenaventura), 75
    CDRG (Citadel Derivatives Group LLC), 245
    CHL (China Mobile Limited), 84, 85
    DELL (Dell), 195
    DO (Diamond Offshore), 82, 83
    DSX (Diana Shipping), 78
    FBCO (Credit Suisse Securities (USA)
        LLC), 245

FCEL (FuelCell Energy), 139
FLS (Flowserve Corp.), 79
FSLR (First Solar), 105
GFA (Gafisa S.A.), 254, 255
GLD (streetTRACKS Gold), 106, 220
GOOG (Google), 62, 63–64, 199, 213
GSCO (Goldman, Sachs & Co.), 245
HPQ (Hewlett-Packard), 195
IMCL (ImClone Symbols), 110
INCA (Instinet LLC), 245
JJA (Dow Jones-AIG Agricultural Total
    Return ETF), 220
JPMS (J.P. Morgan Securities Inc.), 245
LEHM (Lehman Brothers Inc.), 245
LEN (Lennar), 73
LFL (Lan Airlines), 74
LIME (Lime Brokerage LLC), 245
MANT (ManTech International), 114, 115
MCF (Contango Oil & Gas Company), 78
MLCO (Merrill Lynch, Pierce, Fenner &
    Smith Incorporated), 245
MOS (Mosaic Company), 121
MRK (Merck), 159–160, 194
MSCO (Morgan Stanley & Co.,
    Incorporated), 245
MSFT (Microsoft), 195, 242
MVL (Marvel Entertainment), 149–150
NEU (NewMarket), 82, 83
NITE (Knight Capital Group Inc.), 245
PFE (Pfizer), 159, 160
PHI (Philippine Long Distance), 71, 72
REGN (Regeneron Pharmaceuticals), 112
SID (Companhia Siderurgica Nacional),
    254
SIGM (Sigma Designs Inc.), 80, 224
SII (Smith International), 100
SLV (iShares Silver Trust), 220
SNDK (Sandisk), 68, 69, 70, 86
SNY (sanofi-aventis), 159, 160
SPW (SPX Corporation), 91
UBSS (UBS Securities LLC), 245
VG (Vonage), 192
WDC (Western Digital), 81, 104

WEDB (Wedbush Morgan Securities, Inc.), 245
WFR (MEMC Electronics Materials), 97, 126
WRNC (Warnaco Group), 241
WTI (W&T Offshore), 224, 225
XLE (Energy Select Sector SPDR ETF), 220
XME (SPDR S&P Metals & Mining ETF), 220
XOM (Exxon Mobile), 223
YHOO (Yahoo), 227, 228
stop limit orders, 234–236
stop loss level
    automated, 258
    exit strategy based on
        overview, 225–226
        support/resistance level, 226–227
        technical level, 227–228
    setting, 256–257, 283
stop loss orders, 285–286
stop orders, 234
strategies
    cost-focus, 195
    cost-leadership, 195
    differentiator, 195
    differentiator-focus, 195
    exit
        overview, 21–22
        passage-of-time based, 225
        for profitable trades, 221–225
        stop-loss-level based, 225–228
    fundamental, 25
    selling examples, 224
    technical, 25
streetTRACKS Gold (stock symbol: GLD), 106, 220
styles of trading
    discretionary, 25
    mechanical, 25–26
subscriptions
    Barron's, 304
    High Growth Stock (HGS) Investor, 48
    Investor's Business Daily, 48
        paid, 48
    Technical Analysis of Stocks & Commodities magazine, 307
    Zacks Investor Software, 48
supplementing income, 14–15
support levels
    during accumulation phase, 64–65
    defined, 22, 30
    stop loss based on, 226–227
swing lows/highs, 223–224
swing trading. *See also specific topics*
    buy-and-hold approach, compared with, 11–12
    day trading, compared with, 12
    defined, 10
    goal of, 1
    personality fit for, 9
symmetrical triangle chart pattern, 77

• T •

Taleb, Nassim
    Black Swan: The Impact of the Highly Improbable, The, 307–308
target return, 290
taxes
    deferred accounts, 10
    factors determining, 10
    for pattern day traders, 10
tdameritrade.com (Web site), 43
technical analysis
    advantages of, 20, 26–27, 31
    defined, 25
    disadvantages, 32
    fundamental analysis, compared with, 26–27
    how and why it works, 29–30
    overview, 19
    reading charts, 33
    technical indicators, 33–34
Technical Analysis of Stocks and Commodities (magazine), 303, 307
technical exit, 284

technical indicators. *See also* trending indicators
  accuracy of value, 92–93
  analyzing, 90–95
  applying, 33–34, 90
  combining with chart patterns, 114–115
  determining net long/net short positioning, 115–116
  divergences, 95
  exit signal, 125
  limiting, 93–94
  price and volume, 92
  price swings related to, 90–92
  recognizing, 97–107
  settings, 94–95
technical level, 227–228
technical signals, 224–225
technical software providers, 47
telecommunications sector, 185
10K report, 144
10Q report, 144
Theory of Investment Value, The (Williams), 143
TheStreet.com (Web site), 305
thinkorswim.com (Web site), 43
Time & Sales report, 244–246
time commitment, 13–15
time frames, 240
time of day, 19
time-based exit level, 125
time-weighted return method
  breaking time period down, 268–270
  calculating return for time periods, 270–271
  chain-linking time periods, 271–272
  money-weighted return method, compared with, 269
  overview, 266–267
Toll Brothers, 239
top-down approach
  bottom-up approach, compared with, 179–180
  industry assessment, 170–172
  market evaluation
    adjusted Fed Model, 168–170
    Fed Model, 167–168

    long-term P/E ratio, 165–167
    overview, 164–165
  overview, 21, 27, 163–164
  sectors related to, 296
  steps of, 164
  for trending securities, 120–121
total capital at risk
  defined, 215
  limiting, 216–217
trade execution
  full-time
    intraday charting, 238–241
    Nasdaq Level II quotes, 241–246
    order types, 238
    overview, 237
  market mechanics, 231–233
  order types
    limit order, 234
    market order, 233
    overview, 233
    stop limit order, 234–236
    stop order, 234
  part-time
    entry strategy, 236–237
    exit strategy, 237
    overview, 236
trade record, 259
traders.com (Web site), 307
TradeStation charting software, 302–303
tradestation.com (Web site), 43, 47, 258, 303
trading
  changing reasons for, 292–293
  for fun, 290
  journal, 52–55, 259, 286
  for a living, 290
  moving average crossovers, 103–104
  questionnaire, 280
  signals, 243
  strategy selection, 19–23
  techniques, 306–307
  your plan, 279–281
trading plan
  determining securities to trade, 16–18
  overview, 15–16
  risk management, 22–23
  violating, 297–298

trading process
  determining position size
    limiting losses, 257
    overview, 255–256
    setting stop loss level, 256–257
  executing order, 258
  exiting, 259–261
  identifying top industry groups, 250–251
  improving skills, 261–262
  market research
    daily chart, 248–249
    overview, 247–248
    weekly chart, 249–250
  monitoring motion, 259–261
  recording trade, 259
  selecting candidates
    assessing charts, 252–255
    overview, 251–252
    ranking filtered securities, 252–255
    screening securities, 252
trading ranges
  conception of, 119
  entering/exiting, 127–128
  finding strong, 125–126
  overview, 125
  trading trends, compared with, 118–120
trading styles
  choosing, 19–23
  discretionary, 25
  mechanical, 25–26
trading trends
  entering, 122–124
  finding strong, 120–122
  overview, 120
  risk management, 124–125
  trading ranges, compared with, 118–120
traditional brokerage account, 46
trailing twelve months (TTM), 159
trending indicators. See also technical
    indicators
  Directional Movement Index (DMI), 98–99
  limits of, 97
  Moving Average Convergence/Divergence
    (MACD), 105–107
  moving averages, 100–104
  overview, 33
trending markets, 96
trending securities, 95–97
trendlines
  defined, 85
  downtrend lines, 87
  horizontal, 88
  overview, 85–86
  uptrend lines, 86–87
trends
  bearish engulfing pattern, 82–83
  bullish engulfing pattern, 82–83
  defined, 117
  entering, 122–124
  evening star, 83–85
  hammer, 80–81
  hanging man, 82
  long-term, 249–250
  measuring strength of, 85–88
  morning star, 83–84
  short-term, 248–249
triangle chart patterns, 76–77
TTM (trailing twelve months), 159
turnover rate, 11

• U •

UBS Securities LLC (stock symbol:
    UBSS), 245
uptrend lines, 86–87
U.S. dollar, 129–130
usability, 44
utilities sector, 185

• V •

valuation
  defined, 143
  methods, 158–160
  overview, 158
  preferred model, 159

value
  accuracy of, 92–93
  classifying companies according to, 39–40
  fair, 170
  industry examples, 185
  net asset, 17
  screens
    finding leading stocks with, 178
    growth screens, compared with, 175
    overview, 177–178
    shorting with, 178–179
  sector, 184
  stocks, 39–40
valuing shares
  overview, 197
  relative to competitors, 197–198
  share-price justification, 198–200
verifying accuracy of Level II quotes, 244–246
VG (Vonage), 192
violating trading plans, 297–298
volume, 60, 92
Vonage (stock symbol: VG), 192

• *W* •

Wall Street Journal (newspaper), 120–121, 122, 161
Warnaco Group (stock symbol: WRNC), 241
WDC (Western Digital), 81, 104
Web sites
  adrbny.com, 272
  adr.com, 220, 245
  barrons.com, 304
  biz.yahoo.com, 171, 305
  bloomberg.com, 168
  currencyshares.com, 220
  direct access trading firms, 43
  discount broker, 43
  equis.com, 47
  esignal.com, 47
  etrade.com, 43, 47
  fidelity.com, 43, 47
  finance.google.com, 48, 146, 208
  finance.yahoo.com, 48, 146, 208, 305
  fool.com, 196
  Google Finance, 146, 208
  highgrowthstock.com, 47, 301
  interactivebrokers.com, 43
  investors.com, 302
  MagicFormulaInvesting.com, 300
  marketwatch.com, 291
  Motley Fool, 196
  nasdaqtrader.com, 245
  openecry.com, 43
  pimco.com, 304
  reuters.com, 48, 190
  russell.com, 174, 272
  scottrade.com, 43
  SEC (Securities and Exchange Commission), 144, 146
  standard deviation, 275
  standardandpoors.com, 165
  tdameritrade.com, 43
  TheStreet.com, 305
  thinkorswim.com, 43
  traders.com, 307
  tradestation.com, 43, 47, 303
  Yahoo! Finance, 48, 146, 208, 305
  Yahoo! Economic Calendar, 305–306
  zacks.com, 48
Wedbush Morgan Securities Inc. (stock symbol: WEDB), 245
weekly chart, 249–250
Western Digital (stock symbol: WDC), 81, 104
WFR (MEMC Electronics Materials), 97, 126
whipsaws, 92, 94
Williams, John Burr
  (*The Theory of Investment Value*), 143
WRNC (Warnaco Group), 241
W&T Offshore (stock symbol: WTI), 224, 225

• X •

XLE (Energy Select Sector SPDR ETF), 220
XME (SPDR S&P Metals & Mining ETF), 220
XOM (Exxon Mobile), 223

• Y •

Yahoo (stock symbol: YHOO), 227, 228
Yahoo! Finance
  Bond Center, 169
  Economic Calendar, 305–306
  portfolio tool, 305
  statistics on industry groups, 171
  Web sites, 48, 146, 208, 305
YHOO (Yahoo), 227, 228

• Z •

Zacks Investor Software, 48
zacks.com (Web site), 48

Notes

Notes

Notes

Notes

Notes

Notes

Notes

Notes

BUSINESS, CAREERS & PERSONAL FINANCE

Accounting For Dummies, 4th Edition*
978-0-470-24600-9

Bookkeeping Workbook For Dummies†
978-0-470-16983-4

Commodities For Dummies
978-0-470-04928-0

Doing Business in China For Dummies
978-0-470-04929-7

E-Mail Marketing For Dummies
978-0-470-19087-6

Job Interviews For Dummies, 3rd Edition*†
978-0-470-17748-8

Personal Finance Workbook For Dummies*†
978-0-470-09933-9

Real Estate License Exams For Dummies
978-0-7645-7623-2

Six Sigma For Dummies
978-0-7645-6798-8

Small Business Kit For Dummies, 2nd Edition*†
978-0-7645-5984-6

Telephone Sales For Dummies
978-0-470-16836-3

BUSINESS PRODUCTIVITY & MICROSOFT OFFICE

Access 2007 For Dummies
978-0-470-03649-5

Excel 2007 For Dummies
978-0-470-03737-9

Office 2007 For Dummies
978-0-470-00923-9

Outlook 2007 For Dummies
978-0-470-03830-7

PowerPoint 2007 For Dummies
978-0-470-04059-1

Project 2007 For Dummies
978-0-470-03651-8

QuickBooks 2008 For Dummies
978-0-470-18470-7

Quicken 2008 For Dummies
978-0-470-17473-9

Salesforce.com For Dummies, 2nd Edition
978-0-470-04893-1

Word 2007 For Dummies
978-0-470-03658-7

EDUCATION, HISTORY, REFERENCE & TEST PREPARATION

African American History For Dummies
978-0-7645-5469-8

Algebra For Dummies
978-0-7645-5325-7

Algebra Workbook For Dummies
978-0-7645-8467-1

Art History For Dummies
978-0-470-09910-0

ASVAB For Dummies, 2nd Edition
978-0-470-10671-6

British Military History For Dummies
978-0-470-03213-8

Calculus For Dummies
978-0-7645-2498-1

Canadian History For Dummies, 2nd Edition
978-0-470-83656-9

Geometry Workbook For Dummies
978-0-471-79940-5

The SAT I For Dummies, 6th Edition
978-0-7645-7193-0

Series 7 Exam For Dummies
978-0-470-09932-2

World History For Dummies
978-0-7645-5242-7

FOOD, GARDEN, HOBBIES & HOME

Bridge For Dummies, 2nd Edition
978-0-471-92426-5

Coin Collecting For Dummies, 2nd Edition
978-0-470-22275-1

Cooking Basics For Dummies, 3rd Edition
978-0-7645-7206-7

Drawing For Dummies
978-0-7645-5476-6

Etiquette For Dummies, 2nd Edition
978-0-470-10672-3

Gardening Basics For Dummies*†
978-0-470-03749-2

Knitting Patterns For Dummies
978-0-470-04556-5

Living Gluten-Free For Dummies†
978-0-471-77383-2

Painting Do-It-Yourself For Dummies
978-0-470-17533-0

HEALTH, SELF HELP, PARENTING & PETS

Anger Management For Dummies
978-0-470-03715-7

Anxiety & Depression Workbook For Dummies
978-0-7645-9793-0

Dieting For Dummies, 2nd Edition
978-0-7645-4149-0

Dog Training For Dummies, 2nd Edition
978-0-7645-8418-3

Horseback Riding For Dummies
978-0-470-09719-9

Infertility For Dummies†
978-0-470-11518-3

Meditation For Dummies with CD-ROM, 2nd Edition
978-0-471-77774-8

Post-Traumatic Stress Disorder For Dummies
978-0-470-04922-8

Puppies For Dummies, 2nd Edition
978-0-470-03717-1

Thyroid For Dummies, 2nd Edition†
978-0-471-78755-6

Type 1 Diabetes For Dummies*†
978-0-470-17811-9

* Separate Canadian edition also available

† Separate U.K. edition also available

Available wherever books are sold. For more information or to order direct: U.S. customers visit www.dummies.com or call 1-877-762-2974.
U.K. customers visit www.wileyeurope.com or call (0)1243 843291. Canadian customers visit www.wiley.ca or call 1-800-567-4797.

INTERNET & DIGITAL MEDIA

AdWords For Dummies
978-0-470-15252-2

Blogging For Dummies, 2nd Edition
978-0-470-23017-6

Digital Photography All-in-One Desk Reference For Dummies, 3rd Edition
978-0-470-03743-0

Digital Photography For Dummies, 5th Edition
978-0-7645-9802-9

Digital SLR Cameras & Photography For Dummies, 2nd Edition
978-0-470-14927-0

eBay Business All-in-One Desk Reference For Dummies
978-0-7645-8438-1

eBay For Dummies, 5th Edition*
978-0-470-04529-9

eBay Listings That Sell For Dummies
978-0-471-78912-3

Facebook For Dummies
978-0-470-26273-3

The Internet For Dummies, 11th Edition
978-0-470-12174-0

Investing Online For Dummies, 5th Edition
978-0-7645-8456-5

iPod & iTunes For Dummies, 5th Edition
978-0-470-17474-6

MySpace For Dummies
978-0-470-09529-4

Podcasting For Dummies
978-0-471-74898-4

Search Engine Optimization For Dummies, 2nd Edition
978-0-471-97998-2

Second Life For Dummies
978-0-470-18025-9

Starting an eBay Business For Dummies, 3rd Edition†
978-0-470-14924-9

GRAPHICS, DESIGN & WEB DEVELOPMENT

Adobe Creative Suite 3 Design Premium All-in-One Desk Reference For Dummies
978-0-470-11724-8

Adobe Web Suite CS3 All-in-One Desk Reference For Dummies
978-0-470-12099-6

AutoCAD 2008 For Dummies
978-0-470-11650-0

Building a Web Site For Dummies, 3rd Edition
978-0-470-14928-7

Creating Web Pages All-in-One Desk Reference For Dummies, 3rd Edition
978-0-470-09629-1

Creating Web Pages For Dummies, 8th Edition
978-0-470-08030-6

Dreamweaver CS3 For Dummies
978-0-470-11490-2

Flash CS3 For Dummies
978-0-470-12100-9

Google SketchUp For Dummies
978-0-470-13744-4

InDesign CS3 For Dummies
978-0-470-11865-8

Photoshop CS3 All-in-One Desk Reference For Dummies
978-0-470-11195-6

Photoshop CS3 For Dummies
978-0-470-11193-2

Photoshop Elements 5 For Dummies
978-0-470-09810-3

SolidWorks For Dummies
978-0-7645-9555-4

Visio 2007 For Dummies
978-0-470-08983-5

Web Design For Dummies, 2nd Edition
978-0-471-78117-2

Web Sites Do-It-Yourself For Dummies
978-0-470-16903-2

Web Stores Do-It-Yourself For Dummies
978-0-470-17443-2

LANGUAGES, RELIGION & SPIRITUALITY

Arabic For Dummies
978-0-471-77270-5

Chinese For Dummies, Audio Set
978-0-470-12766-7

French For Dummies
978-0-7645-5193-2

German For Dummies
978-0-7645-5195-6

Hebrew For Dummies
978-0-7645-5489-6

Ingles Para Dummies
978-0-7645-5427-8

Italian For Dummies, Audio Set
978-0-470-09586-7

Italian Verbs For Dummies
978-0-471-77389-4

Japanese For Dummies
978-0-7645-5429-2

Latin For Dummies
978-0-7645-5431-5

Portuguese For Dummies
978-0-471-78738-9

Russian For Dummies
978-0-471-78001-4

Spanish Phrases For Dummies
978-0-7645-7204-3

Spanish For Dummies
978-0-7645-5194-9

Spanish For Dummies, Audio Set
978-0-470-09585-0

The Bible For Dummies
978-0-7645-5296-0

Catholicism For Dummies
978-0-7645-5391-2

The Historical Jesus For Dummies
978-0-470-16785-4

Islam For Dummies
978-0-7645-5503-9

Spirituality For Dummies, 2nd Edition
978-0-470-19142-2

NETWORKING AND PROGRAMMING

ASP.NET 3.5 For Dummies
978-0-470-19592-5

C# 2008 For Dummies
978-0-470-19109-5

Hacking For Dummies, 2nd Edition
978-0-470-05235-8

Home Networking For Dummies, 4th Edition
978-0-470-11806-1

Java For Dummies, 4th Edition
978-0-470-08716-9

Microsoft® SQL Server™ 2008 All-in-One Desk Reference For Dummies
978-0-470-17954-3

Networking All-in-One Desk Reference For Dummies, 2nd Edition
978-0-7645-9939-2

Networking For Dummies, 8th Edition
978-0-470-05620-2

SharePoint 2007 For Dummies
978-0-470-09941-4

Wireless Home Networking For Dummies, 2nd Edition
978-0-471-74940-0

OPERATING SYSTEMS & COMPUTER BASICS

Mac For Dummies, 5th Edition
978-0-7645-8458-9

Laptops For Dummies, 2nd Edition
978-0-470-05432-1

Linux For Dummies, 8th Edition
978-0-470-11649-4

MacBook For Dummies
978-0-470-04859-7

Mac OS X Leopard All-in-One
Desk Reference For Dummies
978-0-470-05434-5

Mac OS X Leopard For Dummies
978-0-470-05433-8

Macs For Dummies, 9th Edition
978-0-470-04849-8

PCs For Dummies, 11th Edition
978-0-470-13728-4

Windows® Home Server For Dummies
978-0-470-18592-6

Windows Server 2008 For Dummies
978-0-470-18043-3

Windows Vista All-in-One
Desk Reference For Dummies
978-0-471-74941-7

Windows Vista For Dummies
978-0-471-75421-3

Windows Vista Security For Dummies
978-0-470-11805-4

SPORTS, FITNESS & MUSIC

Coaching Hockey For Dummies
978-0-470-83685-9

Coaching Soccer For Dummies
978-0-471-77381-8

Fitness For Dummies, 3rd Edition
978-0-7645-7851-9

Football For Dummies, 3rd Edition
978-0-470-12536-6

GarageBand For Dummies
978-0-7645-7323-1

Golf For Dummies, 3rd Edition
978-0-471-76871-5

Guitar For Dummies, 2nd Edition
978-0-7645-9904-0

Home Recording For Musicians
For Dummies, 2nd Edition
978-0-7645-8884-6

iPod & iTunes For Dummies,
5th Edition
978-0-470-17474-6

Music Theory For Dummies
978-0-7645-7838-0

Stretching For Dummies
978-0-470-06741-3

Get smart @ dummies.com®

- **Find a full list of Dummies titles**
- **Look into loads of FREE on-site articles**
- **Sign up for FREE eTips e-mailed to you weekly**
- **See what other products carry the Dummies name**
- **Shop directly from the Dummies bookstore**
- **Enter to win new prizes every month!**

* Separate Canadian edition also available

† Separate U.K. edition also available

Available wherever books are sold. For more information or to order direct: U.S. customers visit www.dummies.com or call 1-877-762-2974.
U.K. customers visit www.wileyeurope.com or call (0) 1243 843291. Canadian customers visit www.wiley.ca or call 1-800-567-4797.

Do More with Dummies
Products for the Rest of Us!

DVDs • Music • Games • DIY
Consumer Electronics • Software • Crafts
Hobbies • Cookware • and more!

Check out the Dummies Product Shop at www.dummies.com for more information!

WILEY